Canada Among Nations 2006

Canada Among Nations 2006

Minorities and Priorities

EDITED BY
ANDREW F. COOPER
AND DANE ROWLANDS

Published for the Norman Paterson School of
International Affairs, Carleton University, in cooperation
with The Centre for International Governance Innovation

by McGill-Queen's University Press
Montreal & Kingston · London · Ithaca

© McGill-Queen's University Press 2006
ISBN-13: 978-0-7735-3164-2 ISBN-10: 0-7735-3164-5 (cloth)
ISBN-13: 978-0-7735-3170-3 ISBN-10: 0-7735-3170-x (paper)

Legal deposit fourth quarter 2006
Bibliothèque nationale du Québec

Printed in Canada on acid-free paper

This book has been published with financial support from the Norman
Paterson School of International Affairs, Carleton University, and
The Centre for International Governance Innovation.

McGill-Queen's University Press acknowledges the support of the Canada
Council for the Arts for our publishing program. We also acknowledge the
financial support of the Government of Canada through the Book
Publishing Industry Development Program (BPIDP) for our publishing
activities.

Library and Archives Canada has catalogued this publication as follows:

Canada among nations.
    Annual.
    1984–
Produced for the Norman Paterson School of International Affairs
at Carleton University
in cooperation with The Centre for International Governance Innovation.
Publishers varies.
Each vol. also has a distinctive title.
Includes bibliographical references.
ISSN 0832–0683

ISBN-13: 978-0-7735-3164-2 ISBN-10: 0-7735-3164-5 (bnd)
ISBN-13: 978-0-7735-3170-3 ISBN-10: 0-7735-3170-x (pbk)

    1. Canada – Foreign relations – 1945–   – Periodicals.
    2. Canada – Politics and government – 1984–   – Periodicals.
    3. Canada – Politics and government – 1980–1984 – Periodicals.
    I. Noman Paterson School of International Affairs.

    FC242.C345   327.71   C86-031285-2 rev

This book was typeset by Interscript in 10/12 Sabon.
Cover Photo: CP (Fred Chartrand)

Contents

PART TWO
PRIORITIZING PARTNERS

PART THREE
MINOR PRIORITIES AND PRIOR MINORITIES?

PART FOUR
COMPETING POLICY PRIORITIES

Foreword

Minorities and Priorities, the twenty-second consecutive volume in the *Canada Among Nations* series, contains a number of important and current themes in respect to Canada's international role. Specifically, it explores the new foreign policy priorities of Prime Minister Stephen Harper's minority Conservative government, which won the country's 39th federal election on 23 January 2006. Although the Conservatives ran their campaign on a series of election promises that focused almost exclusively on domestic priorities, international relations quickly forced itself onto the their agenda once they took office. In the initial months after the election, the government had to deal with the growing controversy over the deployments of Canadian troops in Afghanistan; a new US policy that would require identity cards and tighter passport controls at the Canada-US border; continuing trade irritants with the US (especially over the softwood lumber issue); and the looming threat of terrorist attacks on Canadian soil with the discovery of terrorist cells in Toronto. Prime Minister Harper's priorities in the international arena soon became apparent: improve Canada-US relations, which had sunk to an all-time low during Paul Martin's brief interregnum as prime minister; boost defence spending by announcing major, new capital equipment programs; strengthen Canada's national security; renew Canada's commitment to Afghanistan; secure a new deal over softwood lumber; and adopt a 'whole of government' approach to Canada's diplomatic, defence, and development interventions abroad.

The introductory essays in this volume discuss and debate the Conservative government's emerging international priorities. Hugh Segal, in the lead-off chapter, provides a brief overview of the government's agenda, the foundations of conservative foreign policy, and the direction that it is likely to move over the next year. John Kirton and Adam Chapnick offer their own interpretations of the government's priorities and respectively explore the pre-election assumptions of Harper's international agenda and the historical bases for a minority foreign policy. The second section of the volume focuses on Canada's international partnerships: David Malone on the United Nations and the challenges of institutional reform; Marie Bernard-Meunier on Canada's evolving relations with Europe; Christopher Sands on third-country engagements in Canada-US relations; Elinor Sloan on the need for a coherent international security policy; and Ann Denholm Crosby on defence cooperation with the US in respect to ballistic missile defence.

The third section of the volume takes up the theme of 'minorities' and the impact of different sub-national actors and interests on the evolution and development of Canada's international policies. This issue, largely absent from most foreign policy discussions, has recently begun to play out in electoral politics and has greater salience now with the government's minority parliamentary status. Increasingly, immigrants, diaspora communities from countries like China and Haiti, and provincial governments – Québec and Alberta, in particular – have been able to pressure and persuade the government to accommodate their special concerns and interests in Canada's international commitments. Christina Gabriel explores how these pressures have influenced Canada's immigration policies and the government's emphasis on attracting skilled labour, which has yet to translate into better labour market performance. Yasmine Shamsie then looks at Canada's interventions in Haiti and our evolving role in that troubled Caribbean nation – a role that has been motivated, in part, by the large community of Haitian expatriates who reside in Canada. Nelson Michaud looks at the politics behind the prime minister's decision to give Québec representation in the United Nations Educational, Scientific and Cultural Organization (UNESCO) and the wider issues associated with provincial involvement in foreign affairs.

The energy and environmental aspects of Canada's domestic and international policies are taken up in the next section. From a Western Canadian perspective, Wenran Jiang identifies the need for a China strategy, specifically in the areas of resource exports to China and the trade-human rights dilemma. Isidro Morales' chapter looks at Canada's strategic advantages in North American energy market integration. Daniel Schwanen's chapter explores the challenges of developing a new climate change policy for Canada in the aftermath of the government's rebuff of the Kyoto Agreement. The final two chapters of the volume deal with Canada's overseas development assistance programs. David Black looks at Canada's aid programs in Africa, while Roy Culpeper looks at Canada's development policies as a whole and the need to-integrate development more closely into Canada's overall foreign policy priorities.

This is the second time The Norman Paterson School of International Affairs (NPSIA) has collaborated with The Centre for International Governance Innovation (CIGI) in producing the series. We are most grateful for the generous support of CIGI's Executive Director John English, who has significantly contributed to this partnership along with his infectious enthusiasm, energy, and extraordinary good will. Professor Andrew Cooper of CIGI and the University of Waterloo and my colleague at NPSIA, Professor Dane Rowlands, have provided superb editorial leadership in identifying themes, assembling the contributors to this volume, and shepherding it through to publication. As usual, they have produced a volume whose contents are as timely and provocative as the book's subtitle suggests.

Fen Osler Hampson
Director
The Norman Paterson School of International Affairs
Carleton University
Ottawa, Canada

Acknowledgments

In the long running tradition of this series, *Canada Among Nations 2006: Minorities and Priorities* has emerged through a perfect combination of circumstances and collaboration. Early 2006 witnessed the rise of a new government, ending more than twelve years of Liberal rule. With its heavily domestic-focused election platform, it was unclear what role foreign policy would play in the minority Conservative government's priorities. The new prime minister came to office with little expressed interest in world affairs, and chose a cabinet thin on international experience. This uncertainty of direction soon became the focus of this year's collection. As co-editors, we endeavoured to put together a volume that reflected a diversity of views about contemporary Canadian foreign policy and that reached our audience in a punctual manner. The individual chapters capture the scope and immediacy of numerous debates in the field, and identify the surfacing trends of, and challenges to, the new government's international policy agenda. This volume benefited greatly from the professionalism, and generosity of its contributors. Their endless enthusiasm and extensive knowledge kept the volume current and on track despite the rapidly unfolding events in Canadian foreign policy.

This year's volume is again the result of a partnership between Carleton University's Norman Paterson School of International Affairs (NPSIA) and The Centre for International Governance Innovation (CIGI), and we profited from the resources each of these institutions possessed. NPSIA has built up a huge pool of experience and expertise in producing the *Canada Among Nations* series. NPSIA Director Fen

Osler Hampson and Janet Doherty provided support and guidance throughout the endeavour. We would also like to thank Katherine Graham, Dean of the Faculty of Public Affairs and Management at Carleton University, for continuing to support the *Canada Among Nations* series. CIGI showcased its facilities by hosting the Author's Workshop in the spring of 2006. As with all the activities of CIGI this event could not have been held without the enormous support of Jim Balsillie, the Chairman of CIGI's Board of Directors, together with John English, its Executive Director. We also benefited from the insight of Paul Heinbecker, Daniel Schwanen, and Annette Hester.

The CIGI staff once again provided fabulous conference and project management support. In particular, Kelly Jackson reprised her role as organizer of the Author's Workshop and coordinator for the chapter revision process, duties she performed once more with an impressive combination of efficiency and grace. She has earned once again our heartfelt thanks. Our thanks also to Andrew Schrumm who was on board with us once again, and who excelled at the multiple tasks he was asked to take on, often on short notice. We also would like to acknowledge the help of Matthew Bunch with constructing the index, Jennifer Jones, Brian Peebles, and Ivan Capriles for their helpful input.

Finally we would like to thank all the people at McGill-Queen's University Press who worked efficiently to turn the manuscript into a book. Of particular note in this regard we acknowledge with gratitude the efforts of Philip Cercone, Joan McGilvray, and Brenda Prince. Additionally, the production and marketing teams have been of great assistance in compiling and publicizing the many volumes of this series.

Andrew F. Cooper
Dane Rowlands
Waterloo/Ottawa
July 2006

Abbreviations

3D	diplomacy, defence, and development
3T	timing, taxes, and technology
9/11	11 September 2001
ADM	Assistant Deputy Minister
AIDS	Acquired Immune Deficiency Syndrome
APEC	Asia-Pacific Economic Cooperation
ASEAN	Association of Southeast Asian Nations
bb	billion barrels
bd	barrels per day
BMD	Ballistic Missile Defence
BQ	Bloc Québécois
CARICOM	Caribbean Community
CDI	Commitment to Development Index
CERF	Central Emergency Revolving Fund
CF	Canadian Forces
CGD	Center for Global Development
CHR	Commission on Human Rights
CIC	Citizenship and Immigration Canada
CIDA	Canadian International Development Agency
CIGI	Centre for International Governance Innovation
CIVPOL	civilian police
CNPC	China National Petroleum Corporation
CUSFTA	Canada-US Free Trade Agreement
DFAIT	Department of Foreign Affairs and International Trade
DND	Department of National Defence

EPA	Energy Policy Act (US)
ERO	Electricity Reliability Organization
EU	European Union
FAd'H	Forces Armées d'Haïti
FCCC	Framework Convention on Climate Change
FDI	Foreign Direct Investment
FERC	Federal Energy Regulatory Commission
FTAA	Free Trade area of the Americas
G7/8	Group of Seven/Eight (Industrialized Nations)
G77	Group of Seventy-Seven
GATT	General Agreement on Tariffs and Trade
GDP	Gross Domestic Product
GHG	greenhouse gas
GNP	Gross National Product
GNI	Gross National Income
GST	Goods and Services Tax
HIV	Human Immunodeficiency Virus
HLP	High-Level Panel
HNP	Haitian National Police
IADB	Inter-American Development Bank
ICC	International Criminal Court
ICCS	International Control Commissions
ICF	Interim Cooperation Framework
IDRC	International Development Research Centre
IMF	International Monetary Fund
IPS	*International Policy Statement*
IRPA	Immigrant Refugee Protection Act
ISAF	International Security Assistance Force (NATO)
IT	Information Technology
KP	Kyoto Protocol
L20	Leaders' Twenty Summit
LFE	large final emitter
LICUS	Low Income Countries Under Stress
LNG	liquefied natural gas
mb	million barrels
MD	Millennium Declaration
MDGs	Millennium Development Goals
MIF	Multilateral Interim Force (Haiti)
MINUSTAH	United Nations Stabilization Mission in Haiti
MoU	Memorandum of Understanding
MP	Member of Parliament
NAEWG	North American Energy Working Group
NAFTA	North American Free Trade Agreement

NAM	Non-Aligned Movement
NATO	North Atlantic Treaty Organisation
NDP	New Democratic Party
NDRC	National Development Reform Commission (China)
NEPAD	New Partnership for Africa's Development
NERC	North American Electricity Reliability Council
NERO	North American Electricity Reliability Organization
NGO	Non-Governmental Organization
NORAD	North American Aerospace Defense Command
NPSIA	Norman Paterson School of International Affairs
NRCAN	Natural Resources Canada
NSP	National Security Policy
OAS	Organization of American States
ODA	official development assistance
OECD	Organisation for Economic Co-operation and Development
OEF	Operation Enduring Freedom (US)
OPEC	Organization of the Petroleum Exporting Countries
P5	Permanent Five Members of the UN Security Council
PBA	Programme Based Approach
PBSO	Peacebuilding Support Office
PCO	Privy Council Office
PEMEX	Petróleos Mexicanos
PMO	Prime Minister's Office
PQ	Parti Québécois
R2P	Responsibility to Protect
R&D	Research and Development
RCMP	Royal Canadian Mounted Police
REOs	regional electricity organizations
SARS	Severe Acute Respiratory Syndrome
SCO	Shanghai Cooperation Organization
SDI	Strategic Defense Initiative
SPP	Security and Prosperity Partnership of North America
SSA	Sub-Saharan Africa
TCF	trillion cubic feet
UK	United Kingdom
UN	United Nations
UNDP	United Nations Development Programme
UNECE	United Nations Economic Commission for Europe
UNESCO	United Nations Educational, Scientific and Cultural Organization
UNGA	United Nations General Assembly
UNPROFOR	United Nations Protection Force

UNSC	United Nations Security Council
US	United States of America
WCSB	Western Canadian Sedimentary Basin
WMD	weapons of mass destruction
WTO	World Trade Organization

I Positioning Policy Priorities
in a Minority Context:
Prospects for the Harper
Government

ANDREW F. COOPER
AND DANE ROWLANDS

The Canadian federal election of January 2006 brought to an end more than a dozen years of Liberal rule. The shaky year-and-a-half old minority government led by Paul Martin was replaced by the minority government of Stephen Harper and his Conservative Party. This state of transition – with both a dramatic shift between different minority governments and their priorities – is at the heart of the 2006 volume of *Canada Among Nations*. Such a shift provides a stark contrast to the last transition from Liberals to Conservatives. In 1984, Brian Mulroney came to power with a massive parliamentary majority, but with little expertise or interest in international affairs (Michaud and Nossal, 2001: 5). Harper has no such decisive mandate, and moved into office with seemingly even less interest in foreign policy. The world has also changed dramatically since Mulroney left office in the early 1990s. The end of the Cold War brought with it a sense of optimism that was later wiped away completely by the tragedy of 11 September 2001, the Iraq invasion and insurgency, and the extended 'war on terror.'

Amidst these uncertainties, however, the Harper minority government has already indicated in declaratory and operational terms that it is prepared to move in a very different direction than the Martin minority government, and to do so with a sharp contrast in style. The previous government had become bogged down in what ostensibly became an unending international policy review process; an attempt by Martin to put his stamp on government policy that turned sour. Martin's own enthusiasm for an activist foreign policy stands out, but this genuine sense of commitment did not translate into a clear sense of direction. At the centre of this debate at the declaratory level was the 'interests versus values' dilemma that proved to be a huge distraction, a dilemma highlighted in last year's *Canada Among Nations* volume (Cooper and Rowlands, 2005).

The initial operational signal by the Martin government was that it would take a less obvious anti-American posture than that of the previous Liberal government of Jean Chrétien, which held power for a decade between 1993 and 2003. But this pragmatic instinct was not acted upon in any coherent fashion. Nor was there much to show for the activist spirit beyond heightened expectations. Even experienced observers of Canadian foreign policy faced difficulties extracting any meaningful signals from the relatively large amount of noise (see Stairs et al., 2005). For all of its hyperactivity – which surfaced in areas as diverse as promoting a Leaders' 20 Summit, establishing the Canada Corps, and pushing for humanitarian interventionism in Darfur – Prime Minister Martin's administration was widely judged to have generated far more promises than delivery in its performance by the time it was defeated.

Fast forward one year and the noise-to-signal ratio is not the primary problem in trying to understand the new Conservative government's foreign policy. Instead of a surfeit of information we now face a huge knowledge deficit. Neither Prime Minister Harper nor any of his newly appointed cabinet ministers had previously identified foreign affairs as one of their preoccupations or had pursued careers that involved extensive international work. It is perhaps not surprising then, that none of the new government's famous 'five priorities' have much, if any, foreign policy content. Accentuated by the government's suspicion of the national media – which it wants to leave out in the cold – figuring out the likely directions of the new administration's external policy is a demanding task. This constant mistrust shown through its preference for local, rather than national, coverage seems to be only part of a wider strategy. As one journalist expressed, "This is the way they're going to be running the country. It's not just early game jitters. This is part of a deep-rooted belief set. It's almost a culture."[1]

NASCENT INTERNATIONAL PRIORITIES

This is not to say that there have been no indications of what the new government plans to focus on. Although the majority of election promises and the bulk of the first Speech from the Throne focused on domestic issues, the Conservatives have given hints of their international agenda during its initial months in office. Six foreign policy themes do emerge from the statements and activities of the new government thus far. The first theme speaks to the main game of Canadian foreign policy:

our relations with the United States. At the core of the attempt to renew the foundations of this relationship is security. The Conservative government has quickly demonstrated its commitment to the Afghanistan mission, with Prime Minister Stephen Harper and Minister of Foreign Affairs Peter MacKay both making visits early in their tenure to that country, and through a promised extension to the Canadian contribution to the mission of the North Atlantic Treaty Organization (NATO). The high profile given to the Afghanistan mission amidst all its risks is a clear signal to the United States that Canada is a reliable ally in the 'war on terror.' The extent to which the Conservatives have defended and supported Canada's role in Afghanistan has led some observers to suggest that, even though he inherited the mission from the Liberals, it will be remembered as Harper's war (see Madonik, 2006: F1).

The Conservative government has found other ways as well to indicate its willingness and desire to engage with the Americans in a more constructive manner than its predecessor. Flexibility facilitated what looks to be a breakthrough agreement on the perennial Canada-United States trade irritant, softwood lumber (Whittington, 2006: A6). A more congenial approach generally has improved the mood between Ottawa and Washington, and is hardly surprising. Derek Burney (2005), who led Prime Minister Harper's transition team and remains a heavyweight in the Ottawa game, identified the need for such an approach to underpin a more "confident relationship with the United States" in the 2005 volume of *Canada Among Nations*. Whatever the calls for a value-oriented Canadian foreign policy, ultimately there can be no serious denial of the centrality of the United States to Canada's international relations.

At the same time, the Harper government has been careful not to be seen as too cozy with the United States. The anti-American (or perhaps more accurately anti-President George W. Bush) sentiments evident within sections of the Liberal Party, whether in office or not, represent the feelings of a wider segment of the Canadian population that is not easily dismissed in electoral terms, a segment that can help make the difference between majority and minority governments. Facing the very real prospect of another federal election while the profoundly unpopular Bush administration is still in the White House, the minority Conservatives cannot easily afford to be seen as uncritically supportive of American policy.

Through this lens, Harper must have been very thankful to American Ambassador David Wilkins for lobbing him a softball on Canadian sovereignty in the Arctic shortly after the election. Within hours of the Conservative victory, Wilkins spoke out against Harper's plan to station military personnel in the North. "[The American] position is very consistent," he said, "We agree to disagree. We don't recognize Canada's claim to the waters" (cited in Galloway, 2006). The opportunity to lightly chastise the American government on an issue of far greater significance to us than it is to them was played to perfection. Harper responding with enthusiasm, stated that his government had a mandate from the Canadian people, "not the ambassador from the United States" (Ibid.). As long as they remain a minority in Parliament, the Conservative government has to find a way to balance their greater affinity for American-friendly policies with the apparent hesitation of many Canadians to be tied too closely to the United States in general, and to the administration of President Bush in particular.

A second and saliently related theme is the government's commitment to rebuilding the capacity of the Canadian Armed Forces and to improving Canadian security. While not one of its electoral "priorities," the military featured as a prominent sub-theme for the party both before and during the last election. The Liberal government had also indicated its intentions to expand Canada's military capacity, though after a dozen years of relative neglect the Conservatives were able to obtain some electoral mileage by questioning the seriousness of its commitment. Their first budget, entitled "Focusing on Priorities," delivered on the pledge, increasing expenditures by $1.1 billion through the 2007–08 budget cycle and by $5.3 billion over five years. Another $404 million was provided for border security initiatives through to 2007–08 (Canada, 2006).

In conjunction with its commitment to expand military capacity, the Harper administration has provided some clues about how a reinvigorated armed forces are to be deployed. The government has sought to shore up fragile and flagging public support for the mission in Afghanistan by having a parliamentary debate in May 2006 over the extension of the mission. While the debate was highly contentious, the non-binding motion of support was eventually passed by a narrow margin facilitated by the awkward divisions within the opposition Liberal party. In a similar vein – albeit based on a far greater domestic rationale – there has been continued support for a less robust mission in Haiti. Noticeably absent was the commitment of troops to Darfur, a priority of Paul Martin under the auspices of the Responsibility to Protect (R2P) doctrine.

Canada's development policies represent a third area where the new government's intentions are becoming somewhat more visible, though they may perhaps be best characterized as policies of relatively benign neglect. A poll conducted soon after the Harper administration took office, showed that only 11 percent of Canadians expect the new government to do better in aiding the world's poor than the outgoing Liberals

(POLLARA, 2006: 4). These doubts may have been somewhat quelled by the promises made in the Conservatives' first budget. The government has pledged to make good on past commitments made by its predecessor to double Canada's aid budget from its 2001–02 levels by 2010–11. An additional $320 million was made available for various health initiatives, all of which is to be funnelled rather pointedly through multilateral channels rather than through the Canadian International Development Agency (CIDA) (see Canada, 2006: 13). The appointment of Josée Verner as Minister for International Cooperation, responsible for CIDA, itself sent a mixed message. As a key minister from Quebec, she provides some weight to a cabinet post long seen as a temporary parking space for those either on the way up or the way out. Yet, as evident in the early decision by the Conservatives to suspend aid to the newly elected Palestinian Hamas government, Verner was easily sidelined with the decision being made by the prime minister and championed in the media by the minister of foreign affairs (see Adeba, 2006: 5). Furthermore, the lack of any long-standing personal connection to the international development community and the absence of any emphasis on development assistance during the electoral campaign suggest that managing her portfolio may receive somewhat less than her undivided attention. It is expected that much of her effort will be spent in winning the political hearts and minds (or at least votes) in Quebec. For those hoping that the extensive rhetoric on international development generated by the Liberal government would lead to action by its Conservative replacement will be disappointed, at least for the time being.

Migration represents a fourth component of international policy that has emerged in the new government's program. Again the message is a sensitive one that balances the need to nurture Canada's diversity against calls for the curbing of immigration as a means of addressing the threat of terrorism (Mickleburgh, 2006: A1). Thus there are some significant initiatives to appeal to migrants in 'minority groups.' In addition to instituting a reduction in the immigrant landing fee and a commitment to more efficiently facilitate the recognition of foreign credentials, Harper has issued an official apology for the head tax levied on Chinese migrants. In effect until 1923 under the Chinese Exclusion Act (not repealed until 1947), the head tax has remained a black mark in Canada's history, and has been a humiliation to the Chinese-Canadian community. The cabinet has also approved a redress package for those charged the "racist" tax (Campion-Smith, 2006: A15). Choosing to address these specific issues may be seen as an attempt by the government to improve its standing in urban centres, having won no seats in Toronto, Montréal or Vancouver in the January election. At the same time, there is an apparent antipathy to an expansion in immigrant numbers, which the

Liberals had promised, and a harder line on the deportation of unsuccessful refugee claimants. Increasingly, Canada's immigration policies and the perceived insecurity of its borders have been under the watchful eye of Washington, straining the bilateral relationship. The issue of possible 'home produced' terrorism has unfortunately heightened sensitivities, and may not only widen rifts with the US. It may also present difficulties for the Conservatives on the domestic front, specifically on the role of multiculturalism in Canadian society, an issue on which the Liberal Party has long held a monopoly.

A fifth theme centres on Canada's obligations under the Kyoto Protocol on climate change. Despite chairing a UN meeting on Kyoto, the minister of the environment has articulated the government's ambivalence to meeting the targets for emissions reductions. Minister Rona Ambrose has defended the government's position by identifying the poor job done by the previous Liberal government in negotiating and ratifying an unrealistic set of targets for Canada. To those opposed to Kyoto, especially those in Western Canada where the economy revolves around extractive industries, and Conservative members of parliament who speak for these interests, the humbling of Kyoto is long overdue. Environmentalists, in contrast, are outraged. David Suzuki (2006) warns that giving up on our Kyoto commitments puts Canada's "international reputation as a trustworthy, just nation and also as an environmental leader" in serious jeopardy. "Ignoring commitments, politicizing science and dumping on the environment," he argues, "are not exactly sources of pride." Worse yet, from the government's perspective, critics are able to play the anti-American card by linking both anti-environmentalism with an apparent unilateral disregard for international treaties. More instrumentally, the decision to formally remove ourselves from the treaty could take years of legal battles, emissions penalties, and trade sanctions, diverting attention away from actually solving the issue at hand (Reguly, 2006: B2). For a country traditionally reliant on rules and institutions to protect it from the whims of larger powers, Canada cannot lightly cast aside the obligations we enter. At the same time, international institutions and rules need to be practical, and adopting resolutions that are not enforced and targets that cannot be met are also harmful to the construction of a global rules-based system that has been a key foundation of Canadian foreign policy. While the government has not yet resolved this dilemma, in raising doubts about our commitment to Kyoto it has illustrated its preparedness to question the sanctity of this traditional foundation.[2]

Finally, the sixth theme shows the government's amenable inclinations to the opening up of Canadian foreign policy to provincial participation.

The most obvious example is the promise to allow representation from Quebec at the United Nations Educational, Scientific and Cultural Organization (UNESCO). As one commentator noted, this position brought "new life" to an old debate in Quebec, making it an important election issue (Fraser, 2005: B1). The offer could be seen as a hastily conceived way of appealing to soft nationalists in Quebec, or as a manifestation of the kind of flexible and decentralized federalism championed by the new Conservative Party and its predecessors in the Canadian Alliance and Reform Parties (Hébert, 2006: A17). In the end, someone noticed that the initial apparent promise of an independent seat at UNESCO was inconsistent with that organization's rules, and the offer was reformulated as a seat within Canada's delegation. It is not clear whether this absence of clarity reflected a careful electoral calculus or a simple lack of awareness about what the Canadian government can and cannot do within an international institution (see Post, 2006: FP19). In either event, it showed the government's preparedness to dilute its traditional near-monopoly on foreign affairs in response to domestic exigencies.

DISSECTING THESE THEMES

The emerging framework of the new government's foreign policy is mirrored in the themes of this volume. When we first conceived of the possible chapters for this year's volume, we could not be sure what the next government would look like. At the time, the election campaigning had just begun, and various outcomes seemed possible. On one extreme, the Liberal administration of Paul Martin could possibly have been able to hang on for another year, giving us an opportunity to see whether the international policy review process and the *International Policy Statement* could be brought to life. On the other extreme, the election could have generated a new majority government (presumably Conservative) with a mandate to explore in a more unfettered manner its own foreign policy inclinations. In the end neither emerged, and we have instead a new Conservative government that must at least temporarily temper its initiatives in the light of its minority status.

Amidst this uncertainty, we identified two themes that had not received extensive coverage in *Canada Among Nations* in recent years: international development and migration. One of the original ideas was to examine the role of minority groups in the making of Canadian foreign policy. This theme will have to await a future volume, as the presence of a different kind of minority began to consume our attention. Ultimately, the idea of 'minorities' came to encompass the government, as well as regional and migrant groups within Canadian society. The 'priorities' in turn reflected our own initial interest in important policy themes as well as the government's own announced agenda. What has emerged is a review of both what we might expect from the new Conservative government, and what we see as some of the policy challenges and opportunities that they will face.

AN AUTHENTIC CONSERVATIVE APPROACH?

At the time this volume went to press, the government had only had a limited opportunity to articulate its foreign policy program. Therefore, we thought it would be useful to invite the respected Conservative thinker and strategist Senator Hugh Segal to provide the opening chapter for this volume. He provides an outline of how the new government's thinking on foreign policy is embedded in pragmatism and an understanding that Canada can best pursue its interests by constructively engaging with the United States. He is comfortable in speaking of both fundamental values and core interests in the same sentence, although that does not mean he is unaware of the potential complexities of policy and the presence of hard choices to be made. Above all, however, Senator Segal emphasizes the importance of practicality, of process that acknowledges (though not necessarily accommodates) dissent, of ambition that reflects capacity, and of flexibility in tactics and instruments in the pursuit of enduring objectives.

Following from Senator Segal's overview, John Kirton makes the general argument that new governments bring with them a new foreign policy agenda, new concepts to guide and frame their parameters and component policies, and new resource distributions and decisions to put them into effect. And looking through the specific lens of its first 100 days in power, he argues that the Harper government will be not be an exception to this rule.

Kirton asserts that none of the common place predictions of observers have been accurate in anticipating what has occurred so far in terms of the new government's foreign policy. Distinctively, the Harper government has created a "made-in-Canada" foreign policy doctrine, founded on leadership for global democratic development, merging Canadian values in its interest-based operations. This approach is evident in its recommitment to Afghanistan, the strengthening of the tools of national and Arctic sovereignty, the inclusion of Quebec at international cultural institutions, and the advancement of its free trade interests in North America, the Americas, and Asia-Pacific. In examining its first months in power, Kirton contends that the Harper government has been firm and decisive in its foreign policy decisions.

Whereas Kirton emphasizes the Harper government's will and skill, Adam Chapnick identifies a basic contradiction in the Conservative foreign policy approach. He contrasts the pronouncements made by Harper in Afghanistan, where he called for Canadian leadership through international frameworks and alluded to selfless Canadian internationalism, with those made by Minister Ambrose on Canada's inability to meet Kyoto targets and the need for a Canadian-focused approach to climate change. He claims that this paradox can best be explained by locating the Harper government's style within Canada's deeper historical experience as both approaches are consistent with Canadian traditions. Chapnick suggests that Harper's approach to Afghanistan reflects the idealistic, if not also the "messianic rhetoric" of Canada as a leading good international citizen. The methodology on Kyoto signifies, in his view, a more "realistically reflective" approach of a country that has long held conservative views on foreign policy, commonly advancing its own national concerns ahead of those of the world around it.

In his chapter, Chapnick reviews the evolution of the Conservative foreign policy agenda as a sub-set of its domestic agenda, and points to a crisis of branding wherein the Harper government will have trouble distinguishing itself from previous Liberal governments who articulated strong international agendas. With its minority status, the Conservatives have additional limits on how bold they can be. In turning his attention to how best the Harper government can overcome these dilemmas, Chapnick looks back to the experience of the minority governments of Lester B. Pearson. He identifies a number of similarities between these governments recommending that the Conservatives take some liberal internationalist advice, and act conservatively.

PRIORITIZING PARTNERS

This section identifies issues and opportunities for cooperation and leadership outside of our borders and our immediate interests. David Malone's chapter closely examines the state of affairs concerning the modernization and reform of the United Nations (UN). He makes the case that these debates are relevant to Canada's new government as the nature of UN reform may decide much about the future of Canada's diplomacy, and argues that within this process there exists the possibility for Canada to be a global leader. The terror attacks of 9/11, and their aftermath fundamentally changed the atmosphere of optimism surrounding the UN's expanding agenda in the immediate post-Cold War era. Malone highlights how the Security Council debate on Iraq in early 2003 divided major world players; where some lost faith in the UN's ability to prevent war, while others were disappointed in its refusal to support the war. He then outlines the steps taken by UN Secretary-General Kofi Annan to try to reinvigorate the UN through reform measures – the High Level Panel on Threats, Challenges and Change, Annan's response, and the World Summit of 2005.

Malone notes that the adoption of the R2P doctrine by the World Summit was a triumph for Canada. Yet this initiative might not prove to be as influential as hoped. Expectations are high for its implementation, and its ability to force action in humanitarian crises remains uncertain. He introduces the selection of the new secretary-general as a key issue that will be a determinant in the future of reform for the organization. Malone concludes that the new government will work to apply its domestic priorities of accountability, transparency, and program efficiency to the UN reform effort.

Alongside the diplomatic experience of Malone, Marie Bernard-Meunier, a former Canadian Ambassador to Germany, the Netherlands, and UNESCO, proposes that the new government pursue a strategy of renewed engagement with Europe. She asserts that Europe – although largely ignored in Canadian foreign policy – provides the opportunity for cooperation on a range of issues beyond trade with a cohort of reliable, like-minded, multilateral-oriented players with large resources and strong political will. Bernard-Meunier looks at why Canada has lost its European focus. She suggests that this distancing occurred not only because of Europe's own inward-looking mentality over the past decades, but that it is also due to some negative Canadian assumptions about doing business with a highly complex, multi-lingual political union.

She argues that Canada and Europe have much to learn from one another. For Canada, it should attempt to gain from the experience of the European Union integration movement, and appreciate its relevance to its own continental affairs. Equally, Canada is attractive to Europe as a case study for its management of public finances, its immigration policy, and its federalism. Bernard-Meunier affirms that Europe is interested in learning how Canada killed its deficit, and manages a liberal democratic federation while maintaining strong social programs. Furthermore, she argues that there is interest in Canada's ability to increase its cultural diversity and its initiatives designed to accommodate demanding provinces. She concludes that Canada should not be so narrowly focused on its relationship with the US, and that for too long it has ignored other partners with which it may have more common ground, and greater influence. The Canada-Europe relationship has much to offer both parties.

Continuing on a similar theme, Christopher Sands reviews the current state of Canada-US relations, and suggests that analysis of the relationship must be put in the global context, as Canada is one of many middle power countries that are competing for US attention. Some of these countries have found comparatively better methods of adapting to US interests and outlooks. He observes that the new Conservative government has expressed great interest in recasting the relationship, but asserts that there is no simple recipe to strengthen the relationship.

Sands' chapter looks at how third-country issues may be the means for a strategic realignment in Canada-US relations. He identifies Afghanistan as the centerpiece of this approach, as it meets US interests and is concentrated in an area where Canada can excel. He submits that it is important for the new Canadian government to make smart choices in this regard, as such an agenda (especially in the security realm) has the potential to be quite costly. Before Canada can advance successful third-country initiatives, however, there are two misconceptions that need to be overcome. The first of which is the folly of restoration, and the mistaken tendency to reminisce about an equal relationship that never existed between Canada and the US. And the second is the folly of some alternative options. The belief that Canada can become a global superpower on issues such as human rights is but one example of this kind of naïveté. He argues that for Canada to be an effective and attractive partner to the US, it must build on its values and traditions, harnessing its real strengths and capabilities. But in doing so, it must also choose to pursue policies that are appealing to the US. International democracy promotion and domestic counter-terrorism measures are two areas which fit these specific criteria, and are explored in greater detail in his chapter.

Before a renewed strategic relationship is possible with the US, or any other country, Canada needs a comprehensive and clearly articulated international security policy. Elinor Sloan looks specifically at this issue, and analyses the directions of the new Conservative government in this arena. Her chapter provides an extensive examination of the emerging international security policy of the Harper government, which by her definition includes not only national defence, but also an economic element relating to the maintenance of our expected standard of living.

She charts each previous administration's security priorities since the Second World War, and highlights the Martin government's 2004 National Security Policy (NSP), noting that this contained the first recognition of the "homeland" as an important element of our broader security interests. Next, she examines the multilateral, bilateral, and economic dimensions of the Conservatives' security policy, and more specifically, she examines Harper's firm commitment to the Afghanistan mission. She introduces the discussion surrounding ballistic missile defence (BMD), suggesting that in an attempt to gain favour with the

US, the new government may reopen talks on Canadian participation. Sloan critically analyses Harper's "Canada First" strategy, which emphasizes the strengthening of domestic capacities to enforce sovereignty, especially in the Arctic region.

Sloan concludes with an analysis of the challenges and constraints the current government is likely to face as it continues to develop the military component of its international security policy. She identifies funding as the primary constraint, even in a period of large surpluses, yet asserts that the public is much more amenable to spending increases in this area now than it was a few years ago. The Conservatives also, in her view, face great risks in its commitment to our mission in Afghanistan, particularly with respect to the increasingly dangerous nature of the Canadian Forces' missions, the unclear leadership between NATO and the US, and shaky public support. Afghanistan has in many ways become Harper's war, win or lose.

The final chapter of this section merges the themes of international security and Canada-US relations. Ann Denholm Crosby gives a detailed history of Canada's involvement with the BMD system, from Reagan's Strategic Defense Initiative to George W. Bush's advancement of the weaponization of space. In particular, she details the relationship of the North American Aerospace Defense Command (NORAD) to the BMD system. Canada has a long history of opposing the weaponization of space and this position has been reflected in the way Canada's role within NORAD operations has been defined, and through its refusal to participate beyond the identification of missile threats. Denholm Crosby argues that the newly signed agreement, as it has been negotiated and signed after the decision of the Martin government vis-à-vis non-participation in BMD, reflects a contradiction of this long-standing position. She argues that even if the BMD discussions could be reopened with the US, there would be little more that Canada could do to increase our involvement. In her view, Canada is essentially an active participant without officially recognizing its position.

Denholm Crosby argues that although NORAD provides us a "seat at the table" with the US, it has been a forum where US priorities have influenced Canada's, and not the other way around. That is to say, in such an arrangement, the weaker state is "more apt to be influenced than the stronger." Renewal of the Canadian NORAD commitment is thus a recognition of US priorities, BMD being one of them. Denholm Crosby sees the challenge for the minority Conservative government in this regard as twofold. First, it must maintain its Throne Speech commitments and hold a public discussion on this policy decision, and second, to ensure that this discussion is an informed one.

MINOR PRIORITIES
AND PRIOR MINORITIES?

The focus of this next section moves to some of the more specific areas of foreign policy that have emerged, or are emerging, as secondary issues for the government. It begins with Christina Gabriel's review of recent migration policy initiatives. These changes predate the current government, and identify the long-term pressure for migration reform that has emerged in Canada. After describing current policies, Gabriel draws attention to the paradox of Canada's established points based system. Designed to attract migrants with a more desirable economic profile, the evidence she marshals suggests that their performance relative to other Canadians is not improving. Their effect on the economic and political landscape is also examined, as settlement patterns become increasingly concentrated in the three largest metropolitan areas. In addition, Canada's immigration program and its focus on economic selection is raising questions of citizenship, labour rights, and the balance between different categories of migrants.

The question of migration is thus established by Gabriel as worthy of serious attention by the new government, and is fraught with potential pitfalls for them. For countries such as Canada it is becoming increasingly clear that immigration is the only available remedy for declining birth rates and the threat of a dwindling labour supply. In seeking to assure economic expansion and efficiency, Prime Minister Harper cannot ignore the question of migration. As immigration becomes the major source of population growth it will be increasingly difficult to view them collectively as a 'minority.' They will increasingly have to be seen as individuals belonging to distinctive groups, with their own strengths and challenges, just as Gabriel shows in her focus on the divergence between those immigrants identified as skilled, and those seen as unskilled. In addition, immigration is seen as complicating national security, and offering challenges to social cohesiveness in a country that traditionally sees itself as tolerant and multicultural. Finally, the traditional voting and settlement patterns of immigrants affects the electoral calculus of any government, and will be viewed with caution by a government challenged by its paucity of urban seats. Immigration, therefore, is an issue with startling broad linkages to a variety of the government's stated or presumed priorities.

Yasmine Shamsie's examination of Canadian policy in Haiti provides an interesting case study that blends many of the themes of the volume, including security, intervention, migration, development, and Canada-US relations. After reviewing developments in Canada's Haiti policy, Shamsie identifies Canada's unique ability to contribute to Haiti's ongoing effort to find a path of sustainable economic, social, and political development. The various Canadian interests at stake in Haiti in turn provide the justification for action. She argues, in contrast to Sloan, that Canada's international interests lie beyond Afghanistan and Darfur, and that we must be leaders in Haiti – a country that is of greater importance to Canada than mere strategic interests. She identifies a number of areas where Canadian policy can change in order to play a more constructive role, including the need to question development strategies that ignore Haiti's rural population. The case of Haiti highlights the difficulty of defining a coherent multi-dimensional intervention strategy, showing how Canada's 3D (diplomacy, defence, and development) approach to fragile states is in need of reformulation. As a scenario for pursuing our interests in improving relations with the United States, and in acting in accord with our internationalist agenda, however, continued engagement with Haiti offers many advantages for Canada along with the difficult challenges. Amidst the many uncertainties surrounding Canada's involvement in Haiti is the question of whether the 3D approach itself will survive.

One of the political dimensions of Haiti is the role of the Haitian diaspora in Quebec and its ability to affect foreign policy. The role of minority groups and specific regions in modifying international policy is picked up in the next chapter as well. More specifically, Nelson Michaud focuses on the new government's attempt to accommodate Quebec's international aspirations. Michaud traces through the history of this accommodation from previous governments through to Prime Minister Harper's recent efforts. He illustrates that the desire to accommodate, especially for short-term political gain, often runs up against both practical constraints as well as deeply held sentiments in the foreign policy community. In the former case, as the UNESCO promise illustrated, there are rules determining which levels of government can function in an international forum. In the latter case, the long held view that international affairs is and must be the sole prerogative of the federal government, and that it must retain this monopoly in order to be able to articulate a clear and unified foreign policy, has a strong pedigree in Ottawa. Any attempt to carve out a special role for Quebec will inevitably disturb this cherished monopoly.

As Michaud points out, however, clinging to past traditions in the face of the challenges of globalization is itself dangerous. By reviewing the history of Quebec's claims for an international role, and illustrating how increasing international linkages and obligations complicate the exercise of powers distributed by aging constitutional arrangements, Michaud makes a strong case for flexibility in the accommodation of the legitimate international aspirations of the provinces. A strict enforcement of the division of powers in the international context will ultimately make a mockery of international treaties dealing with provincial responsibilities. Instead, Michaud outlines how the lessons of other federations might be helpful in identifying a satisfactory compromise satisfactory in the Canadian context, one that permits provincial voices to be articulated at the international level through a structured engagement with the federal government. This solution, it turns out, is effectively what the Harper government hit on to solve the problem of Quebec's role at UNESCO.

COMPETING PRIORITIES: ENERGY, THE ENVIRONMENT, AND HUMAN RIGHTS

Of course Quebec is not the only province with specific interests. Alberta also has international objectives focused on securing markets for its resource wealth, primarily its fossil fuels. These interests emerge in Wenran Jiang's chapter on China and the Asia Pacific region. The rise of this region as a major consumer of Canadian raw materials has shifted economic power westwards in Canada. At the same time, the rise of China makes it ever harder for the Canadian government to balance its economic interests with its more humanitarian inclinations, as the pursuit of trade interests will come increasingly in conflict with human rights concerns. A final complicating factor is the emerging political importance of Canadians of Chinese origin.

In short, the China case also contains many of the volume's important themes: regional influences on international relations, the debate between values and interests, and the role of diasporas in Canadian policy. Finding the delicate balance between these competing levels of engagement will not be easy. As a consequence, Jiang concludes that the current government will adhere cautiously to the existing "China strategy" that they inherited. This proposed solution, however, can only be a temporary one. At some point, and probably sooner than Prime Minister Harper might wish, the government will have to make some difficult decisions regarding China. Will the government facilitate an expanding trading relationship with important infrastructure investment? Will Chinese ownership of key resources be allowed? Will the Canadian government continue to court business in China, while simultaneously lecturing the Chinese government on human rights? The Conservatives have not yet given any signal on how they will confront these questions.

China, however, is only one market for energy, and a rather distant one at that. There is more than enough continental demand to satisfy producers in Canada and Mexico. Isidro Morales examines the compelling logic of North American energy security and integration. The preoccupation of the United States with secure and reliable energy sources holds great potential for Canada. There are costs to embracing the concept of North American energy integration, however, and these are distributed rather unevenly across the Canadian political landscape. Morales identifies three key avenues for discord within Canada. The first is conflict arising between provinces that produce oil and those that consume it. The former gain politically and financially from energy integration, while the latter face reduced influence and possibly the sacrifice of their own energy security to the demands of the larger American market. The second conflict arises over the implications of expanded energy production for the Arctic region. The pursuit of oil resources above the Arctic circle may have implications for Canadian sovereignty claims in the region, for aboriginal land claims and living conditions, and for the environment. Does a continental energy program mean drilling in sensitive wilderness regions in Alaska and the Canadian territories? If so, would this be politically acceptable to the Canadian public? The third contest will be over wider environmental issues, and particularly over the implications for Kyoto and global warming of a program that fosters petroleum production. The new Conservative government may have an easier time charting a path through these political minefields because of its apparent comfort with markets and cooperation with the United States, its Western power base, and its relative scepticism regarding the need to mollify the environmental mainstream.

These conflicts will inevitably be further exacerbated by the international dimensions of continental energy integration as well. The Americans do not want just energy, they want energy security. That means greater regulatory cooperation and integration on electricity grids, pipelines, and other energy conduits. Regulation often takes place at the state or provincial level, however, and is therefore somewhat hetero-geneous in quality. As the 2003 blackout in Ontario and the North-Eastern United States illustrated, massive portions of the continent can be brought down by one weak link in the transmission chain. In the push to create an efficient and reliable continental energy market the federal government will have to confront the tricky problem of how much integration with the United States will be acceptable to Canadians before there is a sense that too much sovereignty has been compromised, and too much foreign and domestic policy flexibility lost. For example, will our commitments to a continental energy alliance impinge upon our capacity to determine our own environmental policies?

Daniel Schwanen tackles the question of Kyoto and climate change policy directly in his chapter. He tracks Canada's dismal record in meeting its agreed upon targets, and lays much of the blame on the previous government's poor negotiation strategy and subsequent procrastination. The rhetorical hot air expelled in support of Kyoto by the Liberal government stood in stark contrast to the reality of reduced greenhouse gas emissions, serving as a prime example of the dissonance between the expectations it created and the delivery of effective policy. Having inherited the Kyoto debacle, Schwanen suggests that the current government has little choice but to seek a renegotiation of its targets and to get to work on an effective and efficient program to reduce emissions. Thus far the government has moved rather more quickly on the renegotiation component by signalling its disenchantment with Kyoto. While it might be tempting to treat this as an isolated retreat from a poorly-conceived environmental framework, the reality is that Canada has typically placed great faith in the sanctity of ratified international obligations, and violating this principle may have subsequent and undesirable repercussions.

The challenges of environmental policy-making in Canada are exceedingly complex. Governments have long tolerated or fostered an artificial dissonance between the prioritizing of the environment and the economy, thereby facilitating a more extreme discourse than is either necessary or helpful. The middle ground that pragmatically balances ecological capacity and vulnerability with economic and social needs and aspirations has been diluted. Consequently the environmental debate has become more politically charged, making it necessary for governments to consider carefully the electoral consequences of upsetting diametrically opposed provincial and regional sensitivities and powerful interest groups. Schwanen contends that the government must deal with the Kyoto debacle by first coming clean on its views about the science of global warming and its belief about the ecosystem's capacity to tolerate the environmental impact of human activity. The second step is to identify who has the responsibility for action to bring emissions in line with the desired targets. Only then will the government be able to credibly negotiate the distribution of responsibilities amongst different states. These negotiations will not be easy, as it does not simply entail a static division of costs, but a view about how to accommodate the unfolding circumstances of developing countries.

MAKING DEVELOPMENT A PRIORITY

The last two chapters deal with a less formal set of international obligations that Canada has traditionally accepted, even if our execution of them has been less than stellar. Chapters by David Black and Roy Culpeper examine the theme of Canadian development policy. Black does so by focusing on Canada's aid program in Africa. He asks three basic questions. How much real change has the focus on Africa delivered? What have been the consequences of these changes? Will the Conservative government sustain the emphasis on Africa? For the most he is rather pessimistic that significant change has occurred, though there is evidence that donors (including Canada) have been able to introduce some measures that acknowledge the importance of recipient ownership and capacity building. The problems of fragile states and the potential for aid 'orphans' to be shunned by donors, however, remain unaddressed.

Black is unable to discover much interest in development assistance on the part of the new government, which means that in the short run at least it will be carried forward by the inertia of past policy initiatives. Over the longer run, however, Black doubts that the Conservative government will be inclined to devote sustained attention or resources to development assistance generally or Africa specifically, and that a renaissance for Canada's development program is unlikely. In the absence of renewal CIDA programs will likely remain largely subordinate to wider security and diplomatic interests.

The final chapter by Roy Culpeper lays out his view of the possible foundations of such a renaissance. Culpeper weaves a variety of emerging threads in development thinking into a single policy fabric. While gaps remain and details need to be fleshed out, he is able to provide a compelling sketch of the basics of a coherent and multifaceted development policy. Picking up on the construction of a "commitment to development" index, he highlights briefly the important but limited role of traditional development policy instruments such as aid and even trade. Instead, he puts the spotlight on relatively neglected policy areas such as migration and technology transfer regimes. Onto this wider understanding of development policy he attaches greater policy space for the developing country governments themselves, and the need to revisit the components of the traditional restructuring packages that are embedded in policy conditionality. More specifically he suggests that problematic policies such as liberalization and privatization need to be reconsidered, while greater emphasis is placed on redistribution and equity. Instead of echoing past disenchantment with official development ideology, these impulses are derived from a careful re-examination of the development experience by agencies such as the World Bank.

Finally, Culpeper emphasizes the importance of domestic resource mobilization within developing countries, arguing that facilitating reliance on their own political and economic resources is the surest way to bring about growth and development in poorer countries. The emphasis on a more Southern-centric development strategy is complemented by Culpeper's suggestion for greater Northern humility and care, embodied in his suggestion that wealthier countries adopt a Hippocratic, "first, do no harm" principle to guide their development policies.

REVIVING VALUES AND INTERESTS

Some of these suggestions – an emphasis on self-help and a de-emphasis on aid – may well resonate with the new government. Other elements – a focus on redistribution and a questioning of economic orthodoxy – may not hold much appeal for them. In trying to conceive of a coherent approach for an important dimension of foreign policy, however, Culpeper has mapped out one route to shoring up the foundations of Canadian foreign policy in a broader context. Some people will be sceptical about any government's capacity or inclination to pursue such a holistic approach, particularly one in a minority position in parliament. They may with good reason argue that the complexity of the world would inevitably lead such an exercise onto the tortuous path of another full-scale international policy review process. As the chapters in this volume of *Canada Among Nations* demonstrate, however, complexity also bedevils piecemeal responses to global developments, with unintended consequences and inconsistencies arising from seemingly isolated decisions.

Is there a compromise path between these two approaches? It is easy to fall into the trap of creating opposing compartments in which to analyze and agonize over Canadian foreign policy. Coherent and fully articulated structures are contrasted with pragmatic incrementalism, values with interests, continentalism with internationalism. In reality these dichotomies are often more synthetic than natural. What is natural, however, is to ask how a new government will reorient Canada's foreign policy. Do we expect that change will occur because of how different political parties interpret our values and priorities? Or, as Hugh Segal questions in his chapter, do we hope that our Canadian values are perpetual, with differences in policy arising from changing approaches to their pursuit?

As with other contrasts, both answers have merit even if they have different policy implications. Where policies seem to be working (at least in the political sense of not being unpopular) governments of different political stripes will often be content with incremental change. In other policy areas there may be little agreement on the most effective approaches to achieving particular objectives. In this case experimentation is likely, and it is the task of foreign policy analysts to try to make the case for the superiority of one policy over another.

In other cases the source of policy shifts may indeed be competing interpretations of Canadian values and interests. There is no reason to think that in a country as diverse as Canada that all Canadians will be unified by compatible interests and characterized by identical values. On some topics there may well be a significant or overwhelming degree of agreement. Examples of what we may call our core values and interests – our core priorities – might be our recognition of the importance of basic humanitarianism, the importance of rules and institutions, and the centrality of the United States in our economic prosperity and security. Other issues, however, may well be more contentious. Think of the environment, the role of provinces in foreign affairs, perhaps even the desirability of increased migration. In these contestable areas the task falls to the political process to define both our interests and our values, and to build a consensus for them. If they do not transcend the political process and provide an enduring component of policy, perhaps we should be careful in calling them priorities at all.

To belabour the obvious, foreign policy is not formulated in a vacuum in which these debates play out seamlessly. The domestic context makes things far more messy, and the context for all of the analysis in this volume is one of a minority government. The bottom line is that political calculations about how to secure a majority will inevitably influence how the Conservatives define Canada's international priorities.

NOTES

1 The *Ottawa Sun*'s Greg Weston, as quoted in Brown (2006: F1).
2 Funding programs for Kyoto commitments were clearly absent from the May 2006 budget, while no new initiatives on climate change were proposed (see McGregor, 2006: 1).

REFERENCES

Adeba, Brian. 2006. "Cutting Aid to Palestine Could Lead to Humanitarian Emergency," *Embassy Magazine*, no. 92 (22 February): 1, 5.

Brown, Ian. 2006. "In Harper's Regime, Big Daddy Knows Best," *Globe and Mail*, 13 May, F1.

Burney, Derek H. 2005. "The Perennial Challenge: Managing Canada-US Relations," in Andrew F. Cooper and Dane Rowlands, eds. *Canada Among Nations 2005: Split Images*. Montreal & Kingston: McGill-Queen's University Press, 47–62.

Campion-Smith. 2006. "Harper Will Apologize for Head Tax on Chinese," *Toronto Star*, 14 June, A15.

Canada. 2006. *Focusing on Priorities: The Budget in Brief 2006*. Ottawa: Department of Finance. Available at: <http://www.fin.gc.ca/budget06/brief/briefe.htm>

Cooper, Andrew F., and Dane Rowlands. 2005. "A State of Disconnects: The Fracturing of Canadian Foreign Policy," in Cooper and Rowlands, eds. *Canada Among Nations 2005: Split Images*. Montreal & Kingston: McGill-Queen's University Press, 3–21.

Fraser, Graham. 2005. "New Life in Old Québec Doctrine," *Toronto Star*, 31 December, B1.

Galloway, Gloria. 2006. "Harper Rebukes US Envoy over Arctic Dispute," *Globe and Mail*, 27 January.

Hébert, Chantal. 2006. "Harper on a Roll in Québec," *Toronto Star*, 8 May, A17.

Mandonik, Rick. 2006. "Canada at War," *Toronto Star*, 20 May, F1.

McGregor, Sarah. 2006. "Military, Borders Get a Boost; Kyoto and Trade Suffer," *Embassy Magazine*, no. 102 (3 May): 1, 10.

Michaud, Nelson, and Kim Richard Nossal. 2001. "The Conservative Era in Canadian Foreign Policy," in Michaud and Nossal, eds. *Diplomatic Departures*. Vancouver: UBC Press, 3–24.

Mickleburgh, Rod. 2006. "Harper Defends Canadian Diversity," *Globe and Mail*, 20 June, A1.

POLLARA. 2006. *Canadians' Expectations for Stephen Harper's Foreign Policy*. Report on National Poll for the Canadian Institute of International Affairs, February. Available at: <http://www.pollara.ca/library.html>

Post, Isaac. 2006. "Harper Falls into the UNESCO Trap," *National Post*, 9 May, FP19.

Reguly, Eric. 2006. "Kyoto Protocol No One-Night Stand," *Globe and Mail*, 4 May, B2.

Stairs, Denis, David J. Bercuson, Mark Entwisle, J.L. Granatstein, Kim Richard Nossal, and Gordon S. Smith. 2005. *In the National Interest: Canadian Foreign Policy in an Insecure World*. Calgary: Canadian Defence and Foreign Affairs Institute.

Suzuki, David. 2006. "Canada's International Reputation in Jeopardy," David Suzuki Foundation, *Science Matters*, 19 May. Available at: <http://www.davidsuzuki.org>

Whittington, Les. 2006. "US 'Gave Up Nothing' on Softwood," *Toronto Star*, 11 May, A6.

An Authentic Conservative Approach?

2 Compassion, Realism, Engagement and Focus: A Conservative Foreign Policy Thematic

HUGH SEGAL

Canada's foreign policy context springs from its unique position in a world where more often than not, aggression and responses to aggression shape the foreign policy of other countries. The first priority of Canadian foreign policy in these turbulent times must be ensuring the right balance between idealism and robust practicality. What can Canada pragmatically accomplish and are its goals attainable in the world-wide arena? Religious extremist and terrorist groups in the larger world are threatening the values we hold dear; those of civility, democracy, understanding and acceptance of cultural diversity, the adherence to the rule of law, and the common decency not to make innocent civilians terrorist targets. Canada's foreign policy ambitions cannot ignore the mindsets of those who are determined to challenge the rights of Canadians to believe and reflect our own values, and to do so without fear.

The primary purpose of foreign policy is the advancement of a country's fundamental values and core interests abroad. The mindset of the post-11 September 2001 world is one of suspicion and intolerance where Canadian values are constantly being tested. While our Canadian values we hope, are perpetual, the instruments for their achievement have changed over time and may well have to change in the future.

In order for Canada's new minority government to put its own stamp on foreign policy, concessions will be required to balance its goals and objectives with the parliamentary prerequisite of consensus. Furthermore, realistic intentions from members opposite will be crucial to the government's ability to gain support for its proposed initiatives. This country's commitment to international stability, the principles of the United Nation's Charter and the North Atlantic Treaty Organisation (NATO) are generally shared by Canadian political parties of all stripes. Where there is a difference of opinion, and these differences may very well be exacerbated in a minority government situation, they rise to the surface on matters of emphasis and design. But the broad pervasive multi-party support for the new agreement of the North American Aerospace Defense Command (NORAD) on 8 May 2006, speaks eloquently to the areas of consensus that exist.

Canada's new government makes no secret of its belief that our influence, world-wide, is impacted greatly by the apparent success of our relationship with the United States. This does not imply blanket acceptance of US foreign policy in that Canada may differ substantively with the Americans on a host of foreign policy issues. However, the management of our relationship with the United States on all files – from trade to defence, from immigration to the environment – must be a Canadian core priority that is put ahead of all others. Canada cannot and should not minimize the importance of its relationship with the United States and allow shallow anti-American sentiment to distort its priorities for purely political gain. We are geographically intertwined and our undefended border generates a symbiotic relationship that cannot be overstated. Economic and security priorities mean that Canada and the United States have no choice but to work together. Partnering with the United States on common issues affecting security, our environment, our border, and our flow of trade and people is an absolute necessity. Our concurrence (or not) with all of American foreign policy, in no way diminishes the Canadian exigency for stable and cordial relations with the United States overall.

The coincidence of a new Canadian government and a major military procurement programme in support of enhanced deployability for the Canadian forces in humanitarian and combat roles, speaks to a compelling window of opportunity for reshaping Canada's global presence. Not so much in terms of the increase in resources but in terms of the focus and design. The minority nature of the House of Commons as well as the substantial opposition majority in the Senate guarantees that, at some level, this reshaping will need to be inclusive and subtle, and in many ways could be a key opportunity to be seized. As was obvious on 23 January 2006, Canadian voters did not entrust any one party with their complete support and confidence. As a result, no one party is able to totally control and shape the Canadian agenda. A government has a duty to reflect the values of the people it represents, and when in a minority parliament, it has an additional responsibility to listen and hear the views of those parties in opposition. This parliament, its makeup and the message sent by the voters through its election, suggests a foreign policy process with input from all positions on the spectrum. Therefore, voters in their wisdom have authored a joint approach where all parliamentary parties will, out of necessity, need to play a role. In this minority parliament, with the numbers broken down as they are, Canada's foreign policy can be reshaped with the input of the left, the right, and all those somewhere in between.

Foreign policy must be and perceived to be manageable and practicable. Its aims must be acceptable at home and trustworthy abroad. An exaggerated foreign policy frame-work abroad, without the necessary resources or support from home, is as unconstructive as a limited, domestically focused foreign policy frame-work that has no salience or credibility abroad. Canada must be realistic in its undertakings knowing that the material support for the key elements of defence, development and diplomacy are in place. Conversely, Canada must not over-reach in support of defence or developmental goals and then be unable to deliver fiscally. We must move beyond lecturing others and then leave the table before the bill arrives. We must make our values real and interests precise through the aid, diplomacy, or other deployments necessary to have genuine impact.

Canada's foreign policy under the new government has already been subtly shifted by the prime minister in his statements outlining a more pragmatic approach to the United States. As with the new government's overall agenda focus on core priorities, its foreign policy objectives are also assiduously focused. On Canada's foreign policy file, the prime minister has chosen to concentrate on critical values like democratization, the repelling of terrorism, and a stronger continental relationship. This is not a government prepared to throw a myriad of foreign policy suggestions against a wall to see which ones might stick. Foreign policy cannot be all things to all people and Canada's contribution to the international agenda should not be prefaced with excessive promises of unrealistic success. Canada must be open to the world and loyal to its allies. We must be prepared to defend national security at home and, in the spirit of core Canadian values, engage our humanitarian, diplomatic and when necessary, our military capacity against oppression, against deprivation and most definitely, against aggression abroad. The notion of concentrating on clear foreign policy priorities, as opposed to a host of world involvement missions, also implies the politics of making choices. By virtue of the parliamentary make-up, these choices must and will involve the input of all parties.

The new government has committed to bringing all treaties to the House for debate and vote. The commitment also extends to all new military engagements. This undertaking is unprecedented in Canadian history. It embraces the role of parliament in the process of engagement, foreign policy promise-making and its ultimate, successful delivery. In order to speak to these issues, there will be pressure on all parties and parliamentarians to be both well-informed and reasonable in the positions they endorse. The decisions taken in a minority parliament relating to engagement or treaties will have the capacity to dramatically impact the future of Canada's role on the world stage, and the minority make-up of parliament encourages all members of both houses to recognize the influence of their decisions. Similarly, it encourages the government to put forward sensible proposals that can withstand the scrutiny and gain the acceptance of parliamentarians from more than one political party.

In the past, Canada has shown unwavering commitment to the defence of freedom and to the respect for international law. We discharged our duties in both world wars in the same way we took a leading peacekeeping role in the post-Korean War era and the UN-sphere of influence in places like the Congo, Cyprus and the Middle East. Today, there are forces in various parts of the world that do not respond to the old rules of engagement; they operate covertly, assimilate with local innocent populations and specifically target non-combatants. This has resulted in a rethinking of doctrine and practice when forming and implementing national foreign policy. Canada's Foreign Relations Committee in the House of Commons, its Standing Committee on National Defence and the Senate Standing Committees on National Defence, Security and Foreign Affairs have all contributed, in a remarkably non-partisan fashion, to the debate on modern foreign policy doctrine and practice. There is no reason to believe that this non-partisan cooperation will not continue and indeed, the likelihood is that it will be enhanced due to the parliamentary make-up.

The new Conservative government has an established record in advocating a more vigorous commitment to an increased complement of necessary tools for a viable and deployable modern armed force. Parliamentarians of all stripes have been fully engaged in the committees of the House and Senate to frame Canada's policy and subsequent role on the international stage, especially as it relates to the funding and/or the deployment of our forces.

In keeping with Canada's values and traditions, its vital foreign policy interests are reflected in a world where the poorest are making steady and measurable progress towards some economic and social justice; where international law and respect for core civility and democracy are gaining momentum. It is a world where the fanaticism of the left or the right, of the religious or terrorist extremes is marginalized through a growing mainstream that is democratic and tolerant. Make no mistake, Canada's world vision has real enemies, individuals and groups that are well-funded, violent, and nihilistic in intent. They are prepared to target Canada and Canadians, our allies and our trading partners. This does not diminish the traditional Canadian commitment to humanitarian and peaceful outcomes and transitions in areas of the world where a calming Canadian presence is required. But neither does it negate the need for a firm and, if necessary, military resolve to engage in defence of the values and interests we hold dear. We must define 'vital interests' and choose those that require the protection of the Canadian government, namely the national security of our people and territories, the freest possible global movement of goods and services, the rule of law and advance of democracy, freedom and enhanced equality of opportunity.

The successful promotion and defence of these interests requires an integrated strategy that unifies diplomacy, foreign aid, intelligence, and military deployment (when necessary) to address the sources and causes of terrorism. Canadians understand that the root causes breeding terrorism go far beyond religious or extremist views; they also spring from the absence of democracy and the prevalence of oppression and poverty in many geographic centres where terrorist recruitment occurs. In the continued support of freedom and economic progress at home, it is in Canada's vital interest that we develop the necessary strategy to integrate all our resources to promote security and democracy abroad. Canadian citizenship does not cloak us in armour making us impervious to the threats of those who decry our values and ideals.

The nature of migration pressures facing Canada, both within our own hemisphere and from overseas, illustrates that investment abroad to help create economic opportunity and growth remains an important stabilizing opportunity creating options to mass emigration from regions of diminished economic opportunity. For this and other reasons, continuing the push to bring our foreign aid dollars to the proposed Pearsonic level of 0.7 percent of our GNP remains of vital importance. The need, in Africa especially, to engage fully on anti-viral, anti-malarial and nutrition initiatives has never mattered more. Pursuing our own vital interests remains important – but they cannot be disconnected from our collective humanitarian obligations to our fellow human beings. Africa tends to evoke great despair and disengagement at one level because of the size and breadth of the problems; but it is important that areas where progress is being made on development, on democratic engagement, on the rule of law and the broadening of aspects of the economic mainstream not be marginalized or ignored. Africa is a place of challenge, robust courage and immense indigenous strength and resilience. Canada may need to reflect on how best to continue and calibrate our commitment in the region. The commitment remains important and substantive – as should be our preparedness to consider whether there are better ways to advance our partnership with Africa and Africans in the years ahead.

Canada must learn from its failures in Haiti and in Africa, and redouble its engagement in these areas to find better instruments to achieve progress and success. We must not fail to confront difficult issues like North Korea and Iran, even if these result in having to make controversial decisions. Turning away from risk and danger under the guise of Canada's recent history as peace-maker, peace-keeper, and nation-builder is no longer an alternative. It is Canada's duty to be prepared to intervene, either with NATO, the United Nations, or other alliances to combat aggression, repel ethnic cleansing, or counter civil oppression and brutality. In order to do this, we must have the military plans and capacity to contribute when necessary and have the ability to follow through and sustain post-conflict transition. Our presence in Afghanistan is a reflection of those core values of democracy, tolerance, and pluralism. To further our long-term goals, we need to consider more joint and combined operations inviting a broader spectrum of stakeholders to participate, some military, some economic and humanitarian, and some who specialize in the infrastructure of transition and democracy in order to facilitate a healthy post-conflict society.

Canada's relationships with its friends and allies in NATO, in the European Union, and in Asia, need to be strengthened. The depth of these relationships must be developed anew to diminish potential disharmony. As Canadians, we do sometimes have a different view of the world because we have a unique perspective that reflects our social values and expectations. But on the larger core interests of living without fear of intimidation, preserving democracy and an open pluralist society we share far more with our friends and allies than could ever divide us.

Part of our leverage in the larger world – which has diminished over the last while – comes from our capacity to influence the United States. Tending to that relationship, pruning, weeding, seeding, watering and growing that relationship is never wrong nor does it imply lock step agreement with America. During the 1953–93 period, we negotiated the Autopact, the Colombia River Treaty, the St. Lawrence Seaway, NORAD, the Canada-US Free Trade Agreement, the North America Free Trade Agreement, plus a critical mass of agreements that deepened economic integration and a host of protocols for joint training and operations. That period of time also saw disagreements on Cuba, the Bomarc Missile, Central America, South Africa, and Viet Nam. And yet, the relationship continued to deepen and flourish.

The new government may not be able to move forward with a sweeping foreign policy agenda, constrained as it is by its minority status in the

House of Commons. However, Canada's position and standing in the world need not be stalled while we await the results of the next general election, or the one after that. This country and its parliamentarians have been given an opportunity to make their mark on the world stage in a spirit of cooperation, consensus, and compromise.

The ideas and essays in this book are an important part of our foreign policy debate about where this country stands or ought to stand in the world. I agree with many of the ideas and reflections presented and with others, I do not. However, the ideas and analysis are an important contribution to the necessary discussions relating to Canada's place on the world stage; its abilities and its limitations. This book is also a timely reminder that foreign policy discussions must not stagnate regardless of how the parliamentary numbers break down. Members of all parties must recognize the importance of keeping Canada's global presence and capacity at the fore because the intended and real foreign policy capacities of this country are genuine and the grounds for moving forward are powerful. Debate and analysis is profoundly healthy when discussing the protection and advancement of our geopolitical interests. As with my premise that Canadian foreign policy is about choices – some of them obvious and some of them difficult – so do the ideas presented in this book offer thoughtful and intelligent analysis of Canada's choices, instruments, measures and histories that inform the foreign policy debate going forward.

3 Harper's "Made in Canada" Global Leadership

J O H N   K I R T O N

On 23 January 2006, Canadians elected Stephen Harper's Conservatives with a minority government of 124 seats in the 308 seat House of Commons. Two weeks later, the 46 year old western Canadian was sworn in as Canada's 22nd Prime Minister. Even before he assumed the office, the debate over where Canadian foreign policy would go under Harper's leadership had erupted in full force. It continued along much the same lines for his first 100 days in office, which came to a close in mid-May.

The first and most popular school of thought suggested that the Conservatives would pursue a 'restrained retreat to America.' It forecasted a focus on cooperation with the United States, limited by the Conservative's fragile majority position and lack of ideological partners among other parties in the House. Canadian scholar Janice Stein predicted a "greater affinity with US positions internationally," including a pro-American tilt on relations with the Middle East and the United Nations (UN) (cited in McCarthy, 2006). American scholarly observers such as Joseph Jockel, Christopher Sands, David Biette, and Dwight Mason thought the tone and ease of the relationship would improve, that Harper would make good on his defence promises, but that the close, high-level relations of the last Progressive Conservative government would be avoided, given Harper's minority at home (Koring, 2006; Biette, 2006).

A second school foretold a new period of 'ignorant isolationism.' It viewed Harper's government as having little instinct for international activism aimed at America or anywhere else. This flowed from the new prime minister's personal ignorance of, and lack of interest in, international affairs, and the failure of Canadian society to make him change. Columnist Jeffrey Simpson (2006) thought that under Harper's leadership Canada would be a "small, parochial, even self absorbed country" without views on the rise of India and China or crises in Iraq and Iran. This was due, in Simpson's view, to the paltry foreign affairs platform of the Conservatives, their deliberate silence on international affairs during the campaign, a prime minister "with no experience or apparent interest in the world, and a party in power without a single front-bencher qualified by experience or interest to become foreign affairs minister." A harsher version of this strain offered up inexperienced incompetence as the central theme as Harper's government got underway (Ibbitson, 2006).

A third school, in sharp contrast, presented Harper as a decisive self confident calculator, driven by his personal penchant for rational policy analysis and his concern with the next election campaign while facing the constraints of a minority government (see Martin, 2006; McDougall 2006, Campbell, 2006; Galloway, 2006b; and Corcoran, 2006). Supporting evidence first came from Harper's fast and firm assertion of Canada's Arctic sovereignty and his apparent about face in keeping Canada in the Kyoto accord on climate change. As Harper's first 100 days in office concluded, Andrew Coyne (2006) wrote: "The most striking departures have been in the area of foreign affairs: the Prime Minister's bold visit to Afghanistan, with that stirring call to Canadian 'leadership;' the groundbreaking decision to withdraw funding from the Hamas regime in Palestine; the long-overdue designation of the Tamil Tigers as a terrorist group. And capping them all, the softwood lumber deal: evidence, perhaps, that better relations with the United States pays dividends."

The initial questions about Harper's foreign policy were understandable, coming as they did in the immediate wake of the highly familiar and internationally experienced Liberal Prime Minister Paul Martin. But these schools of thought were unable to provide convincing estimates or explanations of what foreign policy challenges the new government would face and how and why it would respond. After the Harper government's first 100 days in office, more convincing answers came. The Harper Conservatives proclaimed a "made in Canada" foreign policy of leadership for global democratic development, based on interest and value based initiatives in demographic diversity, defence, democratization, development and human rights around the world. These directions were driven by a decisive prime minister that took policy analysis seriously, a prime minister and party that fully absorbed the Progressive Conservative tradition it depends on to govern and to deliver the early majority government it sought, and above all by the rationally calculated realist conclusions and self confidence derived from a rapidly changing world, with a more vulnerable America and more capable Canada at its core (Kirton, 2007).

HARPER'S FOREIGN POLICY DOCTRINE

The Harper government's desire for a foreign policy founded on leadership for global democratic development was first seen in its evolving doctrine, from the party's campaign platform, election promises, and victory night address, through to the first Speech from the Throne on 4 April 2006.

The Campaign Platform and Promises

The new prime minister's personal inexperience in international affairs, and his immediate promise, once elected, to "deliver on our commitments" placed a premium on the promises about foreign policy that he and his party had made in their party platform and on the campaign trail. Whereas Simpson and others argued that there was little international content in the platform document *Stand Up for Canada*, there were actually several promises that covered a broad range of issues, countries, and institutions (Conservative Party of Canada, 2006a). Thematically, the platform opened with the imperative to "strengthen national unity and advance our interests on the world stage." It recognized "increased competition from around the world" and the need to protect Canada in its many disputes with America, notably those on softwood lumber, the Canadian Wheat Board, the Byrd Amendment and imported crime (Ibid.: 16).

Economically, it highlighted leadership and initiative in global openness. It pledged to chart a course for the future of the North American Free Trade Agreement (NAFTA), reassert Canadian leadership in negotiations for a Free Trade Area of the Americas (FTAA), and "explore the possibility of free trade negotiations with Canada's democratic and economic partners in the Asia-Pacific, Japan and India." Environmentally, it promised to control greenhouse gas emissions with a plan developed "in coordination with other major industrial countries" and to extend Canada's custodial management in the North Atlantic to the edge of the Continental Shelf, the nose and tail of the Grand Banks, and the Flemish Cap. Its security priorities included defence against the new global vulnerabilities of terrorist attacks, natural disasters, and "outbreaks of disease world-wide." Educationally, it declared it would facilitate recognition of the credentials of immigrants, and (as elaborated by

Nelson Michaud, this volume) it would "invite the Government of Quebec to play a role at the Paris-based United Nations Economic, Social and Cultural Organization (UNESCO) along the lines of its participation in la Francophonie" (Ibid.: 42).

The platform's featured countries were the United States, portrayed in largely negative terms, and Australia, the United Kingdom, India, and Japan, all presented in a positive light. The most frequently noted international institutions were the Group of Eight (G8) major market democracies, the Organisation for Economic Co-operation and Development (OECD) and NAFTA, with la Francophonie, the FTAA, the World Trade Organization (WTO), and UNESCO also on the list. The UN itself in its New York incarnation did not appear at all.

On the campaign trail, in his 'promise a day' electoral strategy that helped produce his electoral victory, Harper issued 23 news releases devoted to international affairs. Thirteen were devoted to security; among them were nine offering to strengthen the military, and two each to do so for Arctic sovereignty and Afghanistan. Three were on immigration and multiculturalism, notably addressing the need to act against Canada's protectionist 'head tax.' Three were about democratization – celebrating Ukraine's 'orange revolution'; condemning Iran's pledge to destroy Israel; and, mourning the death of the leader of the United Arab Emirates. Three dealt with development, headed by a pledge to add C$425 million in official development assistance (ODA), as well as commemorating World AIDS Day and the anniversary of the Asian Tsunami. Only one of Harper's news releases covered trade issues, where he expressed strong support for the Pacific Gateway Initiative.

The Victory Night Address

In his election night victory address, the prime minister-designate said much about international affairs, and offered a single message about Canada's approach – the enduring Canadian value of democracy, for which Canadians had and still fought and "for which too many in our world still yearn" (Harper, 2006a). He proceeded to promise, "We will continue to help defend our values and democratic ideals around the world – as so courageously demonstrated by those young Canadian soldiers who are serving and who have sacrificed in Afghanistan." Two additional messages celebrated immigrants and new Canadians, and promised to "work co-operatively with our friends and allies, and constructively with all nations of the world" (Ibid.). With America absent from his speech, Harper's approach was safely grounded in Progressive Conservative Prime Minister Brian Mulroney's 'constructive internationalism,' and the shared value of democracy and cooperation with friends and allies. Yet

the emphasis was on Canada's distinctive national values of multiculturalism, openness, and globalism, and on Harper's willingness to use force in
Canada's long war in distant Afghanistan (Kirton, 2007: 198).

The First Speech from the Throne

The Harper government's first Speech from the Throne developed this
foreign policy doctrine in a major way. Foreign policy subjects constituted one third of the speech substantively and one fourth of the declared priorities, and appeared from the start, were feature in the
middle and also at the end. Noteworthy for a government apparently
firmly focused on five specific domestic priorities, foreign policy had
become one of the Throne Speech's declared priorities of government,
families, federation, and "our role in the world." The speech opened
with a theme of "Building a Stronger Canada" where foreign policy
was an integral component, and ended with the foreign policy section
entitled "Canada – Strong, United, Independent, Free."

Even by the effusive standards of Throne Speeches, Harper's government offered an exceptionally ambitious conception of Canada's international cadence, relative capability, commitment to leadership, and
capacity to make a difference in the world. Due to the unique "diversity of its people," their "vast country" had become "one of the most
successful the world has ever seen" now at the "leading edge of science, business, the arts and sport," with Canadians from Italy through
Afghanistan to Asia demonstrating "time and time again that they are
leaders." Thus the government pronounced its confidence in "the capacity of Canadians to ... build an even stronger Canada, striving for
excellence, anchored by enduring values, and infused with growing
confidence that they can make a difference at home and in the world"
(Canada, 2006: 3).

As the above passages signal, this vision of international affairs was
driven by both material reality and distinctive national values of demographic openness, multiculturalism, and globalism. Yet national unity
was also a driver of this vision, for in "... the international community,
Canada is stronger when we speak with one voice, but that voice must
belong to all of us." Importantly, it was the "special cultural responsibilities of the government of Quebec" alone that would lead the
Harper government to invite Quebec to play an undefined "role" in
UNESCO (Ibid.: 9).

The speech embraced most major regions, with a focus on the world as
a whole and Afghanistan in particular. Most other regions and countries
were dealt with equally. The two references to the US were evenly balanced, with the first unfavourable reference to "improving the security of

our borders" offset by the subsequent favourable reference to building "stronger multilateral and bilateral relationships, starting with Canada's relationship with the United States, our best friend and largest trading partner" (Ibid.: 9). The speech further highlighted greater resources for both defence and development, including the use of force.

RESOURCE DISTRIBUTIONS

Translating this expansive doctrine into reality were the government's early resource distributions of personnel, departmental machinery, summit and ministerial diplomacy, and budgeting, through to the first formal government-wide budget of 2 May 2006.

Personnel Appointments

In the domain of personnel, the prime minister-designate appointed Derek Burney on 24 January to lead his transition team. Described by Harper as a "former Canadian ambassador," Burney had served as Canada's Ambassador to Washington from 1990 to 1993, and had played a key role in negotiating the Canada-US Free Trade Agreement in 1988 and fostering many other Mulroney-era continental and international policy achievements (see Burney, 2005). He brought to this post a background in the Foreign Service, having acquired his early experience in Asia, in addition to his Ottawa experience of serving as Chief of Staff to Progressive Conservative Prime Minister Brian Mulroney, and internationally as his sherpa for the G7 summits in 1990 and 1991.

Joining Burney on the transition team were several other senior Mulroney-era Progressive Conservatives with extensive experience in priority areas of international affairs. Foremost among these was Michael Wilson, who as Brian Mulroney's finance minister had helped craft Canada's continental free trade agreement with the United States in 1988, secured Canada's admission to the new G7 Finance Ministers' forum in 1986, helped host the 1988 G7 Summit in Wilson's hometown of Toronto, and win the a second Progressive Conservative majority mandate in the general election that fall. In mid-February, Harper appointed Wilson as Ambassador to the United States, replacing the recently resigned Liberal political appointee Frank McKenna. Wilson was well known and liked in Washington, especially among the Republicans who had worked with and were close to President George H.W. Bush. Wilson's first and major achievement as ambassador was to produce a negotiated deal to end to the long-standing softwood lumber dispute.

The premium Harper placed on experience and professionalism was evident in another early appointment. A career foreign service officer,

John McNee, was named as a Permanent Representative to the UN in New York, to replace the departing Liberal political appointee Allan Rock. This confidence in experienced diplomatic professionalism, and an ensuing desire to professionalize rather than politicize Canada's diplomatic corps was reinforced by Canada's mediation in May of a peace agreement in Darfur. Here Rock, flying in from New York, worked with career diplomat David Angel who had long served with distinction in the US, at the Kananaskis summit and in the G8 on the African front.

Departmental Machinery

In the domain of departmental machinery, one of Harper's first decisions as prime minister was to reintegrate the departments of Foreign Affairs and International Trade. It thus undid the divorce instigated by Paul Martin on his first day in office. The decision was consistent with both Burney's declared views on the issue, and the Conservatives' successful opposition to the divorce in the House of Commons the previous year.

Summit Diplomacy

In the domain of summit diplomacy, Harper clearly showed a global vision rather than a continental focus on developing an accommodating relationship with the US. In sharp contrast to Lester B. Pearson, who just days after his election had rushed down to the US to receive America's nuclear weapons and bring the President's American flag back home, Harper's first visit abroad came in mid-March, when he made a surprise visit to distant Afghanistan to visit the Canadian troops there. He thus became only the second Canadian prime minister to visit the country, following Jean Chrétien's stopover there in 2003.

Harper began his multi-day visit late on 11 March, when he touched down at Kandahar airport, to be welcomed by Chief of the Defence Staff General Rick Hillier and Canadian troops. The trip was noteworthy not only for the destination, and for making Afghan President Hamid Karzai the partner for Harper's first summit visit abroad, but for the forum it provided the prime minister to publicly articulate his vision for Canadian foreign policy. Here, Canadian leadership in defence of Canada's national interests and Canadian values was the central theme. He declared that Afghanistan was the most important place in the world for Canada's exercise of leadership. He added, "Canada is not an island. We live in a dangerous world. And we have to show leadership in that world ..." He identified Afghanistan as the best example in decades of "Canada really standing up, going to the front line, articulating our values, not just our opposition to terror, our advancement of democracy, but basic humanitarian values, in terms of development, women's rights, education" (Harper, 2006b). The main message of leadership in global democratic development was unmistakeably clear.

Harper's second summit visit abroad came just over a month later, near the end of March. Again it was not to the United States for a bilateral encounter with George W. Bush but to Mexico. When Mexico's Vicente Fox (fast approaching the end of his term as Mexico's president), extended the invitation for a NAFTA summit, it was unclear whether President Bush would accept. When he did, it was Harper who proved to be reluctant, suggesting it might be too soon for his new government to take the trip. But on 30–1 March he traveled to Cancùn, Mexico, for the second stand-alone North American trilateral summit since 1956. While Harper was following in Paul Martin's 2005 footsteps, both in the visit and in its boost for the work of the new Strategic and Prosperity Partnership (SPP), it was at this second encounter in as many years that this rare event became a regular occurrence. Harper's promise to host the 2007 trilateral summit made him a founding father of a plurilateral summit-level institution, with a defined frequency and hosting order, where the three North American leaders could meet as equals to promote the growing web of trilateral cooperation below. As the 'restrained retreat to America' school had predicted, Harper had not brought back Brian Mulroney's institutionalized 'Shamrock Summitry' with the US. Rather he had helped bring to life a new, more expansive summit institution with Mexico equally and integrally involved.

In the realm of 'direct dial diplomacy' there were also few signs that the United States stood out. While Bush phoned quickly, so did many other world leaders. These included Russia's President Vladimir Putin, who invited Harper to attend the G8 summit in St. Petersburg on 15-17 July 2006. Harper's list of summit visitors to Ottawa further expanded the global vision and francophone dimension of his approach. One such visitor was the newly elected president of Haiti. Another was Australia's John Howard, the first Australian prime minister to address parliament since 1944.

Budgetary Allocations

Another concrete sign of the delivery of a new doctrine came in the form of budgetary allocations. Although, here it appeared by March that funding for the two big expenditure items, defence and development, would increase less quickly than it had earlier seemed. On 13 December 2005, Harper had announced he would "significantly increase defence spending as part of a 'Canada First' defence strategy" to beef-up Canadian sovereignty. He would do so by acquiring "at least three strategic lift aircraft ... a 650 strong airborne battalion ... available for rapid or difficult deployments for emergency, humanitarian, or military operations ... and doubling the size and capacity of the Disaster Assistance Response Team (DART) ... to enhance international disaster relief capability" (Conservative Party of Canada, 2005). A global deployment capability, independent of American or Russian airlift resources, to support international humanitarian relief efforts, was the focus here. He would also do so by strengthening Canada's military presence in the Arctic, through sovereignty patrols in the air and on the sea, and by acquiring three new heavy icebreakers, operated by the uniformed military rather than the civilian Coast Guard.

One month later, on 13 January 2006, Harper promised to "boost overseas development assistance by C$425 million over five years beyond the currently projected level ... to move toward the average level among OECD members." The new money was to be added to the existing commitment to an 8 percent annual increase in ODA until 2010 already scheduled under the previous Liberal administration. The goal was to "articulate Canada's core values of freedom, democracy, the rule of law, human rights, free markets, and free trade – and compassion for the less fortunate – on the world stage" (Conservative Party of Canada, 2006b). The pledge departed from a UN demand for ODA to reach 0.7 percent of GNI in favour of a robust down-payment on a G8 Gleneagles commitment to double aid globally and to Africa within the next few years.

In its first full budget on 2 May 2006, the government, in accordance with its campaign promises and evolving doctrine, boosted international affairs spending by a substantial amount. There was a heavy emphasis on military and broader security affairs, including border security and international public health, with development spending growing substantially as well. In the field of defence, the budget would rise from $14.6 billion in 2005–06 to $16.5 billion for 2007–08. For in addition to the $12.8 billion increase over several years promised by the Liberals in 2005, the Conservatives added another $5.3 billion over five years, with $400 million coming in 2006–07, and $725 billion in 2007–08. While silent on any specific equipment purchases, the budget specified a speeding up of the hiring of 13,000 new full time and 10,000 reserve soldiers as previously promised by Harper.

In the field of development, Canada's international aid would increase to $3.8 billion in 2006–07 and to $4.1 billion in 2007–08. If the 2005–06 budget surplus exceed $2 billion, as seemed likely, an additional $320 million would flow to ODA, with $250 million of it for the

Global Fund to Fight AIDS, Tuberculosis and Malaria, and $45 million for the Global Polio Eradication Initiative. The commitments constituted a continuation of the Martin government's plans to increase ODA, but with no guaranteed early down payment on Harper's promised addition of $425 million during his first mandate.

In other international affairs areas, in accordance with campaign promises, the budget allocated $101 million to arm border guards, and a further $25 million to boost border security. The big budgetary loser was sustainable development, as the $10 billion promised by the Liberals to implement Canada's Kyoto commitment was eliminated, and replaced by a $2 billion promise to back the unspecified purposes in Harper government's "made in Canada" climate change plan when it was produced (see Schwanen, this volume).

DECISIONS

These doctrines and resource distributions were largely and quickly supported by decisions. For even before his swearing in as prime minister, Harper was compelled to make decisions on critical areas of foreign policy by the flow of fast moving changes in the world. Few of these came on the bilateral front on the inherited issues of softwood lumber, ballistic missile defence, or even NORAD, which was due for renewal in a few months. Nor did they come with any proactive moves to launch a new foreign policy review. Rather, in large part, they came on issues dealing directly with Canadian territory and sovereignty, or over the conflict ridden Middle East and Afghanistan.

Arctic Sovereignty

The first of these decisions focused on securing Arctic sovereignty. It arose in response to public comments by the US Ambassador to Canada on 25 January, stating that the US did not recognize Canada's claim to sovereignty over the Northwest Passage, and his public criticisms of Harper's campaign plans to boost Canada's military presence by putting new icebreakers there. At the end of a news conference the next day, Harper went out of his way to respond to the remarks with the words: "The Canadian government will defend our sovereignty. It is the Canadian people we get our mandate from, not the ambassador of the United States" (cited in Galloway, 2006a). In February, the now sworn in Harper government proceeded with plans for the largest ever military affirmation of Arctic sovereignty, by sending five armed patrols toward the North Pole by various routes. The moves showed clearly that Harper would put the national interest of sovereignty and territory, and not the preoccupation with good relations with the US, in first place.

Hamas Funding

The second decision came in response to the surprising victory in the Palestinian Authority election on 25 January 2006 of the political wing of Hamas, which Canada after great reluctance had designated a terrorist organization in November 2002. As prime minister-designate, Harper reaffirmed his support for a secure Israel and a democratic Palestine, but suggested that democratic governments could not support terrorism. His remarks appeared to put on hold, pending a review, a $50 million aid package for Palestine that the Liberals had assembled in response to a G8 commitment at the Gleneagles summit in July. In making this decision, Canada acted in a somewhat liberal internationalist fashion with the likeminded members of the Middle East Quartet – the US, UN, EU, and Russia.

By 27 February 2006, the EU foreign ministers, responding to pleas from the Quartet's Special Envoy, James Wolfensohn, decided the EU would provide US$142 million in emergency aid to the Palestinian Authority. Canada's position, like that of the US and Israel, remained that it would not send any funds to a Palestinian government controlled by Hamas. Having lost its European likeminded liberal internationalist company, Canada's position thus slid, at least temporarily, into a small group dominated by the US and its closest dependent friends. On 29 March 2006, Canada unilaterally cut off aid to the newly sworn in Hamas government of the Palestinian authority, for its continuing refusal to renounce violence and recognize Israel. Canada was the first country in the world outside Israel to stop the flow of funds and cut off such aid. In this case vis-à-vis the Middle East region, Janice Stein's prediction that Harper's Canada would support the US proved to be accurate. Furthermore, this response proved to be a harbinger of the approach adopted to the conflict between Israel and Hezbollah in the summer of 2006.

Afghanistan

The third and more fateful decision came in the more distant and costly theatre of Afghanistan. It was a decision which could well be the defining issue of the entire Harper government's foreign policy stewardship, and with profound implications for Canada's international policy for decades to come. As February 2006 opened, the international community gathered in London to mobilize money for an Afghanistan Compact which had first been forged in Bonn in 2001, in the immediate wake of the terrorist attacks on 11 September 2001. While Canada did not commit to a specific contribution, Prime Minister-designate Harper sent a message through Deputy Minister of Foreign Affairs Peter Harder, that Canada would "stay the course" with its mission. Canada's aid to Afghanistan – by far its largest recipient – had been c$100 million in 2004–05, and was slated to be c$100 million in 2005–06, c$60 million in 2006–07, c$50 million in 2007–08, and c$40 million in 2008–09 (Ghafouer, 2006).

Once sworn into office on 6 February, the Harper government allowed Canada's military presence to grow from 700 troops to the long scheduled increase to 2,200 by March, and for Canada to assume command of the forces in dangerous Kandahar. The decision confirmed the new government's commitment to global democracy promotion, and Canada's willingness to take global military leadership in distant theatres.

During the prime minister's trip to Afghanistan, more details of the new government's approach to this inherited involvement became clear. Harper declared that Canada would not "cut and run" from its military commitment there, implying that it might remain in the country after its current assignment ended in February 2007, as the Afghan government had pleaded with it to do (Harper, 2006b). Yet Harper also suggested that as security was successfully established, Canada's involvement would shift from defence toward other roles. He made no commitment to a further tour of military duty after the current one ended, saying that decision would come in some months. Back in Canada, on 5 April, in a reversal of Harper's earlier position, MacKay announced that a parliamentary debate on Afghanistan would be held on 10 April. April also brought the government's decision, amidst considerable controversy, not to lower the Peace Tower flag to half mast and to keep the public and media away when the remains of four Canadian soldiers killed in Afghanistan came home. In May, Harper defended the practice of Canadian troops handing over suspected Taliban insurgents to the Afghan authorities, despite the concerns of some that the local regime would violate their human rights.

Human Rights

The human rights that Harper had identified as a Canadian value while in Afghanistan were promoted in a series of decisions in several other global locales. Regarding the Middle East, Harper boldly declared the 1915 massacre of the Armenians by Turkey to have been a genocide, leading Turkey to withdraw its ambassador and threaten economic sanctions. In doing so he acted prior to a prospective French government move to do the same thing. Regarding Asia, Peter MacKay threatened to crack down on China's spies stealing Canada's industrial secrets. Canada's behind the scenes diplomacy induced Thailand to release a Chinese human rights activist in April. On 8 April, Canada also moved to declare Sri Lanka's Tamil Tigers a terrorist organization, as the US and Britain had done before. And in mid-May Harper signalled Canada's willingness, in response to request from the leaders of the US and UN, to contribute militarily to a ceasefire in Darfur designed to stop the ongoing atrocities there.

GOVERNMENT DETERMINANTS

The Harper government's growing global assertiveness was driven in the first instance by a prime minister who rapidly developed clear, self-confident views of international affairs, and who immediately assumed strong personal control over the government's foreign policy decision-making process. This self confidence and prime ministerially centered decision-making style were reinforced by Harper's direct international engagement and the early foreign policy successes he delivered, most visibly on softwood lumber, and by the uneven performances of his major international affairs ministers, notably Minister of Foreign Affairs Peter MacKay, Minister of International Trade David Emerson, and Minister of National Defence Gordon O'Connor.

Harper's Foreign Policy Belief System

Stephen Harper entered the Prime Minister's Office, as he acknowledged, with little interest or experience in international affairs. First, his beliefs flowed from his long years as a policy analyst and leader of the National Citizen's Coalition in Alberta in a political context, where principles came first but subsidiary substance mattered as well. Not only did these experiences allow him to become familiar with economic issues and energy affairs, but also shaped his outlook on the foreign affairs field, with the principles of democracy, human rights, and faith in the military standing out.

Second, Harper brought an attachment to the Conservative Party platform, which he had done much to shape as a part of the process of bringing the former Reform/Alliance and Progressive Conservative parties together and achieving the electoral victory this unification brought. His appointment of former Progressive Conservative Party leader Peter MacKay as his foreign minister showed how comfortable he was with the unified platform, in much the same way that Brian Mulroney and Joe Clark had been in 1984. His strong support for democratic Israel, increased development assistance, and the HIV/AIDS cause, reflected these roots.

Third, Harper, aware of his own unfamiliarity, was open to the advice of those who he trusted and who had vast experience in this realm. Standing out here was Derek Burney, who (as noted earlier) Harper appointed to lead his transition team and whose views on the re-integration of Foreign Affairs and International Trade he adopted as his own. Another was Bono, whose meeting with Harper had converted the latter to the African development cause and led to the c$425 million additional oda pledged in the party platform. Indeed, Harper had wanted a higher figure, such as the increase from 8 percent to 10 percent that his party's international affairs professionals had proposed. But the difficulty of securing clear information about the base figure and the need to maintain a credible, deficit-free fiscal framework in the party platform led in the end to the reduced target.

Fourth, much like Mulroney, Harper proved to be a fast learner from the direct experience that his early summit diplomacy brought. His trips abroad to Afghanistan and Mexico, and his visitors to Ottawa, brought a first hand global vision, rather than an American-centric one.

Harper's Executive Branch Decision-Making System

Despite his limited inherited interest or involvement in international affairs, Harper clearly felt confident enough to take the lead himself. He immediately structured a foreign policy decision-making system that placed the Prime Minister's Office in firm control.[1] To reinforce the expertise available to the prime minister, Harper had Derek Burney available. He also had Prime Minister Mulroney, whose advice he had sought during the lead up to the Conservative election victory in 2006.[2]

Harper appointed a very small cabinet of only 27 members, three quarters the size of the previous cabinet of Paul Martin. He appointed as his foreign minister an equally internationally inexperienced Peter MacKay whose foreign affairs acquaintance had been limited to public safety and human rights. As a separate minister of international development he appointed one of his leading new Quebec mps Josée Verner, who had once worked for Quebec's Liberal premier, Robert Bourassa. She was also assigned responsibility for Canada's relations with la Francophonie. As defence minister, Harper chose the one mp who had been the critic of the same portfolio in opposition – Gordon O'Connor. O'Connor brought a wealth of experience to the post, having been a career senior officer in the Canadian army, and briefly a consultant for the defence production industry before his election to Parliament in 2004. As minister of international trade, Harper controversially selected David Emerson, a former forest products executive and Liberal minister of industry, who crossed the floor immediately after his election to join the

Conservatives (much to the chagrin of his Vancouver constituents). As minister of finance, Harper chose Jim Flaherty, who brought with him experience as Ontario's minister of finance, and as the counsel general of Ghana in Toronto. With the cabinet's relatively small size, there was some chance that government-wide coordination could take place within the full cabinet itself.

In constructing this system, Harper was driven in part by necessity, for he had a very limited pool of individuals with extensive international affairs experience on which he could draw. His foreign minister Peter MacKay had even fewer formed foreign policy beliefs, but a natural instinct, as a former party leader, to speak out on his own on a broad range of issues beyond those confined to his precise ministerial brief.[3] The new minister arrived in his department as a very keen, bright individual, eager for new ideas from the department, with a sense of great possibilities. With no personal interests about foreign policy or the management and organization of his department, he was content to follow the direction set in his ministerial mandate letter, which put strengthening Canada's relationship with the US in first place. His fidelity to his mandate letter, and party leader instinct showed when his first public statement on foreign policy was on the softwood lumber file – an issue not in his ministerial brief. It showed again during his first visit to Washington with his lavish, Mulroney-like praise of his American counterpart Condoleezza Rice. His series of public statements requiring clarification were no more serious than those of Joe Clark under Brian Mulroney or Sidney Smith under John Diefenbaker.[4] Internationally, Canadian diplomats stationed in G8 capitals credibly told their foreign counterparts that their minister was a smart, personable politician who had come a long way, accomplished much in domestic politics and who they would likely have to deal with for a long time. At home, MacKay was ably assisted by his parliamentary secretary, Peter Van Loan, a proven bilingual front bench performer, an internationally and G8 experienced practitioner, and a representative of the party's electorally critical greater Toronto area base.

Within the cabinet, MacKay's miscues were less memorable than those of the other major international affairs ministers. Harper himself appointed the newly elected Liberal David Emerson to his cabinet as trade minister, and reversed his own position to finally allow a debate on the Afghanistan deployment in the House. Emerson was forced by deeply dissatisfied constituents in Vancouver to spend much of the first few weeks in office at home justifying his party switch, rather than in Ottawa giving trade initiatives in cabinet a fast start. Defence minister Gordon O'Connor attracted accusations that his previous brief career as a lobbyist for defence firms would compromise his judgment as minister, and subsequently by rumours that he disagreed with his chief of defence staff, the forceful General Rick Hillier, over what military equipment should be purchased first.

These early miscues bred largely by inexperience solidified both Peter MacKay's position and the prime minister's instinct that he should take the lead in foreign affairs.[5] The key Cabinet committee on priorities and planning that Harper designed, selected and chaired, included among its ten other members: MacKay; the public safety minister, former foreign affairs critic, and former Canadian Alliance leader Stockwell Day; and finance minister Flaherty; but not the ministers of trade, development, defence, or environment. The arrangement suggested that MacKay was to be primus inter pares among the international ministers, but that integration across the big international affairs portfolios would take place elsewhere.

Harper's cabinet committee system included a Foreign Affairs and National Security Committee, with a mandate to consider "foreign affairs, international development, security and defence policy issues."[6] Its eight members consisted of MacKay as chair, Day as vice chair, and the ministers of development, defence, and environment, but notably not trade.[7]

Below the cabinet level, the prospects for foreign affairs-led or other forms of coordination were also weak. To be sure, an early Order in Council declared that the foreign minister would be responsible for the "overall co-ordination of Canada's international relations," including trade and aid. It also announced the re-integration of Foreign Affairs and International Trade which had recently been split by the Martin government as one of its first acts. However the three major international affairs ministers – for foreign affairs, trade, and development – were essentially co-equal, ending a tradition in which the trade and aid minister had a reporting relationship to the foreign affairs minister. It gave the foreign minister even less leverage over the Canadian International Development Agency's (CIDA) policy, programs, and resources than it previously had.[8]

Nor were there substitute mechanisms to ensure that communication and coordination among these three major international affairs ministers routinely took place. One traditional mechanism – ongoing contact among the senior political staffers in each minister's office – was compromised by the difficulty in recruiting staff for such positions, given the promise to introduce a new 'Accountability Act' that would make such staffers unemployable as lobbyists for five years after they left public life. The problem was particularly acute in Foreign Affairs. There were thus further incentives for coordination to be produced from the top, through direct clearance by the Prime Minister's Office (PMO).

The Foreign Affairs – International Trade Department Re-Integration

Moreover, the new government's major coordinative move at the departmental level – to reintegrate the Foreign Affairs and International Trade departments – was realized less rapidly in practice than the immediate public announcement made it appear to be. There remained important questions about what the decision meant, how the re-marriage would take place, and how quickly it could be done. Even as the decision was announced to the outside world, internally Foreign Affairs was sending personnel to a new, physically separated trade department building, compounding a practice that had continued even though the legislation to split the department had been defeated in the House in early 2005. While this mentality of 'business as usual' continued, two high level committees, containing three assistant deputy ministers (ADM) from each department, studied how the reintegration should take place. There were several outstanding questions. Would the geographic bureaux get their trade components back?[9] Would they bring back the country desk principle of one stop shopping?[10] Would they restore the traditional structure of three ADMs, thus eliminating the trade department's Global Markets Branch? The process was slowed, and interdepartmental integration further compromised, by the fact that trade minister Emerson remained in Vancouver for the first few weeks after his swearing in as minister, as controversy about his party-switch and appointment raged. While his officials traveled to Vancouver to brief him, his absence from Ottawa made coordinated decisions more difficult to make.

The Afghanistan Debate

Within Ottawa's interdepartmental foreign policy community, the greatest debate beneath the surface arose over the inherited commitment to Afghanistan. Harper's firm 'stay the course' policy began to arouse dissent, not just from outside critics, but from inside doubters. These came not just from a diplomatic and development community against a united Department of National Defence, for consequential voices in the latter also wondered how the new government would manage this potentially open ended promise bequeathed by the departing Liberals, and whether it would consume all the resources for defence equipment, development assistance and diplomacy also badly needed on so many other fronts.

In the domain of policy, the doubters argued that Canada's role in Afghanistan had become one of counter-insurgency, one where Canada had no experience, and one where Canadian public support could not be assured. Indeed, Canada had now moved outside the cover of the International Security Assistance Force in Kabul into the ideological heartland of the Taliban. No one with a mission of pacification, from the British to the Soviets, had ever succeeded in this region. The local Afghans could well assume that the Canadians were just like the Americans they were replacing, and would come with the same brutal tactics of kicking down doors, using drones to send missiles into cars suspected (inaccurately) of containing terrorists, bombing weddings, and shooting to death innocent civilians for speeding or simply not stopping their cars. Canada's front line role in a US-led crusade against the Islamic world could well attract terrorist blowback for unprepared Canadians abroad or at home, as it had for the British, Australians, and Spanish before. At the very least, it would erode Canada's valuable soft power, human security, development partner global brand. It could also destroy (at home and abroad) the credit Canada got for staying out of the American-led coalition invasion of Iraq in 2003.

In the domain of decision-making, the dissidents further felt Canada was charging into Afghanistan due to a failure in foreign policy formulation. This failure was fuelled by an unbalanced militarization arising from joint military planning with the Americans, and a 'gung ho' wing of the Canadian military who wanted to try out the war kit their US colleagues used, and to do some real war fighting too. While they pushed Canada into war-fighting in rural Afghanistan, few in Ottawa focused on what it might mean in the longer term. The political level was preoccupied only by a general desire to placate the Americans and to do something constructive in the war on terrorism. Much like the deadly incrementalism that pulled America into the Viet Nam quagmire, the dissenters worried Kandahar could well become Canada's Khe San, a foreign policy failure brought on by a process where the military tail was wagging the political, diplomatic and development dog.

Indeed, the critics argued, the development wing of a supposedly integrated Canadian foreign policy was not staying the course for the 'long haul' but rather planning on quickly getting out. The largest bilateral recipient of Canadian ODA in 2005-06 was Afghanistan – a country not even on the Martin government's priority list of 24 countries as CIDA aid recipients. Over the next few years the ODA allocations for Afghanistan were scheduled to fall from the hundreds of millions to the tens of millions. CIDA's NGO clients such as Médecins Sans Frontières were already pulling out of an Afghanistan too dangerous for them. They feared that the mission was too much associated with the military and counterinsurgency and would compromise their humanitarianism. On the diplomatic wing, the government had not replaced its senior diplomat killed in Afghanistan the month before. Canada's much pronounced 3D (diplomacy, defence, development) strategy seemed to have lost two of its Ds, and was predominately left with a military mission for counterinsurgency alone.

Public Support

Despite these debates in Ottawa, Harper was encouraged by the growing support from a Canadian mass public not predisposed to giving him and his party a honeymoon or the benefit of the doubt. His personal and party approval ratings increased overall nationally, in Quebec, and in most regions. Polls taken in the first week of May showed majority support for his first budget and government, with approval ratings as high as 60 percent led by strong support in Alberta and Quebec. In particular, a poll conducted between 4-9 May showed that the Conservatives, tied nationally with the Liberals on 6 February at the time of the controversial Emerson and Fortier cabinet appointments, had surged to a comfortable lead of 38 percent to 28 percent, and were in a statistical tie with the Bloc in Quebec and with the Liberals in Ontario (Nanos, 2006). A majority government seemed in sight if an election were to be held.

The trend was sustained by public approval of Harper's performance in foreign affairs, where he came into office surrounded by expectations that he steadily met during his first few months on the job. In a POLLARA (2006) poll conducted between 1–7 February, a majority thought he would do a better job than Paul Martin in improving relations with the United States (57 percent), and making sure the Canadian armed forces had the equipment and training they needed (54 percent), while a plurality picked him as being able to ensure that Canada's peacekeeping forces were ready for their missions (45 percent) and protecting Canada's sovereignty (33 percent, in a tie with neither better nor worse). A plurality felt he would be neither better nor worse on promoting trade with China (41 percent), fighting terrorism (40 percent), and solving the softwood lumber dispute (39 percent). Only on providing aid to people in the poorest countries was Harper seen to do worse, with 32 percent saying worse and only 11 percent saying he would do better than Martin.

These optimistic assessments coincided with those issues Canadians thought most important for Harper to address as prime minister – improving relations with the US and protecting Canada's sovereignty (both at 18 percent), solving the softwood lumber dispute (14 percent), and ensuring Canada's armed forces had the equipment and training they need (11 percent). Here, Harper delivered. His early rebuke of the

American ambassador to affirm Canada's Arctic sovereignty, his soft-wood lumber agreement with the Americans, and his $5.3 billion boost for defence in his 2 May budget showed Canadians he was delivering the foreign policy they preferred.

The one cloud of uncertainty in an otherwise clear blue sky remained Afghanistan. Here Canadians, unused to continuing combat, casualties, and body bags containing dead Canadian soldiers coming home, were a cautious, uncertain and changeable lot, supporting the military in their mission but driven to doubt by periodic outbursts of bad news. One poll conducted between 6-14 February showed that a strong majority of 70 percent supported Canada's expanded military mission in Afghanistan, even though they realized the risk of casualties (Reuters, 2006). Another taken between 16-19 February showed 62 percent were against sending troops to Afghanistan (Laghi, 2006).

By mid-March, as Harper arrived in Kandahar, 78 percent of Canadians felt that the Canadian Forces would have a positive impact on Afghan lives, confirming a broad belief that Canada's armed forces do good deeds abroad, but only a bare majority of 51 percent supported a more active combat role for the troops there (Galloway, 2006b). But when four more casualties came in April, support plummeted, with 54 percent opposing or strongly opposing Canadian involvement (up from 41 percent in mid-March) and 70 percent in Quebec (up from 53 percent) (Blackwell, 2006).

One month later, support for the mission bounced back a little, in the midst of a parliamentary debate and vote on 17 May that approved, by a narrow four vote margin, a two year extension of the mission until February 2009. An Ipsos-Reid poll taken 16-18 May found 57 percent of Canadians backed the mission, but only 44 percent agreed with the government's decision to keep troops in Afghanistan until 2009. Support for the extension was highest in Alberta at 66 percent and lowest in Quebec at 27 percent (Blanchfield, 2006).

CONCLUSION

From the first moment when it secured its election victory, Stephen Harper's Conservative Party sought a foreign policy of global reach, with the principles of democracy, defence, demographic diversity, and the construction of an inclusive international community at its core. The concept of, and self confidence for leadership in order to develop and deliver this foreign policy, there in nascent form from the beginning, acquired growing force during his government's first months.

The resulting "made-in-Canada" foreign policy of global leadership was presented with doctrinal consistency throughout the campaign platform and promises, the election night victory speech, and the first Speech from the Throne. It was backed by real resources, from the prime minister's own globally oriented summit diplomacy to the big boost in the first budget for defence, border and health security, and development. And it was displayed in decisions, over affirming Canada's Arctic sovereignty against American counter-claims, unilaterally and quickly cutting off aid to a Hamas government committed to destroying Israel through terrorism, and committing troops to the Afghanistan mission despite a doubting public at home.

This thrust toward global assertiveness was driven by a rapidly educated, rationally calculating, politically skilled and determined prime minister who assembled his inexperienced ministerial team into a well balanced, coordinated foreign policy decision-making process that he and his loyal group of advisors tightly controlled. The government was thus able to make the accommodations and adjustments required to mobilize support from a sympathetic provincial government in Quebec, a declining separatist movement in the province and in the House, an increasingly united Conservative Party, an opposition Liberal Party distracted by a highly diffuse leadership race, an public approving its overall performance and first budget, if not its approach to Afghanistan, and especially (as Daniel Schwanen will detail in his chapter) its nascent climate change policy. With such strategic unity in Ottawa, and a generally supportive society across the country, the Harper government was easily and rapidly pulled into global leadership by a rapidly changing and more dangerous international system, characterized by a more vulnerable and relatively declining America, and a secure Canada with the surplus capabilities that America and the global democratic community needed most.

During its first months in office, the Harper government started to deliver that global leadership with ever greater confidence and force. But while the aspirations are strong, there is a long way to go before its ambitious vision is achieved. Much of what was done, unilaterally, plurilaterally, and globally, has been broadly supportive of, or consistent with, American policies and purposes in the world, with American adjustment to Canadian stances – over softwood lumber and Arctic sovereignty – still limited in degree. The construction of a new order supporting demographic diversity, democracy and development had started modestly in the home region with the institutionalized trilateral North American summit and the SPP. But the great global test lay ahead as Stephen Harper flew off to his first G8 Summit in Russia where the acceptance of democracy, development, and demographic diversity were all in doubt. And bringing democracy and development to distant Afghanistan and finding the sustainable development formula to effectively control climate change are achievements worthy of all the ambition and leadership a Harper government could muster, even if – like that of Brian Mulroney – it was backed by a majority government for a full two terms. Although the Harper government has made an impressive start, its minority position will hamper its ability to create favourable conditions at home for genuine global leadership abroad.

NOTES

1 His key advisors in the PMO were Chief of Staff Ian Brodie, press secretary Carolyn Stewart Olson, Patrick Muttart, and Senator Marjorie Le Breton (Brown, 2006).

2 The comparable figure, as a trusted, close at hand personal advisor under the Chrétien government was the former foreign affairs and trade minister Mitchell Sharp. Under Paul Martin, such advice was sought from Maurice Strong and Peter Nicholson.

3 The comparison with Joe Clark under Mulroney, while useful in other respects, is severely limited, for while both MacKay and Clark were Progressive Conservative Party leaders, Clark had the unique experience of winning a general election and serving as prime minister, while MacKay did not.

4 The list from the first 100 days includes the softwood lumber statement, and suggesting some Canadian aid could still flow to Hamas. Of more consequence was his failed attempt to hire Graham Fox as his chief of staff (Brown, 2006).

5 Harper was reported to meet his ministers privately before cabinet meetings to listen to their proposals and then present them to cabinet himself, to have the PMO pre-approve all ministers' and MPs' political activities, to manage the media much more tightly and with less access. He also said "I ... expect that all elements of the bureaucracy will be working with us to achieve our objectives" (cited in Brown, 2006). Such instincts, reminiscent of the Diefenbaker government, responded to the many long years of Liberal government before and the culture of familiarity it could breed.

6 The new arrangement eliminated the Global Affairs Cabinet Committee, as well as the Continental Affairs Cabinet Committee which had been chaired by John Manley when it was created.

7 The Economic Affairs Committee had a mandate to consider "economic growth, international trade, sustainable development, natural resources, fisheries, agriculture, energy, transport, infrastructure and communities, and regional development policy issues." Chaired by finance minister Flaherty, it had as its vice chair trade minister Emerson, and as members the ministers of environment and energy. But it excluded the ministers of foreign affairs, development, and defence. Minister of Foreign Affairs MacKay was also absent from the other committees,

for Operations, Treasury Board, Social Affairs, and Economic Affairs. Thus nowhere in the cabinet committee system was there a place to join the international focused ministers of foreign affairs, trade, and development with one another, let alone with the key climate change ministers of the environment and energy. The burden for integration would be on MacKay as the sole member from this community on the key Priorities and Planning Committee.

8 Not that the previous reporting relationship had been a guarantee, as Lloyd Axworthy (2003) had pointed out in his book, *Navigating the New World*.

9 The earlier reorganization eliminated the Africa, Middle East, and Asia Bureau and converted the US Bureau into a North American one. David Mulroney got the rest of the world in his Bureau.

10 The organization tore this asunder when the trade part was ripped out, returning Ottawa to the pre-1980s when trade as entirely separate.

REFERENCES

Axworthy, Lloyd. 2003. *Navigating a New World: Canada's Global Future.* Toronto: Knopf Canada.

Biette, David. 2006. "Whatever Happened to Canada?" *Literary Review of Canada*, 14, no. 5 (June): 25–7.

Blackwell, Richard. 2006. "Support Plummets for Afghanistan Mission," *Globe and Mail*, 6 May, A1.

Blanchfield, Mike. 2006. "Support for Afghan Mission Stays Firm," *National Post*, 20 May, A1.

Brown, Ian. 2006. "In Harper's Regime, Big Daddy Knows Best," *Globe and Mail*, 13 May, F1.

Burney, Derek H. 2005. *Getting It Done: A Memoir.* Montreal & Kingston: McGill-Queen's University Press.

Campbell, Murray. 2006. "Battle with the 'dark side' Just Beginning," *Globe and Mail*, 28 January, A8.

Canada. 2006. *Canada's New Government: Turning a New Leaf.* Speech from the Throne. Ottawa: Office of the Governor General, 4 April. Available at: <http://www.sft-ddt.gc.ca/sft-ddt_e.pdf>

Conservative Party of Canada. 2005. "Harper Calls for Boost to Canadian Forces," News Release, *Stand Up for Canada.* 13 December. 9 May 2006. Available at: <www.conservative.ca/EN/1091/35032>

– 2006a. *Stand Up for Canada: Federal Election Platform*, 13 January. Available at: <http://www.conservative.ca/media/20060113-Platform.pdf>

– 2006b. "Harper Announces Increase in Overseas Development Assistance," News Release, *Stand Up for Canada.* 13 January. 9 May 2006. Available at: <www.conservative.ca/EN/1091/38757>

Corcoran, Terrence. 2006. "Harper Looking Green over Kyoto," *National Post*, 28 February, FP19.

Coyne, Andrew. 2006. "Harper's Show of Accomplishment: Assessing the First 100 Days," *National Post*, 13 May, A1, A6.

Galloway, Gloria. 2006a. "Harper Rebukes US Envoy over Arctic Dispute," *Globe and Mail*, 27 January.

– 2006b. "Polls, History Experts Point to Sea Change in Opinion of Military," *Globe and Mail*, 11 April, A4.

Ghafour, Hamida. 2006. "Leaders Sign Afghan Aid Compact," *Globe and Mail*, 2 February, A15.

Harper, Stephen. 2006a. "Canadians Choose Change and Accountability," Address to the Conservative Party, Calgary, 23 January. Available at: <www.conservative.ca/EN/1004/40299>

– 2006b. Address by the prime minister to the Canadian Armed Forces in Kandahar, Afghanistan, 13 March. Available at: <www.conservative.ca/1004/40850>

Hillmer, Norman, and Garth Stevenson, eds. 1977. *Foremost Nation: Canadian Foreign Policy and a Changing World*. Toronto: McClelland and Stewart.

Ibbitson, John. 2006. "New PM's Icy Comments over Envoy Could Backfire," *Globe and Mail*, 27 January, A5.

Kirton, John. 2007. *Canadian Foreign Policy in a Changing World*. Toronto: Thomson-Nelson.

Koring, Paul. 2006. "Tread Lightly with Bush, Observers Warn," *Globe and Mail*, 25 January, A4.

Laghi, Brian. 2006. "Majority Opposed to Afghan Mission," *Globe and Mail*, 24 February, A1.

Martin, Lawrence. 2006 "A Conservative Pierre Trudeau Is Taking Charge," *Globe and Mail*, February 23, A19.

McCarthy, Shawn. 2006. "Rock's UN Job Seen as Short-Lived," *Globe and Mail*, 25 January, A7.

McDougall, Barbara. 2006. Interview. *Politics with Don Newman*, CBC Newsworld, 26 January.

Nanos, Nikita James. 2006. "Conservatives Lead – Noticeable Tory Pick up in Québec," National Survey, *SES Research*, 11 May.

POLLARA. 2006. *Canadians' Expectations for Stephen Harper's Foreign Policy*. Report on National Poll for the Canadian Institute of International Affairs, February. Available at: <http://www.pollara.ca/library.html>

Reuters. 2006. "Poll Indicates Most Canadians Back Expanded Afghan Mission," *The Epoch Times*, 1 March.

Simpson, Jeffrey. 2006. "Canada's Biggest Challenge Never Made It into the Election," *Globe and Mail*, 24 January, A27.

---

4 Caught In-between Traditions:
A Minority Conservative
Government and Canadian
Foreign Policy

ADAM CHAPNICK

It would certainly be appropriate for a Conservative to suggest
that we must achieve some kind of order if we are to avoid chaos;
an order which is stable, but not static; [an] order therefore which
is reasonably acceptable and which among other things provides a
framework in which enterprise can flourish. That would be a
Conservative tradition.

Robert Stanfield
14 November 1974[1]

On 13 March 2006, in the midst of a public debate at home over the legitimacy of the Canadian mission in Afghanistan, newly installed Prime Minister Stephen Harper boldly traveled to Kandahar airfield to rally support. His speech was notable for its staunch expression of internationalism. "Our Canada is a great place," he said, "but Canada is not an island." Later, in a section called "The Canadian Leadership Tradition," he addressed the soldiers directly: "Your work is about more than just defending Canada's interest. It's also about demonstrating an international leadership role for our country. Not carping from the sidelines, but taking a stand on the big issues that matter ... I want Canada to be a leader ... A country that really leads, not a country that just follows. That's what you are doing. Serving in a UN-mandated, Canadian-led security operation that is in the very best of the Canadian tradition: Providing leadership on global issues; stepping up to the plate; doing good when good is required" (Harper, 2006a).

The message was rather typical of the foreign policy rhetoric that has been broadcast from Ottawa since the Second World War, portraying Canada as a selfless international actor, fully dedicated to improving the state of the world around it. It was also a significant departure from comments made by Minister of the Environment Rona Ambrose (2006:

A19) less than two weeks earlier. In a letter to the editor of the *Toronto Star*, she articulated the Conservative Party's long-standing ambivalent attitude towards the Kyoto Protocol, a UN agreement on environmental security that Canada had ratified eight years earlier: "I want Canadians to know," she wrote, "that our first priority is our commitment to a made-in-Canada solution that actively reduces greenhouse gas emissions by advancing domestic and international policies that reflect our mandate: to clean up *Canada's* air, water and soil" (emphasis added). Although a junior and inexperienced minister, Ambrose should not be thought to have spoken out on her own. Her words came directly from the text of the prime minister's 2005–06 election platform (Conservative Party of Canada, 2006d: 37).

The contrast is startling. Whereas Harper's message emphasized the interconnectedness of the international system, Ambrose's seemed to assume that Canadians could improve the state of the environment by disregarding their commitment to a global protocol and pursuing in its place a self-designed, self-administered, and self-monitored emissions reduction plan. In one instance Canada was a world leader, willing to make sacrifices for the greater good; in another it looked after its own interests first, regardless of its international obligations. Paradoxically, both approaches were consistent with Canadian traditions. The first reflected the idealistic, if not also messianic rhetoric that has increasingly characterized government-sponsored foreign policy pronouncements. The second was more realistically reflective of a country that has long pursued a conservative approach to foreign policy, generally putting its own national concerns ahead of those of the world around it (Chapnick, 2005). Taken together, the two statements left the Conservatives open to the same charges of hypocrisy that dogged the Liberals throughout their most recent time in office. For a party that was elected based on its promise to change the way that government was run,[2] and to introduce a Conservative approach to national governance (which one would assume includes foreign policy), it was a rather disappointing beginning.

It was also entirely predictable. When it took power in January 2006, the Harper administration had no clear foreign policy mission and limited political freedom to manoeuvre.[3] It faced what might be termed a multi-level 'branding crisis' at home, and an historical tradition that pointed the party in conflicting directions. The challenge to the new government is genuinely overwhelming, but it also presents an opportunity to introduce changes that are needed to Canada's foreign policy agenda. In an era of the so-called brand state (Van Ham, 2001), Canada must strive to become the unbranded. This means abandoning the rhetoric of excess that has characterized public statements for too many years and setting aside the impulsive need to emphasize any alleged originality in the new government's approach to foreign policy. Simply put, it must focus on competence instead of headlines. Such a strategy – which is particularly applicable to the crucial issues of security, the Canadian-American relationship, human development, and federal-provincial relations – will require patience, self-discipline, and a commitment to a pragmatic conservatism that might not resonate at first with a public so used to bold pronouncements of idealism. It is an approach that Canadian governments have been (understandably) loath to adopt in the past, but one that might just be particularly well-suited to the current administration. Rather than setting out to consciously shape a new "made in Canada" Conservative foreign policy tradition, the Harper government would best be advised to let good, thoughtful policies speak for themselves.

When the Conservative Party was formed in 2003 (through the merging of the Progressive Conservative and Canadian Alliance Parties), little attention was paid within the party to external affairs. Of its nineteen founding principles, only three had tangible foreign policy implications.[4] Principle fifteen expressed the party's concern for the state of the environment, sixteen stated that Canada should fulfill its international obligations, and finally, number nineteen declared the party's support for a liberalized system of international trade (Conservative Party of Canada, 2006a). The overwhelming emphasis on domestic issues reflected the will of a national public which, in the words of one academic, was in the process of acquiescing to "a substantial transfer of public resources from programs that serve both themselves and others abroad to programs which serve only themselves at home" (Stairs, 2003: 500). The Conservatives' 2005–06 election platform continued to pay only limited attention to world affairs. The forty-six paged document hardly mentioned foreign policy until the forty-second page, where it in fact pledged to reduce the power of the federal government by allowing the provinces greater influence over international decisions that fell under their constitutional jurisdiction. The end of page forty-four included the bland and often-repeated statement, "We need to ensure that Canada's foreign policy reflects true Canadian values and advances Canada's national interests" (Conservative Party of Canada, 2006d: 44). On page forty-five, among other things, the Conservatives promised to increase humanitarian aid, to involve Parliament more regularly in foreign policy debates, and to better fund the military. The final section included proposals to strengthen Canada's international trading relationships. Taken as a whole, there was nothing particularly new in these statements, and certainly nothing that reflected their "Choose Change" motto of the general election campaign.

John Kirton (this volume) over-reaches in suggesting that foreign policy constituted a core component of the Conservative's policy platform. Almost immediately after its election victory, the new minority government laid out its five key priorities. Not one of them related to foreign policy (Conservative Party of Canada, 2006b). Perhaps the Harper administration felt that it might have been able to avoid dealing with external issues explicitly, at least until it had begun to implement its domestic agenda. What was clear within two months, however, was that foreign policy was going to be much more important than the government anticipated. Between 8 February and 23 March, over 50 percent of the news releases coming from the Prime Minister's Office had international implications (Conservative Party of Canada, 2006c). As much as the Tories might have sought to keep their agenda focused on the home front, there was no escaping the world around them.

The problem, it seems, is that when they originally struck their political union, the founders of today's Conservative Party clung too strongly to the old Pearsonian adage that foreign policy was little more than "domestic policy with its hat on" (quoted in Chapnick, 2005: 637). They appear to have assumed that a clear philosophy of governance within the country could easily be translated to the international realm. And they seem to have believed that if Canadians were satisfied with their government's performance at home, they might take for granted the legitimacy of its policies abroad. The Conservatives could therefore 'stand up for change' domestically without having to explain what they were standing up for beyond national borders.

This approach might have been successful had Canadians thought of themselves as less than the fully committed international citizens that a recent survey suggests that they believe themselves to be (Innovative Research Group, 2004: 6). But just like, as an American economist once explained, "It is what we think the world is like, not what it is really like, that determines our behavior" (Boulding, 1969: 423), it is the type of global citizen that Canadians think their country is that determines what they demand of their government on the world stage. A new minority Conservative administration that believes in a hands-off approach to domestic affairs, one that reduces the size and power of government, and limits oversight and regulation in order to deliver greater individual freedom, faces a dilemma in framing its foreign policy platform. What is it supposed to say to a public that seems to be convinced that the world abroad needs more Canada, not less? How can it justify a policy of less government at home and at the same time promote greater governance abroad?

The challenge of defining a Conservative approach to foreign policy for the twenty-first century is only made worse by the Tories' new minority position as Canada's governing party. Not only do they represent a relatively small country on the world stage, they also lack real experience, and their control of Parliament is tenuous. As George Perlin (1980) explained in his study of the Conservatives and their political difficulties in the second half of the twentieth century, whereas a party that has a history of winning elections tends to attract ambitious individuals who can be more easily convinced to compromise their ideals to maintain their grasp on power, those who have served for extended periods in opposition tend to be more ideologically driven and therefore less willing to sacrifice fundamental beliefs. The internal dissent that followed Prime Minister Harper's controversial appointments of David Emerson and Michael Fortier to the cabinet suggests that Perlin's observations remain true today. As a result, the Conservatives must be weary of bold, attention-raising international initiatives (like their decision to be the *first* country to cut aid to Hamas) for fear of disrupting the already delicate Progressive Conservative-Canadian Alliance coalition that keeps the party united, in government, and that maintains support for Harper's leadership.

The government's minority status and the focus of the recent election campaign on the need for change restricts manoeuvrability in external affairs even further. Upon their next trip to the polls, Canadian voters will likely judge the current administration on whether it has kept its promises, and what new initiatives it has introduced. A review of the Conservatives' current foreign policy thinking suggests that, at least thus far, the party that promised change has basically stayed the course. Add to that the limits of a small power like Canada's flexibility on the world stage even if it were to attempt to alter its global attitudes (Farrell, 1969; Nossal, 1988; Stairs, 1982) and the Tories face a formidable challenge. Regardless of whether they had even wanted to formulate a clear and distinct approach to world affairs before they took office, they would have been hard-pressed to develop principles that would have differentiated their party significantly without alienating part of their own base, a significant portion of the general public, or their most important domestic allies. There is simply no room right now, and likely never again will be, for a distinct Conservative foreign policy brand in the traditional sense.

To make matters worse for the Harper team, the language of politics in Canada today favours the Opposition. For instance, while the term 'liberal' might be considered by many to be derogatory in much of the United States, most Canadians still identify themselves that way. It follows that a significant number of Conservative supporters do not consider themselves to be conservatives (Gwyn, 2006: A21). To confuse matters further, the federal Conservatives, with their outspoken commitment to individual freedom and lower taxes, are more classically liberal than the Liberals. The federal Liberals, divided over both missile defence and the war in Afghanistan, are no longer sure where they stand; and the New Democrats, with their outspoken belief in the need for a strong, centralized and powerful state, are in many ways Canada's most classically conservative party (Marzollini, 2003; Gibbons and Youngman, 1996). This leaves the Harper administration in the uncomfortable position of either having to convince the general public that it is Canada's great 'liberal' party without using the word, or having to downplay its own party moniker (as Harper did in the Afghanistan speech by referring to the 'Canadian' leadership tradition), thereby depriving itself of the brand recognition that might help it win the next election.

At the international level specifically, the situation is equally if not more troublesome to a government seeking to brand its policies as Conservative, and to do so advantageously. Canada is home to two co-incidental foreign policy traditions. The first is rhetorical, an expression of a desire to create "a natural affinity between how Canada 'does business' at home and how it wishes to pursue its interests abroad" (Dewitt, 2000: 183), or as one critical report calls it, the promotion of "a naïve and moralistic mythology about the purposes of Canada's foreign policy, one that leads us to conceive of ourselves as holier than others in the world" (Stairs et al., 2005: 13). According to a recent survey, this mythology has become increasingly meaningful to Canadians because there exists in the country "a collective desire to be seen as international promoters of peace and prosperity" (POLLARA, 2004: 3). Perhaps Canadians need to feel that they are contributing to world peace to relieve themselves of guilt over their own financial success or to fulfil what Allan Gotlieb (2004: 27) has called "a missionary impulse which drives us to export our values to the less fortunate peoples of the world." Or perhaps, as Kim Richard Nossal (2003) has argued, Canadians have grown so accustomed to political speeches attesting to the greatness of the "Canadian Way" that they have lost their ability to evaluate these testimonials critically. In either case, bold speeches praising the country's noble contributions to world affairs have clearly become part of the national tapestry.

The second tradition reflects the pattern of Canadian actions on the world stage. These have been more often than not conservative, characterized by a self-interested commitment to peace, order, and good government. Driven largely by the need to broker peace at home, successive federal governments have embraced membership in international institutions while limiting their country's commitments within them. They have praised successful global initiatives but have then responded cautiously and pragmatically when asked to participate. Faced with demands to increase social spending but at the same time to be mindful of running deficits, they have for years under-funded the military. They have provided aid to countries whose human rights records they condemn out of fear of disrupting the international order. And when they have taken leadership roles in world affairs, they have tended to choose issues like landmines and the international criminal court that do not require them to make domestic sacrifices (Chapnick, 2005: 645–8; see also Cooper, 1997).

Both traditions are associated with the most recognizable force in Canadian foreign policy since the Second World War – Lester B. Pearson. For years, Canadians have seen themselves as practitioners of what is often termed Pearsonian liberal internationalism (Simpson, 1999). Ironically, even though Pearson himself took a largely conservative view of foreign policy practice, emphasizing the importance of caution, order, and moderation, Canadians have tended to remember him as an activist hero. They have focused on his morally laudable and idealistic international beliefs and expressions, enshrining him in their minds as a peacekeeper, a staunch critic of the United States (particularly in Viet Nam), and a proud supporter of collective security (English, 2001; Axworthy, 2003b). In doing so, they have neglected to recall that Pearson's vision of international peacekeeping was far more violent, aggressive, and confrontational than what resulted in Suez in 1956, that Canada profited by selling military equipment to the United States throughout the war in Indochina, and that, as prime minister, Pearson hesitated significantly before accepting a UN request to send Canadian peacekeepers to Cyprus.

Over the last forty years opportunistic Liberal governments have taken ownership of this popular view of liberal internationalism, leading Canadians to believe that Liberal foreign policy stands for contributing positively to world affairs. Recently, led most visibly by the former foreign minister, Lloyd Axworthy (2003a: 70), they have managed to convince a substantial portion of the national public that it is "a unique liberal task to help write the primer on global citizenship." Canadians, Axworthy has argued, have to "establish a culture of rights, of social commitment, of negotiation and compromise in a domestic political system and translate that into the same values internationally." Doing so, he has maintained, "would reinforce our basic values and enhance our pride as a people. The extent to which Canadians see their country playing a useful, effective role aboard adds to the sense of cohesion, confidence and pride that is an indispensable part of our national make-up" (Axworthy, 2003b: 59). When Paul Martin inherited the party from Jean Chrétien, he added to this largely Liberal tradition a new mission to restore Canada's place in the world (see Hillmer et al., 2005).

Having governed Canada for so much of the last seventy years, the Liberals have thus managed to appropriate the do-good, feel-good nature of most expressions of Canadian foreign policy to the point that when the Conservative regime under Brian Mulroney proposed to increase the Canadian contribution to worldwide "good governance" initiatives, analysts called it "liberal internationalism, Conservative-style" (Gecelovsky and Keating, 2001: 205).

Today, the general public still believes in the ideals of Lester B. Pearson, and still supports the idea that Canadian foreign policy should be developed within what they call a liberal internationalist framework (no matter how conservative that framework actually might be). Any attempts to re-brand the Canadian approach to world affairs as distinctively Conservative, even if the policies are consistent with the national interest, are therefore likely to disappoint. At the same time however, decisions to stay the course, while potentially popular, will be quickly identified by the opposition as consistent with the preceding Liberal tradition (English, 2001).

Historical precedent offers the Conservatives little immediate solace. Political scientist Don Munton (2002–03: 162) has used survey data to differentiate what he considers to be the various strands of internationalism that have existed within Canadian society. Among them is an historical tradition that he calls "conservative internationalism." This approach to world affairs emphasizes the legitimate role of the national armed forces in conflict resolution and the importance of military strength to domestic and international security. The actions of today's Conservatives in Afghanistan are indeed consistent with this label, but the rhetoric accompanying the mission has at the same time deliberately portrayed the party and its motivations as successors to those whom Munton would label liberal internationalists, more interested in humanitarian causes than in traditional military achievements. In his speech to the troops in Afghanistan, Harper (2006a) noted, for example, that "beyond the threat of terror there's the threat of drugs." And after the section on the "Canadian Leadership Tradition," he devoted a substantial portion of his comments to Canada's "Humanitarian Mission," emphasizing the Canadian contribution to the reduction of poverty in the area, the improvement in the rights of women, and the improved educational prospects for Afghan children. It appears, then, that there is only limited political interest within the government in standing up for conservative internationalism as Munton defines it.

Attempts to seek out another distinctive historical Conservative foreign policy tradition, one which might distinguish the party and its policies from previous Liberal governments, will likely be no more successful. In his analysis of the Mulroney era, Denis Stairs (2001: 28) noted how little focus there had been "on the government's overall foreign policy orientation." Analysts, he wrote, had been "hard put to identify in either its behaviour or its rhetoric an underlying set of premises, much less a doctrine, or 'vision,' of Canada's general role in world affairs. Certainly they [had] not been successful in identifying a *distinctive* vision – one, that is, that would distinguish the Conservative view from those of their adversaries or even from the ones inherent in the eclectic expectations of the public at large." Kim Nossal (1988) reached similar conclusions in his comparison of the Trudeau and Mulroney regimes. And the most comprehensive foreign policy statement of the Mulroney era, the findings of the Special Joint Committee of the Senate and House of Commons on Canada's International Relations, were far too vague to be considered distinctly Conservative. Pronouncements like "international responsibilities should be interwoven with Canada's basic national aims" or "A major objective of Canadian foreign policy should be a broad effort to strengthen the effectiveness of international institutions" could serve as directions to any government, Conservative, Liberal or otherwise (Canada, 1986: 137–8).

Going back to the age of Sir John A. Macdonald, one finds, if anything, the Conservative foreign policy tradition has been to not have one. It was Macdonald, after all, who allegedly once brought two speeches to the House of Commons, one in favour of reciprocity with the United States and the other staunchly opposed. Canada's founding prime minister, it is said, waited for the Liberals to declare their stance on free trade and then chose the appropriate speech to respond. Political expediency, then, and not principle or ideology, seems to have formed the historical basis of Conservative activities in external affairs.

Looking more closely at Conservative minorities for inspiration is equally unhelpful. The rapid failure of the Clark administration of 1979 rules it out as a role model, and John Diefenbaker's experience is in many ways even more problematic. Diefenbaker owes his first minority largely to his ability to envelop the national public in a passionate frenzy of anti-Americanism. Today's Conservatives, in contrast, have condemned the Liberals for using the same tactic repeatedly. During Diefenbaker's second minority government of 1962–63, the prime minister waffled on defence policy, as he found himself unable to decide whether Canada should honour its NATO commitment to accept nuclear weapons. Stephen Harper, on the other hand, has promised to provide Canadians with firm, assertive leadership on national defence.

Today's Conservatives have inherited a situation as a minority which in fact most closely resembles Pearson's Liberal administration of 1963–65. Like Pearson, Stephen Harper was initially unable to defeat a government that had lost credibility in the eyes of the national public. Both leaders also failed to achieve majorities that probably should have been within their grasp. The elections of Pearson and Harper were welcomed in the United States, where it was felt that the new governments would improve what had been a deteriorating bilateral relationship. And just as Pearson's time as prime minister coincided with the escalation of the American war in Viet Nam, Harper faces a similar situation in Iraq. Pearson was forced, at least temporarily, to abandon his opposition to nuclear weapons to ensure an election victory. Harper might well have to abandon or at least compromise the Conservative Party's attitude towards the Kyoto Protocol to have any chance in his next trip to the polls. Both men came to power having pledged to increase foreign aid. Pearson introduced radical reforms to the Canadian military, and Harper is contemplating changes of a similar intensity. Finally, Pearson was the first prime minister to deal in any detail with the role of the provinces in international organizations, yet another challenge that the Conservatives have already begun to accept by granting Quebec a formal role in the United Nations Educational, Scientific and Cultural Organization (UNESCO).

Faced with a nearly impossible challenge, and having already made a number of glaring errors in its first series of foreign policy pronouncements,[5] what can the Conservative Party do? First, it might recognize that aiming to be bold is not always best. The editors of the 2005 volume of this series observed correctly that the recent Liberal administration "had a tendency to oversell its initiatives. Ideas that were promoted enthusiastically raised hackles by raising the level of expectation too high" (Cooper and Rowlands, 2005: 10). Second, rather than focusing exclusively on new ideas, they might consider some old advice. It has been nearly twenty-five years since Denis Stairs (1982: 679) suggested that at times, "good politics" might require "a resigned acceptance of the inconvenience of being weak – a recognition, that is, of the realities of power." As a new party, in a minority position, governing a small country whose relatively meagre population makes its economy largely dependent on international stability, the Conservatives are in an exceptionally poor position to affect global change in a way that will allow them to brand their foreign policy as unique. It is not time, as Lloyd Axworthy (2003b: 370) likes to suggest, "to take on leadership ... [that] will certainly bring howls of protest from other quarters." But nor is it time to "'fix' the image of Canada in the world ... so that people abroad understand what [our] country represents, what it stands for, what it has, what it sells" (Cohen, 2003: 181). Rather, the Conservatives must turn their attention away from the national image and maintain a modest, disciplined – and indeed conservative – approach to world affairs. As David Dewitt (2000: 187) has argued, being "on the margins is not such a bad thing, so long as we are there by choice, understanding what we choose to do, how we choose to do it, and what we forgo in choosing it."

Applying this advice to some of the most significant foreign policy questions that face the new government will not be easy. As an international nation living alongside a hyper-power in the midst of a self-declared war on terror, Canada cannot help but be faced with challenging decisions in the realms of security and defence. The Harper government has attempted to differentiate itself through its commitment to the military, exceeding any and all Liberal efforts to strengthen the armed forces by increasing their size and purchasing new equipment. Realistically, enhancing Canada's military capabilities makes sense. From a popular perspective, a recent poll by the Innovative Research Group (2005) found that, after years of thinking badly of the armed forces, two-thirds of Canadians have come to believe in the importance of an effective military and approve the use of necessary force as a means of contributing to world affairs. At the policy level, in 2005 the Standing Senate Committee on National Security and Defence proposed a dramatic increase in the defence budget (Manson, 2005). And politically, the Martin government had already pledged to increase funding for national defence before it fell from power, making any similar initiative relatively safe for a minority government. In spite of these advantages, however, promising dramatic increases in Canada's ability to defend itself and its so-called values is also dangerous. It has only been four years since Auditor General Sheila Fraser (2002) condemned the state of the recruitment and retention abilities of the Department of National Defence (DND). Although DND has made substantial changes to its strategic approach and has to its credit made progress, recruitment numbers remain relatively disappointing and contingent upon massive sign-up bonuses and expensive retention programs (Fraser, 2006).

The Conservative solution to the recruitment issue thus far has been to promise more money to the recruiters. Certainly, this strategy might work, but it also might not. Young Canadians who will be the target of the enlistment efforts have grown up in a much different environment than that of their parents and grandparents. Apart from some recent immigrants, most youth not only have never experienced a war, but also are not in regular contact with anyone who has. As a result, many lack an appreciation of the contribution of the military to Canada's national history. Without that, it will be more difficult to convince them to join the armed forces (Chapnick, 2006).

A more conservative solution would be to couch pledges to enhance the military in purely dollar terms. Rather than promising to add 15,000 new troops, the government might focus on guaranteeing enough money to support those troops once they have been accepted for service. The financial obligation can be met regardless of the results of the success of the recruitment drive. Similarly, rather than committing to purchase specific pieces of new equipment, the Tories might simply pledge to increase the equipment budget more generally, allowing the military leadership to think through its priorities in light of an ever-changing international situation (Travers, 2006).

For Canada, this situation will continue to revolve around the United States. Here, the Conservatives might recall the early approach of the first Pearson minority. When the new Liberal prime minister took power, he knew that Canadians did not support the war in Viet Nam, and he cleverly argued that to ensure the legitimacy of Canada's position on three international control commissions (ICCs) in Indochina, his country could not actively support its greatest ally. When the ICCs were criticized for their ineffectiveness, Pearson did not deny the charge, but argued (largely through his Secretary of State for External Affairs Paul Martin Sr.) that a voice of any sort in Indochina was better than no voice at all. Stephen Harper could use a similarly cautious strategy in Afghanistan. Instead of trumpeting the mission as an expression of Canadian ideals, he might couch his rhetoric more clearly in terms of Canada's international duty. This is not a time for boasting. Rather, the effort in Afghanistan should be portrayed as evidence of Canada's commitment to making a tangible contribution to an initiative supported not only by its greatest allies, but also by a number of the international organizations to which it belongs.

As Norman Hillmer, Fen Hampson, and David Carment (2005: 10) have argued, "The choice between North Americanism and internationalism is a false one, more of a rhetorical point of reference than a realistic basis of action." The Harper government was therefore correct to recognize that public posturing over disputes such as softwood lumber, while perhaps making for attractive domestic headlines, would not win Canada any permanent friends on the world stage, and could have continued to deceive some ultra-nationalist Canadians into believing that their country could maintain its current level of prosperity if its relationship with America were to rupture. A confrontational approach to the energy issue would be equally unhelpful. The solution is not to give in, but to follow the rather conservative advice of the Merchant-Heeney Report of 1965, that bilateral differences should generally be dealt with through quiet diplomacy. There are indeed times to be bold, but outspoken public quarrels should be reserved for extreme cases, rather than used to score political points at home.

As the Canadian-American relationship improves, rather than seeing Arctic sovereignty as a potentially provocative defence issue, the new prime minister might continue to commit Canada to enhancing the security of *all* of its borders and then use any residual goodwill to explore a bilateral agreement on water resource security. An agreement now, before the United States has clarified its position, could be particularly advantageous. While some might suggest that such policy integration with the United States threatens Canada's long-term independence, Michael Adams has shown that there is "the possibility of … strategic interdependence [with the United States] without the loss of cultural integrity and political sovereignty" (Adams, 2003: 143).

On another environmental, or human security, issue, the Conservatives' position is simply untenable. A policy of arrogantly disregarding an official commitment to the Kyoto Protocol made under United Nations auspices will bring the Tories nothing but criticism at home and abroad. And while the party might argue, quite fairly, that their predecessors' approach of boldly flaunting their alleged leadership during the Kyoto negotiations while at the same time allowing the country's greenhouse gas emissions to increase dramatically was hypocritical, ignorant, and harmful to Canada's international reputation, the solution currently favoured by the new administration, of abandoning the Protocol in favour of the Asia-Pacific Partnership on Clean Development and Climate, is hardly better. It might be more honest, but brushing aside an international obligation to combat the global impact of environmental degradation at any level is still unacceptable, and a poor basis for a Conservative tradition.

It is worth noting that Lester B. Pearson faced a similar type of problem when he took office. Pearson was philosophically opposed to keeping nuclear weapons on Canadian soil but inherited a government that had promised its NATO allies that it would. His solution was to first meet Canada's obligations to accept the weapons, and then negotiate a way to remove them from the country as quickly as possible. The Harper government might consider a similar approach to Kyoto. Canada has a responsibility to keep its word or accept the consequences of failing to meet its reduction targets. These consequences entail a commitment to make up the difference along with a 30 per cent penalty beginning in 2012. Such a pledge will be disturbingly expensive, and likely unpopular among the Tory base in oil and emissions rich Alberta. But it is necessary if the Conservatives hope to develop and maintain a reputation as a government that can be counted on to be true to its word. In the future, rather than balking brutishly, the party might explore means of counting their emissions credits expenditures as part of their promise to increase foreign aid. Canadians believe strongly that their country is generous (Cohen, 2003: 82), and portraying these costs as a consequence of that generosity might lessen the impact of the expense while at the same time making it easier to keep another promise.

Finally, when dealing with federal-provincial relations, the government might take what Nelson Michaud (this volume) calls an administrative approach and revisit the so-called umbrella agreements that were pursued during the Quiet Revolution. The bilateral international accords allowed the provinces to negotiate on their own in areas of external affairs that fell under their constitutional jurisdiction provided that the federal government had already met with the international partner and approved the overall principles of the process. In 1965, for example, Canada and France signed an agreement which allowed the provinces to negotiate cultural exchanges. Working quietly, accompanied by legal experts, the federal and provincial governments should be able to reach similarly acceptable compromises on issues that arise beyond UNESCO representation. Once again, however, the Conservative focus should be on achieving satisfactory agreements, not, as has been the case thus far, to use any negotiated success as public evidence of its ability to govern effectively. The former will convey an image of competence; the latter will suggest a government that is slowly reducing the country to individual pieces.

In 1948, just before he entered politics, Lester B. Pearson (1970: 68) articulated what he felt to be the principles of Canadian foreign policy. "We are not talking of clear-cut, long-range plans and policies under national direction and control," he said. "We are certainly not without power to influence our own external policies – and in many matters the influence is of course decisive. But we needn't exaggerate our power, or deceive ourselves about it, by talk of sovereign rights and unrestricted independence." It was a call for a genuinely conservative approach to foreign affairs, characterized by a focus on what was possible and expectations that were realistic. The Conservatives should feel fortunate that the Pearsonian tradition is hardly remembered that way today. If the new minority government hopes to make a measurable difference on the world stage, it might follow the so-called liberal internationalist advice, and act conservatively.

NOTES

The author would like to thank the editors, the organizers, and participants in the April 2006 authors' meeting; Rob Kidnie; and Erica Berman for their support and suggestions. Financial support for this chapter was provided by the Social Sciences and Humanities Research Council. The views expressed here are the author's alone.

1 Stanfield on Conservative principles, as cited in Christian (1978: 129).
2 Harper (2006b) used the word "change" nine times on the first page of his address to the National Caucus prior to the April 2006 Throne Speech.
3 This comment does not imply, as John Kirton seems to suggest in this volume, that the ignorance of the new government is therefore destined to lead to a policy of isolationism.
4 Kirton's count might be slightly higher, but there can be little dispute as to the dominance of domestic issues in the founding document.
5 Minister of Foreign Affairs Peter MacKay is now best known to some Canadians for his repeated attempts to retract, clarify, or revise his personal statements to the national media.

REFERENCES

Adams, Michael. 2003. *Fire and Ice: The United States, Canada, and the Myth of Converging Values*. Toronto: Penguin.

Ambrose, Rona. 2006. "Mandate to Clean Up Air, Water, Soil," *Toronto Star*, 1 March, A19.

Axworthy, Lloyd. 2003a. "Choices and Consequences in a Liberal Foreign Policy," in Howard Aster and Thomas S. Axworthy, eds. *Searching for the New Liberalism: Perspectives, Policies, Prospects*. Oakville: Mosaic Press, 63–79.

– 2003b. *Navigating a New World: Canada's Global Future*. Toronto: Alfred A. Knopf Canada.

Boulding, Kenneth E. 1969. "National Images and International Systems," in James N. Rosenau, ed. *International Politics and Foreign Policy*. New York: The Free Press, 422–31.

Canada. 1986. *Independence and Internationalism*. Report by the Special Joint Committee of the Senate and of the House of Commons on Canada's International Relations. Ottawa: Parliament of Canada, 27 May.

Catley-Carlson, Margaret. 2005. "The Turbulent World of Water: Threats and Implications for Canada's Foreign Policy," in David Carment, Fen Osler Hampson, and Norman Hillmer, eds. *Canada Among Nations 2004: Setting Priorities Straight*. Montreal & Kingston: McGill-Queen's University Press, 209–24.

Chapnick, Adam. 2005. "Peace, Order, and Good Government: The 'conservative' Tradition in Canadian Foreign Policy," *International Journal* 60, no. 3 (Summer): 635–50.

– 2006. "Bringing the Forces Up to Strength: A Question of Motivating Youth to Service," *Policy Options* 27, no. 6 (July/August): 95–8.

Christian, William. 1978. "Ideology and Canadian Politics," in John H. Redekop, ed. *Approaches to Canadian Politics*. Scarborough: Prentice Hall, 114–37.

Cohen, Andrew. 2003. *While Canada Slept: How We Lost Our Place in the World*. Toronto: McClelland and Stewart.

Conservative Party of Canada. 2006a. "Founding Principles." *Stand Up for Canada*. 1 January. 9 May 2006. Available at: <http://www.conservative.ca/EN/1141/>

– 2006b. "Harper Outlines Priorities for Parliament." *Stand Up for Canada*. 26 January. 9 May 2006. Available at: <http://www.conservative.ca/EN/1004/40354>

– 2006c. "New Releases." *Stand Up for Canada*. 23 March. 9 May 2006. Available at: <http://www.conservative.ca/EN/1091/>

– 2006d. "Stand Up for Canada: Accountable Government That Will Get Things Done for All of Us," Federal Election Platform. *Stand Up for Canada*. 13 January. 9 May 2006. Available at: <http://www.conservative.ca/media/20060113-Platform.pdf>

Cooper, Andrew F. 1997. *Canadian Foreign Policy: Old Habits and New Directions*. Scarborough: Prentice Hall.

Cooper, Andrew F., and Dane Rowlands. 2005. "A State of Disconnects – The Fracturing of Canadian Foreign Policy," in Cooper and Rowlands, eds. *Canada Among Nations 2005: Split Images*. Montreal & Kingston: McGill-Queen's University Press, 3–20.

Dewitt, David B. 2000. "Directions in Canada's International Security Policy." *International Journal* 55, no. 2 (Spring): 167–87.

English, John. 2001. "In the Liberal Tradition: Lloyd Axworthy and Canadian Foreign Policy," in Fen Osler Hampson, Norman Hillmer, and Maureen Appel Molot, eds. *Canada Among Nations 2001: The Axworthy Legacy*. Toronto: Oxford University Press, 89–107.

Farrell, R. Barry. 1969. *The Making of Canadian Foreign Policy*. Scarborough: Prentice Hall.

Fraser, Sheila. 2002. *2002 Report of the Auditor General of Canada* (April). Available at: <http://www.oag-bvg.gc.ca/domino/reports.nsf/html/0205ce.html>

– 2006. *2006 Report of the Auditor General of Canada* (May). Available at: <http://www.oag-bvg.gc.ca/domino/reports.nsf/html/06menu_e.html>

Gecelovsky, Paul, and Tom Keating. 2001. "Liberal Internationalism for Conservatives: The Good Governance Initiative," in Nelson Michaud and Kim Richard Nossal, eds. *Diplomatic Departures: The Conservative Era in Canadian Foreign Policy*. Vancouver and Toronto: UBC Press, 194–207.

Gibbins, Roger, and Loleen Youngmann. 1996. *Mindscapes: Political Ideologies Towards the 21st Century*. Toronto: McGraw-Hill Ryerson.

Gotlieb, Allan. 2004. "Romanticism and Realism in Canada's Foreign Policy." C.D. Howe Institute Benefactors Lecture, Toronto, 3 November.

Gwyn, Richard. 2006. "Is Harper Paddling with the Tide or Against It?" *Toronto Star*, 28 March, A21.

Harper, Stephen. 2006a. Address by the prime minister to the Canadian Armed Forces in Kandahar, Afghanistan, 13 March. Available at: <http://www.conservative.ca/EN/1004/40850>.

– 2006b. Address by the prime minister to the National Caucus, Ottawa, 28 March. Available at: <http://www.conservative.ca/EN/1004/41741>

Hillmer, Norman, Fen Osler Hampson, and David Carment. 2005. "Smart Power in Canadian Foreign Policy," in Carment, Hampson, and Hillmer, eds. *Canada Among Nations 2004: Setting Priorities Straight*. Montreal & Kingston: McGill-Queen's University Press, 3–17.

Innovative Research Group. 2004. "Visions of Canadian Foreign Policy," Conference Report for the Dominion Institute and the Canadian Defence and Foreign Affairs Institute (CDFAI), Ottawa, 4 November. Available at: <http://www.cdfai.org>

– 2005. "The World in Canada: Demographics and Diversity in Canadian Foreign Policy," Report to the CDFAI Annual Conference, Ottawa, 31 October. Available at: <http://www.cdfai.org>

Manson, Paul D. 2005. "In Defence of Defence Spending," *Ottawa Citizen*, 19 November, B7.

Marzollini, Michael. 2003. "Polling Alone: Canadian Values and Liberalism," in Howard Aster and Thomas S. Axworthy, eds. *Searching for the New Liberalism: Perspectives, Policies, Prospects*. Oakville: Mosaic Press, 85–102.

Munton, Don. 2002–03. "Whither Internationalism?" *International Journal* 58, no. 1 (Winter): 155–80.

Nossal, Kim Richard. 1988. "Political Leadership and Foreign Policy: Trudeau and Mulroney," in Leslie A. Pal and David Taras, eds. *Prime Ministers and Premiers: Political Leadership and Public Policy in Canada*. Scarborough: Prentice Hall, 112–23.

– 2003. "'The World We Want?' The Purposeful Confusion of Values, Goals, and Interests in Canadian Foreign Policy," CDFAI Paper. Available at: <http://www.cdfai.org>

Pearson, Lester B. 1970. *Words and Occasions*. Toronto: University of Toronto Press.

Perlin, George C. 1980. *The Tory Syndrome: Leadership Politics in the Progressive Conservative Party*. Montreal & Kingston: McGill-Queen's University Press.

POLLARA. 2004. "Canadian Attitudes toward Foreign Policy," Report prepared for the Canadian Institute of International Affairs (CIIA), April. Available at: <http:www.ciia.org/CIIA_summary.pdf>

Simpson, Erika. 1999. "The Principles of Liberal Internationalism According to Lester Pearson," *Journal of Canadian Studies* 34, no. 1 (Spring): 75–92.

Stairs, Denis. 1982. "The Political Culture of Canadian Foreign Policy," *Canadian Journal of Political Science* 15, no. 4 (December): 667–90.

– 2001. "Architects or Engineers? The Conservatives and Foreign Policy," in
Nelson Michaud and Kim Richard Nossal, eds. *Diplomatic Departures: The
Conservative Era in Canadian Foreign Policy.* Vancouver and Toronto: UBC
Press, 25–42.

– 2003. "Challenges and Opportunities for Canadian Foreign Policy in the
Paul Martin Era," *International Journal* 58, no. 4 (Autumn): 481–506.

Stairs, Dennis, David J. Bercuson, Mark Entwisle, J.L. Granatstein, Kim
Richard Nossal, and Gordon S. Smith. 2005. *In the National Interest:
Canadian Foreign Policy in an Insecure World.* Calgary: Canadian Defence
and Foreign Affairs Institute.

Travers, James. 2006. "Buying Military Hardware Mostly a PR Exercise,"
Toronto Star, 28 March, A21.

Van Ham, Peter. 2001. "The Rise of the Brand State: The Postmodern Politics
of Image and Reputation," *Foreign Affairs* 80, no. 5 (September–October):
2–6.

PART TWO

Prioritizing Partners

5 UN Reform: A Sisyphean Task

DAVID M. MALONE

Calls for United Nations reform have intensified since 2003, the year in which the UN Security Council deadlocked on the use of force against Saddam Hussein's regime in Iraq.[1] The reform process was initiated by a series of reports, instigated by UN Secretary-General Kofi Annan, appearing in late 2004 and early 2005.[2] Since then, progress by member-states towards reform has been halting at best and the atmosphere of *fin de regime* malaise at the UN, in Annan's last year of office, deepened (see Zedillo, 2005; Berdalb, 2005: 7–31; Luck, 2005: 143–52). This chapter examines the origins of the current push for reform; touches on several debates among member-states, notably on Security Council reform, on a new UN Peacebuilding Commission, on the replacement of the Human Rights Commission by a Human Rights Council and on UN management reform and offers conclusions on prospects for the UN. These debates are relevant to Canada's new government as it decides how much of its diplomacy to channel through multilateral institutions.

THE GENESIS OF THE CURRENT UN REFORM EXERCISE

The end of the Cold War, first signalled at the UN by the activism of Secretary-General Javier Pérez de Cuéllar and of the Permanent Five (P5) members of the Security Council in seeking (successfully, through resolution 598 of 1987) to resolve the murderous Iran-Iraq war, introduced an ear of euphoria in the Council, lasting until roughly 1994, during which it tackled many of the crises that constituted the regional wreckage of the superpower confrontation through local proxies after 1950.[3] For a while, this surge in the UN's security-related activities obscured from view continuing tensions within the UN over the core purposes of the organization. These strains have been articulated around a North-South fault-line that has bedevilled the organization since the era of decolonization, that introduced acrid discussions to the UN over the respective responsibilities of developing and industrialized countries for the economic development of the former (see Hagman and Malone, 2002).

Spectacular set-backs for the Security Council in Somalia, the former Yugoslavia and, most catastrophically of all, Rwanda, moderated the enthusiasm for UN-centered conflict resolution and peacekeeping (even though peacekeeping deployments have been rising again steadily since 1998, reaching 85,000 authorized positions in 2006).[4]

A reversion of attention to the broader economic and social agenda of the UN as of the mid-1990s culminated in several important conferences on development financing, notably at Monterrey, Mexico in 2002 and agreement at the UN in 2000 on a declaration involving a number of specific targets and goals (revised to become the Millennium Development Goals) widely hailed as the new blueprint for international efforts to address specific urgent development challenges – notably in the fields of health and education.[5] In 2001, Kofi Annan was triumphantly re-elected secretary-general after a first term which focused on the humanitarian imperative and on his advocacy of greater implementation of human rights standards. Both his and the larger UN's efforts were recognized later that year with the awarding of the Nobel Peace Prize. Thus, the UN seemed better placed than ever to play a central role in international relations.

Additionally, since the end of the Cold War, considerable progress had been made at the UN in re-conceptualizing security and the UN's role therein:

The post-Cold War agenda of the Security Council has supported the concept of "human security," which incorporates socio-economic threats to the well-being of individuals and groups within countries, but more importantly, also insists that safeguarding state security ultimately requires the protection of the security of groups and indivi-duals within the border of states. In parallel with concurrent trends in UN and state decision-making, this normative evolution has qualified the principle of absolute sovereignty that was for decades considered inextricable from the UN's original, state-centric concept of "collective security." (von Einsiedel et al., 2006)

So what went wrong, leading to a crisis in confidence at and in the UN by 2003? In brief, Iraq. The Security Council consensus on how to contain the regime of Saddam Hussein that had already ravaged its neighbourhood twice (by attacking Iran, unprovoked, in 1980 and by doing likewise against Kuwait in 1990), essentially through a strategy of weapons inspections reinforced by a stringent and far-reaching sanctions regime, had been fraying since 1995. The growing discord between the P5 members, with the UK and the US on one side, and France, China, and Russia on the other, might well have continued to be papered over had it not been for the events of 11 September 2001 (see Malone, 1999: 393–411).

The UN membership, particularly in the Security Council, was highly supportive when the US retaliated against al Qaeda and the Taliban regime in Afghanistan that had harboured the terrorist movement, but the US administration soon moved on to a larger target, alleging connections of Saddam Hussein with terrorism, nuclear weapons programs, and weapons of mass destruction. The Security Council deadlocked on the issue, and the UK and US (with a number of allies) nevertheless unseated Saddam Hussein through "Operation Iraqi Freedom" in March and April 2003. The UN's incapacity to prevent war disappointed many, while others were critical of the UN for failing to support action against the odious Hussein (see Daalder and Lindsay, 2003: 92–104). Michael Doyle interpreted the outcome thusly:

The Council's performance on Iraq in March 2003 was both – and in about equal measure – a massive disappointment and a surprising relief. It disappointed all hopes that this essential international forum for multilateral policy could achieve a viable policy. At the same time, it demonstrated to the surprise of many that it would not let itself be bullied or bribed by any power, permanent or even hyper. (cited in Malone, 2006: 644)

But reaction in world public opinion was less sanguine – the UN had failed. Kofi Annan realized that the institution's impotence in a geostrategic arena as vital as Iraq would cost it dearly.

After a further serious set-back, the deaths of UN staffers in the bombing of the UN's Baghdad headquarters in August 2003, Annan (2003) told the UN General Assembly that the UN had reached a "fork in the road." Either it would be able to play a meaningful role on threats against security (defined broadly), or, if it did not, it would wither towards insignificance. In order to provide guidance on how the UN could design for itself a more relevant role in anticipating and embracing necessary change rather than resisting it, he convened a High-Level Panel (HLP), which in December 2004, published a remarkable report, addressing widely and convincingly the evolving security threats facing the UN membership (United Nations, 2004). Responding to a new US security strategy favouring pre-emptive action to deter and arrest security threats, the Panel acknowledged that preventive military action would sometimes be necessary but argued that it would continue to be necessary to convince the Security Council of the merits of each individual case.[6] The Panel made many other useful points, not least on evolving conceptions of sovereignty, of threats arising from growing international organized crime (championed by French uber-jurist and HLP member Robert Badinter). Summing up the Panel's conclusion, Bruce D. Jones (2006), a senior HLP staff member and prominent Canadian on multilateral issues writes:

Given the current state of interconnection between states and peoples, and given the growing divisions in international politics, nothing short of a broad new security consensus could serve as a basis for effective response to security threats old and new. The first requirement for a security consensus is to recognize the interlinkage between six clusters of threat: war between states, war within states, organized crime, proliferation, mass casualty terrorism and the spread of poverty and infectious disease. The second requirement is to recognize that in a global world, collective security is only as strong as its weakest link – and therefore, there is an overriding interest for the international community in building the capacity of states in the developing world to tackle transnational threats. If UN reform is to work, it must be built on such a consensus and geared towards making the UN relevant to its implementation.

Vaste projet! While the inter-linkages were widely accepted at the UN, the focus on security rather than on development rankled many. The study led by Jeffrey Sachs and published by the UN Millennium Project (2005: xxii) in January 2005 was more to the liking of these critics, particularly his seventh recommendation (of ten):

High-income countries should increase official development assistance (ODA) from 0.25 percent of donor GNP in 2003 to around 0.44 percent in 2006 and 0.54 percent in 2015 to support the Millennium Development Goals, particularly in low-income countries, with improved ODA quality (including aid that is harmonized, predictable, and largely in the form of grants-based budget support). Each donor should reach 0.7 percent no later than 2015 to support the Goals and other development assistance priorities. Debt relief should be more extensive and generous.

The report also outlined many sensible recommendations to the governments of developing countries, but these were widely overlooked in the debate that ensued, focused very much on the *supply* of development assistance rather than the *demand* of countervailing responsibilities. Indeed, under strong pressure from UK Prime Minister Tony Blair and

UK Chancellor of the Exchequer Gordon Brown, who choreographed the Gleneagles G8 Summit in July 2005 around the issues of Climate Change and Africa, most public and media interest revolved around the need for more development assistance to Africa (which was rather divorced from any assessment of the results of previous such ODA).[7]

The overlap and clash among these various debates was reflected in UN corridor discussions and was not defused by Annan's own synthesis report, topically (in view of themes in vogue in Washington) titled *In Larger Freedom*, was released on 21 March 2005 (Annan, 2005a).

In early 2005, Annan frequently argued that meaningful UN reform was a make or break issue for the organization and that specific measures needed to be agreed by the time of the UN Summit of September 2005. To raise the stakes so dramatically certainly drew attention to very serious problems, but it also gave reform 'wreckers' more leverage than they otherwise might have had. To some, notably the thoughtful Mats Berdal (2005a: 8), this tactic was a "strategic error":

This is especially so if success comes to be measured in terms of whether agreement on "far-reaching institutional reforms," specifically expansion of the Security Council, can be reached by September 2005. This focus has already proved deeply divisive, and risks squandering the opportunity presented by the panel's innovative thinking. The result could be a period of prolonged tension and mutual recrimination among member states, and the kind of inertia and paralysis of which UN bodies have often been accused.

Berdal's worries proved prescient.

SECURITY COUNCIL REFORM

Midway through the HLP's debates in 2004, and possibly yielding to the backroom pressures of certain member-states, Annan urged the HLP to address the highly contentious issue of Security Council reform. Several HLP members and, reportedly, some of its staff thought this a mistake. But his wishes, which were shared by some panel members, were heeded, with predictable results – the issue initially sucked all of the oxygen out of the rest of the reform debate.[8]

The HLP suggested two models for reform of Council composition, one involving the creation new permanent seats (without veto), the other premised on the creation of a new category of non-permanent seats to be held for four years and to be allocated to a new configuration of four regional groupings (rather than the current five – Canada would have moved from the current West European and Other Group to a new group covering all of the Americas).[9]

Brazil, Germany, India, and Japan (known as the G4) then advanced jointly a scheme for reform involving new permanent seats for themselves plus two extra for Africa, and several non-permanent seats to boost representation from the developing world (with an additional non-permanent seat added late in the game as an added inducement for African support).[10] They were countered by determined resistance of group of countries (including Canada) initially known as the "Coffee Club" and later as "Uniting for Consensus." Consensus, not surprisingly, proved elusive, all the more so as African countries developed a scheme of their own close to that of the four aspirants, but not quite overlapping with it.[11] Canada's position was that permanent seats are essentially undemocratic and that all Security Council members should have to face the discipline of election and re-election in order to remain accountable to the membership at large.[12]

Canada, which argued that Security Council reform was not among its top priorities, favoured the addition of a small number of elected seats and some further attention to greater transparency and inclusiveness in the Council's working methods. It opposed new permanent seats, particularly with vetoes, as undemocratic and as building in future sclerosis of the body (just as several of the permanent members designated in 1945 no longer seemed entirely fitting with great power status). Canada did not engage extensively on reform of the veto, although successive Canadian governments have viewed many past vetoes and veto threats as unhelpful.[13]

The debate focused on legitimacy in terms of the representativity of the Council's composition, completely ignoring what Ramesh Thakur (2006) has described as the (increasingly tattered) "performance legitimacy" of the body, unlikely to be addressed positively by the dynamics of committee decision-making by a larger number.

Why does this matter, beyond the fact that the HLP's important substantive recommendations were largely ignored while this went on? Amidst the welter of dysfunctional UN decisional bodies, only the Security Council has shown itself as capable (occasionally) of rapid and meaningful action. It is this effectiveness of the Council that needs to be preserved and enhanced if the UN is to continue to matter in a world where conceptions of legitimacy are splintering and in which the UN's central role is increasingly in doubt. In attempting to address the very real democratic deficit in the Council, the Pavlovian UN response of enlarging decision-making bodies in fact runs the risk of neutering them (as we have seen with the Economic and Social Council [ECOSOC], for example).

Thus, not only was the UN at risk of a train wreck in terms of the diplomatic confrontation between the champions of proliferating models of Council reform, but it ran the much greater risk of debasing the Council's key currency – its capacity for decisiveness.[14]

Canada's position throughout aimed for a measured tone. Ottawa argued that Security Council reform was not its priority, and that other reforms of UN management, human rights, and on peacebuilding mattered more.[15]

After much bitter talk, with emotions running very high, the debate petered out during the summer of 2005, as delegations began to focus on the need to debate the HLP's and Annan's other recommendations before the September Summit. In 2006, this debate resumed listlessly, with Japan relying on US support for its claim, and India, South Africa and Brazil seeming to band together in pressing the claim of 'the South.' Undoubtedly, the issue will be back and some form of expansion is likely in the medium-term future. This particular debate, ill-conceived, hastily and poorly timed, was all the more unfortunate as nobody doubts the major contributions of each of the aspirants to the UN system and to international relations more broadly and few wished to see them publicly frustrated.

SOME REFLECTION ON NEGOTIATIONS TOWARDS THE SEPTEMBER 2005 UN SUMMIT

The 2005 World Summit was held from 14 to 16 September, at UN Headquarters in New York, bringing together 151 Heads of State and Government. The negotiating process on a Summit outcome document proved tortuous and negotiations themselves made abundantly clear that outstanding differences among UN member-states were not minor disagreements that could be easily papered over – they represented fundamental splits. The fault lines on terrorism, human rights, and WMD/ non-proliferation were particularly notable.

Although it is a gross oversimplification, there is some truth to the contention that the negotiations pitted the interests of developed countries on security concerns (non-proliferation, counter-terrorism), human rights, the protection of civilians and improvement of UN management and oversight, against the predominant concentration of Third World countries on development, particularly more ODA, debt relief and trade concessions.[16] In fact, while the report of the High-Level Panel clearly recognized the inextricable links between security and development, the negotiations ended up with a tendency to trade off commitments in the two areas in an attempt to reach a consensus text addressing also issues of order and justice.[17]

The prospect of 191 member-states negotiating on all of these issues with each other daunted even the most optimistic. The President of the

General Assembly (Gabonese Foreign Minister Jean Ping, generally thought to have performed creditably, particularly in the early innings) was first inclined towards a 35-member "Core Group," but it soon became apparent that an even smaller negotiating group was required. That smaller configuration of roughly twenty eventually formed, with some help from Ping, and included the P5, the Group of 77 chair, Canada (representing also Australia and New Zealand), the Netherlands, Sweden (representing the Nordic countries), the European Union presidency, Japan, India, Pakistan, Algeria, South Africa, Mexico, Brazil, and Chile.[18]

Discussion of the document, even by that smaller group, raised questions about the merits of negotiating in a consensus-driven context (the UN's default mode, not least because the US has often feared being outvoted, not least on financial issues). Had the credible threat of a vote on the draft document in plenary been available, power would have shifted away from 'spoilers' to the more creative, moderate and flexible majority. This is true both among the industrialized and among the developing countries, and would have resulted in a text producing a Human Rights Council with teeth, a non-proliferation chapter and possibly more action-oriented language on the Responsibility to Protect. It might also have produced a better outcome on UN management reform.

The endorsement of the concept of the Responsibility to Protect in the Summit document was achieved against the predictions of almost everyone inside the UN and outside and is testament to the power of a good idea, presented well and defended to the last.

Global leadership in negotiations on the Summit outcome was absent. The secretary-general, perhaps distracted by the Volcker Inquiry into the Iraq Oil for Food Program and by urgent political challenges in the security sphere, was largely invisible during negotiations – and did not contribute much behind the scenes either. Similarly, very few national leaders were engaged. There were almost no public leader-to-leader discussions on the document or the wider issue of UN reform at any stage. Canada, the US, and the UK were exceptions in this regard. Interestingly, Cuba's political leadership made a major eleventh-hour contribution, dissuading Venezuela in the waning hours of the Summit from calling a paragraph-by-paragraph vote on the Summit Document (United Nations, 2005a). But this was crisis-management, not advocacy.

Active US involvement remains vital to key UN negotiations. The absence of a US Permanent Representative throughout much of the Summit preparatory process (John Bolton took up the position only in mid-August 2005) frequently stalled and sometimes undermined the negotiations. Many member-states simply were not prepared to negotiate seriously without hearing the opening bid of this kinetic figure.

That many of them did not much like his position when they did learn of it takes nothing away from the basic dynamic. (Late in the day, the presentation by the US of some 750 suggested amendments to the draft document gave member-states a target at which to direct their fire.) The eventual adoption of many of the US suggestions resulted in the end in a much stronger document. But a consistent hard line of the United States in matters of disarmament and the failure of the Nuclear Non-Proliferation Treaty Review Conference in May 2005 contributed to ensure that the outcome document was devoid of any reference to these important issues – an astonishing outcome for onlookers and described by Annan (2005b) as a "disgrace."

A TRIUMPH FOR THE RESPONSIBILITY TO PROTECT?

In the wake of the Kosovo crisis, during which NATO ultimately acted militarily to protect Kosovar civilians without a Security Council mandate (as attempts were blocked by Moscow's veto threat), Kofi Annan – who had made clear his sympathy for NATO's predicament – encouraged international debate on the conditions under which humanitarian intervention could and should be practiced.[19] Lloyd Axworthy, then Canada's foreign minister, understanding the saliency of the precedent created by NATO's Kosovo intervention, soon thereafter convened the International Commission on Intervention and State Sovereignty (ICISS).[20] This Commission concluded on two important notions: 'sovereignty as responsibility' and the related concept of the Responsibility to Protect (R2P), the latter to be exercised in the first instance by states in support of their own populations, and by others internationally where states do not act to protect their populations (or act to oppress them seriously or to deny their basic rights).[21] The HLP endorsed the R2P concept, as had Kofi Annan all along. It thus became a plausible matter for the Summit outcome document, but improbable in terms of acceptance because so many rights-violating countries would be party to negotiations on the text and because many member-states are attached to traditional notions of sovereignty – even though the Genocide Convention, for one, qualifies absolute conceptions of sovereignty.

The negotiating dynamic featured a small group of deeply recalcitrant member-states (Iran, Egypt, Russia, Pakistan, India, and Jamaica as G77 chair) that strongly resisted any reference to qualified sovereignty or to the Responsibility to Protect phrase. On the other side, most European and many Latin American and Caribbean countries were keen. The US was generally supportive, but very sensitive to any language Washington believed would limit its military options in the future. As a consequence, all language on use of force in relation to R2P died quietly and quickly. (Some in Washington feared that the R2P principle would create new obligations on the US to intervene forcibly in situations of massive human rights violations or crimes against humanity, while others argued that such obligations already existed.) Among the P5, the UK was particularly helpful as was, latterly, France. The Non-Aligned Movement (NAM) chair Mauritius and also South Africa were helpful in shading into the G77 position a strong sense of African support for the R2P principle (often linked in debate linked to the Rwanda genocide of 1994). China was silent, and ultimately acquiescing (its effort was focused more on negotiations over the Human Rights Council). It is this range of positions that the outcome document language had to bridge.

In view of the wide divergence of positions in the room, the last few days of negotiations required adjustments in language to overcome a variety of specific objections. But several drafting issues proved particularly tricky. To address American concerns, Canada accepted a move from "we accept our shared responsibility" to "we are prepared to take collective action" in support for R2P. Further, each of the P5 expressed reservations over the Canadian proposal that the P5 undertake not to use their vetoes in cases relevant to the R2P principle. Although many in the negotiations supported the Canadian approach, eventually, it was dropped (much to the chagrin of some spoilers who were hoping the P5 would torpedo any hope of agreement on the text). On the final day of negotiations, opponents of the concept attacked the title of the draft text's relevant section, wanting to replace the words "Responsibility to Protect" with the inadequate "Protection of Civilians." Fortunately, the clock ran out on that debate.

Late in the negotiations, delegations essentially deadlocked on the text, which at the UN, would have meant no inclusion of any reference to R2P in the Summit outcome document. On the advice of Allan Rock, Canada's Permanent Representative in New York, the prime minister entered the fray, placing calls to several leaders of countries opposed to the Canadian text (McCarthy, 2005: A15). (Several other capitals were contacted by senior Canadian officials.) These personal interventions had an effect that surprised even the most veteran observers of Summit-level contacts. In every case, whatever the local view of Canada's substantive arguments, the delegations in question essentially folded in New York. It was thus the last-minute involvement of leaders that allowed the will of the majority at the UN to prevail, with R2P enshrined in the outcome document (United Nations, 2005a: paras. 138–40).

Important as this negotiating success proved on its own terms, it is equally important to recognize that international acceptance of a concept or principle (even by a Summit of international leaders) will not necessarily translate into its early implementation. Thus the critique of some activists, that the advance represented by R2P's inclusion is at best incomplete, has merit. It is in the field that the Security Council's resolve and that of the UN membership more broadly will be tested. The battle on R2P thus now shifts to its application in specific circumstances. The Security Council's resistance to endorsing the Summit's language on R2P – which it finally did on 28 April 2006, after much debate, suggests this will be no easy battle (United Nations, 2006: para. 4). Not coincidentally perhaps, the Council's belated endorsement occurred at a time of heightened debate over mass killings in Darfur (with violence beginning to spread to neighbouring Chad). The situation in Darfur raised questions for Canadians of whether consensual or forcible humanitarian intervention was the right response, and of what contribution Canada could make to this effort, with Canadian troops already heavily committed in Afghanistan.[22]

The Summit outcome document is in itself significant on this issue alone, yet on this issue it is highly significant, directing a major blow at absolute conceptions of state sovereignty. And on this issue, Canada demonstrated that if it is prepared to focus its effort, take some risks and brave some criticism, it can still achieve notable victories internationally in the normative field.

THE UN PEACEBUILDING COMMISSION

The Security Council has often done a creditable short-term job of tackling conflicts, helping to restore the peace and ensuring that early steps towards sustainable stability are taken (see Malone, 2003: 487–517). But it has done poorly in ensuring the sustained attention to peacebuilding societies emerging from war, and particularly civil war, require. While in the early post-Cold War period, peacebuilding was often understood to be a largely mechanical, development-oriented project, its political complexities, indeed its centrality to politics, soon came to be better appreciated (see Cousens et al., 2001; and, Cousens and Cater, 2001). Indeed, the recent special representative of the secretary-general (SRSG) in Burundi, Carolyn McAskie, a Canadian who oversaw the successful conclusion to the UN's peacekeeping operations in Bujumbura in March 2006, underscored the key role of politics domestically and regionally in UN peacemaking and peacebuilding during a series of lectures in Canada in May of that year.

The concept of a United Nations Peacebuilding Commission was first formally introduced in December 2004 by the HLP. The Panel identified the lack of a UN mechanism to assist in war to peace transitions and to prevent countries from sliding back into conflict as a "key institutional gap" preventing the UN from acting effectively along the conflict continuum – from early warning to preventative action to post-conflict peacebuilding. The Panel suggested that the Commission identify countries at risk and organize preventative international assistance where required. Annan endorsed the recommendation in his own subsequent report.

In the ensuing inter-governmental negotiations, broad support for the Commission emerged, as did differences over whether the Commission should focus solely on the post–conflict period or include conflict prevention. Predictably, developing countries saw the Commission mostly as a tool for resource mobilization and for ensuring a longer-term donor commitment to reconstruction efforts, while others focussed more on the potential benefits of better international coordination of peacebuilding efforts.

The issue of the reporting relationship of the body (to or through the Security Council or the moribund but symbolically potent for some ECOSOC) became a polarizing question. There were also veiled threats by some to tie an agreement on creation of the Commission to progress on negotiation of other, more controversial elements of the outcome document, such as the creation of the Human Rights Council and substantive management reforms.

Ultimately, the Commission emerged as an instrument for post-conflict recovery rather than a proactive conflict prevention mechanism. The outcome document tasks the Commission to marshal resources, to advise and propose integrated strategies for post-conflict recovery, focussing attention on reconstruction, institution-building and sustainable development, in countries emerging from conflict. The document also notes that the Commission should be supported by a "small" Peacebuilding Support Office (PBSO) and by a Peacebuilding Voluntary Fund, the parameters of which were not specifically defined and left to further negotiation.[23]

Canada was among the countries that had first identified weak Security Council policy on and commitment to peacebuilding as problematic. However, it did not believe that new machinery was necessarily the answer (as so many UN commissions and committees wind up as anachronistic and irrelevant.) Given the HLP's call for a Peacebuilding Commission, Canada argued for a Commission as small and action-oriented as possible, with strong links to the Security Council, and an effective secretariat for the Commission. It has, so far, committed $5 million to the Peacebuilding Fund, a sum that will doubtless rise in months ahead.

After lengthy wrangling over the size of the Commission (and corresponding balance between membership categories that include ECOSOC, the General Assembly (UNGA), the Security Council, Donors and Troop Contributing Countries), concurrent resolutions of the Security Council and of the UNGA were adopted in December 2005 establishing the body.[24]

Considerable dissatisfaction was expressed (particularly among the G77 but also by other non-Security Council members) that control over the Commission's agenda was ultimately biased in favour of the Security Council. This resentment was reflected in renewed polarization of discussions over how the 31 seats on the Organizing Committee would be divided between the regional groups. Of greater concern has been the absence of meaningful debate over the Commission's actual agenda, internal structure and working. The failure by April 2006 to constitute an Organizing Committee after four months of negotiation was holding back progress on all fronts, including the terms of reference of the Peacebuilding Fund and the size and functions of a Peacebuilding Support Office in the UN Secretariat, which were both vital for action as opposed to talk.

The Peacebuilding Fund was agreed in principle as a $250 million revolving instrument that some (G77) would like to see firmly under the control of the Commission while others (donors, UN Secretariat) see it as a more independent resource to be guided by the Peacebuilding Support Office upon recommendation of UN Country Teams and SRSGs, in concert with host nations. Further complicating the issue, the Secretariat subsequently proposed that the Fund's administration be guided by an eminent persons group rather than the now-traditional donor committee method, a suggestion that has met with an unfavourable response from contributors. Given the relatively small size of the Fund and the significant expectations surrounding the Peacebuilding Commission as a resource mobilization tool for developing countries, more tension can be expected to emerge over its control.[25]

FUNDING THE UN'S RESPONSE TO EMERGENCIES

The UN is a major provider of emergency relief and protection, a catalyst for international action and an often powerful advocate on behalf of individuals impacted by emergencies, as its telegenic and effective humanitarian coordinator, Jan Egeland, has frequently demonstrated in Sudan. This willingness to alleviate human suffering is not without risk – attacks against UN aid workers have increased dramatically over the last ten years, often with impunity. Since 1992, 240 Consolidated and Flash Appeals have raised some US$33 billion for UN agencies, NGOs, and others.

Three challenges continue to stand out and impact on UN humanitarian action: coordination, resources, and the willingness and ability of states to fulfill their responsibilities towards affected populations. Each was addressed in the secretary-general's report *In Larger Freedom* and in the 2005 Summit outcome document. However, the most difficult to manage has been the proposed increase from US$60 million to US$500 million of the Central Emergency Revolving Fund (CERF) – allowing the UN to trigger humanitarian response before the detailed appeal process plays out – to provide more timely and equitable funding across crises (some crises, in part due to selective media attention, attract a great deal more attention and donor support than others of equivalent seriousness).[26] In July, in hopes of promoting greater donor engagement in the expanded CERF, the UK admirably indicated it would provide $1 for every $3 contributed by others.

Following very difficult negotiations, the General Assembly approved the creation of the expanded CERF in December 2005. Key sticking points included the nature of the oversight mechanism for the fund and triggers for its use, and, as a backdrop, the desire of some G77 countries to exert as much control over CERF use as possible. On 9 March, it was formally launched by Kofi Annan in New York. Thirty-eight countries made pledges totalling $254,845,586. Canada stands at number five in terms of amount pledged, behind the UK, Sweden, Norway, and the Netherlands. The CERF, which is now very likely to reach the $500 million goal, will be replenished as required on an annual basis.[27]

IS MONEY THE CENTRAL CHALLENGE IN UN REFORM?

The willingness of donor states to agree to pony up $250 million for the Peacebuilding Fund and an additional $440 million for the CERF strongly suggest that the UN is not being starved of funds by the industrialized countries. Rather, there is strong concern over how large amounts in assessed contributions are allocated and spent by member-states and UN staff in processes that are opaque to most and worrying to many. Where objectives are clear, leadership is strong (as with Egeland) and the cause a worthy one, donor countries continue to work through the UN, often with generous voluntary funding.

HUMAN RIGHTS COUNCIL

The UN Commission on Human Rights (CHR), established 60 years ago, early on made significant contributions to the development of human rights norms and practice.[28] However, growing concern regarding its recent ineffectiveness and loss of credibility led to calls for its abolition and replacement. (In particular, membership of such notorious human rights violators as Zimbabwe and the election of Libya as chair undermined the Commission's standing.) The High-Level Panel did not go so far in its suggestions for CHR reform, but Kofi Annan did in his own recommendations.[29] The 2005 Summit outcome document agreed on the importance of human rights to the work of the UN as one of its three pillars, and "resolved" to establish a Human Rights Council (to replace the CHR).

Responsibility for follow-up was given to the new President of the General Assembly, Jan Eliasson of Sweden – a stalwart of UN diplomacy going back to the days when he served as the UN special envoy for the Iran-Iraq conflict, through which he did much to help end in 1987–88 (see Hume, 1994). Discussions took place fitfully from November 2005 until February 2006. Canada was active throughout, often in collaboration with Australia and New-Zealand (in the 'CANZ' formation). Canada championed the new concept of universal periodic review of Council members by each other.

Eliasson produced a text in late February that appeared to be acceptable to most delegations and called for its adoption in early March. The US delegation raised concerns, primarily on Council membership on which they thought the text insufficiently robust to exclude persistent human rights abusers and states subject to UN sanctions (Leopold, 2006). Other delegations then threatened to propose amendments of their own that would weaken the text or introduce political factors. Canada and others expressed their support for strong criteria for membership and the need to review this issue specifically when the Council and its mandate are reviewed in five years.

On 15 March 2006, the UN General Assembly adopted Resolution 60/251, formally establishing the Human Rights Council. The vote was 170 in favour (including Canada) to 4 against (US, Israel, Marshall Islands, Palau), with 3 abstentions (Belarus, Iran, Venezuela). The United States indicated that while Washington stood by its concerns on the text of the resolution, it continued to support strengthened human rights mechanisms and that it would therefore contribute to, and participate in, the Council in the future (United States, 2006a). That said, Washington subsequently announced that it would not run for membership in the Council at its outset, and it is clear that for a number of actors in Washington, this new UN body is "on probation" (United States, 2006b). Because many of the US reservations over the terms under which the Council was set up are sensible, and because it will be important for the Council's future that the US buy into it, it will be vital that the Council not include among its founding membership a raft of notorious violators, and that, early on, it achieve concrete results that represent an improvement over the Commission's track-record. It is on these objectives that much of Canada's subsequent UN human rights diplomacy will be focused (Canada, 2006).

To date, the main innovations and improvements in the Council's mandate relative to that of the Commission include: an elevated status – the HRC is a subsidiary body of the General Assembly; four sessions annually instead of one will allow for more timely responses and interventions; and the introduction of the system of "universal periodic review" championed by Canada. Members will be elected individually and directly, precluding election without a vote through "agreed slates." In addition, the UN General Assembly would have the ability to revoke the membership of the most egregious human rights violators. While the members would not be elected by a 2/3 majority (of those present and voting, a key US and objective shared by Canada), the requirement for an absolute majority (i.e. 50 percent of all UN members) is nearly as onerous. Finally, the Council will preserve key features of the UN human rights architecture and procedures, such as a system of independent rapporteurs and the participation of NGOs.

Elections to the Council on 9 May 2006 were the first test. They were particularly challenging for members of the Western European and Other Group, of which Canada is a member, with 11 candidacies for only 7 seats.[30] Several candidate states, including Canada, presented pledges regarding their commitment to the Council and to the standards it set for itself and by implication for election of others on the body. Canada was duly elected to a full three-year term.[31] (Many others had to settle for single or two-year terms, all of this being determined by chance.) Among human rights "malefactors," Zimbabwe and Libya did not present candidacies, doubtless sensing that the new deck was stacked against them. Cuba and China, both with considerable clout within the NAM and G77 were elected. Importantly, Iran was defeated.

SELECTION OF THE UN SECRETARY-GENERAL

The selection of the UN secretary-general is one of the most significant collective decisions made by its member-states. The office of secretary-general is a very prominent but a remarkably ill-defined one.[32] A few articles of the UN Charter assign to the incumbent mainly the task of administering the organization, while Article 99 offers an opening to the secretary-general for a more overtly political role in relation to the Security Council. Early secretaries-general worked hard to expand the leeway for initiative of the incumbent under this article (see Cockayne and Malone, forthcoming).

Today the position is more often seen in terms of moral and global political leadership than in relation to mundane administrative duties. But the so-called Volcker Report into irregularities within and mismanagement of the Iraq Oil for Food program once again shone a spotlight on the wide-ranging administrative responsibilities of a secretary-general overseeing $6 billion of peacekeeping operations annually and many other programs, beyond the UN's regular budget of roughly $1 billion annually (IIC-OFFP, 2005a; 2005b).

Annan delivered a superb first term, focused on human rights and the humanitarian imperative, crowned by the millennial Nobel Peace Prize and early re-election to the office. But after the deadlock in the Security Council over Iraq in March 2003, everything seemed to go wrong for him – even the ambitious reform process he launched (the topic of this chapter) as a way of reviving the UN's fortunes and burnishing his own reputation proved difficult and remains, at the time of writing, incomplete. His predecessor, Boutros Boutros-Ghali, served only one term after developing stormy relations with the US and poor ones with several other UN member-states, seeing himself more as General than Secretary.

Thus, by late 2005, the position itself no longer seemed as attractive as it once had. Further, the opaque selection process is widely perceived as one of back-room deal-making by the P5. Each of these more powerful members can veto candidates in the straw-polling conducted in the Security Council, as under the provisions of Article 97 of the Charter, it is the Security Council that recommends to the General Assembly *the* candidate to be appointed.[33]

With Annan's second term expiring in December 2006, Canada, in February of that year, drawing on innovations in the method of selection of the heads of the World Trade Organization (WTO) and of the Organisation for Economic Cooperation and Development (OECD), circulated a 'non-paper' at the UN and in world capitals on adjustments it wished to see in the opaque methods of selection of the secretary-general.[34] It took aim at the lack of transparency and inclusiveness of the exercise in the past, and offered suggestions aimed at ensuring that candidates faced more systematic scrutiny by the General Assembly as well as the Security Council.[35] All of this, Canada argued, would serve to engender the widest possible support for the new secretary-general among member-states and, simultaneously, serve to revitalize the role of the General Assembly.

The ultimate objective of Canada's initiative was not a General Assembly power grab, but rather an effort to develop the broadest possible support among member-states for the new secretary-general and to stimulate an informed decision-making process in the Council.

Canada suggested a five-point program to this end:

1 The qualities sought in a secretary-general should be articulated. The very process of considering, discussing and identifying the key characteristics of a successful incumbent would establish a useful framework for member-states as they consider candidates.[36]
2 A systematic means should be put in place by which potential candidates can be identified. This might take the form of a search committee, appointed jointly by the president of the Security Council and the president of the General Assembly.
3 Means should be devised to allow member-states to hear from candidates well before recommendation and appointment – under circumstances that permit assessment of their qualities, evaluation of their aptitude and determination of their vision for the office and for the United Nations (preferably in open session). Member-states would then be able to make known to the Security Council their views with respect to the various candidates.[37]
4 Member-states should consider establishing a date by which persons must declare their interest in the position of secretary-general in order to be considered as candidates. The advantages of an orderly and systematic process (and the opportunity for member-states to learn about candidates, their qualities and their vision) is lost if emergence at the eleventh hour of candidates is permitted.[38]
5 Member-states should consider limiting the candidate to a single term in office as secretary-general, whether for five or seven years. By ruling out a second term, member-states would remove any basis for suggestion that the secretary-general's conduct was influenced by expectations of re-appointment (Rock, 2006).

Several other considerations arose. By its Resolution 11(1) in 1946, the General Assembly decided that the Security Council should recommend a single name for appointment as secretary-general. Some experts and several member-states have floated the idea of opening up the process by amending or revoking this resolution, so that two (or more) names are forwarded by the Security Council to the General Assembly. In May 2006, Egypt and India were leading the charge to do just this, possibly as a tactic in the broader struggle for dominance between the Council and the Assembly. For Canada, this issue was not a priority and the prospect of a battle for election in the General Assembly raised the risk of the election of a candidate whose authority would be weakened at the outset.

An important element in the debate among governments and UN delegates on selection of the secretary-general has been the principle (for some) and practice (for others) of regional rotation of successful candidates. In 2006, this led to a claim by some Asian countries that it was 'Asia's turn' – not actually true as Eastern Europe has never fielded a successful candidate. Canada systematically argued that the best candidate – from whatever region – should win and that if Asian countries attached importance to the position, they should take care to field the best candidate. In discussion, Canada was more interested in promoting gender equality, encouraging the candidacy of as many qualified women as possible.[39]

It would be difficult if not impossible to implement this year all of the foregoing changes, not least because other, highly contentious issues continue to weigh down the reform agenda. But it was important to make a start. And Canada is now very much identified with this element of the reform agenda.

UN MANAGEMENT REFORM

In Larger Freedom did not focus heavily on management issues but the secretary-general made proposals that extended beyond the previous, rather timid reform initiatives.[40] Several key ideas stand out in the secretary-general's various proposals: the urgent need to overhaul human resources management, the need to manage budgeting more rationally, and the need to enlarge the managerial authority and flexibility of the secretary-general to respond to changing operational circumstances.[41] He also advocated a review of the many General Assembly mandates older than five years.[42]

Annan's recommendations provided the point of departure for 2005 Summit outcome negotiations, but, the Volcker Inquiry served more acutely to focus minds of major contributor countries on management issues – compounded by the arrest of several UN officials in connection with graft allegations and an unfolding scandal relating to sexual exploitation by UN peacekeepers. All of these issues raised serious ethics, oversight, and management concerns that could not be ignored.

But underpinning subsequent difficulties in negotiation, were three politically-freighted issues: a fundamentally different view between the G77 and most major budget contributors as to the appropriate balance of power between the Secretariat and the General Assembly. The first being that budgetary flexibility for the secretary-general is feared by the G77 as a means of loosening General Assembly control over the implementation of mandates. The second, that mandate review was perceived by many in the G77 as a vehicle to attack politically sensitive mandates, such as those relating to Palestine. And the third, that resentment by many in the G77 of pressure to adopt Volcker recommendations to satisfy American congressional demands.

After the Summit, Eliasson designated Allan Rock of Canada and Munir Akram of Pakistan as co-chairs of discussions on management reform. Progress was slow and fitful, marked by procedural wrangling and high levels of suspicion among delegates. The Secretariat did not always play its hand well. Meanwhile, discussions on the UN budget for 2006–07 were unfolding joylessly. The central issue in that negotiation was the insistence by the United States that a full budget not be approved pending progress on management reform, resulting in a decision to fund UN spending only for 6 months, until the end of June 2006 (United Nations, 2005b).

In due course, the secretary-general produced another report, *Investing in the United Nations: For a Stronger Organization Worldwide*, a document that contained governance proposals that were immediately unpopular with the G77 (Annan, 2006). Its governance proposals fanned fears of disenfranchisement among G77 members, and in a sour atmosphere, the G77 pressed a resolution that would have set them aside altogether. Because management governance is at the core of any serious management regime, the major contributors (with a few exceptions, including Russia and China) could not accept this approach, particularly with important budget discussions soon to be renewed. An EU compromise proposal (that Canada and some other contributors disliked) to take the governance issues off the table for four months as a face-saving device failed to impress the G77.

Breaking with the long-standing tradition of consensual decision-making on UN budget and management matters, the G77 forced a vote on 28 April 2006, with disappointing results for itself (considerably less than its full membership voted for the measure, while 50 states opposed it outright), but with potentially serious consequences.[43] US Ambassador Bolton made clear that Congress was likely to view the vote as a provocation (see Hoge, 2006).

As usual at the UN, under the surface of debate on principles, personality clashes loomed large. The new Deputy Secretary-General Mark Malloch Brown (an accomplished former head of the UN Development Programme) was to have been given greater authority under Annan's governance proposals. However, the G77 viewed Malloch Brown as having deferred excessively to the US Congress, while its highly regarded South African chair in New York, Dumisani Kumalo, reportedly still smarted from a clash with the United States over the Security Council's involvement in discussions on peacekeeping procurement which the G77 regarded as an issue exclusively for the General Assembly.

While the issue of mandate review initially aroused fewer passions than that of management governance, it was not clear where any 'early harvest' of mandates to retire would come from.[44] As with national parliaments, much mandated activity enjoys committed constituencies, even when these are narrowly based. Reporting relative to existing mandates is overwhelming for both the Secretariat and member-states, so changes in reporting procedures may be agreed, but member-states are not practiced at giving up on pet projects at the UN (no matter how dated).

Where does this leave UN management reform and the reform agenda more broadly? First, some real progress needs to be recognized: stronger oversight by the Office of Internal Oversight Services has been achieved and, further to the Volcker Inquiry, steps have been taken to strengthen staff financial disclosure, the UN's ethics policy and capacity, and its whistleblower protections. But, it is hard to be optimistic that an institution in which the majority of the members (and hence the majority of the votes) to date have regarded serious management renewal as an optional extra but such renewal matters considerably for major contributors and especially to the US. Japan, unhappy with its failure to secure a permanent seat and rightly irritated that it pays nearly as much to the UN general budget as does the US, is pressing for adjustments to the scale of assessments (in which many developing countries enjoy sizeable special discounts) that would reduce its payments. For Canada, the principal issue is how to secure better management of an institution that has mattered greatly in Canadian foreign policy but may not forever do so unless Canadians can be convinced of its effectiveness and efficiency.

CONCLUSIONS

One important element of Kofi Annan's strategy since the fall of 2003 has been to retain US engagement in the UN. It is hard to overstate how disappointed the Bush Administration and many in Congress were with the deadlock in the Security Council over Iraq in early 2003 (see Malone, 2006). Stephen Stedman (2006) of Stanford University and highly-regarded staff director for the HLP remarks: "Many commentators miss what a big part of the crisis was in September 2003 – that the US would walk away from the organization." However, with the US unhappy over the terms under which the new Human Rights Council was created, in addition to its frustration with the G77 on important aspects of UN management reform, and with Congress once again toying with the idea of withholding dues (a pattern that bedevilled US relations with the UN in the 1990s), it is not clear that the US will re-engage beyond those forums that demonstrably serve its own interests. Even at the Security Council, its level of commitment varies from year to year, from issue to issue. Its engagement with the Council, as that of all other P5 members, is essentially instrumental.[45]

The UN is one element of a multilateral system imagined by President Franklin D. Roosevelt in the early 1940s, on which many additional elements have been grafted since the Bretton Woods institutions and the UN emerged mid-decade. Because decision-making power is diluted within many of these organizations, because their *raison d'être* sometimes is not as clear-cut as it was at the outset, and because vested interests always argue powerfully against reform, the multilateral system as a whole is aging poorly in its seventh decade. At the International Monetary Fund there are early, timid, signs of adjustment to an altered world economic order through a reallocation of quotas, and, as noted earlier, the OECD and the WTO have succeeded in addressing some specific reform challenges. That said, most regional organizations, and many regional and global economic institutions are widely perceived as less dynamic and effective (intellectually as well as managerially) as the private sector or the thriving and expanding, although perhaps excessively self-regarding, non-governmental sector.

Canada's new Minister of Foreign Affairs Peter MacKay visited the UN early in his tenure and made a strong impression there, arguing for a more robust and focused Canadian foreign policy. For Canadians, increasingly the value of multilateral institutions is likely to be assessed in terms of the results they achieve. Anecdotally, one senses among Canadians that support for the UN and other multilateral institutions remains strong in the abstract, but that it is shallower than it used to be in real terms. Further, along with the rest of the world, multilateralism is likely to be seen increasingly by Canadians as a means to various ends rather than as an end in itself (as it often was in Canadian foreign policy during the Cold War years). In keeping with its existing five domestic priorities, the new Canadian government will doubtless emphasize that the UN needs to achieve much higher levels of accountability and that it must provide value for money relative to other available channels for Canadian policy and program delivery.[46]

The creation of the Peacebuilding Commission and the Human Rights Council, significant new funding for the Peacebuilding Fund and the Central Emergency Revolving Fund, as well as the willingness of Leaders at the 2005 Summit to endorse the Responsibility to Protect suggest that the UN continues to harbour the capacity for change. But the quality of implementation of these various initiatives will be critical to the evaluation of their successes or failures.

It would take a cataclysm to sweep away the existing multilateral system, but this has happened before, with the outbreak of the Second World War for example. It would be highly distressing if the atrophy of multilateral capacities and commitment such as we may be witnessing at the UN were to bring closer the prospects of just such a cataclysm.

NOTES

The author is very grateful for the input of Sebastian von Einsiedel, Bruce D. Jones and Stephen John Stedman, all cited here, and for valuable suggestions by his DFAIT colleagues Heidi Hulan, Heather Jeffrey, Wendy Drukier, Deborah Chatsis and Jerry Kramer.

1 On the influence of events related to Iraq over the UN reform process, see Malone (2006: 222–64).
2 The most important were United Nations (2004), and Annan (2005a).
3 On the pivotal role of the Council's efforts and those of Pérez de Cuéllar to end the Iran-Iraq war, see Hume (1994).
4 On the revival of UN peacekeeping in the late 1990s, see William Shawcross, *Deliver Us From Evil: Peacekeepers, Warlords and a World of Endless Conflict* (New York: Simon and Schuster, 398–413).
5 The Millennium Summit in September 2000 adopted the Millennium Declaration, which contained a core group of goals and targets, some of which were later refined in an Report of the Secretary-General (UN Document A/56/326, September 2001), that offered what have now more widely come to be known as the MDGs. These eight goals (involving numerical targets) are essentially centered on national targets for poverty, education, gender equality, and environmental sustainability. The report of the International Conference on the Financing of Development at Monterrey, Mexico, March 2002, can be found in UN Document A/Conf.198/11.
6 Annan had earlier come to grips with hard issues relative to military intervention after NATO's action to protect Kosovo in March 1999 (unauthorized by the Security Council) in perhaps his finest speech, to the UN General Assembly in September 1999 (see SG/SM/7136, 20 September 1999).
7 See Tempest (2005); *South African Press Association* (2005); and, Dugger (2005). See also G8 Summit Chairman's Summary, available at: <http://www.g7.utoronto.ca/summit/2005gleneagles/summary.html>, and, Bayne (2005).
8 Discussion of Security Council reform is often a charged topic at the UN. See Bailey and Daws (1998: 382–90), and Fassbender (2004: 341–57).
9 A number of Canadian officials in recent years have favoured an Americas group, particularly given a tendency of some European Union (EU)

members only to support candidacies of other EU members within the Western European and Other Groups (WEOG) voting bloc. However, because, on balance, Canada performs well in UN elections, the issue has not been an urgent one for Ottawa.

10 On the inherently unpromising international dynamics underpinning this effort, see Zacher (2004: 211–26).

11 On these manoeuvres, see Malone (2005: 370–2).

12 For a full statement on Canada's position on the issues under the previous government, see Rock (2005). At time of publication, the new Canadian government's position on UN reform had not been formulated.

13 Professor Thomas M. Franck, that great Canadian authority on international law who has spent a life-long career largely devoted to UN law from his perch at the NYU School of Law, argues persuasively that any expansion of the Security Council, particularly if it involves new permanent members, should be accompanied by new understandings among the permanent members to reduce the use and threat of the veto. He spoke along these lines both in a public lecture at the Department of Foreign Affairs and International Trade and at the International Law Association meeting in Toronto, in early June 2006.

14 The aspirations of key emerging powers to participate in the discussions that matter might better be partially met in a larger body modelled on the Group of Eight. Former Canadian Prime Minister Paul Martin made just such a proposal for a Leader's Twenty (L20) Summit. See Martin (2005: 2–6).

15 For a similar view from a leading scholar, see Weiss (2005: 367–9).

16 For interesting reflections on how poverty and state failure can be relevant to the fight against terrorism, see Rotberg (2003).

17 For a trenchant essay on how order and justice issues at the UN, consult Roberts (2003: 49–79).

18 For Canadians, it is worth noting that the number and many of its members recall former Prime Minister Martin's advocacy of an L20 as a new forum for exchange of views on major global issues.

19 In early 2000, Annan himself undertook some serious reflection on the subject, through the International Peace Academy, drawing *inter alia* on Thomas P. Franck, Adam Roberts, Mats Berdal, Robert Badinter, and Alain Pellet, but this group was unable to produce any agreement on "criteria" for intervention.

20 The debate over humanitarian intervention in the years 1999 and beyond produced many excellent contributions. As a sampling, see Wheeler (2000), McDermott (1999), and Ignatieff (2003). For two interesting chapters on legal dimensions of the debate, see Byers and Chesterman (2003: 177–203), and Franck (2003: 204–31).

21 For a summary of ICISS conclusions, see "The Responsibility to Protect," Ottawa: International Development Research Centre (IDRC), 2001. Most International Commissions produce little of lasting value. Some, like ICISS, continue to resonate in debate years after their work is done. On such

Commissions, see Thakur, Cooper, and English (2005). On Axworthy's role in championing the concept of "human security," see in extenso, McRae and Hubert (2001). It is worth remembering that renewed debate in Canada on the need for humanitarian intervention was sparked by Brian Mulroney in his celebrated Stanford University centennial convocation speech of 29 September 1991.

22 Prime Minister Harper told the House of Commons he was in touch with Kofi Annan on the issue (Salot, 2006).

23 In May 2006, Carolyn McAskie of Canada was appointed the first leader of the PBSO at Assistant Secretary-General level.

24 The General Assembly passed Res. 60/180, UN Doc. A/RES/60/180, on 30 December 2005; and the Security Council passed Res. 1645 (2005), UN Doc. S/RES/1645 (2005), on 20 December 2005.

25 As of May 2006, the fund was only partially subscribed as most donors wished to have the terms of reference firmly entrenched before offering contributions. Nevertheless, about US$70 million had been offered already by then.

26 This expansion target was more modest than the US $1 billion advocated by UK Minister for International Cooperation Hilary Benn, but a huge leap nevertheless.

27 Two-thirds of the CERF grant facility is to be reserved for life-saving rapid response initiatives (programs of no more than 3 months, maximum of $30 million for any one crisis). One third of the grant facility will be allocated to cover critical needs in neglected and chronically under funded crises.

28 On the development of rights through various UN treaties and treaty bodies, see a seminal new volume, Wiess, et al. (2005). See also Brody (2004), a terrific essay on the struggle for human rights amidst conflict since 1980.

29 For a critique of the HLP's stance, see Hicks (2005: 378–80).

30 While the overall membership of the Council was only a few seats less than the Commission, the allocation of seats for the WEOG group dropped from 10 to 7.

31 Canada, which enjoyed strong support from New Zealand and Australia for its election, has committed to stepping down from the Council after a single term and supporting New Zealand for election in 2009.

32 On the secretary-general's role, see see Brian Urquhart and Erskine Childers, *A World in Need of Leadership: Tomorrow's United Nations – A Fresh Appraisal* (Uppsala: Dag Hammarskjold Foundation, 1996).

33 China repeatedly vetoed Kurt Waldheim's over-reaching candidacy for a third term, while the United States, Soviet Union and even France have vetoed candidates, in some cases as recently as in 1996, when Annan was elected. See Bailey and Daws (1998: 238).

34 The highly competitive OECD process – leading to the election of Mexican candidate Angel Gurria, requiring each of six candidates to lay out their platforms and to convince not only OECD Council members, but also OECD capitals (during a flurry of visits) of their qualifications, leadership potential and policy acuity – was considerably shaped by Canada. Our accomplished

OECD ambassador (and former Clerk of the Privy Council), Jocelyne Bourgon, was one of three individuals selected to oversee the consultations leading to his formal nomination. See <www.oecd.org/secretarygeneral/gurria>.

35 This is not the first time that the UNGA has considered its role in the selection of the secretary-general. In August 1997, it adopted Resolution 51/241, setting forward some conclusions picked up in Canada's proposals. At the time, no meaningful follow-up action was taken.

36 Such an exercise in definition, repeated periodically, would also serve as a barometer of how member-states see the role of secretary-general in a changing political landscape.

37 Some UN experts argue that candidates for the SG slot should identify those they would appoint as deputy secretary-general, given the important role, not least on management of the system, of the latter position. So far, there has been no uptake among declared candidates.

38 Historically, several candidates did emerge late in the straw-balloting process within the Council, most recently Javier Pérez de Cuéllar in 1981.

39 A Canadian, Louise Fréchette, was the UN's first deputy secretary-general (DSG) from 1998 to 2006. Several other Canadian women played very prominent roles at the UN in 2006, notably High Commissioner for Human Rights Louise Arbour.

40 For earlier reform proposals, see *An Agenda for Further Change* (UN Document A/57/387, 9 Sept 2002).

41 The SG early on rejected a Volcker Report recommendation of transforming the DSG into a full Chief Operating Officer, preferring a cabinet-style decision-making structure (that has failed repeatedly at the UN, it might be noted). See *Secretary-General's Bulletin* (UN Document ST/SGB/2005/16, 8 August 2005).

42 One specific proposal, for staff buy-outs, proved particularly controversial with some due to its costs, although the unsatisfactory competency of a range of UN staffers suggests this would be a wise one-off investment (if accompanied by better hiring practices).

43 UNGA Resolution on *Investing in the United Nations: For a Stronger Organization Worldwide* (UN Doc. A/C.5/60/L.27/Rev.1, 28 April 2006). Canada viewed the prospect of taking any key aspect of UN management reform off the table for any amount of time as so irresponsible that it would have voted against the EU compromise, along with a few others, had the G77 been able to accept it, which it did not.

44 On mandate review, see *Mandating and Delivering: Analysis and Recommendations to Facilitate the Review of Mandates* (UN Document A/60/733, 30 March 2006).

45 For a sophisticated analysis of instrumental multilateralism, see Rosemary Foot, S. Neil MacFarlane and Michael Mastanduno, "Conclusions: Instrumental Multilateralism and US Foreign Policy" in *US Hegemony and International Organizations* (Oxford: Oxford University Press, 2003: 265–72).

46 Students of the UN and of international assistance programs will know that
some UN agencies, funds and programs are more impressive than others.
UNICEF, the World Food Program and the World Health Organization are
generally very impressive indeed. At the other end of the spectrum, in the early
1990s, Canada decided to withdraw from the UN Industrial Development
Organization (UNIDO) and has never had reason to regret the decision.

REFERENCES

Annan, Kofi. 2003. Address by the Secretary-General to the UN General
Assembly, New York, 23 September. Available at: <http://www.un.org/
apps/sg/sgstats.asp?nid=517>
– 2005a. *In Larger Freedom: Towards Development, Security and Human
Rights for All*. Response to the High Level Panel Report. UN Doc. A/59/
2005, 21 March.
– 2005b. Transcript of Press Conference by Secretary-General, UN News and
Media Division, New York, 13 September. Available at: <http://www.un.org/
News/briefings/docs/2005/sgsm10089.doc.htm>
– 2006. *Investing in the United Nations: For a Stronger Organization
Worldwide*, UN Document A/60/692, 7 March 2006.
Bailey, Sydney D., and Sam Daws. 1998. *The Procedure of the UN Security
Council*. Oxford: Oxford University Press.
Bayne, Nicholas. 2005. "Overcoming Evil with Good: Impressions of the
Gleneagles Summit, 6–8 July 2005," University of Toronto, G8 Information
Centre, 18 July. Available at: <http://www.g7.utoronto.ca/evaluations/
2005gleneagles/bayne2005–0718.html>
Berdal, Mats. 2005a. "The UN's Unnecessary Crisis," *Survival* 47, no. 3
(Autumn): 8.
– 2005b. "The United Nations at 60: A New San Francisco Moment?"
Survival 47, no. 3 (Autumn): 7–31.
Brody, Reed. 2004. "Right Side Up": *Twenty-five Years of the Human Rights
Movements. In World Report 2004: Human Rights and Armed Conflict*.
New York: Human Rights Watch, 376–89.
Byers, Michael, and Simon Chesterman. 2003. "Changing the Rules About Rules?
Unilateral Humanitarian Intervention and the Rule of Law," in J.L. Holzgreve
and Robert O. Keohane, eds. *Humanitarian Intervention: Ethical, Legal and
Political Dilemmas*. Cambridge, UK: Cambridge University Press, 177–203.
Canada. 2006. "Canada Welcomes United Nations Human Rights Council,"
News Release. Ottawa: Department of Foreign Affairs and International
Trade (DFAIT), 15 March.
Cockayne, James, and David M. Malone. Forthcoming. "Relations with
the Security Council," in Simon Chesterman, ed. *Secretary or General?*

The Role of the United Nations Secretary-General in World Politics. Forthcoming.

Cousens, Elizabeth, et al. 2001. *Peacebuilding as Politics: Cultivating Peace in Fragile Societies.* Boulder, CO: Lynne Rienner.

Cousens, Elizabeth M., and Charles K. Cater. 2001. *Towards Peace in Bosnia: Implementing the Dayton Accords.* Boulder, CO: Lynne Rienner.

Daalder, Ivo H, and James M. Lindsay. 2003. "American Foreign Policy and Transatlantic Relations in the Age of Global Politics," in Gustav Linstrom, ed. *Shift or Rift: Assessing US-EU Relations After Iraq.* Paris: Institute for Security Studies, 92–104.

Dugger, Celia W. 2005. "Trade and Aid to Poorest Seen as Crucial on Agenda for Richest Nations," *New York Times,* 19 June.

Fassbender, Bardo. 2004. "Pressure for Security Council Reform," in David M. Malone, ed. *The UN Security Council: From Cold War to Twenty-First Century.* Boulder, CO: Lynne Rienner, 341–57.

Franck, Thomas M. 2003. "Interpretation and Change in the Law of Humanitarian Intervention," in J.L. Holzgreve and Robert O. Keohane, eds. *Humanitarian Intervention: Ethical, Legal and Political Dilemmas.* Cambridge, UK: Cambridge University Press, 204–31.

Hagman, Lotta, and David M. Malone. 2002. "The North-South Divide at the United Nations: Fading at Last?" *Security Dialogue* 33, no. 4 (December): 399–414.

Hicks, Peggy. 2005. "Correct Diagnosis, Wrong Prescription: The Human Rights Component of Security," *Security Dialogue,* 35, no. 3 (Autumn): 378–80.

Hoge, Warren. 2006. "Third World Bloc Thwarts UN Reform Plan," *New York Times,* 29 April.

Hume, Cameron R. 1994. *The United Nations, Iran and Iraq: How Peacemaking Changed.* Bloomington, IN: Indiana University Press.

Ignatieff, Michael. 2003. *Empire Light: Nation-Building in Bosnia, Kosovo and Afghanistan.* London: Vintage Press.

IIC-OFFP (Independent Inquiry Committee into the United Nations Oil-for-Food Programme). 2005a. "Report on the Management of the Oil-for-Food Programme," 7 September. Available at: <http://www.iic-offp.org/Mgmt_Report.htm>

– 2005b. "Report on the Manipulation of the Oil-for-Food Programme," 27 October. Available at: <http://www.iic-offp.org/story27octo5.htm>

Jones, Bruce D. 2006. Correspondence with the author, Ottawa, 10 April.

Leopold, Evelyn. 2006. "US Rejects New UN Rights Council, Wants More Talks," *Reuters,* 28 February.

Luck, Edward C. 2005. "The UN Security Council: Reform or Enlarge?" in Paul Heinbecker and Patricia Goff, eds. *Irrelevant or Indispensable? The United Nations in the 21st Century.* Waterloo, ON: Wilfred Laurier University Press, 143–52.

Malone, David M. 1999. "Goodbye UNSCOM: A Sad Tale in UN-US Relations," *Security Dialogue* 30, no. 4, (December): 393–411.

– 2003. "The Security Council in the Post-Cold War Era: A Study in the Creative Interpretation of the UN Charter," *Journal of International Law and Politics* 35, no. 2 (Winter): 487–517.

– ed. 2004. *The UN Security Council: From Cold War to Twenty-First Century.* Boulder, CO: Lynne Rienner.

– 2005. "The High-Level Panel and the Security Council," *Security Dialogue* 36, no. 3 (September): 370–2.

– 2006. *The International Struggle over Iraq: Politics in the UN Security Council, 1980–2005.* Oxford: Oxford University Press.

Martin, Paul. 2005. "A Global Answer to Global Problems," *Foreign Affairs* 84, no. 3 (May-June): 2–6.

McCarthy, Shawn. 2005. "Deep rifts threaten UN summit; PM phones world leaders to help forge declaration, avert crisis at world body," *Globe and Mail*, 13 September, A15.

McDermott, Anthony, ed. 1999. *Sovereign Intervention.* Oslo: International Peace Research Institute (PRIO).

McRae, Rob, and Don Hubert, eds. 2001. *Human Security and the New Diplomacy: Protecting People: Promoting Peace.* Montreal & Kingston: McGill-Queens University Press.

Roberts, Adam. 2003. "Order/Justice Issues at the United Nations," in Rosemary Foot, John Lewis Gaddis, and Andrew Hurrell. *Order and Justice in International Relations.* Oxford: Oxford University Press, 49–79.

Rock, Allan. 2005. Address by Canada's Permanent Representative to the UN to the General Assembly, New York, NY, 12 July. Available at: <http://www.international.gc.ca/canada_un/ottawa/statements/unga-en>

– 2006. Statement by Canada's Permanent Representative to the UN to the General Assembly on the Selection of the Secretary-General, New York, NY, 19 April. Available at <http://www.international.qc.ca/Canada-UN/New_York/statements/ungaen.asp?id=6268&content_type=2>

Rotberg, Robert I., ed. 2003. *State Failure and State Weakness in a Time of Terror.* Washington, DC: Brookings/WPF.

Salot, Jeff. 2006. "Harper Won't Send Soldiers to Darfur: But Canada Will Help Peace Mission," *Globe and Mail*, 12 May.

South African Press Association. 2005. "Gleneagles Redefines Africa-North Relations: Mbeki," 15 July.

Stedman, Stephen John. 2006. Correspondence with the author, Ottawa, 10 April.

Tempest, Matthew. 2005. "G8 Leaders Agree $50bn Africa Package," *Guardian Unlimited*, 8 July. Available at: <http://www.guardian.co.uk/g8/story/0,,1524305,00.html>

Thakur, Ramesh. 2006. *The United Nations, Peace and Security: From Collective Security to the Responsibility to Protect.* Cambridge, UK: Cambridge University Press.

Thakur, Ramesh, Andrew F. Cooper, and John English, eds. 2005. *International Commissions and the Power of Ideas.* Tokyo: United Nations University Press.

United Nations. 2004. *A More Secure World: Our Shared Responsibility.* Report of the High Level Panel on Threats, Challenges and Change. UN Doc. A/59/565, 2 December.

– 2005a. "2005 World Summit Outcome," General Assembly Resolution. UN Doc. A/RES/60/L.1, 16 September. Available at: <http://www.un.org/summit2005/documents.html>

– 2005b. "Resolution Adopted by the General Assembly," UN Document A/RES/60/246, 23 December.

– 2006. "Security Council Resolution 1674 (2006)," UN Doc. S/RES/1674 (2006), 5430th Meeting, 28 April, para. 4.

UN Millennium Project. 2005. "Investing in Development: A Practical Plan to Achieve the Millennium Development Goals," Report to the UN Secretary-General. New York, NY: United Nations Development Programme (UNDP).

United States. 2006a. "Explanation of Vote on the Human Rights Council Draft Resolution," News Release. Geneva: US Mission to the United Nations in Geneva, 15 March. Available at: <http://geneva.usmission.gov/Press2006/0315Bolton.htm>

– 2006b. "The United States Will Not Seek Election to the UN Human Rights Council," Press Statement. Washington, DC: Department of State, 6 April. Available at: <http://www.state.gov/r/pa/prs/ps/2006/64182.htm>

von Einsiedel, Sebastian Graf, Heiko Nitzschke, and Tarun Chhabra. 2006. "Evolution of the United Nations Security Concept: Role of the High-Level Panel on Threats, Challenges, and Change," in Hans Günter Brauch, et al., eds. *Globalisation and Environmental Challenges: Reconceptualising Security in the 21st Century.* Heidelberg: Springer-Verlag.

Weiss, Thomas G. 2005. "An Unchanged Security Council: The Sky Ain't Falling," *Security Dialogue,* 36, no. 3 (September): 367-9.

Weiss, Thomas G., Tatiana Carayannis, Louis Emmerij and Richard Jolly. 2005. *UN Voices: The Struggle for Development and Social Justice.* Bloomington, IN: Inidiana University Press.

Wheeler, Nicholas J. 2000. *Saving Strangers: Humanitarian Intervention in International Society.* Oxford: Oxford University Press.

Zacher, March W. 2004. "The Conundrums of International Power Sharing: The Politics of Security Council Reform," in Richard M. Price and Mark W. Zacher, eds. *The United Nations and Global Security.* New York, NY: Palgrave Macmillan, 211-26.

Zedillo, Ernesto, ed. 2005. *Reforming the United Nations for Peace and Security.* New Haven: Yale Center for the Study of Globalization.

6 Did You Say Europe?
How Canada Ignores Europe
and Why That Is Wrong

MARIE BERNARD-MEUNIER

Canada's old obsession with the United States and new obsession with emerging markets leave little room for Europe, old or new, as described so famously by Donald Rumsfeld. While both obsessions may be quite legitimate they reflect an international agenda dictated by trade interests alone. The focus of this chapter on Europe is meant to illustrate the advantages of taking a broader view of our interests, and that there is more to Canada than foreign trade. If Canada wants to play a role in the world that matches its rhetoric, it will need to enter into strong partnerships with countries that share its values and its over-arching goals. Reliable, like-minded, multilateralist players with enough resources and political will to make a contribution do not come in such numbers that Canada can afford to ignore Europe. What Europe has to offer is substantial, and it is not limited to the field of foreign policy. Our domestic challenges are not so different from theirs and we can learn from them as they can learn from us.

This chapter is divided into two parts. The first will look at the reasons why Europe has disappeared from our radar screen as well as the reasons why it should come back on it. The second will focus on what is going on in Europe that is of interest to Canada and what is going on here that is of interest to them.

WHY HAS EUROPE DISAPPEARED
FROM THE CANADIAN RADAR SCREEN?

There are many reasons why Europe has slipped from Canada's international focus. The growing integration of Europe and its successive waves of enlargement have had an obvious impact on Canada's relations with all European countries. Over the years, nearly every country in Western Europe, in Central Europe and soon in Eastern Europe has either become a member or an aspiring member of the European Community or of the European Union (EU), as it is now known. The impact was felt with particular acuteness when the United Kingdom (UK) joined because it spelled for Canadian foreign trade the end of the Commonwealth preferential treatment. Even then, trade was paramount. Canada was not only losing markets in Europe as Europeans were trading more and more amongst themselves, but Canada was and still is losing market shares to Europe in third countries because of policies like the Common Agricultural Policy and the heavily subsidized exports it produces.

Various attempts were made to form a structured and fruitful partnership with this increasingly unified Europe. Back in the early 1970s, Trudeau's 'Third Option' was geared not only, but primarily, towards Europe. However, it never produced the expected results. A substantial diversification of our bilateral relations did not occur and after the signature of the Canada/US Free Trade Agreement, the assumption was that it never would. This did not prevent Prime Minister Jean Chrétien from pursuing the objective of a Free Trade Agreement with the European Union, beginning in 1995. Years later, in 2003, Canada and the EU finally agreed to negotiate a Trade and Investment Enhancement Agreement, "a twenty-first century type of agreement" to quote the then European Commissioner for Trade, Pascal Lamy (2004). Progress, however, has been slow and high expectations have been, shall we say, contained. Responsibility for this state of affairs lies on both sides of the Atlantic, but it feeds the cynicism of many in Canada about the possibility of moving forward with Europe.

There is also an important series of negative assumptions about the future of Europe, that has contributed to Europe's disappearance from the Canadian radar screen. Common assumptions include: that there is too much national and regional bureaucracy; that labour markets are too rigid and markets themselves are saturated; that the resistance to change remains strong; and that a rise in protectionism is to be expected. Furthermore, in recent years most European countries have experienced slow economic growth, and demographics suggest a rather bleak future unless Europeans reconcile with themselves that the idea of increased immigration is key to ensuring their prosperity. In addition to this already rather distressing list is the notion that European countries, taken individually, have ceased to matter and that Europe as a new international player does not matter yet.

Despite the fact that there is an impressive amount of academic, scientific and cultural cooperation between Europe and Canada, and the fact that Canadian business has been investing very significantly in Europe over recent years,[1] there is no organized pro-Europe lobby in Canada. The closest thing to such a lobby is the Canada-EU Roundtable born to promote a Canada-EU Free Trade Agreement and which remains to this day the high-level forum where Canadians and Europeans seek to define and pursue a common agenda.

Last but not least, the Europeans are not on the Canadian screen because Canada is not on theirs. Europeans are perceived as too inward-looking or too interested in countries other than Canada. They can probably hold the same grievances against Canada and this vicious circle is not easily broken. Unfortunately, Canada is never more visible in Europe than when it is at odds with the United States, be it on a multilateral or a bilateral issue. Our active support for the International Criminal Court, our position on Iraq, and our ratification of Kyoto all caught the attention of the Europeans. Our softwood lumber dispute did too but other opportunities to grab their attention do exist, and as will be discussed later in this chapter, the appetite in Europe for made-in-Canada solutions is real.

WHY EUROPE SHOULD BE BACK ON THE RADAR SCREEN

While there is probably still a majority of Canadians that can trace their ancestry back to Europe, this can not be the only reason to keep Europe on the radar screen. Within a generation, a majority of Canadians may well come from all the other regions of the world, yet this is not to say that our European roots will become irrelevant. Our institutions, our political culture, and both of our official languages have come from Europe, helping to forge our national character. The big break-away from Europe that the American Revolution represents in the United States never happened here and accordingly our views on domestic as well as on foreign policy issues remain quite close to those of Europeans to this day. Evidence of this is provided by the data produced regularly by the Pew Global Attitudes Project (2004). Also, some like Michael Adams (2003) have further argued that the gap between American and Canadian public opinions continues to grow wider.

In his book, *The European Dream: How Europe's Vision of the Future Is Quietly Eclipsing the American Dream*, Jeremy Rifkin (2004) provides at least an interesting description of the differences between the American and European visions of the world. According to Rifkin, for example, the American culture of individualism versus that of European solidarity is a significant difference. Other differences include, respectively; mass culture versus diversity, accumulation of wealth versus quality of life, unconstrained economic growth versus sustainable development, property rights versus human rights and nature rights, and unilateral exercise of power versus global cooperation. One can denounce the Manicheism or oversimplification of his arguments but called upon to determine where Canadians would stand on most if not all of those issues, one would have to recognize that Canadians are more European than American. In his recent book, *America at the Crossroads*, Francis Fukuyama (2006) adds another element of comparison – the promotion of democracy. He argues that the Europeans, in their democratic development agenda, tend to achieve better results than the Americans. He mentions the impact of the integration of Europe on the democratization of the whole continent, and he argues that it remains the best, if not the only, example of how to overcome deep-rooted regional hostility and ensure the spread of strong democratic values.

For those who are not driven by such lofty ideals, there a number of more modest reasons to put Europe back on the radar screen. Europe is a formidable source of foreign investment and Canada is only attracting a small portion of it. In recent years, Canadian investment in Europe has grown at a faster pace than European investment in Canada,[2] although recent European investments in the Alberta oil sands may soon alter those numbers. Europe is also a major centre for technology research and development, and the opportunities for scientific cooperation are as great as they are under-utilized. On the trade front, the European market of 450 million consumers should be attractive, but Canadian exporters have for a long time preferred to focus on the neighbouring and highly accessible American market, and more recently on the emerging markets due to their size and impressive rates of growth. If Europe is not attractive as a market it should at least be kept on the radar screen as a competitor. Germany alone, despite the strong euro, huge domestic challenges, and high production costs, is still the number one exporter in the world. They ought to be doing something right, and perhaps accordingly some of the more negative assumptions about Europe should be re-visited.

In the field of foreign policy, the cooperation between Europe and Canada has always been quite close, partly because of converging views, and partly because of NATO which remains Canada's strongest anchor point in Europe to this day. Canada has often sought and ob tained the support of the Europeans in the pursuit of its foreign policy agenda. On issues like land-mines, the International Criminal Court, or the Responsibility to Protect doctrine, they have proven to be strong and reliable partners. A shared commitment to an effective multilateral system has been at the heart of that fruitful cooperation.

The current international security agenda also brings Europeans and Canadians together. Most Canadian foreign military missions have been carried out in close cooperation not only with the United States and Australia, but also with European countries. It was the case in the Balkans and it is now the case in Afghanistan – it is little known in Canada that the Germans have many more on the ground there. Many other European countries are also doing their fair share. In the fight against terrorism, it is worth underlining that the cooperation among allies across the Atlantic (such as the sharing of intelligence, and the planning and execution of joint counter-terrorism operations) never stopped, even when the US and key European players like France and Germany were very much at odds over the war in Iraq. For Canadians, it is also worth reflecting on how the Europeans and the Americans have managed those tensions and sought to quickly restore a climate of mutual understanding and confidence. The visit of President Bush to Europe in February 2005 and the many visits of Condoleezza Rice since then, show how keen the American administration now is to acknowledge the importance of its European allies (Bernard-Meunier, 2005b: 21). Angela Merkel's first visit to Washington as German Chancellor also provides a good example of how to overcome a crisis in a bilateral relationship. Her strong commitment to a renewed partnership with the US allowed her to be more critical of the US on Guantanamo than her predecessor ever was.

If the case for close cooperation with the Europeans in the area of foreign policy should be made, the case for closer cooperation in other areas is less obvious but can and must be made. Canadians can learn from the achievements and failings of Europe, as many of the things that are occurring in Europe are of direct relevance to Canadian experiences. Conversely, much of what is happening here is of real interest to Europeans. The next section of this chapter will examine both. Looking first at lessons from Europe, the section will address two key questions: first, what does the integration of Europe tell us about our own continental integration process?; and second, is there a distinct and viable European economic model worth considering? The section will then turn to examining what Canada has to offer to solution-hungry Europeans, through the use of three examples: first, our victory against budgetary deficits; second, our immigration policy; and third, our federal system.

THE LESSONS OF THE INTEGRATION OF EUROPE

The integration of Europe has been a complex process, characterized by the simultaneous combination of political and economic integration, of supra-national and inter-governmental mechanisms, and of liberal and interventionist economic policies. In the minds of the founders, the *economic* integration of Europe was a means to an end – the end being political integration. The former was intended to bring about the latter. This was clear from the beginning, with the establishment of the European Coal and Steel Community. When, a few years later, the Treaty of Rome was negotiated, the focus was obviously on removing obstacles to trade, but the Treaty went well beyond that. The stated objective was not to create a free-trade zone but to lead member countries towards the adoption of common policies, starting with the Common Agricultural Policy. Over the years, many other common policies were created to support regional development, to build up a monetary system or to put in place a single market that required common competition and industrial policies. The political calling of the construction of Europe was encapsulated in the decision taken at Maastricht in 1992 to change the name from the European Community to the European Union. The draft constitution that was submitted to the member-states in 2004 was later ratified by many, but rejected by France and The Netherlands, continued the move towards a political union, with new rules for the designation of the President and the appointment of a European Minister of Foreign Affairs. The ratification process of the draft Constitution has now been suspended but the expectation is that the Constitution itself will be resurrected in some form as early as next year, after the French elections and during the German presidency of the EU.

The institutional mechanisms of the EU are of two kinds, the supranational and the inter-governmental ones. The Commission is the supranational body *par excellence*. It exercises the powers surrendered to it by the member-states and it is meant to be the incarnation of the European ideal. The Council of Ministers, on the other hand, reflects the lasting inter-governmental nature of Europe. In some areas member-states have an actual right of veto, but in a growing number of areas the rule of qualified majority applies. In other words, member-states can be overruled by their fellow member-states. The complexity of this institutional framework requires equally complex coordination mechanisms – horizontal ones to coordinate among member-states and the vertical ones to coordinate between the Commission representatives and national and local representatives. The coordination itself can be indicative or coercive. For instance, the Lisbon Strategy aimed at increasing Europe's competitiveness is indicative, the Stability Pact that limits national budget deficits to 3 percent of the GDP is coercive (i.e. non-compliance can generate sanctions).

The mix of liberal and interventionist economic policies has evolved over time. The policy mix was, from the outset, more liberal than interventionist and that tendency was accentuated with the entry of the UK in 1972. It is of course difficult to carry very far the notion of state intervention when there is no European state, but member-states that have left-of- the-centre governments have in the past and will in the future influence, in some measure, the policies of Europe. When the Maastricht Treaty was negotiated and signed in 1992, the prevailing mood was clearly pro-liberal. Since then, the mood has changed and those who oppose the draft Constitution (which brings under one single economic chapter the content of treaties previously negotiated) often do so on the grounds that it is too liberal.

How successful has Europe been? In terms of reconciling former enemies, and contributing to the democratization of Central and Eastern Europe, the Union has been most successful on the political front. On the economic front, the record is more mixed. The homogenization of the numerous national economies has been remarkable. Differences among early member countries were not very significant, but when countries like Greece, Spain, and Portugal and later Ireland joined, the challenge was quite formidable, and Europe lived up to it. Time will tell how much more difficult the integration of Central European countries will be. The smooth introduction of the euro and long years of price stability are also to be put to Europe's credit.

Up until the mid-1980s, Europe was closing the gap with the United States. Since then the gap has begun to grow again. While there are significant differences between countries, Europe as a whole has experienced slow growth and high unemployment in recent years, for the euro, the single market, and the last wave of enlargement have not produced the boom originally expected by economists.

Where did Europe go wrong? Too much welfare? Too much rigidity in the labour market? Intractible resistance to change? An excessive focus on the need to limit inflation and budgetary deficits? Insufficient investments in R&D and information technologies? All of the above? Probably. More interesting are the questions of what will happen next. Given the unique nature of this European construction and the kinds of combinations that have been described above, the questions that will need to be answered are the following; will the current difficulties accelerate or slow down the construction of a political union in Europe?; will the present trend towards a more inter-governmental than supra-national Europe be confirmed or will it be questioned?; and finally, will the predominantly liberal game plan be altered? One can only speculate on the answers that will be given, but it seems quite obvious that diverging views could prove so difficult to reconcile that in the end there will be either a regression into some kind of a free trade zone or a renewed impetus for European political integration. Unless there is an unstoppable evolution towards a multi-speed Europe with a hard-core of countries committed to the process of ever greater integration, surrounded by several concentric circles on which other countries will position themselves in relation to this core, then it remains to be seen how integration will proceed. The core countries committed to deeper political integration would probably want both the UK and Turkey on the most outer circle!

Irrespective of whether we think that the European model is the one to follow or the one to avoid, we can draw from their experience lessons that are quite relevant to our own integration agenda in North America (Bernard-Meunier, 2005c). First and foremost, does Canada have a continental integration agenda? Many of Europe's problems today stem from the fact that the integration agenda that was there at the beginning is not always subscribed to by new members, let alone founding ones. Clarity of purpose is key. What is Canada's agenda? Who is defining it and who will defend it? What is the integration agenda of our partners? Do the Americans or the Mexicans have an integration agenda? The assumption seems to be that our free trade agreement will naturally evolve into some kind of economic integration. The European example does not provide any evidence of that. Their economic integration was wanted and pursued from the outset.

If after 50 years of experience with a form of economic integration, which goes way beyond anything envisaged in North America, the Europeans are divided between those who claim that a free trade zone may be all they really want and those who think that European governance must be significantly strengthened, the 'three amigos' should perhaps determine what their long-term goal is before moving too far into an economic integration process.

The question of whether future institutional mechanisms should be supra-national, inter-governmental, or both, is also vital. Again the European experience shows that the interests of the smaller member-states are best protected by supra-national mechanisms. It may not be a sheer coincidence that what Canadians like most about NAFTA is the dispute settlement mechanism! How much supra-nationalism however are our partners in North America prepared to envisage?

Finally, can Canada face the challenges of globalization alone or is it vital to the defence of its interests that it close ranks with its neighbours and partners. There again the European experience clearly suggests that there is no other way to go. It may be more obvious to some members of the EU than to others, but there is little doubt that challenges from the outside are what will keep Europe united.

THE DEBATE AROUND A DIFFERENT ECONOMIC MODEL

One can hardly talk about a single European model. There are major differences among countries – very different prescriptions, with very different results. Some models are more inspiring than others. France, for instance, currently gives the image of a society that is almost dysfunctional. The UK has fared better than many continental Europeans but it cannot stand as a regional model, as the British seldom define themselves as Europeans, and in turn, the Europeans do not perceive the UK as truly being a part of the continent. The recent decision from British Aerospace (BAE) to withdraw from the Airbus consortium will do nothing to alter that widely spread perception. Moreover, despite Tony Blair's professed commitment to the 'Third Way', the UK is mostly seen in Europe as the epitome of Anglo-Saxon neo-liberalism. One can only regret it and note the fact that Europe and the UK go on having a distorted view of each other.

Is Rhineland capitalism still alive? If defined as the combination of broad access to public services, the search for consensus among all stakeholders and the role of the state in managing disparities, then it is still very much alive. One could even argue that the coming to power of a 'Grand Coalition' last fall expresses the wish of the Germans to hold on to their economic model. Angela Merkel's temptation to move too close to the Liberal Party was held against by her own electorate. She ended up with no alternative but a coalition with the SPD (Bernard-Meunier, 2005a: 9). The German model still enjoys broad support despite the fact that, since the mid-1990s, it has failed to deliver on two major points; growth and employment. How much of Germany's economic difficulties are linked to the high costs of reunification? A fair share. Which other country in the western world could have shouldered transfer payments of £75 billion a year for the last fifteen years and signed on for the next ten? In recent months, economic indicators in Germany have been improving steadily. If the Germans were not ready to give up on their model before, they are not likely to do it now.

The Scandinavians (Sweden, Denmark and Finland) have for years secured the strongest economic performance in Europe. It is difficult to argue that welfare costs and high taxes lie at the heart of Europe's problems, when the countries in the lead are those who have first-rate welfare systems and the highest taxes. How is this possible? The recipe is a mix of pro-active industrial policies with government support, strategies to contain welfare costs, greater flexibility for companies to hire and fire, greater job security for the unemployed who receive personalized help to find new jobs and upgrade their qualifications, and long-term investment in education, R&D, and IT.

Despite all these national variations, a recent study of the UN Economic Commission for Europe (UNECE) argues that there is such a thing as a European economic model that can serve as an alternative to the American model (UNECE, 2005: ch. 7). The study begins by challenging the notion that the gap between Europe and the United States is growing. The basic argument maintains that while there is a large difference in GDP per capita, the difference between Europe and the United States is quite small in GDP per hour worked. Moreover when social and environmental indicators are added to the economic ones, the difference between Europe and the United States, the study claims, tends to be considerably less significant. The UNECE does recognize that some European countries out-perform the others and their so-called European model is very much inspired by the policy choices and administrative practices of Scandinavian countries. What they present as the new European model is a one that combines welfare and sustainability on the one hand, and economic incentives on the other.

Let us assume for a moment that there are indeed two models, a European and an American one. Is one of them bound to prevail? What if the two were to converge? Some analysts have already declared victory. Henry Hansmann and Reinier Kraakman (2001) argue that the American system has established itself as the normative role-model. That conclusion is based on the premise that all countries are competing for foreign investment and whatever policies work best to attract such investment will be copied by all. Paul Wolfowitz seems to be of the same persuasion. He decided recently to disband the research unit of the European office of the World Bank. Joseph Stiglitz, when he was at the World Bank, used to think that this unit provided a different and useful perspective on development strategies (Caramel, 2006).

Andreas Busch (2005) takes a different view. He argues that the jury is still out on the issue, as countries like Germany wish to retain their specificity and tend to do so. In his judgment, the resistance to the American economic model comes from its excessive focus on shareholder value and from a system of corporate governance that has failed to demonstrate its superiority in terms of economic performance.

What if models tended to converge? Can one find evidence of mutual influence? Aren't American companies worried about rising health insurance costs and slowly recognizing the advantages of a universal public health system? Isn't General Motors looking at new ways to fight its way out of the current crisis, including a different way of sharing the costs and the benefits among all stakeholders? (*La Presse*, 2006a). Aren't Europeans acknowledging the need for greater flexibility in labour markets and better cost-balancing of welfare programs?

There is a very lively debate in Europe about the mortal sins of hyper-capitalism: indecent profits, shareholders tyranny, overpaid bosses, highly profitable financial operations backed by no visible increases in economic activity, corruption, and much more. As one should expect, the debate is particularly passionate in France, fuelled by books with engaging titles such as *L'horreur économique, Le capitalisme est-il moral?, Le Nouvel Age du capitalisme, Au Coeur de la Folie financière,* and *Le capitalisme est en train de s'auto-détruire.* Those who fought, not long ago, to give socialism a human face are now working on giving capitalism a human face. This can only be described as a positive development, especially in light of the fact that, according to Alain Minc (2004), the Chinese version of capitalism, a form of which the world has only seen the first humble manifestations, will be nothing less than apocalyptic!

For Canadians, the mere existence of such debate in Europe should be of interest because it provides a little conceptual breathing space. If the situation in Europe confirms that there is more than one way to reconcile the seemingly conflicting objectives of economic growth, social justice, and environmental protection, then Canadians should feel entitled to fight for their own vision of what the right mix of policies should be. The notion that you can only compete with American companies if your companies operate under the same constraints (or lack thereof) may simply be untrue. The ability of European companies to succeed in the US and to win market shares in third countries makes this abundantly clear.

The American economic model is of course less foreign to Canadians than to most Europeans, and one can observe that Canada has been moving in the direction of more liberalism and less welfare state for some time. That being said, it may prove unnecessary and unhelpful to declare the victory of the American model before it actually happens. Moreover, should the movement away from the welfare state be accentuated, as one might expect with the election of a Conservative government, one may see a reaction in the opposite direction on the part of significant segments of the Canadian population. Canada may have its own debate on the virtues of different economic models. An examination of what has worked and what has not worked in Europe could substantially enrich that debate. Not surprisingly, in Quebec, where access to European sources is more widely spread than in the rest of Canada, the debate is already going on.

Experience shows that the best economic model is always the one that works. When Germany was an economic powerhouse, the German model was in fashion. Sustained growth and job creation in the US has made the American model the quotable one for decades. We may however be coming to the end of a cycle. To meet the new challenges, creative thinking will be required and those countries with the most open mind and the greatest ability to pick and choose the best part of every recipe may well be the winners.

If Europe can be a source of inspiration for Canada, the reverse is equally true. In several areas, Canada is perceived by Europeans as having found pragmatic and effective solutions to the problems with which they are wrestling. Three examples come readily to mind: first, the management of public finances and in particular the control of budgetary deficits; second, immigration; and third, federalism.

There are many reasons why the Canadian story on public finances has made such an impact in Europe. First, they know where Canada came from. Because Canada is a member of the G8 and of the OECD, the Canadian numbers (good or bad) make their way into the European press. With this in mind, it did not go unnoticed that Canada quickly went from being one of the worst economic performers in these groups to being the best. Many Europeans were struck by the fact that in 1993, the Canadian numbers, particularly on the debt to GDP ratio, were actually much worse than what their own numbers are today. This is most encouraging for them when dealing with their own economic issues. Second, for governments that cannot adhere to the discipline of the Stability Pact, which limits budgetary deficits to 3 percent of GDP, the example of a government that generates huge budgetary surpluses year after year is very impressive. Third, that Canada was able to introduce the GST, reduce the size of the public service, and freeze the salaries of its employees without coast-to-coast street demonstrations is a source of great envy!

European countries generally do not have the kind of federal structures that Canada has and therefore do not have the option of cutting economic transfers to the provinces. Furthermore, none of them can even dream of the kind of majority in Parliament that the first Chrétien government enjoyed and all of them are trying to fix their public finances in a period of very limited growth. The Canadian 'miracle' therefore, will not be easily reproduced, yet the interest in the Canadian example is very real. Laudatory articles are written in the press, research institutes dissect the Canadian model, study tours are organized, and even films are being made![3] The attraction of the Canadian story resides of course in its success, but not exclusively. To Europeans, one of the most important features of the story is the fact that it happened in a country that shares their basic social values. In order to balance its budget, Canada did not do away with its welfare programs. In their eyes, the right compromise was reached between the need to cut costs, the need to maintain an adequate level of protection for the weakest, and the need to keep solidarity as a key organizing principle in society.

It is only in recent times that European countries have come to acknowledge that there was little point in maintaining the fiction of 'guest workers' going back home when no longer needed. Not only are migrants there to stay, more immigration will be required to solve the problems of a quickly aging population. European countries are therefore busily drafting new immigration laws and, for inspiration, they turn to so-called 'immigration countries' and in particular to Canada.

The Independent Commission on Migration to Germany studied the Canadian model in depth and recommended to Parliament many features of the Canadian legislation. The French maintain that the Canadian success with immigration is linked to the fact that Canada chooses its immigrants. Whether France will follow that example is still the subject of considerable public debate. While some argue that a selection process is the only way to get the kind of immigrants the country needs, others argue that such a selection is contrary to the country's tradition of liberty, equality, and fraternity, or question a strategy aimed at depriving developing countries of their best and brightest.

In the debate over immigration in France or elsewhere, the good reputation of Canada is often used to allay the fear that selecting immigrants could be morally objectionable. In Germany, when a point system to evaluate potential immigrants was considered, but finally rejected on the grounds that people should not be assigned a numerical value, many voices rose to say that if a country like Canada did it, surely it could be done.

The European interest and positive impression of Canada's immigration policy does not extend to Canada's multiculturalism policy. Europeans tend to believe that Canada's good track record on the integration of immigrants has a lot more to do with the selection of immigrants than it has to do with multiculturalism. To Canadians, the misgivings (not to say the outright opposition) of Europeans towards multiculturalism often comes as a surprise. Yet the reality is that Europeans tend to see multiculturalism as a threat to the universality of human rights and they reject what they see as an attempt to define individuals through their links to a particular community. They also see it as contrary to the principle of national cohesion through shared values. The fact that these generous principles do not translate into much real integration for immigrants in Europe does not seem to alter the discourse. The Supreme Court of Canada decisions based on the Charter of Rights and Freedoms do however attract considerable interest in Europe. They become part of their public debates, and even more so it seems, than in Canada.

The issue of federalism arises in Europe in very many different contexts. It is seen as a solution to the problems of fragile multi-ethnic states – the Balkans for instance. It is also seen by some as a possible institutional response to growing regionalisms in several European countries. For those European countries that already have federal structures, the challenge for central governments is to deal with the combined pressure of a European entity (to which they have already conceded significant areas of jurisdiction) and that of sub-national entities (that want more power and are getting it through the principle of subsidiarity[4]). Finally, the long-term project of a European federation is not doing very well at this particular juncture but it is still alive, even if only as an option for a selected few.

In all these contexts, Canada is an interesting example for Europeans because the Canadian federation, despite the fact that it faces its own set of challenges, is perceived as a well functioning one. It is seen as capable of adapting to changing circumstances, as the conclusion of the debate over the federal-provincial fiscal imbalance or the international role of provinces will hopefully demonstrate. More fundamentally however, what lies at the heart of Europe's interests in the Canadian federation, is the Quebec factor. Those who believe that the solution to the problems of war-torn countries resides in federal multi-ethnic states will want to go on quoting the Canadian example. Those who already have to deal with sub-national entities will want to see how far centrifugal forces can be or should be tolerated. Those who fight for the recognition of regional identities will argue that they are only asking for a fraction of what Quebec already has. Finally, those in favour of a European federation will argue that Quebec is proof that you don't lose your identity by joining a federation. Domestic challenges sometimes have very far-reaching international implications, and domestic actors would do well to be aware of this influence.

CONCLUSION

Canada has often argued that it can bring to Europeans a North American perspective and a knowledge and understanding of the United States that is unparalleled in Europe. That is absolutely true, but the purpose of this chapter has been quite different. My contention is that Canada has more in common with Europe than it readily acknowledges and that it has much to gain (in domestic as well as in foreign policy terms) from increasing its interaction with European countries. In this world, in these times, and given the nature of the challenges that are confronting us all, Canada should see the importance of having such partners. As already stated, reliable, like-minded partners with the will and the means to make a difference do not come in such numbers that Canada can afford to ignore Europe. They can help us as we can help them deal with the complexity of many issues and find workable solutions. There is more than one way to analyze and solve a problem, there is more than one way to define growth, and there is more than one way to define progress. The weight of its big neighbour and the quick rise of emerging markets should not prevent Canada from realizing that keeping Europe off its screen is simply wrong. This is simply a plea for a broadening of the horizon.

NOTES

1 McCain, Alcan, and Bombardier all have more employees in Europe than in North America. La Caisse des Dépôt et Placement du Québec just invested US$1 billion in Germany (*La Presse*, 2006b). Between 1989 and 2004, Canadian FDI in the US has gone down by 20 percentage points and is now at 41 percent. For the same period, Canadian FDI in Europe has gone up almost 10 percentage points and is now at 27 percent (Statistics Canada: 2005: 3).

2 65 percent of FDI in Canada is coming from the US, 25 percent from Europe and 10 percent from the rest of the world (Statistics Canada, 2005: 3). European investment in the US is at the level of US investment in Canada, representing more than 62 percent of FDI inflows (United States, 2003).

3 A ninety minute documentary entitled, "Pourquoi le Canada fait-il rêver?," which examines the exceptionalism of contemporary Canada, was produced in 2005 by France2, the French Public Television Network.

4 The principle of subsidiarity means that what the lesser entity can do adequately should not be done by the greater entity unless it can do it better. Taken over into EU policies, it is used as an instrument for determining when the Union is to act in areas not coming under its exclusive competence. This principle was first introduced in the Treaty of Maastricht, and is generally applicable to all areas of non-exclusive competence. Further explanation is available at: <http://www.euractiv.com/en/constitution/future-eu-subsidiarity/article-117271>

REFERENCES

Adams, Michael. 2003. *Fire and Ice: The United States, Canada, and the Myth of Converging Values*. Toronto: Penguin Canada.

Bernard-Meunier, Marie. 2005a. "Germany: From an electoral Stalemate to a 'Grand Coalition' of the CDU and SDP," *Policy Options* 26, no. 9 (November): 7–10.

– 2005b. "La visite du Président Bush en Europe," *Policy Options* 26, no. 4 (May): 17–21.

– 2005c. "The 'Inevitability' of North American Integration?" *International Journal* 60, no. 3 (Summer): 703–11.

Busch, Andreas. 2005. "Globalisation and National Varieties of Capitalism: the Contested Viability of the German Model," *German Politics* 14, no, 2 (June): 125–39.

Caramel, Laurence. 2006. "Le grand ménage," *Le Monde*, 14 March.

Fukuyama, Francis. 2006. *America at the Crossroads: Democracy, Power, and the Neo-Conservative Legacy*. New Haven, CT: Yale University Press.

Hansmann, Henry, and Reinier Kraakman. 2001. "The End of History for Corporate Law," *Georgetown Law Journal* 89, no. 2 (January): 439–67.

Lamy, Pascal. 2004. Speech by the EU Trade Commission to the Canada-Europe Roundtable for Business (CERT), The National Club, Toronto, 18 March.

La Presse. 2006a. "GM répartit les sacrifices," 8 February.

La Presse. 2006b. "La Caisse mise sur l'Allemagne," 25 April.

Minc, Alain. 2004. *Ce Monde qui vient*. Paris: Grasset & Fasquelle.

Pew Global Attitudes Project. 2004. *Americans and Canadians: The North American Not-so-odd Couple*. Washington, DC: The Pew Research Center, 14 January.

Rifkin, Jeremy. 2004. *The European Dream: How Europe's Vision of the Future Is Quietly Eclipsing the American Dream*. New York: Penguin.

Statistics Canada. 2005. "Foreign Direct Investment 2004," *The Daily* (17 May): 2–4.

UN Economic Commission for Europe (UNECE). 2005. "Towards a New European Model of a Reformed Welfare State: An Alternative to the US Model," in UNECE, *Annual Report 2004–5*, Geneva, 105–14. Available at: <http://www.unece.org/ead/pub/051/051c7.pdf>

United States. 2003. *Foreign Direct Investment in the US: Balance of Payments and Direct Investment-cost Basis, 2003*. Washington, DC: Bureau of Economic Activity (BEA). Available at: <http://www.bea.gov/bea/di/fdipos/fdipos-03.htm>

CHRISTOPHER SANDS

The Conservative government of Prime Minister Stephen Harper is committed to the improvement of Canada's relations with the United States, just as the Liberal government of Prime Minister Paul Martin claimed to have been prior to the January 2006 general election. The efforts of the Martin government were modestly successful, in that Martin was able to exert greater discipline against outbursts of anti-American comments by members of his party caucus and staff than had been his immediate predecessor, Prime Minister Jean Chrétien. Martin also improved the sense of professionalism in the Canadian management of the relationship. Yet, notwithstanding these efforts, the relationship between the governments in Ottawa and Washington remained strained throughout Martin's tenure.

Will Prime Minister Harper have greater success? Before answering this question, it is important to consider how the challenge of managing this bilateral relationship has changed in the post-Cold War period, and in particular following the 11 September 2001 al Qaeda organized terrorist attacks on the United States. This chapter will argue that the scope of policy flexibility in bilateral relations for Canadian governments is more narrowly constrained and that as a result, Canadian governments are in the frustrating position of having to do a number of major new things that the US government considers to be *de minimus* efforts that merit no special credit. But if Canada fails to meet American expectations, the US government is prone to react harshly. Furthermore, as continental economic integration continues to deepen, US pressure on Canadian policy and regulation affecting US interests is growing, even in areas heretofore considered to be exclusively in domestic domains. This has strong political implications. If Canada concedes too much in these areas, the cost will be high in lost public support.

The limited room to manoeuvre on domestic and bilateral policy has increased the importance of third-country issues for Canada's relationship with the United States. Third-country issues are international, but not primarily bilateral. As a realm of interaction among Canadian and US interests, they are generally overshadowed by the interaction of the two countries' interests at the domestic and bilateral realms. Yet for a number of reasons, third-country issues are becoming more critical and provide the best chances for Canada to demonstrate both its policy independence from Washington and its value as a strategic US ally. Skilful management of third-country issues could determine whether or not Harper's management of the Canada-US relationship is seen as an improvement on the record of his predecessor.

The perception of the health of the relationship, on the part of US and Canadian observers, influences the substance of relations directly. For example, the Canadian public may resist perceived concessions to Washington, and the US public may demand action based on the perception that Canada is not taking the danger of terrorism seriously enough – and politicians in both countries will interpret this as a constraint. Officials are also attuned to the perceptions. When provocations from the Chrétien government led President George W. Bush to cancel a planned state visit to Canada in May 2003, subsequently many mid-level political appointees in the Bush administration cooled to initiatives proposed by their Canadian counterparts, slowing progress and momentum in response.

The role of the media in shaping perceptions on both sides of the border has changed in recent years, due to the fluid information flows across the Canada-US border. For years, these flows seemed to run northward, as Canadians consumed US media, from newspapers to radio broadcasts and later to television and satellite programming. More recently, the advent of web-logs and the internet have given US and Canadian audiences immediate access to one another's media. Yet, while Canadians have enough grounding in American politics to discount television commentator Patrick Buchanan's reference to Canada as "Soviet Canuckistan" as bluster, Americans have less context with which to interpret the significance of anti-American comments from Ontario Member of Parliament Carolyn Parrish (Sands, 2002). Media reporting everywhere tends to cover conflict rather than cooperation, due to the drama inherent in clashes between personalities and policies. This can lead to distorted perceptions, such as when President Bush's failure to make a public statement in April 2002 following the deaths of Canadian soldiers in Afghanistan from US friendly fire was portrayed by the media as evidence of Bush's indifference to the Canadian deaths, or his stubborn unwillingness to sympathize with Prime Minister Jean Chrétien's government. Such an interpretation, for which there was no real proof and seems absurd on its face, nonetheless contributed to the perception of poor relations and the virtual impossibility of improving them on the basis of US leadership.

An improvement in the bilateral relationship may now be particularly important for Canada, as the United States is in the process of consolidating its position for a long struggle against global terrorism. If a similar consolidation like that which followed the end of the Second World War and launched the Cold War era is a reliable guide, the next president of the United States (who will take office in January 2009) is likely to formalize new US strategic alliance structures. There can be no assumption that Canada will be a core member of these alliances without a sufficient improvement in the Canada-US relationship in the intervening years to render Canada an attractive prospective global partner for the United States once again.

CONSTRAINTS IN BILATERAL RELATIONS

Notwithstanding recent concerns over the cordiality of relations between Canadian prime ministers and US presidents, the day-to-day relationship between the two countries is in excellent shape. The main reason for this is the progressive removal of economic issues on the bilateral agenda from the vagaries of politics through memoranda of understanding, agreements, and treaties. Thanks to the Canada-United States Free Trade Agreement (CUSFTA), the North American Free Trade Agreement (NAFTA), and the creation of the World Trade Organization, trade and investment relations between the two countries are largely harmonious. Businesses and investors can, for the most part, proceed with confidence in the rules of the depoliticized economy.

This generally positive atmosphere does not mean that the two countries have trade no disputes, as the long-running softwood lumber issue is just the most highly visible case in point. For the most part though, recent disputes have been confined to primary products, for which commodity price swings lead to demands for protection from producers on a periodic basis. In the conduct of negotiations over softwood and other outstanding trade problems, it should be noted that the governments have formally constrained themselves to handle dispute settlement in an orderly fashion with recourse mechanisms in various trade agreements have been made available to private interests that seek government help in resolving their trade problems. Media reporting in Canada tends to suppose political motives behind the actions of one or both national governments in disputes such as the softwood case. In the United States, the approach to dispute settlement is highly litigious, and so the room for political interference is limited. Conversely, those in Canada who have suggested that trade dispute mechanisms in CUSFTA and NAFTA are legally binding overstate the implications of an administrative review process that most often results in a decision by the unsuccessful litigant government to remand and correct errors.

Canadians have tended to freight such disputes with symbolic meaning, looking for signs in the US government's response to a dispute that suggest how Canada is viewed in Washington. Anything short of US capitulation to the Canadian position will predictably lead to cries of outrage and accusations of American bullying. Canadian impatience is expressed as bitter frustration at American indifference to Canada's claims. Governments in Canada play on these emotional responses to portray Ottawa as either bravely standing up to Washington's vested interests and power brokers, or forthrightly lecturing forgetful and even wilfully purblind American counterparts about the importance of Canada as a trading partner.

This type of response makes for good politics in Canada, even if it does not advance the Canadian cause. Yet in Washington, it appears part of a familiar script. Not as nationalism, but as an expression of the long-standing American pastime of 'running against Washington.' State politicians, city councillors and mayors, candidates in congressional races, and even presidential candidates throughout American history have made eloquent use of outrage against Washington to win elections and bring about change. If Canadian politicians have begun to engage in this practice, it only makes their concerns seem more domestically opportunistic to American leadership, which is in turn generally unmoved by such rhetoric.

Yet this ingrained Canadian habit may not be entirely harmless to Canadian interests in the United States. While California Governor Arnold Schwarzenegger may run against Washington's failure to secure the Mexican border, and District of Columbia Mayor Anthony Williams may protest cuts to Homeland Security funds for Washington, the appeals are made to US voters who will ultimately decide the fate not only of these politicians, but of federal politicians as well. When then Canadian Prime Minster Martin ran against Washington in his 2004 and (even more blatantly) in his 2006 election campaigns, federal officials in the United States were once again reminded that Canadians do not vote in, nor have any influence on US elections. Any credible US policymaker will note that Canada relies on the United States for 86 percent of its exports and 87 percent of its imports, and the majority of its foreign direct investment. In the realist political calculations of Washington power brokers, this makes Canada's politicians running against Washington more irritating than California's, since it is both less legitimate and ultimately less consequential.

Therein lies the peril for Canadian politicians in dealing with issues on the bilateral agenda: posturing against Washington, though popular with Canadian voters, further weakens Canada's negotiating position in Washington. The extent to which the Canadian economy is integrated with the American, reflected in bilateral trade and investment, broadens the scope for actions the United States may take to damage Canadian interests in retaliation of cheap election rhetoric. The generally held perception of Canadian weakness and vulnerability may tempt Americans to take such actions without fear of Canadian responses if provoked enough. Since the bilateral relationship is currently in excellent shape, despite the existence of disagreements in specific sectors, accentuating these disagreements may come at a significant opportunity cost for Canadian politicians.

DOMESTIC CONSTRAINTS AND RELATIONS WITH THE UNITED STATES

In the years since the terrorist attacks of 11 September 2001, the political expense of showing Canadian weakness to Washington has increased, as policymakers in the United States have become concerned with the quality of Canadian domestic policy in a range of new areas. This changing attitude honed in on Canada's immigration policies. Of particular concern was its failure to amend its approach to account for the impact of the pivotal Supreme Court of Canada ruling of 1986 in the Iqbal Singh case – a judgment that limited Canada's ability to restrict aliens after they had entered Canada. In the wake of 9/11, rumours of terrorists infiltrating the US from the porous Canadian border swirled uncontrollably. These allegations were soon followed by the expression of a host of US concerns over Canadian security policies by the administration and media pundits alike. With huge media coverage on both sides of the border, these concerns reached such a peak that they prompted the federal and provincial governments of Canada to move quickly to improve the capacities of domestic security legislation, law enforcement, and domestic intelligence in tandem with upgrades in these areas being undertaken in the United States.

These evolving dynamics on domestic security legislation and enforcement in Canada and the United States are instructive, since they reveal the different way in which US pressure on bilateral and domestic policy in Canada generates an altered response. At no time did

Canadian officials risk exploiting nationalist sentiment to resist US calls to upgrade domestic security arrangements. One reason for this may have been that the United States was making similar changes. Another was a pragmatic consensus that took shape among Canadians that the overall relations with the United States would not withstand a Canadian refusal to make security changes – with an appreciation that 9/11 changed the mood of the American public about domestic security.

Yet when it came to Canadian domestic security, US officials applied enormous and focused pressure on Canada to follow the US lead. Canadian officials may have felt they had less room to manoeuvre in this area, but they may also have feared that US demands for Canadians domestic governance changes would expand beyond law enforcement related to terrorism if Canada did not move swiftly to restore American confidence in its security measures. Additionally in 2003, Members of Congress and media personalities began discussing Canada's proposal to decriminalize marijuana possession in limited quantities and the potential impact of this on the United States. Many advanced the notion that such possession could be 're-criminalized' by US border officials if it appeared on the criminal record of a Canadian requesting entry into the United States, even as a misdemeanour. And during the 2004 election campaign, politicians from Democratic presidential candidates Howard Dean and John Kerry to a number of state gubernatorial candidates considered how they could expand access for American citizens to the low priced Canadian prescription drugs. In this sense, the existing soft border and thereby the easy access to the Canadian market (especially for comparatively cheaper products) was seen as an asset.

The best defence Canadians policymakers can take is on the enhancement of Canadian sovereignty, and it is here that the increased opportunity cost of 'running against Washington' as a bilateral strategy is paid in full. Unlike California, Canada cannot resort to the protections of the US Constitution for individual state sovereignty, or to the opinion of a shared electorate, to resist pressure from Washington. In most cases, pressure on Canada to harmonize its policies with those of the United States, or extend benefits to American citizens, will earn voter support for Washington politicians. By advertising Canada's vulnerability to US actions and its weakness when compared to US states, Canadian politicians invite more intrusion into Canadian domestic affairs by US policymakers, not less. Thus, in domestic policy, Canada has to avoid the temptation towards exposure and linkage, limiting its room to manoeuvre in domestic policy conflicts with the United States even more severely than in bilateral relations.

THE VALUE OF THIRD-COUNTRY ISSUES

In light of the limited political manoeuvrability in relations with the United States over bilateral issues and Canadian domestic policies, it is easier to see why Canadian governments have emphasized changes in the tone of Canadian conduct of the relationship over changes in its substance. The Martin government's limited success at improving Canada-US relations could possibly be attributed in part to this difficulty, which may in turn prove a limiting factor on the Harper government's efforts as well, for it (like its immediate predecessor) holds only a parliamentary minority. In this case, its agenda must bend to the will of the parties in opposition, further constraining its policy manoeuvrability.

In light of this context, third-country issues will become increasingly pivotal to Canada's management of its relationship with the United States in the coming years. Third-country issues are valuable because by addressing them in a manner congruent with US interests, Canada reinforces its ability as a sovereign state to engage in international relations in a manner beyond that of California or any other US sub-federal entity. If Canadian policymakers must act defensively to protect domestic policy independence, and must strike a balance in bilateral relations between assertiveness and jingoism, third-country issues provide Canada the opportunity not to be limited by bilateral concerns, rather to be limited only by its capabilities. Through its successes internationally, Canada can go on the offensive and earn political capital in Washington that can be used to defend Canadian interests in the domestic and bilateral realms.

A key factor in the ability to project Canadian action on third-country issues to accrue benefits is the voluntary nature of Canadian engagement. Canadian action to improve domestic law enforcement countering terrorist threats does not garner much credit in Washington – any respectable country should do so in its own interest, so why should Washington applaud Canada for this *de minimus* action? Civility in bilateral relations is likewise a policy in the rational self-interest of a small country dealing with a larger neighbour, as well as the most basic way to earn respect. A change in tone in Canada's approach to the relationship will be appreciated in Washington, but is not likely to translate further into political capital.

Yet Canada is not bound to contribute to the liberation or stabilization of Afghanistan, nor to a contribution to strengthening Haitian democracy and Haiti's impoverished economy. Canada could opt not to spend the C$1 billion it pledged to contribute over a ten year period to decommission Russian nuclear weapons stockpiles, and it might beg off its commitment to interdict illicit shipments of components for potential weapons of mass destruction under the multilateral Proliferation Security Initiative. Each of these undertakings is voluntary, and quite costly. In the case of Afghanistan, aside from financial outlays, the cost can be measured in Canadian casualties. Canadians might imagine that the United States has the power, wealth, and influence to make up for any such contribution that Canada chooses not to make, and this may be true in many cases. However, even the United States has limits to its power, wealth, and resources and welcomes contributions that lighten US burdens around the world. Gratitude for assistance on third-country issues translates easily into appreciation from Members of Congress and by the American voters and taxpayers.

The Harper government has appeared to grasp this truth very quickly, sending the prime minister to Afghanistan in March 2006 for visits with Canadian troops engaged in security and reconstruction efforts in the more turbulent Kandahar province, and for meetings with the Afghan government. Harper's visit did more than rally troop morale; it drew attention to the Canadian contribution in Washington. President Bush and Prime Minister Stephen Harper talked about Afghanistan during their first meeting at a trilateral summit with Mexican President Vicente Fox in Cancún, Mexico, later that month. Canada's contributions in Afghanistan provided a pivot from which to leverage discussions in the bilateral realm, such as mitigating the impact of the US Western Hemisphere Travel Initiative (Primiani and Sands, 2006).

These activities signal a further evolution of Canadian policy toward leveraging third-country issues to improve bilateral relations with the United States. In Canada's first national security statement, *Securing an Open Society: Canada's National Security Policy*, most security measures are portrayed as Canadian actions taken in the Canadian interest, and the United States is rarely mentioned (Canada, 2004). Indeed, in most instances the 2004 document refers to the 9/11 attacks without mentioning the country or the cities in which they occurred (although Madrid and other sites of terrorist attacks are mentioned more specifically). Certainly, the authors of this report make no reference to the potential for collateral benefits of their recommendations for the Canada-US relationship. The authors of the multi-volume *International Policy Statement: A Role of Pride and Influence in the World* were moved closer to linkage between third-country issues and the US relationship, but the extent to which they did so varied in each volume. The "Commerce" volume is logically centered on the United States, a traditional emphasis in this area (Canada, 2005a). "Defence" has a section on Canadian cooperation with the United States, but opens with a discussion of Canadian expeditionary missions and their contribution to allied security goals (Canada, 2005b) – exactly what

Washington readers might hope to read. The volume on "Diplomacy" does separate out North American relations from other international relations, but attempts to link the two explicitly in several places, and its section on "New Multilateralism" echoes the agenda of the Bush administration on good governance and democratic values (Canada, 2005d). This is similar to the approach of the "Development" volume, which mentions the United States only in citing figures for global poverty in US dollars (Canada, 2005c). Yet the agenda for Canadian development assistance mirrors that of the United States Agency for International Development (see United States, 2003). Although Harper's administration has not signalled that it will follow the *International Policy Statement*, the centrepiece of Martin's external agenda, the document serves as a strong indication of the mind-set of the practitioners of Canada's international policy in the numerous government departments, and as a policy basis for constructive third-country engagement.

The value of third-country issues to Canada's management of its relationship with the United States would not be news to veteran diplomats (see Gotlieb, 2005; Burney, 2005). Nor would it surprise them that at times, third-country issues might eclipse bilateral issues in importance to the globally-minded United States government. But the rise of third-country issues in Canada's relations with the United States may be more than a phase. It may present Canada with a window of opportunity to enhance and secure its position within the United States core alliances for the US campaign against the asymmetric threat posed by international terrorist groups such as al Qaeda and its affiliates, a struggle that President Bush has suggested will last a generation or more – that is, beyond the end of the present administration. As such, the window of opportunity may come as early as this administration's last days, with the inauguration of its successor.

THE POTENTIAL OPPORTUNITY OF 2009

This chapter has argued that a rise in the importance of third-country issues to relations between Canada and the United Sates in the coming years is likely because such issues provide a greater room to manoeuvre for the Canadian government, as well as because they provide valuable opportunities for Canadian leverage in managing the more constrained relationship with the United States on bilateral and even domestic issues. There may also be a significant long-term reason for Canada to improve its profile on third-country issues affecting US interests: the potential that the next US president, regardless of party affiliation, will take a historic opportunity to consolidate US alliances to combat terrorism. The early years of the Cold War provide a precedent for this, for at the time Canada was well-positioned to be 'present at the creation' of the Cold War institutions, such as the North Atlantic Treaty Organization (NATO), that structured US relations with its principal allies. Will Canada be similarly well-positioned in 2009?

Although an ally in the last war, Canada cannot assume a place at the alliance table in the next. And if it is absent at the creation of the next alliance, it will signal a downgrading of the Canada-US relationship that will, in turn, make it more difficult for Canada to engage the United States on other priorities, such as the management of North American economic integration.

The 2009 hypothesis, of course, remains just that. Although it now seems unlikely that President George W. Bush will be in a position to offer a new Grand Bargain to allies during the remainder of his term, his administration has certainly established the foundations of the US strategy for fighting al Qaeda and related threats. The reorganization of a number of US federal agencies to create the Department of Homeland Security; support for a dramatic transformation of the US military and the introduction of many new offensive and defensive technologies; and commitments made to new and renewed bilateral pacts with Australia, Bulgaria, the Czech Republic, India, Iraq, Japan, Poland, and Romania (among others) have established a framework for a new system of international partnerships. Old alliances such as NATO have been reoriented to new missions, and new alliances of willing partners have included the Proliferation Security Initiative to interdict shipments of materials that could be used in fashioning weapons of mass destruction. So profound and far reaching are these changes, they will continue to influence US wartime policymaking under nearly any imaginable future president, drawn from the current pool of prospects for the Republican or Democratic Party nominations.

With the outlines of the US strategy now visible, prospective partners such as Canada can begin to consider how they can contribute, and how their interests may be affected, by the short-term consequences of US action. Thus, even if 2009 does not present Canada with a golden chance to negotiate a role for itself in the new ranks of US allies, this backdrop is the appropriate context for the Harper government to plan to advance its international role. At a minimum, for a 'change in tone' in Canada's approach to the United States to lead to a more harmonious partnership, it is crucial for the Harper government to listen to the tune to which Washington is marching. This is because Ottawa is caught between the decentralizing pressures of continental integration and a bilateral agenda that, while largely copasetic, is no longer considered by Washington to be a partnership between equals, but one defined by asymmetries of power and concern that put Ottawa at a disadvantage. The greatest latitude for the Harper government to take initiative today lies in the international arena, on third-country issues that are neither constrained by integration and the battles of federalism, nor by the limitations of leverage in a relationship of bilateral asymmetry. And if Harper can regain a reputation for Canada as an ally worth courting for its ability to contribute helpfully to US interests on third-country issues, then he may be able to translate this renewed reputation and attendant political capital in Washington into a partnership with Washington that will last into 2009 and beyond, providing Canada with a greater ability to manage continental integration and bilateral issues.

The new dynamics of the Canada-US relationship were transfigured by the 11 September 2001 terrorist attacks on New York and Washington, but have their origins in the difficulty of managing the rapidly growing asymmetry of power between the two countries. The original framework for managing the relationship – under the pretence that the two countries were sovereign equals despite their power differences – had become more and more unworkable before the urgent needs of US national security manifested themselves and made it impractical for the United States to carry on the basis of this assumption. Yet it is not clear that this approach benefits Canada so much as it once did. Canada was originally pleased with a bilateral partnership of equals with the United States, since it managed third-country issues not in relation to its neighbour but as part of the British Empire. Arguably, for much of its history, Canada made greater positive contributions to international affairs outside the confines of its bilateral relationship with the United States that the United States, in its isolationism, cared to do. Today, in an era of globalization, the fiction of a partnership of equals anchored in local affairs and irrelevant to either countries global position is perhaps unworkable for both Canada and the United States.

For nearly a century following the 1905 Boundary Waters Treaty, Washington treated Ottawa as a sovereign equal despite differences in power status that were apparent even then, when Canada was still a British colony. One explanation for why the rise of the United States to global power status did not upset this arrangement is the ambivalence about the US post-war role of the generation that came to power in the United States during and after the Second World War (Cohen, W., 1993; Gaddis, 2004). Following as it did on a long period of isolationist sentiment in the United States, the growth in the scope and scale of the US government was dramatic in the post-war period, and many of the new civil servants and politicians who came to Washington were ill at ease with US dominance in international relations. As the Cold War took shape, they took comfort in allies who could share the burdens of the new struggle.

For their own comfort as well as pragmatic reasons, they treated the recovering countries of Western Europe in a fashion that assumed that their diminished status was only temporary. The first international institutions designed as part of the Grand Bargain between the United States and its allies, the collective security pledge of the United Nations and the economic security arrangements of the Bretton Woods institutions ran into separate difficulties; the UN, after the police action in Korea, seemed unable to serve as a functional collective security guarantor (Buchan, 1976), and the International Trade Organization debated in Havana failed to secure the ratification of the signatories (Jackson, 1991). To address these weaknesses, a second round of international institutions was launched, such as the General Agreement on Tariffs and Trade in 1947 and NATO in 1949, each with a more narrowed focus and membership.

Canada, the star pupil of the British Empire, was also rising in status and therefore US leaders eagerly promoted Canadian membership in each of the post-war multilateral institutions. In 1947, Canada was just as eager to participate with the democracies of the world to build a rules-based world order (Holmes, 1982). As with Europe, the asymmetries of this relationship were considered likely to narrow over time and to be more manageable in the context of a larger Canadian role outside North America; Charles Doran (1984) would later call this the "forgotten partnership" when it appeared that the US no longer wished to manage its relations with Canada on the basis of bilateral equality and international cooperation. Yet Canada was thereafter a great joiner of international organizations (Cohen, A., 2003).

Canada did rise, and Europe did recover, and the costly Cold War burdens of the arms race with the Soviet Union, the Korean War, and the Viet Nam War kept the United States in need of allies to share these burdens. Yet the allies generally reduced their contributions to collective security, while capitalizing on concessionary access to the US market to grow their economies through exports. This contradiction gave rise to a persistent theme in US foreign policy thinking, that of relative decline. After all, if the US had to bear an increasing share of the burden of the Cold War, and the allies made decreasing contributions to collective security while demanding a greater voice in allied decision-making, this too would come at the expense of the United States. Richard Rosecrance (1976) argued that the United States had to adjust to being an "ordinary country," gradually withdrawing its Herculean commitments to the security of its allies as a way of weaning them from dependence on the United States; the hope was that the allies would rise to the occasion and spend more. Some viewed this as a return by the United States to its traditional nationalistic isolationism (Detsler, Gelb, and Lake, 1984); others viewed this as a reflection of a loss of national self-confidence, rather than of real power and influence. Historian Robert Dallek (1983) identified the periodic temptation to retreat as a trend driven by US public confidence in the universality, and universal acceptance (by key allies at least) of American ideals.

The end of the Cold War opened a period of "unipolarity" that challenged US leadership in a manner similar to the end of the Second World War. With the military threat of Soviet power gone, many scholars agreed that an era of economic primacy and advancing globalization was likely, although analysts differed on their prescriptions for US policymakers. Typical of the period, Peterson and Sebenius (1992) saw a drive to regain the global competitiveness of the US economy as the new focus of national interest with the domestic agenda at last taking center stage, while Nau (1992) saw the US as powerful as ever in the global economy, retaining global leadership in the shift to an economic era. An argument was made to revive the successful post-war strategy that followed the end of the Second World War by offering the Soviet Union a new Grand Bargain of massive, sustained, western investment in exchange for market and democratic reforms (Allison and Blackwill, 1992). The point of recalling these selected few arguments today is not nostalgia, rather it is to note that the assumptions about the world at the end of the Cold War shaped the sense of possibility in that period; the options for US policymakers seemed numerous and generally positive.

In the end, the administrations of George H.W. Bush and Bill Clinton opted for a cautious approach. They re-examined the extant alliances of the Cold War period with a bias toward their maintenance, but both administrations emphasized strengthening economic and trade linkages to major allies, leaving the reform of security alliances for a time when the threats to US interests would be clearer. In Canada's case, this occasioned the negotiation of new trade agreements, CUSFTA and NAFTA, each conformed to what had by then become the prevailing US strategic view at the time that economic rivalry would characterize the post-Cold War era.

Yet the major US allies also felt free to re-examine their Cold War commitments and to envision a new approach to independent action and multilateralism in the absence of the Soviet threat. Freed from the need for even cosmetic solidarity with the United States, many countries spoke out on global issues with new vigour, and speaking out against the United States was the logical way to exercise independence. Yet, emerging globalization emphasized the economic interdependence of western countries, and the limited freedom of action governments had to act independently in economic policymaking. In effect, the Cold War constraints on security policy were now replaced by globalization's constraints on economic policy. Once again, the United States was on top, and had greater freedom of action than any other country. From this discomfiting observation arose a new approach to multilateralism, designed to bind US power to the service of the international community priorities; from the Kyoto Protocols to the International Criminal Court to the UN Convention on Racism, the international community moved to establish rules for the post-Cold War period that would right old injustices and limit the ability of the United States to wreak new ones.

Henry Kissinger observed of this moment that the United States was adrift and that European leaders were heading in a different direction when 9/11 hit, radically altering the American perceptions of their national security. The US reaction was swift, and initially threw the Europeans off-balance:

Americans have traditionally sought to overcome a challenge, once it is recognized, in a conclusive manner; European societies have rarely had the resources to do so and have a predisposition, honed by history, to seek to manage problems, rather than to solve them. (Kissinger, 2002)

Terrorism presented an asymmetrical challenge to US security, and the small but deadly threat of terrorist groups led US policymakers to seek small but capable allies to cooperate in small but necessary ways. Intelligence and law enforcement cooperation were requested and received from nations large and small. Cold War alliances that had structured the asymmetric security interaction between the United States and its closest allies, such as NATO and NORAD, were forced to adjust to this new era of uncertainties. The post-Cold War era was now viewed in Washington as an interbellum period, as a war against terrorist groups and their state supporters began.

The 2002 *National Security Strategy of the United States* presented the new security environment in this way:

Defending our Nation against its enemies is the first and fundamental commitment of the Federal Government. Today, that task has changed dramatically. Enemies in the past needed great armies and great industrial capabilities to endanger America. Now, shadowy networks of individuals can bring chaos and suffering to our shores for less than it costs to purchase a single tank. Terrorists are organized to penetrate open societies and to turn the power of modern technologies against us. (United States, 2002b)

In 2002, Canada was poorly positioned for this new environment. Canadian governments had disinvested in international capabilities during the 1990s, reducing its diplomatic corps, military readiness, and the generosity of its international development assistance. Andrew Cohen (2003) noted this dramatic decline:

The truth is that Canada is in decline in the world today. It is not doing what it once did, or as much as it once did, or enjoying the success it once did. By three principal measures – the power of its military, the generosity of foreign aid, the quality of its foreign service – it is less effective than a generation ago. In other areas – such as the relative strength of its economy, the diversity of its trade, the persuasiveness of its diplomacy, the quality of its foreign intelligence, and the awareness of the world among its people, and of its people among the nations of the world – it is also in retreat.

Consequently, policymakers in the United States came to view Canada as a peer of countries such as the Netherlands, Denmark, or Portugal: small, prosperous, friendly, western countries that are liberal in matters of trade and economics and have very limited capacity for the projection of force outside their own borders. This was not a judgment rendered formally, but by an informal consensus about the inescapable facts of Canada's capabilities. Economic factors that would have made Canada more significant were not weighted as heavily as the new war placed a premium on the capacity of allies to assist globally in US security concerns. This was a shift made without animus toward Canada, but it was disconcerting to Canadian leaders who were confronted with an abrupt end to the management of the US-Canada relationship as an equal partnership *de jure*, if not *de facto*.

The 2002 *National Security Strategy of the United States* reflected this mentality, mentioning Canada by name just twice in thirty-one pages, and always in combination with Mexico as an expression of US vulnerability, rather than as a partner (United States, 2002b). Elsewhere in the document, Canadians might be comforted by references to NATO, the Organization of American States, and the Group of Eight countries – all multilateral groupings where Canada could make its presence felt. Later that year, Canada was mentioned by name four times in the *National Strategy for Homeland Security* (United States, 2002a), and here there were aspirations for US partnership with Canada building on the Smart Border Declaration signed by the two countries in December 2001. But taken together, these two documents appear to place US interests in cooperation with Canada firmly in the bilateral, if not domestic realms, rather than on the kind of third-country challenges for which Britain is considered.

The 2006 *National Security Strategy of the United States* confirms the new configuration of US priorities, needs, and alliances (United

States, 2006a). Canada appears just once, in a reference to post-conflict stabilization efforts worldwide. Dov Zakheim (2006) notes the significance of Canada being mentioned in this section of the updated National Security Strategy:

The choice of governments that receive specific mention is interesting – the United Kingdom, Canada and the EU. Canada, which was placed on the notorious list of states whose firms could not win contracts in Iraq, is now rightly seen as part of America's solution for reconstruction, not its problem.

This shift in Canada's fortunes is doubly-significant since it occurs over a third-country issue. In April 2006, the Office of the Coordinator for Counterterrorism within the State Department devoted two pages in its *Country Reports on Terrorism 2005* (United States, 2006b) to Canada alone, recognizing Canadian contributions in Afghanistan in addition to the references to Canadian efforts at home and bilaterally with the United States (and trilaterally, with Mexico and the United States under the aegis of the Security and Prosperity Partnership negotiations launched in 2005). At a time when the attention of US policymakers is concentrated overseas, and on the threats of new terrorist attacks, the recognition of Canada in this context shows that hope for a Canadian contribution has not been lost among senior US leaders.

It would be easy to conclude from this shift that the only contributions to third-country problems that will get noticed by Washington are those that involve the Canadian military. Yet this claim overlooks an area of international activity that has become of paramount importance to the United States, and to which Canada could make an enormous contribution: assistance to developing democracies. In keeping with the theme of President Bush's second inaugural address, the 2006 *National Security Strategy of the United States* places aid to new democracies and to people struggling against tyranny at the center of US strategy for fighting and winning the struggle against the ideologies of global terrorist organizations – in particular, the openly anti-democratic al Qaeda (United States, 2006a).

The United States has a long tradition of supporting the development of democracies abroad, having placed the establishment or restoration of democratic government at the heart of its strategy for fighting and winning the Cold War. This began with a commitment to constitutional democracy in occupied West Germany and Japan, and was reinforced by Marshall Plan economic aid, which was designed to engage local leaders in their own development. President Ronald Reagan (1989) called for non-governmental institutions to provide assistance to democrats around the world, and the efforts of these organizations greatly eased the transitions to democracy in Central and Eastern Europe after the fall of the Berlin Wall and in Latin America as military regimes surrendered power.

Long before 11 September 2001, there were calls for a greater effort to assist struggling democrats around the world as an imperative for US global leadership in the post-Cold War era (see Muravchik, 1992; 1996; and Travis, 1998). Yet prior to those same attacks, Canada was earning praise for its record of supporting democratic principles through its foreign policy from observers in the international human rights community, too (Herman and Piccone, 2002). Most Canadians share a strong conviction on the virtue of democratic governance, and as a country that has managed fractious regionalism and ethnic nationalism with constitutional reforms, creative federalism, and democratic referenda, Canadians have a wealth of experience to share with other peoples. Les Campbell (2004) argues that Canadians must look past President George W. Bush's embrace of democracy assistance and recognize that it is a natural global calling for a country like Canada.

Charles Callan Tansill (1943) describes a previous low point in the Canada-US relationship, just after the Canadian public rejected the offer of reciprocity in the general election of 1911 in these words:

It is evident that there were many reasons for the defeat of reciprocity in Canada in 1911. Not the least of these was the resentment caused by the adverse attitude toward repeated Canadian overtures in the period from 1865 to 1895. The decision of the Alaskan Boundary Tribunal deepened this feeling of hostility which found vehement expression in the elections of 1911. But this storm of anti-Americanism blew itself out in the excesses of that year, and prepared the way for a new climate of opinion that was increasingly friendly. Joint efforts in the First World War on behalf of a new design for living that incorporated many of the ideals that lay closest to Canadian hearts, gave indisputable evidence that Americans shared Canadian dreams of a new world order, and were willing to die to preserve a common heritage.

From the low point of 1911, the common cause in the First World War, itself an example of a third-country issue, helped to restore mutual confidence in a manner similar to what this chapter proposes. Canada's major effort in Afghanistan demonstrates its shared values and commitment in the war on global terrorism on the side of the United States, and has became pivotal to Canadian interests in a larger sense than anything it does in the bilateral or domestic policy realms. If sustained, this and other contributions on third-country issues should ensure that Canada will once again be present at, and party to, the creation of a new Grand Bargain between the United States and its new principal allies for the twenty-first century.

Inclusion in this Grand Bargain would be both a significant and concrete dividend from improved Canadian management of the relationship with the United States, and Prime Minister Harper and his government would deserve credit if they laid the foundation for this arrangement, whether or not they continued to form the government in 2009.

NOTES

The author would like to thank John Ferris at the Centre for Military and Strategic Studies at the University of Calgary and Commander Bob Edwards, CD, at the Centre for Foreign Policy Studies at Dalhousie University for providing opportunities to test the main ideas in this chapter before learned conference audiences in the Spring of 2006. In addition, the author is grateful to Andrew Cooper and Dane Rowlands for the invitation to contribute, and to Kelly Jackson and Andrew Schrumm at CIGI for their patience and support during the manuscript's development.

REFERENCES

Allison, Graham, and Robert Blackwill. 1992. "The Grand Bargain: The West and the Future of the Soviet Union," in Graham Allison and Gregory F. Treverton, eds. *Rethinking America's Security: Beyond Cold War to New World Order*. New York: W.W. Norton & Company.

Buchan, Alastair. 1976. "United States Foreign Policy and the Future," in Richard Rosecrance, ed. *America as an Ordinary Country: US Foreign Policy and the Future*. Ithaca: Cornell University Press.

Burney, Derek H. 2005. "The Perennial Challenge: Managing Canada-US Relations," in Andrew F. Cooper and Dane Rowlands, eds. *Canada Among Nations 2005: Split Images*. Montreal & Kingston: McGill-Queen's University Press, 47–62.

Campbell, Leslie. 2004. "Canada Alert – Democracy Canada: Turning Canadian Democratic Experiences into International Action," *CSIS Hemisphere Focus* 12, no. 4 (13 January). Washington: Center for Strategic and International Studies.

Canada. 2004. *Securing an Open Society: Canada's National Security Policy*. Ottawa: Privy Council Office, April.

– 2005a. "Commerce" in *Canada's International Policy Statement: A Role of Pride and Influence in the World*. Ottawa: Department of Foreign Affairs and International Trade (DFAIT), 19 April.

– 2005b. "Defence" in *Canada's International Policy Statement: A Role of Pride and Influence in the World*. Ottawa: Department of National Defence (DND), 19 April.

– 2005c. "Development" in *Canada's International Policy Statement: A Role of Pride and Influence in the World*. Ottawa: Canadian International Development Agency (CIDA), 19 April.

– 2005d. "Diplomacy" in *Canada's International Policy Statement: A Role of Pride and Influence in the World*. Ottawa: Department of Foreign Affairs and International Trade (DFAIT), 19 April.

Cohen, Andrew. 2003. *While Canada Slept: How We Lost Our Place in the World*. Toronto: McClelland and Stewart.

Cohen, Warren I. 1993. *America in the Age of Soviet Power, 1945–1991*. The Cambridge History of American Foreign Relations, vol. 4. New York: Cambridge University Press.

Dallek, Robert. 1983. *The American Style of Foreign Policy: Cultural Politics and Foreign Affairs*. New York: Oxford University Press.

Destler, I. M., Leslie H. Gelb, and Anthony Lake. 1984. *Our Own Worst Enemy: The Unmaking of American Foreign Policy*. New York: Simon and Schuster.

Doran, Charles F. 1984. *Forgotten Partnership: US-Canada Relations Today*. Baltimore, MD: Johns Hopkins University Press.

Gaddis, John Lewis. 2004. *Surprise, Security and the American Experience*. Cambridge, MA: Harvard University Press.

Gotlieb, Allan. 2005. "Romanticism and Realism in Canada's Foreign Policy," *Policy Options* 26, no. 2 (February): 16–27.

Herman, Robert G., and Theodore J. Piccone. 2002. "Canada" in *Defending Democracy: A Global Survey of Foreign Policy Trends 1992–2002*. Washington, DC: Democracy Coalition Project, Open Society Institute.

Holmes, John W. 1982. *The Shaping of the Peace: Canada and the Search for World Order*, vol. 2. Toronto: University of Toronto Press.

Jackson, John H. 1991. *The World Trading System: Law and Policy of International Economic Relations*. Cambridge, MA: MIT Press.

Kissinger, Henry. 2002. *Does America Need a Foreign Policy? Toward a Diplomacy for the 21st Century*, 2nd ed. New York: Simon and Schuster.

Muravchik, Joshua. 1992. *Exporting Democracy: Fulfilling America's Destiny*. Washington, DC: American Enterprise Institute Press.

– 1996. *The Imperative of American Leadership: A Challenge to Neo-Isolationism*. Washington, DC: The American Enterprise Institute Press.

Nau, Henry R. 1992. *The Myth of America's Decline: Leading the World Economy into the 1990s*. New York: Oxford University Press.

Peterson, Peter G., and James K. Sebenius. 1992. "The Primacy of the Domestic Agenda" in Graham Allison and Gregory G. Treverton, eds. *Rethinking America's Security: Beyond Cold War to New World Order*. New York: WW Norton & Company.

Primiani, Tanya, and Christopher Sands. 2006. "Canada Changes the Tone on Passports," *CSIS Hemisphere Focus* 14, no. 4 (9 June). Washington, DC: Center for Strategic and International Studies.

Reagan, Ronald W. 1989. "Address to Members of the British Parliament, Palace of Westminster, June 8, 1982" in Ronald W. Reagan, ed. *Speaking My Mind: Selected Speeches*. New York: Simon and Schuster.

Rosecrance, Richard. 1976. "New Directions?" in Richard Rosecrance, ed. *America as an Ordinary Country: US Foreign Policy and the Future*. Ithaca: Cornell University Press.

Sands, Christopher. 2002. "The Eavesdropping Problem," *CSIS Canada Focus* 3, no. 1 (January). Washington, DC: Center for Strategic and International Studies.

Tansill, Charles Callan. 1943. *Canadian-American Relations, 1875–1911*. New Haven: Yale University Press.

Travis, Rick. 1998. "The Promotion of Democracy at the End of the Twentieth Century: A New Polestar for American Foreign Policy?" in James M. Scott, ed. *After the End: Making US Foreign Policy in the Post-Cold War World*. Durham: Duke University Press.

United States. 2002a. *The National Strategy for Homeland Security*. Washington, DC: Office of Homeland Security, July.

– 2002b. *The National Security Strategy of the United States of America*. Washington, DC: The White House, September.

– 2003. *Security, Democracy, Prosperity Strategic Plan: Fiscal Years 2004–2009, Aligning Diplomacy and Development Assistance*. Washington, DC: Department of State and United States Agency for International Development, August.

– 2006a. *The National Security Strategy of the United States of America*. Washington, DC: The White House, March.

– 2006b. "Canada" in *Country Reports on Terrorism 2005*. Department of State Publication, no. 11324. Washington, DC: Office of the Coordinator for Counterterrorism, Department of State, April.

Zakheim, Dov S. 2006. "The Bush Foreign Policy, Take Two: A Symposium," *The National Interest*, no. 84 (Summer).

8 Canada's International Security Policy under a Conservative Government

ELINOR SLOAN

One of the most important considerations that must weigh in the mind of anyone becoming prime minister of Canada is how to guarantee the security of the country's citizens. This is an enormous responsibility and is the primary obligation of any federal government. International security policy is concerned with developing strategies to guard against threats to national security, which can be defined as actions or sequences of events that threaten to degrade – drastically and over a relatively brief span of time – one or more of the values citizens hold essential to their way of life. It is impossible to talk about national security policy without acknowledging the importance of the international political climate.

This chapter examines Canada's emerging international security policy under Prime Minister Stephen Harper's Conservative government. Security policy includes defence policy in that defence pertains to those situations where the military is seen as the best tool for responding to a particular range of threats. It also has an important economic dimension, since a certain level of economic prosperity is inevitably one of the values a nation's citizens will hold dear. Security policy cannot be seen in isolation from foreign policy since security inevitably has the international component noted above. As a result, this chapter will provide analysis of elements of Canada's foreign policy that are relevant to Canadian security, as well as more detailed aspects of Canadian defence policy under Stephen Harper. The first section places the discussion in context by providing a brief overview of Canadian international security policy from the early post–Second World War period to the January 2006 federal election. The second section examines the multilateral, bilateral, and economic dimensions of Stephen Harper's security policy. The final section high-lights some constraints and challenges the current government is likely to face as it continues to develop the military component of its international security policy.

CANADIAN INTERNATIONAL SECURITY POLICY FROM ST LAURENT TO MARTIN

Canada's Implicit International Security Policy

Successive Canadian governments since the Second World War have developed international security policies for Canada, but most of these have been implicit, rather than explicitly written down. Louis St. Laurent, both as secretary of state for External Affairs in the administration of William Lyon Mackenzie King and later as prime minister, saw Canada's security as being best guaranteed through a combination of collective security through participation in and promotion of the United Nations system, collective defence through membership in the North Atlantic Treaty Organisation (NATO), strong bilateral relations with key allies like the United States, Britain, and France, as well as maintenance of broader relations with Europe and the Commonwealth. Military spending, although cut significantly from the Second World War levels, remained relatively high.

Prime Minister John Diefenbaker's security policy continued to support St Laurent's multilateral approach through NATO, the UN, and the Commonwealth, but Diefenbaker's defence policies towards the US were inconsistent. The government supported greater defence integration through the creation of the North American Aerospace Defense Command (NORAD), yet at the same time refused to arm the Bomarc missiles on Canadian soil with their nuclear warheads, and was slow to put Canadian forces on alert during the Cuban Missile Crisis. Additionally, he sought to decrease Canada's economic dependence on the US by redirecting Canadian exports to Britain.[1]

Prime Minister Pierre Trudeau's security policy was more consistent, seeking to decrease both Canada's economic *and* military dependence on the United States – the former through the 'Third Option' of economic ties with other areas of the world, and the latter through the promotion of east-west confidence building initiatives like the Helsinki Final Act. With the failure of détente, the familiar strategy of guaranteeing Canadian security through NATO and bilateral relations with the United States returned. Moreover in the early 1970s, after downgrading the role of the military in Canadian security policy, Trudeau was compelled by changing circumstances later in the decade to support a NATO agreement to increase defence spending to 3 percent of GDP, a level not seen since.

Prime Minister Brian Mulroney shared the strong belief in multilateralism and in bilateral ties with key allies that had first been expressed by St. Laurent. Additionally, Mulroney strongly advocated close economic links with the United States, and thus negotiated the Canada-US Free Trade Agreement, which would come to be an important guarantor of Canadian security.[2] Under his administration, the role of the military was accorded a high priority, most famously in the 1987 White Paper. However, the unexpected end of the Cold War quickly rendered this document obsolete. As the Berlin Wall crumbled, Secretary of State for External Affairs Joe Clark supported the notion of cooperative security as an alternative means of assuring Canadian international security (Dewitt and Leyton-Brown, 1995: 14).

When the Chrétien government came to power it readily signed the already-negotiated North American Free Trade Agreement (NAFTA) and thus supported economic integration with the United States. But the remainder of its tenure was marked by internationalist initiatives designed to distinguish some independence of action from the United States.[3] This was demonstrated most notably in the human security agenda promoted by Minister of Foreign Affairs Lloyd Axworthy, which included both strong promotion of the Landmines Convention and the creation of the International Criminal Court. As the use of soft power tools seemed to become of growing importance in the post-Cold War period in achieving foreign policy objectives, the role of the military in the government's security policy diminished significantly, and with it military spending and the size of the Canadian Forces (CF).

Canada's Explicit International Security Policy under Martin

Prime Minister Paul Martin's two short-lived governments were the first in Canadian history to explicitly define what constitutes Canada's international security policy. *Securing an Open Society: Canada's National Security Policy*, released in April 2004, along with the "Defence" and "Overview" chapters of *Canada's International Policy Statement: A Role of Pride and Influence in the World*, released a year later, provide a detailed articulation of how Canadian security is conceived and practiced through a combination of measures at home and activities abroad.

The Martin government's approach to Canada's security was unique in that it was the first to include the dimension of homeland security. Aide of the civil power has always been one of Canada's military responsibilities, dating back to Confederation, but this function has never been integrated into a broader concept of homeland security that encompassed the participation of civilian officials and related to Canada's overall international security policy. The instigating factor in this change was the terrorist attacks of 11 September 2001.

Canada's National Security Policy states three core national security interests: protecting Canada and Canadians at home and abroad; ensuring Canada is not a base for threats to our allies; and, contributing to international security. The document itself has a strong domestic focus and is primarily concerned with the first two priorities. It centers especially on responses to natural and manmade disasters, health pandemics, border and transportation security issues, and intelligence findings. In doing so, the approach responds not only to threats on Canadian soil, but also to the imperative of addressing perceptions of a leaky border and upholding Canada's 1938 pledge to America that it would not allow security threats to enter the United States via Canadian land, sea, or air space. Yet the document also stresses that "given the international nature of many of the threats facing Canadians, national security also intersects with international security" (Canada, 2004: 3). The document's final section sets the stage for a review of how Canada could best contribute to international security.

Canada's International Policy Statement (IPS), particularly the Overview and Defence chapters, fills out the international dimension of how the government can best provide security for Canadians. Many of its concepts reflect elements of Canadian security policy that have appeared in the actions and policies of Canadian governments since the Second World War, including multilateralism, bilateral relations, and the economic dimension of security. But the details of Canada's approach in each of these areas point to significant changes in the contemporary international security environment.

Whereas multilateralism through the United Nations was once a central component of Canada's international security policy, the IPS speaks of "building a new framework of [multilateral] governance" (Canada, 2005b: 26). The United Nations can make a useful contribution in some areas, such as helping to reduce poverty, but this organization and others that were created at the end of the Second World War "now exist alongside myriad informal rules and relationships that contribute to global governance" (Ibid.: 27). Notably, Prime Minister Martin championed the creation of a new informal organization, the L20, an annual summit for the leaders of the twenty most influential countries in the world, as a better reflection of the contemporary international system than the UN Security Council. Throughout the document, NATO is advanced as a key institution for military missions, with the rebuilding of failed states being the most important area of overseas emphasis, yet it also notes that broader (and informal) coalition operations have a role to play (Canada, 2005a: 6). The Martin government promised substantial increased funding for the Canadian Forces, primarily for participating in missions abroad but also to boost our sovereignty at home.

When it comes to bilateral relations the IPS speaks of the necessity of revitalizing our North American partnership, including the security dimension. The document stresses the importance of renewing the NORAD Agreement, as well as strengthening cross border law enforcement and counterterrorism activities that figure within the broad framework of the Security and Prosperity Partnership for North America (SPP), which has been an outgrowth of the Smart Border Accord and the *National Security Policy*. But in taking the decision not to participate in America's ballistic missile defence system, the Martin government also attempted to stem further continental defence integration. Moreover, both the "Overview" and the "Defence" chapters stress a renewed focus on Canada (through the creation of Canada Command and an emphasis on the Arctic, for example) rather than on Canada-US defence relations. At the same time there is no mention, as there would have been in previous decades, of bilateral security relations with traditional allies like Britain and France.

The bilateral economic dimension of security is stressed in the SPP, and NAFTA has a significant position in the IPS. Yet at the same time there is marked emphasis not only on Mexico, which is mentioned just as often as the United States, but also on "emerging economic powers like China, India and Brazil [which] are the key drivers of a new era of global economic growth" (Canada, 2005b: 17). The expanding European Union is also highlighted as an emerging economic giant (Ibid.: 6). As if to underline a renewed 'Third Option' approach, the document states explicitly that securing prosperity "is no longer simply a question of negotiating trade agreements" (Ibid.: 16). Rather, it lies in securing investment access to overseas markets and attracting capital to our shores.

CANADA'S INTERNATIONAL SECURITY POLICY UNDER A CONSERVATIVE GOVERNMENT

Multilateral Security and Missions Abroad

Unlike its immediate predecessor, it is improbable that Stephen Harper's minority government will release a comprehensive foreign or defence policy statement. This is in part because the bulk of its energies will be concentrated on turning its minority into a majority, but also because the two documents produced by the Liberals provide a well-written and flexible framework within which the Conservatives can tailor their particular areas of interest. As a result, the government's international security policy – similar to most of its predecessors – is unlikely to be explicit but rather will be revealed in the actions of the government. Already there are some clear signs as to the direction it will take.

The Harper government, like that of Paul Martin's before it, sees the rebuilding of failed states as central to Canada's security. Failed states can pose a security threat to Canada because some (although by no means all) can provide a safe haven in which terrorists can train and build their expertise, and from which they can plan attacks on North America. The role of Afghanistan as a failed state where the perpetrators of the 9/11 terrorist attacks on the United States took refuge and planned the attacks is the clearest example of this, although other failed states could play this role in the future. Thus, Harper (2006: 7) has stressed that "Canada is not an island. What happens in places like Afghanistan threatens and affects all of us back home in our own country" – a clear statement of the international component of a national security policy. He has repeatedly drawn the link between failed states and the security of Canada, tying it to the more than two dozen Canadian fatalities in the attacks of 9/11 (see Laghi, 2006: A4). Harper travelled to Afghanistan himself in March 2006 to highlight Canada's commitment to Afghanistan, stressing that Canada would not 'cut and run' before it becomes a stable country, a potentially decades-long undertaking.

Canada's objective in playing a strong role in Afghanistan is not solely security related. It also reflects a desire on the part of the new Canadian government to play a more prominent role on the world stage after more than a decade of being seen as an increasingly marginal player, beset by a combination of declining defence budgets and by a reduced commitment to overseas development aid and Canadian diplomacy.[4] In its first Speech from the Throne, the Harper government committed itself to "a more robust diplomatic role for Canada, a stronger military and a more effective use of Canadian aid dollars" (Canada, 2006: 10). "The work of our soldiers is about more than just defending Canada's interests," Harper (2006: 7) has further argued, "it's also about demonstrating an international leadership role for our country." Thus, although Canada has been in Afghanistan since soon after 9/11, and although the Canadian redeployment from Kabul to the much more dangerous Kandahar region in February 2006 was a decision taken by the previous Liberal government, it was only after Harper's election that such a firm and visible link was made between our mission in that country and our place in the world.

Multilateral organizations like the United Nations and the Commonwealth are not mentioned in the Conservative Party's election platform, *Stand Up For Canada*, nor in the April 2006 throne speech. This may be an indication that for the Conservative government, like that of the Liberals before it, collective security through the United Nations is perceived to be of declining importance to Canada. Tellingly, Canada closed out its last major commitment to a United Nations peacekeeping mission in March 2006, the UN Disengagement Observer Force on the Golan Heights, bringing to an end half a century of significant involvement in such missions (Ward, 2006b). As of summer 2006, Canada had only about 125 personnel involved in UN missions, with the majority operating in Sudan. By contrast, roughly 2600 CF members are taking part in NATO-led missions. While multilateralism remains important, and the Harper government stressed in the throne speech it will seek to build stronger multilateral relationships with friends and allies in order to advance common interests (Canada, 2006: 10), these are likely to be informal multilateral relationships and coalitions of the willing that are perceived to be better at responding to the new security environment. NATO remains relevant because it has adapted to the post-Cold War and post-9/11 security environment in this manner. It can facilitate and be the foundation of coalitions of the willing, as is the case with the NATO-led International Security Assistance Force, which includes many non-NATO countries. In his first meeting of NATO defence ministers in February 2006, Minister Gordon O'Connor underlined that Canada is committed to the Organisation and would remain a strong and engaged partner in NATO's Afghan mission (O'Connor, 2006).

Bilateral Defence Relations

In comparison to the previous Liberal government, the Harper administration has placed greater importance on close bilateral defence relations with the United States, and has iterated the goal of strengthening military ties with our neighbour to the south (CBC, 2006). Closer Canada-US military ties centre on a renewed NORAD agreement, now expanded to include maritime surveillance, but the bulk of the agreement's negotiations were carried out by Martin's Liberal government. Similarly, the SPP, established under Martin, will continue to be an important element of closer Canada-US relations (Boehm, 2006). As is the case with the multilateral efforts, these concrete bilateral security and defence initiatives are not new; they were already in place or underway in the previous government.

One area where there could be a difference in approach is with regard to ballistic missile defence (BMD). The Conservative government appears to be willing to entertain the idea of Canadian participation in America's BMD system at some point in the future, an invitation that was rejected by former Prime Minister Martin in February 2005. Minister O'Connor has indicated that he "has no difficulty with ballistic missile defence" (cited in Ward, 2006a). Nonetheless, any discussion in this area is unlikely to take place under a minority government given the strong opposition to participation on the part of the Canadian public. For his part, US Ambassador to Canada David Wilkins has stated that the US has no plans to re-open missile defence talks with Canada, nor has President Bush raised the issue in his discussions with Harper (Panetta, 2006).

Economic Relations

Echoing its change in tone on bilateral defence relations, the new government has stressed that it will build stronger bilateral economic relations. The focus though here is really on "Canada's relationship with the United States, our best friend and largest trading partner" (Canada, 2006: 9). Leaving for a meeting in Cancùn with his American and Mexican counterparts, Prime Minister Harper made it clear that his government would put the dialogue between Canada and the US "on a more mature and productive wavelength" (Panetta, 2006) after a number of incidents during the Chrétien and Martin years that damaged the working relationship with the United States. This is a clear indication that the Conservative government sees economic security for Canada as being best achieved by good relations with the US. For America, this is a welcome change in tone from north of the 49th parallel, and it may have played a role in securing the softwood lumber agreement between the two countries in April 2006.

At the Cancùn Summit, Harper also indicated a certain 'third way' inclination with plans to increase trade with Mexico by 50 percent by 2010 (Woods, 2006). But beyond this, it is too early to tell whether security policy under a Conservative government will seek the diversified economic relations often attempted by Liberal governments since the 1970s (and expressed most recently in the Martin government's IPS), or if it will focus on the strengthening of economic relations with the United States that was prominent in the security policy of Canada's last Conservative government.

CANADA FIRST

Stephen Harper's government has announced a "Canada First" strategy designed to strengthen Canadian sovereignty at home and abroad.

During the election the Conservatives committed to all of the things the Liberal government had previously supported, including Joint Support Ships and amphibious transport vessels for the Navy, but in sharp contrast to the Liberals they also committed to purchasing three strategic lift aircraft, something the Liberals had flat-out rejected. Moreover, rather than increasing the Canadian Forces by 5,000 regular force troops and 3,000 reserves, as the Liberals had planned, the Conservatives raised those figures to 13,000 and 10,000 respectively.

The most significant change in Canada's security policy approach as represented by the Canada First strategy is in regards to the link between Canadian territory and sovereignty. During the election campaign Stephen Harper said that a Conservative government would:

- Station three new armed naval icebreakers in the north, including 500 regular force personnel to man these ice breakers;
- Build a deep water port in Iqaluit on Baffin Island;
- Establish an underwater sensor system in the north, designed to detect submarines;
- Build an army Arctic training centre in Cambridge Bay;
- Purchase new fixed wing search and rescue aircraft and station them in Yellowknife;
- Create two unmanned aerial vehicle squadrons, one each in Goose Bay and Comox, to conduct regular surveillance of the Arctic; and,
- Create a new airborne battalion at CFB Trenton designed for operations in the Canadian north (Conservative Party of Canada, 2005).

If these initiatives were to be carried out they would be nothing less than transformative in how Canadians think about their security. Historically, Canada has looked primarily overseas to guarantee its security. During the Cold War, Canada and the United States placed much greater emphasis on measures abroad to provide for their security than on measures at home. This approach made sense, given the nature of the threat at the time. The primary threat to Canada was from intercontinental ballistic missiles and there was little we could do defensively against such a threat. The four decades of the Cold War solidified a Canadian political and military culture of looking overseas to address threats to Canada, and the predominance of intrastate conflict around the world during the 1990s supported a continued emphasis on looking overseas.

Under Prime Minister Martin, the Canadian government initiated a new approach to conceive of Canadian security. The Liberals argued that Canada had to pay more attention to security and defence at home and created a new Canadian Forces command structure to reflect this change in emphasis. But their proposed capital acquisitions for the Canadian

Forces did not fully reflect the shift. The Liberals highlighted, for example, the acquisition of amphibious transport vessels and air-to-ground precision munitions for our fighter aircraft – things that would only be appropriate for overseas missions. By contrast, Stephen Harper's election announcements appeared to give concrete evidence of his desire for a re-balancing between the focus on activities at home and missions abroad. Unfortunately, the May 2006 budget was silent on all of these issues, leaving significant questions as to just how committed the government is to this new approach.

The Homeland Dimension

The Harper government has not explicitly indicated whether or not it supports the Martin government's *National Security Policy*. Nonetheless, in maintaining the Department of Public Safety and Emergency Preparedness created under Martin, and in appointing a powerful minister to the portfolio, Stockwell Day, the government has given implicit support to the Liberal approach. In fact, all of the major homeland security institutions established under Martin's landmark reorganization of government in December 2003 have remained in place (see Sloan, 2005). In *Stand Up For Canada*, the Conservative Party election platform, Harper indicated that his government would push homeland changes even further than that of Martin's, most notably by arming Canadian border officers with pistols, increasing the government's ability to deport people connected to organized crime or terrorist organizations, revitalizing the Coast Guard, and creating a national security commissioner to coordinate the work of CSIS, the RCMP, and the Canada Border Services Agency (Conservative Party of Canada, 2006: 26–7).

ISSUES FOR THE FUTURE

There are several issues this Conservative minority government will need to consider as it continues to develop the military component of its international security policy. Some pertain to constraints it will face in implementing its defence policy, while others encompass broader policy issues.

Costs and Budget

It probably goes without saying that the principal constraint the Harper government has in implementing its defence policy is the cost of its proposed program, combined with the fact that it is in a minority government situation. In February 2005, the Liberal government announced a C$12.8

billion increase in the defence budget over five years to fiscal year 2009–10. In May 2006, the Conservatives announced a further c$5.3 billion increase over five years to fiscal year 2010–11, over and above what the Liberals had promised. And yet these commitments are still not enough to address the personnel increases and re-equipment programs that are necessary if the CF is to be able to carry out its missions. A large part of the problem centres on the fact that both the Liberal and Conservative programs are heavily back-loaded. There are relatively small increases in years one and two of the programs, while the majority of increases will not arrive until late in the respective five-year windows. Moreover, almost half of the Liberal government's year one commitments were clawed back for other government priorities.

But even assuming all the Liberal and Conservative committed funding arrives, a rough addition of the costs of sustaining operations, paying for an increased force size, and buying new equipment reveals an c$8–10 billion shortfall in defence funding in the period to fiscal year 2010–11. And this does not account for a potential increase in operations – say, for example, a deployment to the Darfur region or to Haiti. Nor does it account for things that will be required just shortly after this window, notably replacements for Canada's frigates, destroyers and fighter aircrafts.

Generally speaking the Canadian public is more amenable to increased defence expenditures today than they were, say, five years ago. The Canadian Forces have had a lot of visibility since 11 September 2001, and, especially after the PM's recent visit to Afghanistan, the public is largely supportive of the CF's overseas missions in this new environment. Nonetheless, increasing the capabilities of the CF, or even making a broader commitment to Canada's international role, is not among the government's set of five priorities to which it has been unwavering in its first few months in office. Moreover, as much as it may want to devote increased resources to defence, it is still a minority government that must take the views of three other parties into account that, again generally speaking, are less supportive of increased military expenditures. In its May 2006 budget the government kept its campaign promise of increased funding for the Canadian Forces, but the full requirement for military investments is unlikely to be addressed unless the government is returned with a majority after the next election.

Recruitment

Increased funding is only part of the story. One of the biggest challenges the CF faces in the future is recruiting. Finding and training the additional 5,000 regular forces and 3,000 reserve forces that were originally promised by the Martin government in 2004 was thought to be a major challenge. Now those figures have been increased to 13,000 and 10,000 troops respectively by the Conservative government – a three-fold increase that will be even more difficult to bring about.

The challenge comes in three parts. First, there is a need to fill out existing units that are undermanned. The Harper government has announced plans to increase the size of the CF from the 62,000 that currently exists on paper to a force level of 75,000, but the CF's effective strength stands at only about 53,000. So a lot of recruiting and training has to be done just to fill existing positions; only then can the CF start to build up the size of its forces. Second, the CF has to find enough suitable recruits to meet the announced 13,000–person increase in regular forces. In the fall of 2005, defence experts argued that the changing demographics of the Canadian population would make it "exceedingly difficult if not impossible" to meet the Liberal government's recruiting targets (Pugliese, 2005: 32). These conclusions are supported by a May 2006 Auditor General's Report which found that the CF was barely keeping pace with attrition, and that there were serious shortfalls in some of the key trades and classifications (see Den Tandt et al., 2006). And finally, there is a requirement to have enough highly trained personnel who are not away on deployment or on exercise to train the new recruits. This is perhaps the greatest challenge and the biggest reason why increasing the size of the CF is not something that can be done too rapidly. Already the Minister of National Defence has raised the possibility of scaling back Canada's Afghanistan commitment in future years so there are enough people at home to train new recruits (Campion-Smith, 2006: A8).

Procurement

Another major challenge to increasing military capabilities is equipment. The CF has been quite successful in recent years in increasing its military capability by buying smaller pieces of equipment and individual off-the-shelf kits. Examples include the unmanned aerial vehicles and precision guided artillery that were bought for Canadian troops in Afghanistan. But the Canadian Forces remain hampered by the lengthy procurement times it faces for major capital acquisitions like helicopters, fixed-wing aircraft, ships, trucks, and armoured vehicles. A report released by the Conference of Defence Associations Institute in Spring 2006 argues the problem arises from a combination of three things. First, that the detailed statement of requirements procedure within the Department of National Defence (DND) is an administrative nightmare, as it can run into the thousands of pages. Second, that there is a "plethora of interdepartmental processes" for approval involving the Treasury Broad Secretariat, Public Works and Government Services, Finance, Industry Canada and the Privy Council Office. And third, that there is a shortage of people within DND who are qualified in managing major procurement programs (CDAI, 2006: 16). Furthermore, a major problem, at least in recent years, has been changes in government brought on by the succession of minority governments. The long-awaited Hercules replacement purchase that the Liberals almost had in place in late 2005, for example, was put on hold by the Conservatives pending a discussion of an alternative mix of tactical and strategic lift aircraft.

Changing procurement practices is especially important today because of the fast pace of technological change and the need to have equipment that is not technologically out of date before it even arrives. Both the minister and the chief of defence staff have stressed that the CF can no longer afford to take years and years to obtain major pieces of equipment, and that the acquisition system needs to give the CF the equipment they need, when they need it. But to date there have been no concrete proposals as to how to bring about this desired end state.

Hands Tied

The result of all this is that the government is likely to find its hands tied when it comes to missions it would like Canada to undertake in the near to medium term, but that the CF simply does not have the forces to do so. A longstanding deployment principle holds that it is necessary to have four battalions (or ships or aircraft) at home for every battalion deployed overseas. This is meant to ensure that a soldier (or sailor or airman) is at home for two years before being deployed overseas for his or her next six-month tour. With only nine battalions it is very difficult to maintain this deployment principle should Canada decide to take on more than one major international commitment. The CF is in the process of recruiting a new battalion-sized Special Operations Regiment which, once in place in about five years time, will help alleviate some of the pressure. Equally, if not more important will be to fill out the ranks of the combat support and combat service support personnel that are crucial to missions such as that which the CF has undertaken in Afghanistan. But these people are not there now, so when it comes to international missions the government will have fewer options.

A good example is Canada's response to the crisis in the Darfur region of Sudan. It has been several years since the International Commission on Intervention and State Sovereignty released its *Responsibility to Protect*

(R2P) report. Canada played a key role in the document's formulation and was instrumental in getting the ideas of this report reflected in the UN's World Summit outcome document in September 2005. In recent years there have been calls for Canada and NATO to move the R2P concept from theory to practice with a deployment to the Darfur region. But the Minister of National Defence has been forced to concede that the current deployment in Kandahar has put a significant strain on the CF and that the Forces will therefore not be able to take on any additional overseas commitments. Prime Minister Harper has stressed that Canada's contribution could come in the form of increased humanitarian assistance or technical support, but that the army will not be able to send any more than the approximately 50 Canadian Forces personnel that are already in Darfur. Even Canada's humanitarian assistance contribution is likely to be limited by the fact that Canada has no strategic air transporters and only a very stretched tactical airlift capability – a situation that will not be remedied until at least 2008 (Blanchfield, 2006). In this sense, the current government is constrained in its foreign policy activities by failures on the part of previous governments to commit to maintaining Canada's military capability since the mid-1990s.

Afghanistan

Beyond budgets, recruiting, and procurement, there are broader policy challenges that the Harper government is likely to face. Perhaps the most pressing pertain to the mission in Afghanistan. In the more than three years since NATO took over leadership of the International Security Assistance Force (ISAF) in Afghanistan, ISAF's geographic reach and mission have expanded significantly. Originally tasked with creating a safe and secure environment in and around Kabul, ISAF has now expanded its geographic reach to include the north, west and south of the country, and it will also expand eastward. Meanwhile, ISAF's missions have expanded from stability and security operations, security sector reform, and training the Afghan National Army, to include commanding the military component of numerous provincial reconstruction teams and supporting Afghan government programmes to disarm illegally armed groups.

The move to more dangerous areas of the country, and to a more pro-active mandate, has entailed more robust rules of engagement than was previously the case. In making these mandate changes NATO has stressed that ISAF's mission continues to be stabilization and security, and that it remains distinct from that of America's Operation Enduring Freedom (OEF), which has its own rules of engagement. But in the minds of the Afghan people it will likely be increasingly difficult to make the distinction between a new and more robust stabilization and reconstruction mission and America's warfighting counter-terrorism mission. NATO (2006) also implicitly acknowledges this problem when it notes that its operational plan includes clear arrangements for "de-conflicting" the two missions.

The international community's experience in Bosnia more than a decade ago exposed the difficulty of trying to undertake two kinds of mission in one location, at the same time, with overlapping sets of players. In that case there was the UN Protection Force (UNPROFOR) mission and NATO air strikes taking place concurrently. The UN peacekeepers were increasingly seen as partial to the Croats and the Muslims and they therefore became the target of Serb hostilities. Today, in Afghanistan, there is the NATO-led ISAF with a large US component, and the US-led Operation Enduring Freedom. This arrangement, too, is likely to lead to attacks against soldiers engaged in the stabilization mission. In May 2006, for example, OEF launched an attack against an Afghan village which killed many Taliban but also inadvertently killed a number of innocent civilians. ISAF was quick to stress that it was in no way involved in the attack, but the reaction on the part of some Afghans highlighted the fine line between the missions when it comes to Afghan perceptions. "We cannot tell the difference between Canadian and American soldiers," argued one bystander who was injured in the attacks, "They are all Americans to us. They have been very cruel to us" (Farrell, 2006: A5). Along similar lines, a high ranking British officer has noted that the distinction between a British soldier conducting stabilization operations as part of ISAF and a British soldier eradicating poppy fields as part of OEF is likely to be lost on most Afghan farmers (Stanhope, 2006). Maintaining the perceptual, if not operational, distinction between ISAF and OEF will be even more difficult since ISAF took command of the multinational brigade in southern Afghanistan in July 2006.

A better approach may be to create one operation, with one set of missions, and one set of rules of engagement that are matched to the prevailing, currently very dangerous, circumstances on the ground. In this context, during its tenure the Harper government may be faced with the challenge of presenting the case to the Canadian public for the need to create one mission in Afghanistan. This will be in addition to continuing to explain, as casualties mount, why it is important that Canada be there in the first place. Minister of Defence Gordon O'Connor presented the case during the House of Commons debate on 17 May 2006 which led to the extension of Canada's contribution to the Afghan mission to February 2009. O'Connor argued that the extension was necessary in light of a request for support by the Afghan government, our commitments to our allies and, most notably, Canada's own national security interest in ensuring Afghanistan does not once again harbour terrorists.

Ballistic Missile Defence

A second and equally potentially explosive issue pertains to the familiar theme of ballistic missile defence. With the recent NORAD renewal, and as time reveals the true impact of Canada's decision not to participate in America's BMD system, the Harper government may be compelled to revisit the wisdom of not participating. Over time, it is likely to become increasingly apparent that Canada is being progressively cut out of access to ballistic missile early warning and space surveillance information.

All of the land, space, and now sea-based systems involved in gathering ballistic missile early warning and space surveillance information belong to the United States; Canada has none. Since the early 1960s, this information has been gathered by a US-only command and channelled into the NORAD command centre for threat assessment. In August 2004, Canada agreed that this assessment information from NORAD could be sent to Northern Command for ballistic missile defence purposes, a set-up that is analogous to the Cold War information sharing framework. At that time, such assessments were sent to the US command that controlled nuclear weapons. But the United States did not intend to shoot down missiles coming from the Soviet Union. Rather, it was going to respond in kind after absorbing a first strike. By contrast, ballistic missile defence involves what is often described as 'shooting a bullet with a bullet.' Assessment and response timelines would be far shorter in the case of ballistic missile defence, making it difficult, if not impossible, to divide assessment and response capabilities between organizations.

The August 2004 agreement is unlikely to be a long-term solution. As processing systems are modernized the US could set up a separate assessment centre within either Strategic Command or Northern Command, and there are already indications that this is starting to happen. NORAD (read Canada) could be progressively cut out of space surveillance and ballistic missile early warning information. This matters because Canada benefits from having information about ballistic missile launches around the world, including not only missiles that may be headed our way but also situations like scud missile launches in the Middle East. We also benefit from having space surveillance information about objects orbiting or coming at the earth.

In around 2010 Canada will launch a satellite that will conduct the surveillance of space, called the Sapphire system. Part of its role will be to feed information into America's space surveillance network. It will be unique in that it will be the first space-based, space surveillance system. But Canada's Sapphire contribution may not be enough to keep the window open to the vast amount of information collected by America's far more extensive systems. As a result of all this, the Harper government may be faced with the challenge of reconsidering Canada's decision not to participate in BMD.

CONCLUSION

Developing Canadian public policy on any area of federal jurisdiction is never an easy task during a minority government (see Chapnick, this volume), and this is no different when it comes to putting forth a Canadian international security policy. Historically, Canada's security policy has almost always been implicit in the actions and statements of the government of the day, with the exception being the two short-lived Martin governments that produced *Canada's National Security Policy* and *Canada's International Policy Statement*. These two documents set out the first explicit framework for providing Canadian security.

The Harper government is unlikely to develop its own security and defence policy. If anything, it seems to be taking the key themes of the defence component of the Liberal's IPS – rebuilding failed states and an increased focus on Arctic security – and running with them. It has also worked to stress the importance of strong bilateral defence and economic relations with the United States. But, with the possible exception of the softwood lumber agreement, the Harper government's change in approach is far more rhetorical than substantive. The renewed NORAD agreement was largely negotiated by the Liberals. The May 2006 budget contained no reference to the strategic airlift and Arctic icebreakers that were announced with much fanfare during the election campaign. This safe approach is no doubt the inevitable result of minority government imperatives; concrete change in Canada's international security policy awaits a majority government.

NOTES

1 Diefenbaker's goal was to redirect 15 percent of Canadian exports to Britain and it involved, in part, opposing Britain's entry into the European Community. Although Britain's entry was ultimately delayed until 1973, this had little effect on the structure of Canadian trade (see Keating, 2002: 62–3).

2 For a discussion of Canada's implicit international security policy from the end of the Second World War until the early 1990s, see Dewitt and Leyton-Brown (1995).

3 For a discussion of the internationalist versus continentalist perspective, see Hampson et al. (2001).
4 These trends are well documented in Cohen (2003).

REFERENCES

Blanchfield, Mike. 2006. "Tories Set to Sink Billions into Cargo Planes for Military," *Ottawa Citizen*, 3 June, A2.

Boehm, Peter. 2006. "The Security and Prosperity Partnership of North America: One Year Later," Presentation by the Assistant Deputy Minister of Foreign Affairs (North America) to Carleton University, Ottawa, 17 March.

Campion-Smith, Bruce. 2006. "Mission Being Re-evaluated: Canada Mulls Scaling Back on Its Troop Commitment," *Toronto Star*, 19 April, A8.

Canada. 2004. *Securing and Open Society: Canada's National Security Policy.* Ottawa: Department of Public Safety and Emergency Preparedness (PSEP), 27 April.

– 2005a. "Defence," in *Canada's International Policy Statement: A Role of Pride and Influence in the World.* Ottawa: Department of National Defence (DND), 19 April.

– 2005b. "Overview," in *Canada's International Policy Statement: A Role of Pride and Influence in the World.* Ottawa: Department of Foreign Affairs and International Trade (DFAIT), 19 April.

– 2006. *Canada's New Government: Turning a New Leaf.* Speech from the Throne. Ottawa: Office of the Governor General, 4 April.

CBC News. 2006. "Canada's Military Priorities: More Troops, Closer Relations with US," 23 February. Available at: <http://www.cbc.ca>

Cohen, Andrew. 2003. *While Canada Slept: How We Lost Our Place in the World.* Toronto: McClelland & Stewart.

Conference of Defence Associations Institute (CDAI). 2006. "Creating an Acquisition Model that Delivers," *Vimy Paper*, no. 1 (April): 15–63.

Conservative Party of Canada. 2005. "Harper Stands Up for Arctic Sovereignty," News Release, *Stand Up for Canada*, 22 December. Available at: <http://www.conservative.ca/EN/1091/36512>

– 2006. *Stand Up for Canada: Federal Election Platform*, 13 January. Available at: <http://www.conservative.ca/media/20060113 Platform.pdf>

Den Tandt, Michael et al. 2006. "Shortfalls in Military Recruitment, AG Says," *Globe and Mail*, 16 May. Available at: <http://www.theglobeandmail.com>

Dewitt, David, and David Leyton-Brown. 1995. "Canada's International Security Policy," in Dewitt and Brown, eds. *Canada's International Security Policy.* Scarborough, ON: Prentice Hall.

Farrell, Jim. 2006. "Afghans Direct Anger at Canadians," *Ottawa Citizen*, 23 May, A5.

Hampson, Fen Osler, Norman Hillmer, and Maureen Appel Molot. 2001. "The Return of Continentalism in Canadian Foreign Policy," in Hampson et al., eds. *Canada Among Nations 2001: The Axworthy Legacy*. Don Mills, ON: Oxford University Press, 1–18.

Harper, Stephen. 2006. "The Canadian Way: Efforts in Afghanistan Represent the Country's Core Values," *Edmonton Sun*, 19 March, 7.

Keating, Tom. 2002. *Canada and World Order: The Multilateralist Tradition in Canadian Foreign Policy*, 2nd ed. Don Mills, ON: Oxford University Press.

Laghi, Brian. 2006. "Afghanistan Is 'Our War' Too, Harper Says," *Globe and Mail*, 25 March, A4.

North Atlantic Treaty Organisation (NATO). 2006. "Revised Operational Plan for NATO's Expanding Mission in Afghanistan," *NATO Topics-Afghanistan*. 10 March. 9 May 2006. Available at: <http://www.nato.int/issues/afghanistan_stage3/index.html>

O'Connor, Gordon. 2006. Address by the Minister of National Defence to the Canadian Defence Associations Institute Annual General Meeting, Ottawa, 23 February.

Panetta, Alexander. 2006. "Harper Predicts Better Relations with US," *Canadian Press*, 28 March. Available at: <www.canada.com>

Pugliese, David. 2005. "Canada's Ambitious Plan Sparks Questions," *Defence News*, 12 September, 32.

Sloan, Elinor C. 2005. "Homeland Security," *Security and Defence in the Terrorist Era*. Montreal & Kingston: McGill-Queen's University Press, 44–69.

Stanhope, Admiral Sir Mark. 2006. "Understanding NATO Military Transformation," Presentation to the Centre for Security and Defence Studies, Carleton University, Ottawa, 2 June.

Ward, John. 2006a. "Defence Minister Open to Missile Plan," *Canadian Press*, 23 February. Available at: <http://cnews.canoe.ca>

– 2006b. "Era of Canadian Peacekeeping Dwindles as Canada Pulls Out of the Golan Heights," *Canadian Press*, 24 March. Available at: <http://www.canada.com>

Woods, Allan. 2006. "Bush, Harper Seek to Finally End Long-Running Softwood Feud," *Ottawa Citizen*, 31 March. Available at: <http://www.canada.com>

9 The New Conservative Government and Missile Defence: Is Canadian Participation Back on the Agenda, or Was It Ever Off?

ANN DENHOLM CROSBY

In response to public pressure, the Liberal government announced on 24 February 2005 that Canada would not participate in the American missile defence system. The government subsequently argued that, "Canada's principle approach to address the missile threat is prevention, through non-proliferation, arms control and disarmament (NACD) measures" (Canada, 2005: 2). Clearly, it seemed, the Liberals preferred prevention through arms control over deterrence through military means.

By apparent contrast, less than one month after the Liberal announcement of Canadian non-participation, Stephen Harper, the leader of the Conservative Party, announced that his party supported "Canada's participation in negotiation of a North American Missile Defence System on the clear understanding that any agreement must serve Canada's interest" (Conservative Party of Canada, 2005). Subsequently, Harper argued that he would re-open discussions with the United States and if a formal invitation was extended to participate in missile defence, he would put the issue to a free-vote in Parliament (Radio Canada, 2006).

The Conservative Party won the federal election of January 2006 and was sworn in to form a minority government on 6 February. Due to its minority status and with the Liberal, New Democratic (NDP), and Bloc Québécois Parties' positions of Canadian non-participation, it was reasonable to suspect that the Conservatives would not re-open the issue. Indeed, on 24 February 2006, US Ambassador David Wilkins stated that neither Canada nor the US had made efforts to re-open discussions and that in fact, the issue of Canadian participation in the US missile defence system was off the agenda in the US (Curry, 2006).

Public pressure in Canada, it seemed, had effectively shaped Canadian defence and security interests, in the process, distancing Canada from US foreign and defence policy initiatives supported by its missile defence system – including US plans to develop space weapons as part of that system. But it now appears that this is not so. The US missile defence system depends significantly on the functions of The North American Aerospace Defense command (NORAD), the joint Canada-US military command responsible for the aerospace defence of the continent. In May 2006, the NORAD Agreement was renewed with changes to the command's mandate that entrench Canadian participation in missile defence through the NORAD command.

The new Conservative government signed this new agreement but it had been largely negotiated by the preceding Liberal government. Both parties voted to support the renewal in the House of Commons on 8 May, and both parties claim that Canada is not participating in missile defence. The subject of this paper is thus an exploration of the contradiction between the terms of the new NORAD Agreement and the claims of the two major political parties in Canada. A discussion of the policy implications of this contradiction for the minority Conservative government follows a review of the US missile defence system and Canada's increasing involvement in it through the NORAD command.

THE US MISSILE DEFENCE SYSTEM

In the early 1990s, following the use of rudimentary missile defences during the first Gulf War, most specifically the early version of the Patriot missile, the US established legislation and funding for the development of a missile defence program.[1] The Strategic Defense Initiative, announced by President Reagan in 1983 as a research program involving space weaponry, was replaced by the Ballistic Missile Defense Organization with a mandate for the research, development and deployment of three missile defence programs. The Theatre Missile Defense Program was to address the use of short and medium range missiles in regional conflicts. The Global Warning Program was to further develop and deploy a land, sea, air, and space-based layering of radars, sensors, and communication technologies to provide the US military with global surveillance, communication and battle management tools.

The third program, the National Missile Defense Program, was designed to address an accidental, or hostile launch of a limited number of long-range missiles aimed at the US by intercepting and destroying the missiles in mid-course, either in space or at high altitudes. At the time, it was thought that an accidental launch could come from the arsenals of Russia or China, while the 'hostile' missiles were expected to be launched from North Korea, Syria, Iran, or Iraq – states that did not then, and will not for the foreseeable future, have long-range ballistic missile capability (see Cirincione, 2005).

Throughout the 1990s, funding, research, and development were focused on the first two components of the program, theatre missile defense and global warning. By 2000, and particularly after 9/11, attention turned to the National Missile Defense Program. To facilitate its development and eventual deployment, the US unilaterally withdrew from the ABM Treaty in 2002, after Russia's President Vladimir Putin failed to agree to retire the Treaty. The ABM Treaty was the flagship Cold War arms control agreement between the USSR and the US that prevented all but rudimentary research, development, and deployment of missile defences and thus prevented the development of an arms race in missile technologies and defences.

The same year, the US budgeted $8 billion for its missile defence programs and has funded them at similar levels each year since. The US also restructured its military command system and created the Northern Command (NORTHCOM), its mandate being the defence of the continent including Mexico and Canada. It is NORTHCOM that is responsible for missile defence on the continent.[2] Further, in 2002, President Bush announced plans to field initial long-range missile defence capabilities by 2004–05. Ten interceptors were to be deployed with eight at a site in Alaska and two in California. This has been accomplished although at this point the sites are primarily test beds rather than operational defence installations. There are also now plans to field an additional ten interceptors; to have three Aegis Ballistic Missile Defense Cruisers at sea equipped with short to medium range interceptors; and, to add engagement upgrades to thirteen destroyers now equipped with long range surveillance and tracking technologies. All of these plans are to be accomplished by the end of 2006. In addition, the research and development of airborne laser weapons is well advanced and the US has long range plans to develop a range of space-based weapons including space-based interceptors for which they hope to have a test-bed in space by 2012.[3]

Finally, in 2002 also, the Ballistic Missile Defense Organization was renamed the Missile Defense Agency partly in recognition that the original three missile defence programs were in fact inseparable, that the US National Missile Defense program, together with its plans to eventually weaponize space, is part and parcel of, and cannot be separated from, the constantly evolving US global missile defence systems. These now consist of sophisticated land, sea, air, and space-based surveillance, warning, communication, and battle management systems designed to address short and medium range missile activity anywhere in the world. With North American missile defences in place, the system will also detect and respond to limited long range missile attacks on the North American continent. The Agency's mission is to "Develop and field an integrated Ballistic Missile Defense System capable of providing a layered defense for the homeland and its deployed forces, friends and allies against ballistic missiles of all ranges in all phases of flight" (MDA, 2005: 4).

NORAD'S RELATIONSHIP TO MISSILE DEFENCE

The North American Aerospace Command was established in 1958 as a joint Canada-US military command responsible for the air defence of the North American continent during the early Cold War years when it was thought that a Soviet attack against the United States would be launched from bombers flying over Canada to US targets. For their intercept role in this regard, Canadian air forces had access to US nuclear weapons stored on Canadian soil. As the USSR developed long-range ballistic missiles, the bomber threat decreased and NORAD's role became one of passive defence involving air and aerospace surveillance and warning. By the end of the Cold War, NORAD had surveillance, warning, and communication systems that were global in scope and was, therefore, poised to play a pivotal role in the development and operations of the US missile defence system (see Denholm Crosby, 1998: 56–105).

Canada, however, had a history of policy positions against missile defences and the weaponization of space. In terms of the latter, the Canadian government has worked consistently since the 1960s within the United Nations disarmament fora to establish a ban on space weapons. As for the former, Canada had an ABM clause written into the NORAD Agreement in 1968 stating that the agreement did "not involve in any way a Canadian commitment to participate in an active ballistic missile defence" system (Canada, 1968). For the 1981 renewal of the NORAD Agreement, that specific clause was deleted, ostensibly because it's inclusion suggested that Canada did not trust the US to abide by the ABM Treaty.[4] It was at that time, however, when plans were developing for the US Strategic Defense Initiative (SDI), popularly known as Star Wars, an initiative mandated to research and develop a space-based layer of missile defences.

SDI became controversial in Canada in 1985 when the NORAD Agreement was again scheduled for renewal and it became public knowledge that the clause preventing Canadian participation in missile defences had been removed from the agreement in 1981. Partly in response to the public controversy, and partly in keeping with Canada's position against the weaponization of space, the Progressive Conservative government of Brian Mulroney refused the US invitation to participate in SDI. The government's refusal, however, did not close any doors. Prior to renewing the NORAD Agreement in 1986, representatives of the Departments of National Defence and External Affairs (as the present Department of Foreign Affairs and International Trade [DFAIT] was then known), were informed during a meeting with NORAD's commander-in-chief, General Robert T. Herres, that, although future NORAD activities would become increasingly involved in missile defence, the agreement could be renewed in its present form without compromising Canadian policy positions as US missile defence planning was still in its formative stages (Denholm Crosby, 1998: 87).

By 1996, when the agreement was again scheduled for renewal, the future had become the present. The US had had legislation and funding for its missile defence program in place for five years and the NORAD facilities in Colorado Springs had been providing US commands with much of the surveillance, warning, and communication information required for US security purposes in general, and in particular, for regional battle management purposes such as during the first Gulf War (Ibid.: 91). In recognition that the NORAD Agreement was the vehicle for Canadian participation in missile defences, it was rewritten to allow for Canada's formal participation in the future. In the meantime, the rewritten NORAD Agreement mandated NORAD military personnel at NORAD Headquarters, including Canadians, to work within other US commands in the Cheyenne Mountain Operations Center to perform NORAD duties and it is clearly stated in the rewritten agreement that "NORAD personnel performing NORAD duties in other commands may be called upon to support the mission of that command" (Canada, 1996: 3).[5] At that time, the United States Space Command and NORAD shared a Commander and headquarters space and both worked out of the Cheyenne Mountain complex in Colorado.

As General Joseph Ashy, Commander-in-Chief of both NORAD and United States Space Command, announced to the US Senate Armed Services Committee at the time of the signing of the 1996 NORAD Agreement, the new agreement established the NORAD Command as part of a "system of interdependent [US] commands that make important contributions to the security of the United States and Canada, and bring the power of space to US military operations worldwide" (Ashy, 1996). Despite the hyperbole, this is the mindset and projected reality in which NORAD, a Canadian Command, was grounded.

When the US military command system was reorganized in 2002, the US Space Command was merged with a new US Strategic Command, a command with a global mandate including missile defence. NORTHCOM assumed responsibility for continental missile defence operations, while the Commander of NORTHCOM was assigned to simultaneously be the Commander of NORAD. All three commands, plus the US Air Force Space Command, work out of the Cheyenne Mountain Operations Center. Under the terms of the 1996 NORAD Agreement, Canadian military personnel assigned to NORAD headquarters were mandated to perform NORAD duties within these other commands and to support their missions. Indeed, during the Iraq War, an initiative in which Canada chose not to participate, NORAD surveillance and warning information was transferred instantaneously to the US Central Command (CENTCOM) in Iraq, the command responsible for conducting the war. CENTCOM then operated the theatre missile interception system in the region. (Regehr, 2004a: 5).

Still, because NORAD's global surveillance and warning information was relayed to the military commands operating abroad, it was possible to maintain that Canadian military personnel at NORAD Headquarters were working in a passive situation with regard to missile defence. With an increasing focus on National Missile Defense in the US in 2002, the illusion of passivity could no longer be sustained. As Ernie Regehr (2004a: 1) explains, for continental missile defence;

… the early warning and assessment functions would have to be directly linked to the command and control of the missile defence interceptor forces. NORAD's tracking of the path of the incoming missile would in this case be the primary source of the coordinates that would be needed to direct the intercepting BMD missile toward the incoming attack missile. So, the NORAD warning and assessment functions would be virtually inseparable from the planned BMD interception functions.

Under these conditions, Canadian military participation in missile defence is effectively an overt activity.

The Liberal government entered into discussions with the US in May 2003 on possible Canadian participation in the North American missile defence program and in January 2004 there was an Exchange of Letters between the two governments establishing the basis of negotiations for participation through NORAD. Following these discussions, it was announced in August 2004 that the NORAD Agreement had been amended to allow NORAD to share its global missile surveillance and warning information with the "designated commands responsible for missile defence of North America," and that all other "provisions of the NORAD Agreement shall remain valid and effective."[6]

DFAIT was explicit about the amendment not constituting Canadian participation in the missile defence system, stating that "Allowing NORAD to share information on missile warning is not the same as participating in the US system: missile warning involves detecting missile launches and tracking their flights, while missile defence involves shooting down incoming missiles. US Northern Command (NORTHCOM) is responsible for the missile defence of the United States" (Canada, 2005). Yet, given Regehr's argument that missile tracking and interception cannot be separated, and putting the amendment together with the rewritten 1996 NORAD Agreement which mandates Canadian NORAD personnel to work within other US commands to perform NORAD duties, and in doing so to support the mission of those commands, the conditions are set for Canadian military personnel at NORAD Headquarters to fulfil the range of functions – including interception – required by continental missile defence within both NORAD and NORTHCOM.

Subsequently, the Liberal government announced in February 2005 that Canada would not participate in the US missile defence system (Pettigrew, 2005). It is difficult, however, to argue that the new NORAD Agreement reflects this position.

THE 2006 NORAD RENEWAL

On 8 May 2006, following a four hour debate on the issue in the House on 3 May, members of the House of Commons voted overwhelmingly (257 to 30) to renew the NORAD Agreement, the vehicle for Canadian participation in missile defences. The agreement was substantially rewritten for the renewal,[7] and the most apparent changes involve the addition of a maritime warning mandate, and the jettisoning of the requirement for periodic renewal. It is now an agreement in perpetuity to be reviewed by both governments every four years and to be amended as agreed upon at any time. As with previous agreements, it can be terminated by either government upon twelve months notice.

In terms of missile defence, the document contains mixed signals. As with the previous agreement, the primary missions for NORAD are "Aerospace warning for North America" and "Aerospace control for North America." Aerospace warning involves "processing, assessing, and disseminating intelligence and information related to man-made objects in the aerospace domain and the detection, validation, and warning of attack against North America whether by aircraft, missiles or space vehicles." Aerospace control involves "providing surveillance and exercising operational control of the airspace of Canada and the United States. Operational control is the authority to direct, coordinate, and control the operational activities of forces assigned, attached, or otherwise made available to NORAD." There is a clear distinction here between warning and control, with NORAD's control mandate being limited to activities in the airspace. Although there is no explicit statement in the document reflecting Canada's position of non-participation in missile defences, active participation would seem to be effectively denied by the agreement's mission statement.

However, in two ways, the new agreement actually increases Canadian participation in missile defence activities. First, it replaces the August 2004 amendment which allowed for NORAD's aerospace warning capabilities to be used "in support of the designated commands responsible for missile defence of North America," with a clause allowing NORAD's aerospace warning capabilities to be used in support of US missile defence activities in general, not just North American missile defence.

Second, the clause in the previous agreement that mandated Canadian military personnel assigned to NORAD to work within other US commands at the Cheyenne Mountain Operations Center to perform NORAD duties has been modified. In the new agreement, NORAD assigned personnel are mandated specifically to perform NORAD support functions for non-NORAD activities within other commands working out of the Operations Center. In the process, their mandate is to support the missions of those US commands "as appropriate." As noted earlier, those commands responsible for both global and non-NORAD continental missile defence activities are NORTHCOM, the US Strategic Command, and the US Air Force Space Command.

What is meant by "as appropriate" is not explained. It may mean that it is not appropriate for Canadian NORAD personnel to perform active support functions for non-NORAD activities in other US commands, that they are indeed confined to a passive role in terms of the processing and dissemination of aerospace warning intelligence and information. However, it may also not mean this. The document contains no reflection of Canada's policy position of non-participation in missile defence; it does not distinguish between US and Canadian NORAD personnel supporting the missions of other US commands; and it does not specify what is involved in the mandate to support the missions of those commands. In this regard, the document is more specifically permissive, rather than specifically restrictive, of Canadian military participation in US missile defence activity.

Under these conditions, Canadian 'non-participation' in the US missile defence system is a bit of a misnomer, or at least, it is very narrowly defined. Had the Conservatives been able to re-open the issue, there is very little more participation to be achieved. There is no need for Canadian territory for siting missile defence radars or interceptors (see

Calder, 2003), and as Ernie Regehr (2004a) argues, the US would not likely be interested in having their missile defence system placed under joint management, which would be the case if NORAD was to assume a missile interception role. What the US did want was a formal declaration of Canadian participation. Prior to Canada's decision, President Bush pressured for such a declaration during his visit to Canada in December 2004. In February 2005, after it was announced that Canada would not participate, the American ambassador, Paul Cellucci, expressed his country's displeasure with the decision. More recently, the present American ambassador, David Wilkins, explained that the US wants to build a global missile system and Canada's "formal participation" would "help sell the project internationally." Such an announcement, he added, would be largely symbolic (Curry, 2006).[8]

So too, it can be argued, was the Liberal government's announcement of non-participation, a position now also assumed by the new Conservative government. As Peter MacKay, the Conservative Minister of Foreign Affairs, argued during the Parliamentary debate on the renewal, "This country has made it clear that we have no intention of being part of this system [missile defence] ... . Norad [sic] ... is not involved in a US missile defence system" (House of Commons, 2006: 1830). Yet, NORAD's global surveillance, communication, and warning functions are vital supports of the US missile defence system in both its continental and global contexts, and Canadian military personnel assigned to NORAD have been mandated to work within and support the missions of the US commands responsible for both continental and global missile defences.

For a brief moment, it appeared that the issues involved in Canadian participation in the US missile defence system might have gone away, but instead, with the signing of the new NORAD Agreement, they are reinforced in that Canada is de facto participating; expanded in that participation is mandated on a global scope; entrenched in that the NORAD Agreement no longer requires renewal; and subverted by the illusion of non-participation maintained by both the Conservative minority government and the Liberal opposition. In short, the issues are still salient but far more difficult to address by those concerned. Such issues have been made invisible by the prevailing view that there is no clear missile intercept role assigned to the NORAD command, and Canada is accordingly not participating in missile defence. The following section highlights some of those issues and attempts to give an indication of the minority Conservative government's position on them as expressed, primarily, during the debate on the new NORAD Agreement in the House of Commons on 3 May 2006.

SUPPORT OF US FOREIGN POLICY

As a bi-national military command, NORAD activities have to be seen as reflecting elements of Canadian foreign policy. The NORAD command, however, is one part of a system of interdependent US commands designed to support American defence and foreign policy, including its present policy of pre-emptive war. Furthermore, the global missile defence system works to facilitate such policy. By its very nature then, NORAD institutionalizes Canadian support for US military and US foreign policy initiatives. This was most readily apparent when, despite the Canadian government's decision not to participate in the US war on Iraq, Canadian military personnel through NORAD performed key support functions for that war.

Such a disconnect between Canadian foreign policy and Canadian military activity will remain a possibility unless the Canadian government decides to either retire its membership in the command, or design its foreign and defence policy to reflect US interests. The first option is not even in the range of thinkable alternatives for the Conservatives. As Peter MacKay put it, "I suggest that nobody believes it would be in Canada's interest to withdraw from Norad [sic]" (House of Commons, 2006: 2000).

The second option is not outside the realm of possibility given the Final Report of the Canada-United States Bi-National Planning Group, a committee established by the Canadian and US governments in 2002 as a forum for joint Canada-US planning for continental defence and security. The Report recommends the creation of a Canada-United States "Comprehensive Defense and Security Agreement," the goal being "to achieve the level (although not necessarily the form) of cooperation that now exists in NORAD in all other domains." Such an agreement would be designed to "bring unity of effort and direction to each of the defence, security and foreign policy organizations, including NORAD" (Canada and United States, 2006: i). During the House debate, the Conservative Minister of National Defence Gordon O'Connor said that although the Bi-National Planning Group's term had expired, a number of organizations will be taking up its work (House of Commons, 2006: 1845).[9]

Hence, efforts to integrate and institutionalize Canadian and US defence, security, and foreign policy interests are afoot. The new Conservative government's Speech from the Throne committed the government to submitting "significant international treaties for vote in Parliament" (Canada, 2006: 11). In keeping with this commitment to openness and transparency on security and defence issues, the implications of Canada's membership in the bi-national NORAD command, as well as any steps taken to advance the recommendations of the Bi-National Group's Final Report, should be the subjects of informed public discussion.

A SEAT AT THE TABLE

Many analysts, if not most, argue that NORAD supplies Canada with a much needed 'seat at the table' and hence, access to US intelligence, to US defence planning for the continent, and a position from which to influence US decision-making. This was also a central theme of the House debate on 3 May. The history of NORAD, however, is a history of the US influencing Canada, rather than the other way around. It was US influence that brought nuclear weapons to Canadian soil in 1963, that saw the removal of the ABM Clause from the NORAD Agreement in 1981, that brought the testing of US cruise missiles over Canadian territory in the 1980s and on into the 1990s, and that has now involved Canada in missile defence and may still involve the country in the weaponization of space.[10] Each of these activities involved, or will involve in the case of space weapons, a reversal of previously held government policy preferences, and taken together they indicate exactly what one would expect in relations between a strong and a weaker state – it is the weaker state that is more apt to be influenced than the stronger.

Besides, there are other 'seats at the table' that could achieve similar objectives. At present, the Permanent Joint Board on Defence and the Military Cooperative Committee exist for mutual consultation and the sharing of defence planning and information. Canada also has access to US intelligence and planning, including for the North American continent, through its membership in NATO. There too, Canadian influence on US decision-making can be exercised in concert with other NATO members. It is also possible to devise and create any number of bilateral Canada-US protocols, committees, and agreements that cover the full range of information and intelligence sharing for land, sea, and aerospace surveillance and warning functions, and for the training of Canadian and US forces for mutual operational support purposes (see Regehr, 2006: 4).

There is little doubt that a seat at the table is important, but whether that table needs to be within a bi-national military command is a subject for the kind of informed public discussion to which the Conservative government has registered its commitment.

SPACE WEAPONIZATION
AND ARMS CONTROL

The US has long-range plans to develop an array of space-based weapons for their missile defence programs including space-based interceptors for which they hope to deploy a test bed in space by 2012. However nebulous and technologically challenging these plans may be at the moment, the Bush Administration, reflecting continuing efforts along these lines since the early 1980s, has been clear in its intention to use space as an operational arena for military combat. Historically, Canada has unambiguously supported the international norm opposing the weaponization of space and has worked within UN disarmament committees to convert this norm into law. However, the Letters of Intent exchanged to establish the basis for negotiating Canadas participation in NORAD did not raise the issue of space weaponry. Rather, they stated that "the technical extent of protection afforded by the US ballistic missile defence system will evolve over time," and that "our bilateral co-operation in this area should also evolve" (Canada, 2004).

The new NORAD Agreement also acknowledges "that space has become an important dimension of national interest and ... that a growing number of nations have acquired or have ready access to space services that could be used for strategic or tactical purposes against the interests of Canada and the United States." On the one hand, this statement simply provides justification for NORAD's aerospace surveillance and warning functions. On the other hand, however, it also provides a basis for the evolution of "bilateral cooperation in this area." This concern was raised in the House debate by Alexa McDonough, the NDP member for Halifax, but it was not addressed directly by the minister of foreign affairs (House of Commons, 2006: 2005).

A further pressure to reverse Canada's position on the weaponization of space potentially resides with both major parties' interest in protecting the Canadian defence production industry. The Letters of Intent, signed by the preceding Liberal government, propose pursuing avenues of increased "industry-to-industry cooperation on missile defence." Similarly, the Harper government has also expressed a strong interest in ensuring that the "Canadian defence industry has access to the United States defence procurement market" (Conservative Party of Canada, 2005).

In any case, the prospects for an agreement on the Prevention of an Arms Race in Outer Space at the UN are dim in a security environment that advances missile defence. Addtionally, there are a number of international arms control issues that are complicated by such an environment. Specifically, the retiring of the ABM Treaty, a necessary condition for deployment of the US national missile defence system, was followed by Russian announcements that it was no longer bound by the Strategic Arms Reduction Treaty and that it had tested a new generation of ballistic missiles capable of avoiding ballistic missile defence (BMD) detection. China too is developing BMD countermeasures and has plans to increase its long-range ballistic missiles from 20 to 60 by 2010 (Regehr, 2004b). Indeed, the US missile defence program in its totality provides incentives for states and terrorists alike to develop a full range of missile defence-immune weapons, and in so doing to challenge the Missile Technology Control Regime, the Hague Code of Conduct on Ballistic Missiles, the Nuclear Non-Proliferation Treaty, the Biological and Toxin Weapons Convention, and the Chemical Weapons Convention. These are all areas of Canada's non-proliferation and arms control interests and activities.

It may be that Canada can maintain its membership in a bi-national command that performs vital functions for the US global missile defence system and at the same time work effectively in the international arms control fora that are seriously challenged by that same missile defence system. This contradiction, however, should be fully explored in the kind of informed public discussion involving significant international treaties that the Conservative government promised in its April 2006 Speech from the Throne.

SECURITY OR PROVOCATION?

As noted earlier, the land-based missile defence system presently being deployed in Alaska and California is designed to intercept and destroy an accidental or hostile launch of a limited number of long-range ballistic missiles in either in space or at high altitudes. The missile threat to the continent is hardly palpable given that the countries that are deemed 'hostile' in this context do not have a long-range ballistic missile capability now or for the foreseeable future.[11] Further, although there have been some successes in the testing of the system's intercept capability, these have been under highly controlled experimental conditions that have little resemblance to battle conditions. There have been no tests of the system as a whole and indeed, the Alaska and California sites now being prepared are meant to be test beds before they are considered defence installations. As Ernie Regehr (2004c: 2) points out, the system offers only "theoretical protection from a theoretical threat."

There is also no scientific consensus as to what will happen to the warhead on the attacking missile if intercept takes place and this is particularly worrisome if the missile is carrying a nuclear weapon (Calder, 2003). Will the warhead simply be destroyed, as some suggest, or will an intercept result in a nuclear explosion? Where would such an explosion occur, in space, at high altitudes, or on the ground if the warhead survives? What effects would these types of explosions have? Definitive answers to these questions are not known.

In terms of provocation, and quite apart from issues of weapons proliferation, the US missile defence system in its entirety is designed to project and protect US power worldwide, and as such, it enables the US to shape global and regional security environments to suit its own interests, including its economic interests. This is provocative on at least two counts. First, it seriously compromises the ability of peoples, particularly non-western peoples, to define for themselves what constitutes their security and to pursue that definition within a environment that enables negotiation and cooperation.

And second, the forces of the global market have been propelled by the western industrialized countries, led by the US. These forces have produced insecurities for vast numbers of the world's peoples. They have contributed to the growing economic gap between the 'have' and the 'have-not' peoples both within and among states, and they have propelled the processes of environmental degradation and resource depletion. As such, they are also complicit in the range of insecurities that are produced by poverty, economic and political instability, and competition for resources, including internal state conflicts, disease, human rights abuses, mass movements of peoples, and terrorism. This is what Lloyd Axworthy (1999), as minister of foreign affairs in the Chrétien Liberal government, described as "the dark underside" of globalization.

American military power is also complicit in this regard. As Joel Sokolsky writes, "In seeking to protect itself by sustaining its dominant military position in the world, the United States makes possible the stable international environment that all but eliminates any major challenge to the security of the West. And in so doing, it provides the basis for global trade and the whole panoply of commercial relations" (Sokolsky, 2005: 313). When US military power is used to secure the economic interests of the west, and when those economic interests produce insecurities for others, then the systems that allow the projection of that power can be seen as provocative in that they reinforce relations of inequity amongst the world's peoples.

The issue of Canada's membership in a bi-national military command designed to facilitate the projection of US power worldwide should be, as per Conservative government commitments, subjected to an informed public discussion about how security is defined in a missile defence context, who exactly is being secured by these defence systems, and at what costs to others.

INFORMING CANADIANS ABOUT NORAD AND MISSILE DEFENCE

The above issues, it has been suggested, need to be addressed through informed public discussion. Although a public discussion of these issues is not difficult to mount, and indeed, such discussions influenced Martin's Liberal government to take its 'non-participation' decision, an informed discussion is difficult to come by. Apart from public debates in the late 1950s and early 1960s about Canadian forces having access to US nuclear weapons stored in Canada for Canada's air defence role within NORAD, and again in the mid-1980s when public controversy surrounding SDI and Canada's possible participation in that program, Canadians have been poorly informed about NORAD issues. Indeed, even in those two instances, independent researchers and journalists provided the primary source of comprehensive and reliable information, not the Canadian government (see Denholm Crosby, 1998: 145–94). In the post-Cold War era, the Canadian government has also been a particularly poor source of information about NORAD and missile defences, with the 1996 NORAD renewal being the most egregious case in point.

As described earlier, the agreement was completely rewritten for the 1996 renewal and was seen, by Canadian and American officials alike, as the vehicle for future Canadian participation in the developing national and global US missile defence programs. There were no public hearings prior to the renewal, as had occurred with most renewals during the Cold War, and although Parliament discussed the renewal, it did so without access to copies of the new agreement. The only new information presented to the House of Commons for discussion was that it was "a substantially revised agreement" but that there was "no anti-ballistic missile system in any way connected to this NORAD Agreement" (Axworthy, 1996). Moreover, the parliamentary debate on the issue took place on 11 March 1996 by which time the new agreement had already been prepared for signing on 28 March.[12] So, the House debate was both uninformed and too late to matter.

When the agreement was again renewed in 2000, a year earlier than scheduled and this time approved for a period of six years instead of the usual five, it was simply announced after the fact, as was the August 2004 amendment. When the Liberal government announced this amendment, it also stated that any Canadian decision to participate further in the US missile defence program would not be undertaken without the input of Parliament, a position subsequently reflected by the Conservative government. The Conservatives, however, despite the House debate on 3 May 2006, have continued in the post-Cold War Liberal tradition of keeping the Canadian public less than fully informed.

It was from the US State Department, not the Canadian government, that members of the House learned that the new NORAD Agreement had actually been signed by the Minister of National Defence Gordon O'Connor and the US Ambassador to Canada David Wilkins, in Ottawa on 28 April 2006, six days before the House debate (House of Commons,

2006: 1950). The agreement, however, was not to take effect until an exchange of notes between the two governments indicating the completion of related internal procedures had occurred. The agreement was tabled in the House two days before the debate, giving very little time for parliamentarians to consider the implications of the document and, in any case, the vote was to be an "accept or reject vote," or in the present parlance of the House, an "up or down" vote. There could be no discussion of possible amendments to the agreement and requests for a short term renewal to allow full consideration of the issues involved were denied on the basis that the old agreement was due to expire on 12 May (Ibid.: 2000). During the debate, neither the Liberals nor the Conservatives, the two parties with hands-on experience of the terms of the new agreement, broached the subject of the degree of participation in the US missile defence system afforded Canada by the document, nor was there a discussion of what constituted non-participation.

Without being fully informed as to the vital role NORAD's surveillance, communication, and warning functions play in support of the US continental and global missile defence system, and with public assurances that Canada is not participating in these systems, the Canadian public is left with a general understanding that missile defences are somehow disconnected from NORAD. In the absence of a full and informed discussion of the range of issues involved and their implications, they are also left thinking that renewing the NORAD Agreement is really only about unproblematically maintaining cheap defence, a seat at the table, and a tradition of cooperation with the US. It may be that continuing the arrangement is to Canada's benefit, but this should be the subject of a public discussion that is considerably better informed by the Canadian government than such discussions have been in the past.

CONCLUSION

During the Cold War, a joint Canada-US military command for the air/aerospace defence of the continent arguably made sense, given Canada's geographical position between the and the US, and the Canadian government's support of the US policy of nuclear deterrence. It is not clear that such a command makes sense in the post-Cold War era, particularly in the context of the US missile defence system. The issue of Canadian participation in that system is, at the same time, the issue of Canada's continued membership in the bi-national NORAD military command. It is through this command that Canada performs vital support functions for missile defences in both its continental and global contexts, and it is through this command that Canadian military personnel assigned to NORAD are mandated to perform duties in support of non-NORAD activities within the US continental and global missile defence system and, in so doing, to support the mission of the program. In this way, Canadian support of US foreign policy initiatives that depend upon the activities of the US military has been institutionalized.

However, as the Liberal government's decision to not participate in the Iraq War indicates, Canada does not automatically support US foreign policy or military initiatives. The Conservative government's support of Canada's position of non-participation in the US missile defence system as expressed during the House debate, however narrowly that is defined, also indicates a degree of policy independence for Canada. It might, therefore, be time to rethink membership in a military command that is designed to act in concert with other US commands in support of US foreign policy and military initiatives, including its continental missile defence system that is, at the same time, a global missile defence system.[13]

The challenge for the minority Conservative government in this regard is twofold. To reflect its commitments in the Speech from the Throne, it needs to mount a public discussion conducive to such rethinking, and second, it needs to ensure that that public discussion is well informed. This is not likely to happen. The House debate on 3 May was indicative of the Conservative government's unwillingness to commit the time, or to disseminate the information required for a fully informed public discussion of the issue. The NDP voted against renewing the NORAD agreement largely for these reasons. The other parties, however, including the Bloc Québécois, a party that has been most adamant and persistent in its pursuit of Canadian non-participation in missile defence, voted for renewal. Hence, the issue is effectively off the government's agenda for now, and because the agreement no longer requires a periodic renewal, for the foreseeable future. The issue, then, offers no constraints for the minority Conservative government.

The overwhelming House support for the NORAD renewal, however, reinforces the perception that the US missile defence system and the NORAD command are discrete areas of activity. It also reinforces the process whereby defence programs that are introduced to Canada through the NORAD command eventually become policy in the country, compromising previously held policy positions in the process. Efforts to gain Canadian participation in the US missile defence system have been afoot since the mid-1990s and, apart from a public declaration, the degree of participation sought has now been achieved.

There is little doubt that, in the same manner, the issue of Canada's participation in the weaponization of space will be on the agenda in about ten years. By that time, if history repeats itself, Canada's ability to distance itself from US space defence systems will have been compromised by NORAD's inevitable involvement in the evolution of space-based systems, by any support the government may have given the Canadian defence production industry in contracting to these systems, and by a continuing government refusal to provide the conditions for a meaningful public exploration of viable alternatives to membership in a bi-national military command for Canadian aerospace security.

NOTES

Parts of this paper were presented at the conference "Canada and the New American Empire," hosted by the Centre for Global Studies, University of Victoria, 26–8 November 2004.

1 For a full history of the US missile defence interests from the inception of the Cold War until 1996, see Denholm Crosby (1998).
2 See the NORTHCOM website at <http://www.northcom.mil>; and Lagrasse (2003).
3 For details of these and other missile defence programs see MDA (2005).
4 This reason was given by Joe Clark as the Secretary of State for External Affairs in the Mulroney Conservative government. For details, see Denholm Crosby (1998: 78).
5 The rewritten agreement also contains a clause that allows for amending the agreement without going through a renewal process, and hence the August 2004 amendment.
6 Text of Amendment is available at: <http://www.fac-aec.gc.ca/department/note_0095-en.asp>
7 The agreement is available at: <http://www.treaty-accord.gc.ca>
8 The Deputy Commander of NORAD said, during an interview with the author in June 1995, that Canadian participation was being sought because it would lend credibility to the program and help reduce any "liability associated with the product." For the context, see Denholm Crosby (1998: 93–4).
9 The primary organizations Minister O'Connor referred to are Canada Command, NORTHCOM and, as the Final Report mentions, Public Safety and Emergency Preparedness Canada.
10 For details see Denholm Crosby (1998: 38–55) for the nuclear weapon issue; (73–90) for the ABM clause removal and cruise missile testing; (90–105) for missile defences.
11 For an exploration of the pro and con arguments on the issues raised in this section see Hildreth (2005).
12 The final draft of the new agreement was actually ready for signatures by November 1995, the date on the copy sent to the author by NORAD Headquarters in Colorado Springs.
13 As an example of this rethinking, Regehr (2006) offers four alternatives to the NORAD command.

REFERENCES

Ashy, Joseph W. 1996. Testimony of General Ashy to the Senate Armed Services Committee, 21 March. Washington, DC: Federal Document Clearing House.

Axworthy, Lloyd. 1996. *House of Commons Debates*, 35th Parliament, 2nd Session, 11 March. Available at: <http://www.parl.gc.ca/35/2/parlbus/chambus/house/debates/010_96-03-11/010GO1E.html#495>

– 1999. Message from the Minister of Foreign Affairs to The Hague Appeal for Peace, The Hague, Netherlands, 13 May.

Calder, Kenneth. 2003. Testimony of the Assistant Deputy Minister (Policy), DND, to the Standing Committee on National Defence and Veterans Affairs, Ottawa, 13 February.

Canada. 1968. "NORAD Agreement," *Canada Treaty Series 1968*, no. 5. Ottawa: Department of External Affairs.

– 1996. "NORAD Agreement," *Canada Treaty Series 1996*, no. 36. Ottawa: Department of Foreign Affairs and International Trade.

– 2004. "Letters Exchanged on Missile Defence," *Department of National Defence*, January. 12 May 2006. Available at: <http://www.forces.gc.ca/site/Focus/Canada-us/letter-e.asp>

– 2005. "The Basics: Missile Defence Facts and Definitions," *Department of Foreign Affairs and International Trade*, 15 June. 12 May 2006. Available at <http://www.dfait-maeci.gc.ca/foreign_policy/missile-defence-en.asp>

– 2006. *Canada's New Government: Turning a New Leaf.* Speech from the Throne. Ottawa: Office of the Governor General, 4 April.

Canada and United States. 2006. *Final Report on Canada-United States Enhanced Military Cooperation.* Peterson Air Force Base, CO: Bi-National Planning Group, 13 March.

Cirincione, Joseph. 2005. "The Declining Ballistic Missile Threat, 2005," *Policy Outlook*, The Carnegie Endowment for International Peace (February).

Conservative Party of Canada. 2005. "National Defence and Security," *Policy Declaration*, 19 March, 40–2. Available at: <http://www.conservative.ca/media/20050319-POLICY%20DECLARATION.pdf>

Curry, Bill. 2006. "U.S. Puts Missile Defence Talks on Ice, Ambassador Says," *Globe and Mail*, 24 February. Available at: <http://www.globeandmail.com>

Denholm Crosby, Ann. 1998. *Dilemmas in Defence Decision-Making: Constructing Canada's Role in NORAD, 1958–96.* Hampshire: Macmillan Press.

Hildreth, Steven A. 2005. "Missile Defense: The Current Debate," A Congressional Research Service Report for Congress, 19 July.

House of Commons. 2006. *Debates*, 39th Parliament, 1st Session, 3 May. Available at: <http://www.parl.gc.ca/39/1/parlbus/chambus/house/debates/015_2006-05-03/HAN015-E.htm>

Lagrasse, Phillippe. 2003. "NORAD, NorthCom, and the Bi-National Planning Group: The Evolution of Canada-US Defence Relations – Part 1," *Canadian American Strategic Review* (July). Available at <http://www.sfu.ca/casr/ft-lagasse1.htm>

Missile Defense Agency (MDA). 2005. "A Day in the Life of the BMDS," *BMDS Booklet*, 3rd ed. Washington: Missile Defense Agency. Available at: <http://www.mda.mil>

Pettigrew, Pierre. 2005. Address by the Minister of Foreign Affairs to the House of Commons, Ottawa, 24 February. Available at: <http://w01.international.gc.ca/minpub/Publication.asp?publication_id=382190&Language=E>

Radio Canada. 2006. "Le point des chefs: Stephen Harper," *Téléjournal*, 12 January.

Regehr, Ernie. 2004a. "BMD, NORAD, and Canada-US Security Relations," Project Ploughshares, *Briefing* 04, no. 4 (March). Available at: <http://www.ploughshares.ca/libraries/Briefings/brf044.pdf>

– 2004b. "BMD and Arms Control Implications," Project Ploughshares, *Briefing* 04, no. 2 (March). Available at: <http://www.ploughshares.ca/libraries/Briefings/brf042.pdf>

– 2004c. "Ballistic Missile Defence and Canada=s Vital Security Interests," Project Ploughshares, *Briefing* 04, no. 5 (June). Available at: <http://www.ploughshares.ca/libraries/Briefings/brf045.pdf>

– 2006. "NORAD Renewal: Considerations for the Parliamentary Debate," Project Ploughshares, *Briefing* 06, no. 4 (May). Available at: <http://www.ploughshares.ca/libraries/Briefings/brf064.pdf>

Sokolsky, Joel J. 2005. "Between a Rock and a Soft Place: The Geopolitics of Canada-US Security Relations," in Hugh Segal, ed. *Geopolitical Integrity*. Montreal: The Institute for Research on Public Policy.

PART THREE

Minor Priorities and Prior Minorities?

CHRISTINA GABRIEL

Immigration policy and politics is located at the intersection of international and domestic realms. The right to control the entry and exit of persons to a territory and the distinction between nationals and non-nationals is a critical aspect of state sovereignty. The governance of international migration is shaped by relations between states and is the subject of joint state actions (Weiner, 2006: 96–9). This said, immigration policy is also squarely situated within the realm of domestic politics as immigration affects population demographics, labour market dynamics and the provision of social goods. This chapter reviews some key directions in Canadian immigration policy since 1993 in relation to broader trends within the field of migration policy. Specifically, it examines the Canadian points based selection model, frequently held up as an exemplar for other countries, and suggests that it enshrines an increasing tension. On the international level the model selects 'the best and brightest' people – the skilled – often from countries that can ill afford to lose them, while on the domestic front there is increasing evidence to suggest that recent immigrants experience significant labour market disadvantages.

The latter issue has come to the fore and informs public discussions on immigration directions. To the extent that Canada continues to focus on skilled migration, whether permanent or temporary, a number of policy issues need to be addressed including how should these migrants be selected; should skilled migration be prioritized within the program; what mechanisms, if any, should be put in place to allow temporary workers to become permanent residents; and lastly, and importantly, what can the state do to ensure effective labour market integration for immigrant workers? Recent announcements suggest that the new minority government will take up some of these matters as part of its domestic agenda. However, the broader issues associated with selective migration policy or what is sometimes termed "brain picking" (Ramamurthy, 2003:12), such as which migrants will be able to access citizenship rights and the socio-economic impacts on source countries of emigration, will continue to remain sidelined.

PART I: MIGRATION AND THE
INTERNATIONAL ARENA-GLOBAL
TRENDS AND CHALLENGES

International migration has emerged as a key political issue in the post Cold War period for states in the global economic North (Castles, 2002: 1143). Here, as Myron Weiner (2006: 98) has emphasized, a relational approach to the analysis of migration is important, as it addresses "how states make their access and entry rules, how states influence one another in shaping these rules, and how these rules in turn affect the relations between states." Within this international context a number of common trends have emerged that have an impact on migration politics and the trajectory of national immigration policies. Three trends are particularly noteworthy.

Global Flows of People

The United Nations (2002: 2) reports that 175 million people (or 3 percent of the world's population) live in a country other than the nation of their birth. While large cross border flows of people are not new, analysts have suggested that the significance of this contemporary movement rests in the fact that it tends to be directed towards certain areas. UN data, for example, demonstrates that net growth in the migrant population took place in more developed areas of the world while the migrant population of less developed regions declined (Ibid.). Stephen Castles, for example, has pointed out that these flows are an important factor in social transformation with the developed world far more affected by immigration than developing countries (Castles, 2002: 1147). This uneven distribution of international migrants is captured in recent UN figures: "In 2000 they [international migrants] constituted 8.7 percent of the population in developed countries, while they accounted for just 1.5 percent in developing countries" (United Nations, 2002: 11).

Analysts have outlined the ways in which migratory pressures on people in countries of the South have increased. Differences in wealth and flows of capital underscore the gap between countries in the North and South. The motivations to migrate from countries in the economic South, as Daiva Stasiulis and Abby Bakan argue, are rooted in histories of colonialism, imperialism, and poverty. But, as they go on to emphasize, these factors are further complicated by neoliberal globalization, liberalization and structural adjustment. Simultaneously states in the global economic North, with more developed welfare states and higher wages, have moved toward more selective policies and stricter entry and control measures (Stasiulis and Bakan, 2003: 25–7). This said, there has been some recognition that action must be directed at the 'root causes' of mass migration by improving the social and economic conditions in sending countries. Stephen Castles and Mark Miller (1998: 100–1) identify foreign aid as having the potential to improve the conditions of people and thereby reducing the incentive to emigrate. However, they argue, "if it is to help reduce migration, future aid policy will have to be much more concerned with social and demographic issues."

The flows of people raise a range of political, social and economic policy issues for nations in the global economic North. While many of these countries have moved to liberalise trade and investment rules to permit the freer movement of goods and services the same logic does not necessarily apply to the movement of all persons.

Changing Demographics

Immigration debates are also linked to the broader concern of demographic change, as many countries in the global economic North are confronted with declining birth rates and ageing populations. What comes to the fore here is the issue of replacement migration, defined as "the international migration that would be needed to offset declines in the size of population, the declines in population of working age, as well as to offset the overall ageing of the population" (United Nations, 2000: 1). According to UN projections, the population of Japan and virtually all countries in Europe are expected to decrease over the next 50 years, while at the same time experiencing a rapid ageing process (Ibid.). Although there is variation in these projections, these same broad demographic trends are evident in Canada. Consider for example, the findings of a study using Statistics Canada data (Dolin and Young, 2004: 6):

– Canada's fertility rate was 1.51 in 2001 ... At current fertility rates, deaths are predicted to exceed births in Canada in 20–25 years. At that point immigration would account for all population growth;

- In the first half of the 1990s, immigration accounted for 70 percent of net labour force growth;
- By 2011 immigration is expected to account for all net labour market
  growth.

International migration itself is not necessarily *the* solution to declining
and ageing populations but within this context the question as to what
is an 'appropriate' immigration level to help address demographic
changes becomes more salient.

Migrant Categories

International migration flows are also differentiated by category – labour, family related and humanitarian/refugee. Thus immigration policy addresses, either implicitly or explicitly, the question of whom to let
in and relatedly what the mix between these categories should be. Increasingly, the response to these questions is shaped by an emphasis on
the need to attract skilled workers[1] to address the imperatives of a globalizing economy. As the *Economist* put it: "Already, many governments have realized that the market for top talent is global and
competitive. Led by Canada and Australia they are redesigning immigration policies not just to admit, but actively to attract high skilled immigrants" and goes on to suggest "that the case for attracting the
highly skilled is fast becoming conventional wisdom" (Cairncross,
2002: 4). Consequently, even as many countries in the global economic
North move to enact tighter control policies toward some groups of
migrants, they are easing regulations to attract and facilitate the entry
of those people designated as skilled. Mobility rights and the privilege
to access citizenship in developed countries is increasingly limited by
very selective immigration policies.

Canada's Selection Model and the Phenomenon
of Managed Migration

Canada pioneered a points based model in the late 1960s to select independent applicants, or what are now referred to as skilled workers,
within the economic component of the program.[2] Initially, under this
system points were awarded in nine categories including education,
age, employment opportunities in Canada, official language ability and
suitability. The heaviest weighting was in the occupation and skill categories. Applicants had to obtain a pass mark of 50 out of 100 in order
to be eligible (Knowles, 1997: 158). Since that time the model and its
occupational classification system have been fine-tuned a number of

times (Foster, 1998: 69–75). The introduction of a points based model represented a departure from the explicit discriminatory elements that characterized previous Canadian policy. The Chrétien Liberal government retained a points model when it introduced the Immigration Refugee Protection Act (IRPA) in 2001. The new model emphasized official language ability, education, and work experience. Additionally, the list of preferred occupations was eliminated in favour of flexible, transferable skills (Rekai, 2002: 4–5). This rationale is intimately connected to the view that national immigration policy has a role to play in maintaining a country's economic competitiveness in a globalizing world. As David Stewart-Patterson (2005: 14), Executive Vice President of the Canadian Council of Chief Executives, stated:

By adding to both to the quantity and quality of our labour force, immigration helps to increase the competitiveness of Canada's economy. Indeed, Canada's strong flow of immigration from many different countries may provide one of our countries most important competitive advantages in an increasingly global economy.

The most recent incarnation of the selection model is compatible with this view and has been characterized as the "human capital approach" (Dolin and Young, 2004: 17). Human capital theory is based on the assumption that a person's education and training is an individual 'investment,' and according to this rationale will provide a return, in the form of higher wages, in the labour market. The rationale "that links earning to human capital has been adopted to evaluate the productivity and potential economic contribution to Canada of immigrants" (Li, 2003: 100–1). While it can be argued that a human capital approach has always informed the points based selection system, within the current model the logic is much more pronounced:

Under the original point system, of the total 100 points used in evaluating prospective economic immigrants, 20 points were assigned to the category 'education and training', and another 10 points to 'occupational skill' ... Under the new immigration regulations announced in June 2002, as much as 70 points can be given to economic immigrant workers ... on the basis of formal education, official language capacity, and work experience. (Ibid.: 102)

A number of criticisms can be directed at the workings of the selection model and the way in which gender, race and class exclusions find expression (Abu-Laban and Gabriel, 2002). Firstly, the model privileges those individuals who have the opportunity and financial means to obtain the appropriate education and training, and whose resulting credentials are recognized in Canada (Ibid.: 50). A second and related issue is the assessment of skill which, while at the heart of the selection model, is problematic and tends to be premised on formal education. Tradespeople, for example, might not be classified as "highly skilled" despite their specific expertise whereas "university graduates with some types of degree may have few marketable skills" but still receive that designation (Gent and Skeldon, 2006: 2). Gender also comes into play. Depending on the gender relations in the country of origin women may not be able to access higher formal education or training. The definition of high skill itself is gendered – much of what counts as 'women's' work is not usually considered skilled work. Further the points system does not offer points for women's unpaid work whether it be childcare, voluntary work or participation in family run businesses (Abu-Laban and Gabriel, 2002: 50–2; Gabriel, 2004: 172). Additionally, as will be illustrated in the next section, the points based selection model is not necessarily an indicator of immigrant success in terms of either labour market integration or earnings advantage.

This said, the Canadian points based selection model is often held up as an exemplar for the selection of migrants, and has influenced immigration policy in other countries. Australia adopted a similar scheme in the 1970s. Today many European states look to 'countries of immigration' for lessons on how to manage and set levels for migration (Kofman, 2005: 457). Canada's selection model is of particular interest to Britain and Germany (Cairncross, 2002: 7). In Britain, for example, the Blair government recently unveiled proposals for a new points based system of selection. In its White Paper, *A Points-Based System: Making Migration Work for Britain*, the Home Secretary Charles Clarke stated; "The UK needs a world class migration system to attract the brightest and the best from across the world, while at the same time being more robust against abuse" (United Kingdom, 2006: iv). The White Paper outlines proposals for a five-tier points framework.

Tier 1: Highly skilled individuals to contribute to growth and productivity.
Tier 2: Skilled workers with a job offer to fill gaps in the UK labour force.
Tier 3: Limited numbers of low skilled workers needed to fill specific temporary labour shortages.
Tier 4: Students.
Tier 5: Youth mobility and temporary workers: people allowed to work in the UK for a limited period of time to satisfy non-economic objectives. (Ibid.: 15)

People within Tier 1 and 2 will have the opportunity to settle in the UK while those entering under Tiers 3–5, temporary categories, are expected to return to their home countries and will not be allowed to switch tiers. The exception will be for persons in Tier 4 as the Home Office acknowledges it might be desirable to retain some of these students for the UK workforce (Ibid.). Whether we are talking about Canada's current system to select economic migrants or Britain's proposed changes to its selection process, the emphasis is on attracting 'the best and the brightest' people and this is equated unproblematically with skilled migrants. However, despite the prevailing orthodoxy, the composition of the best and brightest is still a political question.

A number of consequences flow from this rationale which privileges those migrants designated as "skilled" in a globalizing economy. Referring to the European case, Eleonore Kofman has argued that the ability to migrate and ultimately access citizenship is increasingly being limited to the high skilled. She argues that states are pursuing a policy in which different categories of migrants and asylum seekers have different rights of entry, residence and access to citizenship as a result of a managerialist approach which "applies an economic and political calculus not only to labour migration but also to forms of migration more closely aligned to normative principles and human rights, such as family formation and reunification and asylum" (Kofman, 2005: 453). The privileging of skilled migration results in the concomitant devaluing of those perceived to be not as desirable, such as the less skilled. The latter are constructed as possible drains on social programs and as direct competitors with national workers (Ibid.: 458). Yet it should be noted that the work of those constructed as low skilled is in fact integral to the functioning of the global economy despite the overvalorization of the high skilled (Sassen, 1998: 86–9). For example, there are critical shortages in work associated with social reproduction such as childcare, eldercare, household services, nursing, and other healthcare work prompting the movement of women migrants from South to North (Maher, 2004).

In Canada, despite the stated emphasis on skilled economic migrants, public debate has not directly addressed the issue of who should be classified as a potentially desirable future citizen. As the Maytree Foundation (2001: 5–6) told a Parliamentary Standing Committee in 2001:

We often hear about Canada's need to compete with other countries for the world's best educated, most skilled, wealthiest immigrants. But why should we restrict "economic" migration to these; why not expand our focus to include anyone who truly wants to adopt this country as their home and who has the skills and ability to land on their feet?

Additionally, the attempt to attract 'the best and the brightest' raises other questions about the often unequal relations between sending and host countries. In other words, while it might be desirable for skilled individuals to migrate on the basis of personal advantage or professional considerations, their mobility is facilitated through migration policies, such as Canada's or Australia's, that actively seek to recruit skilled workers (Stalker, 2000: 108). The movement of skilled workers raises the broader issue of 'brain drain.' This phenomenon, which has been studied since the 1960s, generally refers to the "exodus of skilled professionals from developing to developed countries" (Ramamurthy, 2003: 56). It has been reported that more than 40 percent of the Caribbean's university educated cohort live in a member country of the Organisation of Economic Co-operation and Development (Reynolds, 2005) and that Africa in particular has suffered the loss of professionals, many of whom are health workers (Stalker, 2000: 107). The United States, Britain, Canada, and Australia figure prominently among the destination countries receiving doctors from Africa and the Caribbean (*Migration News*, 2006). The loss of skilled workers from the global economic. South may have considerable repercussions in the countries they leave behind. For example, of the 16 countries (over 5 million people) with "more than one quarter of their educated population abroad, seven fall within the United Nations category of 'low human development'. Excluding Haiti, six of these seven are in sub Saharan Africa" (Gent and Skeldon, 2006: 3). In their work on the consequences of skilled emigration, Devesh Kapur and John McHale (2005: A17) argue that "since the most sought-after immigrants are also the ones most capable of driving institutional development at home 'creaming' the most talented, especially from small, poor countries, risks undermining their political and economic development." They also question the view that remittances sent home offset this loss by pointing out "countries that receive the most remittances relative to the size of their economy from Haiti to Somalia – have not developed as a result." Among the measures Kapur and McHale advocate is the active fostering of circular migration through the use of temporary visas, portable pensions and incentives to return to the country of origin.

In Canada, the debate around the brain drain has taken a particular form. Specifically, the chief concerns are not around the way in which Canadian immigration policy may or may not be implicated in poaching skilled workers from developing countries or what strategies Canada should pursue at the international level to develop an ethical approach to skilled migration. Canada's attempt to fast track the applications of health care workers from other countries to address shortages in the health field, for example, is not the subject of sustained debate. But rather, the public debate has been dominated by the perceived loss of Canada's own professionals and skilled workers to other countries, most notably the United States (DeVoretz, 1999; Iqbal, 1999; Zhao et al., 2000). As a result, the ethical issues attached to brain drain have been downplayed in public debate.

At the international level, the governance of migration in the global economic North is increasingly shaped by South to North cross border mobility, and demographic challenges and policies that seek to attract desired individuals such as skilled workers while actively policing borders against those categories of migrant viewed as less desirable. The attempt to actively select economic migrants, through mechanisms such as the points system, has impacts on countries of origin and raises broader political and ethical questions. To what extent, for example, is development compromised by the exodus of skilled migrants?

PART II: CANADA AND IMMIGRANT LABOUR EXPERIENCES

The selection and indeed privileging of skilled economic migrants was a hallmark of Canadian immigration policy through the 1990s. Immigration reform and the fine-tuning of the much-celebrated selection model have worked to admit more skilled migrants than in the past. But the selection of prospective migrants is only one part of the story. At the domestic level, as this section demonstrates, the increasing focus on skilled workers has not necessarily been coupled with an equivalent emphasis on ensuring favourable labour market experiences for these newcomers. Indeed, data demonstrates that recent immigrants are experiencing labour market disadvantages.

The Immigrant Population

Canada's immigrant population is an important and significant proportion of Canada's total population. According to the 2001 Census, immigrants accounted for 18.4 percent of the country's population, reaching its highest level in 70 years. Only Australia has a higher proportion of people born outside the country (Statistics Canada, 2003a: 5). Under current immigration regulations the Government of Canada presents annually planned targets for immigration to parliament each year. During the 1993 election the Liberal Party proposed a 1 percent target of Canada's population. But during its tenure, annual immigration levels were in fact set below this pledge (Rekai, 2002: 2). For example, in 2003 the target range was 220,000 – 245,000 and the actual number of new immigrants entering Canada was 221,352 (Canada, 2004a: 14). The 2005 *Annual Report to Parliament on Immigration* made a commitment to admit between

225,000 and 255,000 newcomers (Canada, 2005). Between 1991 and 2000, 2.2 million immigrants were admitted to Canada (Statistics Canada, 2003a: 6). It should be noted that the government does not prepare estimates of the number of people who are in Canada without documents, however in all likelihood these numbers are "far less than the proportionate number in the United States due to Canada's lack of a shared border with any third country" (Rekai, 2002: 2).

Historically, the primary source countries of immigrants to Canada were the United Kingdom, Italy, Germany and the Netherlands. In fact European immigrants accounted for 90 percent of immigrants before 1961 (Statistics Canada, 2003a: 7). Today, recent immigrants are more likely to come from Asian countries. Citizenship and Immigration Canada (CIC) reports that in 2004 the top five source countries of permanent immigration were: China (15.4 percent), India (10.8 percent), Philippines (5.6 percent), Pakistan (5.4 percent), and the United States (3.2 percent) (Canada, 2004b: 32). Not surprisingly, immigration largely accounts for the growth in Canada's visible minority population because newcomers are more than likely to have been born in countries outside of Europe (Statistics Canada, 2003a: 10). Additionally, immigrant settlement tends to be concentrated in Canada's urban centres. "Seventy-three percent of the immigrants who came in the 1990s lived in just three metropolitan areas: Toronto, Vancouver and Montreal" (Ibid.: 7).

These trends were coupled with the other major change in the 1990s, namely the shifts in numbers between the three different immigration categories. This period saw an increasing emphasis on the economic category, and notably on skilled workers. Table 1 illustrates the steady increase in the percentage of migrants arriving under the 'economic immigrant' classification, generally at the expense of 'family class' migrants. The 2005 *Annual Report to Parliament on Immigration* continues this pattern by proposing to maintain the ratio between economic and what is termed 'non-economic' categories (family class and humanitarian) at 56 to 44 (Canada, 2005). This official discourse reinforces a dichotomy between those immigrants selected on the basis of human capital criteria and 'unsolicited' or 'self-selected' individuals in the family or refugee class, implying that the former have more to contribute to the country whereas the latter are less productive (less skilled) and may prove more costly to integrate (Li, 2003: 177). Yet, as some observers have also pointed out, many skilled workers enter under the family and refugee categories (Rekai, 2002: 2).

Table 1
Percentage of Immigrants in Different Migrant Classifications

Year	1984	1993	2004
Economic	29.5	41.2	56.7
Family Class	50.4	43.9	26.4
Humanitarian	17.4	11.9	13.9
Other	2.6	3.0	3.0
Total	100.0	100.0	100.0

Source: Citizenship and Immigration Canada (2004b: 8–9)

CHARTING RECENT DIRECTIONS IN CANADIAN IMMIGRATION POLICY: SKILLED WORKERS

The shifts in distribution between the three categories are the outcome of some deliberate changes to Canadian immigration policy. Jean Chrétien's Liberal government came to power in the fall of 1993 and shortly after began a process of immigration policy consultation and reform which culminated in the 2001 Immigration Refugee Protection Act. In contrast to its public persona as a "party of immigration," the Liberal policies for the most part continued and extended what the previous Progressive Conservative government under Brian Mulroney initiated (Knowles, 1997: 200). These changes were underwritten by the assumption that by attracting the right kinds of people – skilled workers – immigration policy can position Canada to better compete in a globalizing world. Throughout this period, economic criteria became the sine qua non of the policy and neo-liberal values of competitiveness, individual self-sufficiency, economic performance and fiscal restraint were championed (Abu-Laban and Gabriel, 2002: 61–97).

Early in their mandate the Liberals engaged in a sweeping public consultation on immigration. In 1994, then Minister of Citizenship and Immigration Sergio Marchi announced an immigration policy review and eight month public consultation to "forge a comprehensive, forward looking, and progressive immigration framework to take Canada into the next century" (Abu-Laban and Gabriel, 2002: 62). He subsequently announced changes in the composition of the immigration streams with greater importance being placed on the economic category as well as proposals to modify the selection model. These changes directly affected the family class of immigrants. Consequently, whereas family reunification was historically touted as important by all political parties, developments through the 1980s and 1990s sidelined this priority and in fact introduced more stringent requirements as to which family members could be sponsored (Rekai, 2002: 4).

A series of budget measures were also enacted that were ostensibly directed at cost recovery. The 1995 budget, for example, introduced a new controversial "right of landing fee." Under this scheme all adult immigrants including refugees would have to pay $975 upon entry to Canada. This cost added to the application fees previously imposed by the Canadian government in 1992. These fees were justified as a means to offset the costs of integrating newcomers to Canada (Abu-Laban and Gabriel, 2002: 67–9). Peter Li's analysis of CIC data offers an interesting insight. For example, in 2000–01 immigrants paid more than $460 million dollars in processing and landing fees and that "the revenue contributed by new immigrants was higher than the amount spent in each respective year by the federal government on various programs for integrating immigrants and resettling refugees" (Li, 2003: 168).

In 2001, the 1976 Immigration Act was replaced by the IRPA. The selection model governing the entry of those in the economic category introduced more stringent eligibility criteria and emphasized the need to select skilled workers with sound transferable skill sets (Abu-Laban and Gabriel, 2002: 79–80). Points were awarded for a number of factors – educational attainment, official language ability, employment experience in a range of skilled occupations, age, arranged employment and adaptability (Dolin and Young, 2004: 18). Additionally, the list of preferred occupations, which had previously been used to identify national labour market demand for particular occupations, was rejected in favour of the new human capital criteria (Rekai, 2002: 5). However the stringent new requirements coupled with a pass mark of 75 (out of a possible 100) led many to suggest that it would be difficult to enter Canada as a skilled worker. As a result, the pass mark was reduced to 67 and came into effect in December 2003 (Dolin and Young, 2004: 18).

In addition to the policy emphasis on skilled immigrants, the provisions governing the entry of temporary foreign workers also focused on skilled workers. These provisions are of increasing importance insofar as they are being used to address skill shortages, but ironically have been overlooked in the debate around immigrant selection criteria (Rekai, 2002: 9). Canada has used temporary work provisions in a variety of areas including, agriculture through the Seasonal Agricultural Workers Program (see Basok, 2004) and carework through the Live-in-Caregiver Program (Stasiulis and Bakan, 2003). Both of these programs have been constructed as 'low-skilled.' However, in the 1990s the federal government developed a pilot project to attract and expedite the processing of software workers. This project became the basis for new provisions that allowed employers to sign agreements with the government to fast-track the entry of desired skilled temporary workers. Coupled with these changes were new provisions allowing the spouses of skilled temporary workers to obtain work permits for any kind of work in Canada (Gabriel, 2004: 174). These added inducements, however, do not apply to the either the Seasonal Agricultural program or to the Live-in-Caregiver program. Consequently, in the area of temporary workers the same dichotomy between skill and unskilled prevails insofar as the provisions governing entry and regulation differ considerably between different programs. Increasingly, the regulations governing temporary skilled workers are being liberalized in Canada and elsewhere.

Labour Market Experiences

Immigrants' experiences and success (or lack of success) in the labour market can be used as measure of integration into broader Canadian society. As Grace-Edward Galabuzi has pointed out, "For immigrants, labour market attachment is critical to integration, identity formation, ability to claim a sense of belonging and ultimately, full citizenship" in addition to being important for financial well being (Galabuzi, 2005: 53). However, as many analysts have highlighted (Li, 2003; Reitz, 2005), recent immigrants have not fared as well as their predecessors in the labour market. These poorer outcomes have occurred despite the recent changes in the selection model which placed greater weight on formal education, official language ability and work experience. Canada's human capital approach within the points system effectively stands at odds with the labour market experiences of recent immigrants. This dichotomy can be demonstrated by examining the following three indicators of labour market success.

Employment Rates

Statistics Canada (2003b: 12) data indicates that a gap persists in the labour market conditions between recent immigrants and those workers born in Canada. According to the 2001 Census, 65.8 percent of recent immigrants were employed compared to 81.8 percent of those born in Canada. In contrast, in 1986 not only were a higher percentage of recent immigrants employed (71.1) but their rates of employment were broadly comparable to that of non-immigrants (75.8). The unemployment rates of recent immigrants in 2001 was almost twice that of their Canadian born counterparts. While recent immigrants experienced a higher level of unemployment (11.8) than non-immigrants (9.4) in 1986 the rates of unemployment were much closer than in 2001.

The data also indicates significant gender differences. The employment rate for male recent immigrants was 8.9 percentage points lower than the rate for their Canadian-born counterparts. However the 2001 employment rate for female recent immigrants was 21.8 percentage points lower than Canadian-born women. This is a considerable difference from 1986 figures which indicate a much smaller difference of 5.1 percent between recent immigrants and non-immigrant women workers' employment rate.

Wages

Citizenship and Immigration Canada's *The Monitor* reported that immigrants have also experienced declining earnings from the 1980s to the year 2000. This decline "has been widespread, but more pronounced for those with high levels of education" and has had a greater impact on males (Canada, 2004d: 5). Census figures indicate that during this period the full time earnings of recent male adult immigrants dropped 13 percent, while the earnings of Canadian born men working full time rose 10 percent (Ibid.: 7). A recent CIC review of the earnings of skilled worker principal applicants highlighted:

In 1981, the employment earnings for a skilled worker principal applicant one year after arrival were $37,400 compared to the Canadian average of $30,300 (all inflation adjusted to the year 2000). In 2000, a skilled worker principal applicant, who had arrived one year earlier, earned $28,500 compared to a Canadian average of $32,500. (Ibid.: 6)

Additionally, the earnings of foreign-born immigrants are affected by underemployment. Jeffrey Reitz has estimated that these individuals earn $2.4 billion less than their Canadian born counterparts with comparable skills. Significantly, he suggests that immigrants who belong to racial minorities are more adversely affected by the earning disadvantage and skill underutilization than those of European origin (Reitz, 2005: 3).

Low Income

Related, the share of the foreign born population defined as having low incomes stood at 20.2 percent in 2000, up from 17 percent in 1980. Recent immigrants have higher rates of low income than those immigrants who have been in Canada longer. However, the gap between low income rates for immigrants and persons born in Canada has widened over the last 20 years (Canada, 2004c: 6).[3]

Taken together, employment rates, earnings and low income prevalence illustrate how recent immigrants to Canada have been less successful than those immigrants that arrived earlier. While there is agreement on this point, there is not necessarily a consensus as to why immigrants, selected under increasingly more stringent criteria, are experiencing worse labour market outcomes relative to their predecessors. Explanations have focused on the role of professional bodies in accreditation, difficulties in assessing foreign training and the requirement of Canadian employment experience. But as Li (2003: 123) has argued "many factors influence the earnings of immigrants – human capital, gender, race, place of origin ... earnings differentials should not be simply interpreted as individual differences in productivity or in investment strategies in human capital, but should take into account larger structural forces of inequality."

The labour market experience of recent immigrants has not gone unnoticed by the popular press, think tanks and policymakers. As Reitz (2005: 3) has pointed out, "the underutilization of immigrant skills, although by no means new, is increasingly pressing." The previous Liberal government recognized this issue in its 2003 Speech from the Throne by placing responsibility for foreign credentials with the Parliamentary Secretary to Citizenship and Immigration Canada (Dolin and Young, 2004: 35).

New Directions in Immigration?

The newly elected Conservative government of Stephen Harper will have to address the same immigration policy challenges the previous administration had to contend with: What should the level of immigration be? Should Canada maintain current levels, increase them or scale back numbers? What should the mix be between economic, family and refugee categories within the immigration stream? Should emphasis remain on recruiting highly skilled economic immigrants, or should other models, such as employer driven ones, be considered? Lastly, how should issues beyond the selection of immigrants, such as integration and settlement, be addressed?

These types of questions were not explicitly debated during the recent 2006 election (Collacott, 2006: A15). However, in the run up to the election the previous Liberal administration made a number of immigration related announcements. In October 2005, then Liberal Minister of Citizenship and Immigration Joe Volpe announced a number of changes including: plans to raise immigration targets up to 300,000 over the next five years; a major allocation of new spending to address a backlog of 700,000 applications in the system; and proposals to bring in more temporary workers (Jiménez, 2005: A1). The backlog in applications had been identified by the Auditor General of Canada as early as 2000 when the Auditor reported that Citizenship and Immigration Canada was unable to process applications to meet target goals because the department was under resourced (Dolin and Young, 2004: 3). Volpe also indicated that he was interested in a "limited amnesty plan" to regularize the status of undocumented workers (Jiménez, 2005: A1). These proposals were coupled with an earlier announcement that CIC would expedite the sponsorship applications of parents and grandparents coming under the family class provisions. There was speculation that these announcements coming so close to a federal election were designed to garner Liberal support within immigrant communities (Tandt, 2005: A8).

The electoral calculus may have also been a critical factor in the Conservative's recent positions on immigration during the past two elections. In a marked contrast to the Reform Party of the 1980s that spoke out against both increased immigration levels and multiculturalism (Kirkham, 1998: 250; Patten, 1999), the Conservative Party's public pronouncements in this area have been measured. Their 2006 election platform, *Stand Up for Canada*, called for "a fair and sensible immigration plan that works for Canada" and it pledged to:

– cut the $975 Right of Landing Fee in half
– create a Canadian Agency for Assessment and Recognition of Credentials
– support Canadian parents who adopt foreign-born children by extending automatic citizenship. (Conservative Party of Canada, 2006:38)

Despite this platform the Conservatives were unable to secure any seats in the country's three largest cities where most newcomers reside. Immigration issues do not figure in the Conservatives five key priorities outlined in the April 2006 Speech from the Throne. This said, and while it is still early in the mandate of the new government, some directions have been signalled. Firstly, the Conservatives have moved quickly to fulfill the promises made during the election. The Right of Permanent Residence Fee was cut from $975 to $490, effective 3 May 2006 (Canada, 2006: 10). Interestingly, it is not to be immediately eliminated completely despite the fact that its original justification – cost recovery to address deficits – is no longer applicable in a period of surplus and, as noted above, revenues generated from this fee surpassed CIC's settlement budget. Secondly, in an effort to address the recent experience of immigrants in the labour market the Conservative government has earmarked $18 million toward the establishment of a Canadian Agency for the Assessment and Recognition of Credentials. According to statements made during the election, the agency will:

provide a pre-assessment of international credentials and experience before immigrants even come to Canada. It will collect information on foreign credentials to evaluate appropriate comparisons with Canadian credentials. It will work with provinces and professional associations to encourage the recognition or adaptations of foreign credentials in as timely a manner as possible. And it will work with employers to encourage a better understanding of these credentials. (Harper, 2006)

To date, however, the government has only made a pledge to conduct consultations regarding the credentials (Ibbitson, 2006). While this is a laudable starting point and certainly a marked departure from the actions of previous federal administrations, much of what is needed to address this issue lies outside the scope of the federal government itself and rests in the actions and decisions of professional groups and the provinces.

In some respects it appears that the Conservatives will continue with some of the broad directions outlined by the previous Liberal administration. The new Minister of Citizenship and Immigration, Monte Solberg, indicated shortly after the election that the government is not planning to change the overall annual target number for newcomers or the numbers of people coming in under the family category. He also indicated that perhaps it may be time to explore an expansion in the use of temporary work visas for skilled workers (Cheadle, 2006: A10). The expansion of skilled temporary work programs need to be considered carefully. On the one hand, these programs are flexible, driven by employers, have the potential to address short term critical labour shortages and encourage circular migration. This expansion is of importance to provinces, such as Alberta, which are experiencing significant labour shortages. Additionally, Solberg has floated the idea of "earned citizenship" for these type of workers (Ibid.), but again this should be scrutinized more carefully. Even 'best practice' temporary worker programs raise issues around the vulnerability of workers in these situations – would their status be dependent on continuing employment with the same employer? How would worker rights be protected? These types of questions have all been raised in relation to Canada's live-in-caregiver program. Others have questioned how to ensure that people leave the country once their temporary employment has ended. As Jeffrey Reitz, has pointed out, considerable resources would have to be allocated to enforce the conditions of a visa on a large scale (Vu, 2006: 1).

The previous Liberal government indicated that it would direct funds to address the backlog in immigrant applications but to date there are few indications as to what the current administration will do in this area (Ibid.: 4). Also, it is highly unlikely that the new government will follow-up on Volpe's suggestion for a limited amnesty. They too would face similar challenges insofar as such an initiative would require agreement and cooperation between several federal departments including the RCMP, CSIS, Finance, Justice, and Human Resources Skills Development Canada (Jiménez, 2005: A1). However, pursuing such a proposal would stand at odds with the Conservatives' stated commitments to "secure borders" and "effective deportation laws," as outlined in the 2006 party platform. It is not surprising that Solberg has indicated that the issue is of "low priority" for his government (Jiménez, 2006: A1).

The Conservatives moved quickly to ensure that they kept the 2006 election promises in the area of immigration. Additionally, Stephen Harper has gone on the record to extol the virtues of Canadian cultural diversity and defend Canada's immigration program as some critics drew links between terrorist threats and immigration in the wake of an alleged terrorist plot in Toronto (Mickleburgh, 2006: A1). Nevertheless, the Conservatives currently find themselves between a rock and a hard place. As a minority government it will be difficult to pursue radical new directions within the field of immigration. However, as *Globe and Mail* columnist John Ibbitson (2006: A4) recently noted, "if the Conservatives cannot place their stamp on an aggressive immigration policy they can forget about winning urban ridings, they so desperately need to solidify their shaky electoral base."

CONCLUSION

This chapter has sought to highlight the ways in which Canadian immigration policy is located at the interface between international and domestic realms. At the international levels, a number of factors, including demographics, immigrant mix, and the liberalization of immigration rules for some groups (notably skilled workers) shape, and are shaped by, international migration policy. But the broad issues attached to high skilled labour mobility, especially from the South to the North, such as the brain drain, do not figure in Canadian debates about immigration, despite the fact that the Canadian selection model actively selects and promotes the recruitment of migrants with human capital. As a result, a greater proportion of recent immigrants to Canada enter with higher educational degrees. However, recent immigrants have experienced declines in the labour market in terms of employment and earnings, raising questions about how well Canada, as a country, addresses immigrant settlement and integration.

NOTES

1 It should be noted that the definition and measurement of 'skilled' or 'highly skilled' worker is the matter of some debate that has important policy ramifications (see OECD, 2002; and Gabriel, 2004).

2 Different rules and regulations govern the entry of economic class members (skilled workers, business immigrants, provincial nominees), family class members and those in the humanitarian/refugee category as well as those people admitted on a temporary basis – workers, visitors, and students.

3 This data, published by Citizenship and Immigration Canada, highlighted the findings of a study by Garnet Picot and Feng Hou, "The rise in low-income rates among immigrants in Canada" (Ottawa: Statistics Canada, 2003). This study used a low income measure based on the low income cut off (LICO) – "a review of expenditure patterns and is calculated for different sized families and different sized cities" (Canada, 2004c: 5).

REFERENCES

Abu-Laban, Yasmeen, and Christina Gabriel. 2002. *Selling Diversity: Immigration, Multiculturalism, Employment Equity, and Globalization.* Peterborough: Broadview Press.

Basok, Tanya. 2004. "Post-national citizenship and social exclusion and migrant rights: Mexican seasonal workers in Canada," *Citizenship Studies* 8, no. 1 (March): 47–64.

Cairncross, Frances. 2002. "The Longest Journey," *Economist*, 2–8 November, 3–6.

Canada. 2004a. *Annual Report to Parliament on Immigration.* Ottawa: Citizenship and Immigration Canada (CIC).

– 2004b. *Facts and Figures 2004: Immigration Overview.* Ottawa: Citizenship and Immigration Canada (CIC). Available at: <http://www.cic.gc.ca/english/pdf/pub/facts2004.pdf>

– 2004c. "Low Income Trends among Immigrants," Citizenship and Immigration Canada, *The Monitor* 7 (Fall): 5–7.

– 2004d. "The Economic Performance of Immigrants," Citizenship and Immigration Canada, *The Monitor* 5 (Spring): 5–8.

– 2005. *Annual Report to Parliament on Immigration.* Ottawa: Citizenship and Immigration Canada (CIC).

– 2006. *Focusing on Priorities: The Budget in Brief 2006.* Ottawa, Department of Finance Available at <http://www.fin.qc.ca/budget06/brief/briefe.htm>

Castles, Stephen. 2002. "Migration and Community Formation under Conditions of Globalization," *International Migration Review* 36, no. 4 (Winter): 1143–68.

Castles, Stephen, and Mark Miller. 1998. *The Age of Migration. International Population Movements in the Modern World*, 2nd ed. London: MacMillan Press.

Cheadle, Bruce. 2006. "Ottawa Looks at Changing Immigrant Mix," *Globe and Mail*, 15 February, A10.

Collacott, Martin. 2006 "Open Doors, Closed Minds," *Ottawa Citizen*, 4 January, A15.

Conservative Party of Canada. 2006. "Stand Up for Canada: Accountable Government That Will Get Things Done for All of Us," Federal Election Platform: *Stand up for Canada*, 13 January: 9 May 2006. Available at: <http://www.conservative.ca/meda/20060113-Platform.pdf>

DeVoretz, Don. 1999. "The Brain Drain Is Real and It Costs Us," *Policy Options* 20, no. 7 (September): 18–24.

Dolin, Benjamin, and Margaret Young. 2004. *Canada's Immigration Program*. Ottawa: Parliamentary Information and Research Service, Library of Parliament, October. Available at: <http://www.parl.gc.ca/information/library/PRBpubs/bp190-e.htm>

Foster, Lorne. 1998. *Turnstile Immigration: Multiculturalism, Social Order and Social Justice in Canada*. Toronto: Thompson Educational Publishing.

Gabriel, Christina. 2004. "A Question of Skills: Gender, Migration Policy and the Global Political Economy," in Libby Assassi, Kees van der Pijl and Duncan Wigan, eds. *Global Regulation: Managing the Crisis after the Imperial Turn*. London: Palgrave.

Galabuzi, Grace-Edward. 2005. *Canada's Economic Apartheid: The Social Exclusion of Racialized Groups in the New Century*. Toronto: Canadian Scholars' Press.

Gent, Saskia, and Ronald Skeldon. 2006. "Skilled Migration: New Policy Options," Development Research Centre on Migration, Globalisation and Poverty, *Briefing* 5 (March): 1–4.

Harper, Stephen. 2006. "Promoting Opportunities for New Canadians," Address by the Leader of the Conservative Party, Mississauga, ON, 4 January.

Ibbitson, John. 2006. "It All Comes Down to Immigration," *Globe and Mail*, 24 February, A4.

Iqbal, Mahmood. 1999. "Are we Losing Our Minds?" *Policy Options* 20, no. 7 (September): 34–8.

Jiménez, Marina. 2005. "Canada Opens Door for 700,000," *Globe and Mail*, 31 October, A1.

– 2006. "Foreign Labourers Shown the Door," *Globe and Mail*, 28 March, A1.

Kapur, Devesh, and John McHale. 2005. "Are We Losing the Global Race for Talent?" *Wall Street Journal*, 21 November, A17.

Kirkham, Della. 1998. "The Reform Party of Canada: A Discourse on Race, Ethnicity and Equality," in Vic Satzewich, ed. *Racism and Social Inequality in Canada*. Toronto: Thompson Educational Press.

Knowles, Valerie. 1997. *Strangers at Our Gates: Canadian Immigration and Immigration Policy, 1540–1997*. Toronto: Dundurn Press.

Kofman, Eleonore. 2005. "Citizenship, Migration and the Reassertion of National Identity," *Citizenship Studies* 9, no. 5 (November): 453–67.

Li, Peter. 2003. *Destination Canada: Immigration Debates and Issues*. Toronto: Oxford University Press.

Maher, Kristen Hill. 2004. "Globalized Social Reproduction: Women Migrants and the Citizenship Gap," in Alison Brysk and Gershon Shafir, eds. *People Out of Place: Globalization, Human Rights and the Citizenship Gap*. New York: Routledge.

Maytree Foundation. 2001. "Brief to the Standing Committee on Citizenship and Immigration regarding Bill C-11, *Immigration and Refugee Protection Act*," 26 March. Available at: <http://www.maytree.com/HTMLFiles/BriefC-11.htm>

Mickleburgh, Rod. 2006. "Harper Defends Canadian Diversity," *Globe and Mail*, 20 June, A1.

Migration News. 2006. "World Bank: Brain Drain, Migrants," *Migration News* 13, no. 1 (January). Available at <http://migration.ucdavis.edu/mn/more.php?id=3175_0_5_0>

OECD. 2002. "International Mobility of the High Skilled," *Policy Brief* (July). Paris: Organisation for Economic Co-operation and Development (OECD).

Patten, Steve. 1999. "The Reform Party's Re-Imagining of the Canadian Nation," *Journal of Canadian Studies*, vol. 34, no. 1 (Spring): 27–51.

Ramamurthy, Bhargavi. 2003. *International Labour Migrants: Unsung Heroes of Globalization*, Sida Studies 8. Stockholm: Swedish International Development Cooperation Agency.

Reitz, Jeffery. 2005. "Tapping Immigrants' Skills: New Directions for Canada's Immigration Policy in the Knowledge Economy," *IRPP Choices* 11, no. 1 (February): 2–18.

Rekai, Peter. 2002. "US and Canadian Immigration Policies: Marching Together to Different Tunes," C.D. Howe Institute, *Commentary* 171 (November).

Reynolds, Jeremy. 2005. "The World's Population: Trends, Prospects, and Challenges," Presentation to the Geography Teachers' Association of Victoria. Victoria, Australia: Department of Sustainability and Environment, Demographic Research.

Sassen, Saskia. 1998. *Globalization and Its Discontents: Essays on the New Mobility of People and Money*. New York: New Press.

Stalker, Peter. 2000. *Workers without Frontiers: The Impact of Globalization on International Migration*. Boulder, CO: Lynne Rienner Press.

Stasiulis, Daiva K., and Abigail B. Bakan. 2003. *Negotiating Citizenship: Migrant Women in Canada and the Global System*. London: Palgrave.

Statistics Canada. 2003a. "Canada's Ethnocultural Portrait: The Changing Mosaic," *2001 Census Analysis Series*. Ottawa: Statistics Canada, 21 January.

– 2003b. "The Changing Profile of Canada's Labour Force," *2001 Census Analysis Series*. Ottawa: Statistics Canada, 11 February.

Stewart-Patterson, David. 2005. "Immigration and Diversity: A Key Competitive Advantage for Canada," in *Diversity in Canada: Regions and Communities*. Ottawa: Centre for Research and Information on Canada. *The CRIC Papers*, no. 18 (October): 14–6.

Tandt, Michael Den. 2005. "$700-Million Earmarked for Immigration Backlog," *Globe and Mail*, 25 November, A8.

Travis, Alan 2006. "Immigration Shakeup Will Bar Most Unskilled Workers from Outside EU," *The Guardian*, 8 March.

United Kingdom. 2006. *A Points-Based System: Making Migration Work for Britain*. London: Home Office. Available at: <http://www.homeoffice. gov.uk/documents/command-points-based-migration>

United Nations. 2000. "Executive Summary," in *Replacement Migration: Is It a Solution to Declining and Ageing Population?* New York: Department of Economic and Social Affairs, Population Division. Available at: <http://www.un.org/esa/population/publications/migration/execusum.htm>

– 2002. *International Migration Report*. New York: Department of Economic and Social Affairs, Population Division. Available at: <http://www.un.og/esa/ population/publications/ittmig2002>

Vu, Uyen. 2006. "Slight Shift Signaled in Immigration Policy," *Canadian HR Reporter*, 13 March, 2.

Weiner, Myron. 2006. "On International Migration and International Relations," in Anthony Messina and Gallya Lahva. *The Migration Reader: Exploring Politics and Policies*. Boulder, CO: Lynne Rienner Press.

Zhao, John, Doug Drew and T. Scott Murray. 2000. "Brain Drain and Brain Gain: The Migration of Knowledge Workers from and to Canada," Statistics Canada, *Education Quarterly Review* 6, no. 3 (Spring): 8–35.

11 It's Not Just Afghanistan or Darfur: Canada's Peacebuilding Efforts in Haiti

YASMINE SHAMSIE

It is difficult to exaggerate the severity of Haiti's longstanding humanitarian crisis or the tenacity of the problems underlying it: abject poverty and inequality, a non-functioning judiciary, corrupt and inept law enforcement, and a declining agricultural base. But despite Haiti's complex and constantly shifting political context, Canada has made it a foreign policy priority, sending peacekeepers to the island nation ten times in the last twenty years, and contributing c$90 million per year in the last two years. This makes Canada the third largest donor, behind the United States (US) and the European Union (EU); on a per capita basis we are the most generous.[1] On the diplomatic front, Ottawa has been at the forefront of all developments as a 'Friend of Haiti.'[2] The appointment of Haitian-born Michaëlle Jean (a daughter of Haitian exiles) as Canada's Governor General symbolizes the many links between our countries.

Still, Haiti's fractious political environment has been a major barrier to effecting change in the nation's desperate social and economic environments. Civil unrest in late 2003 culminated in an armed insurgency comprised primarily of thugs (calling themselves the "Cannibal Army"), former soldiers, and death-squad leaders. When the insurgents threatened to march on Port-au-Prince, President Jean-Bertrand Aristide chose exile over the potential for chaos. His departure triggered the establishment of a US-led Multilateral Interim Force (MIF), which was replaced in June 2004 by a United Nations Stabilization Mission (known by its French acronym, MINUSTAH). MINUSTAH's extended mandate, coupled with the election of René Préval as President on 19 February 2006, signalled the beginning of a new peacebuilding effort, with Canada at the forefront.

This chapter reviews Canadian actions regarding Haiti since 2004 in three key areas: promoting democracy, economic development and poverty reduction, and security. The three spheres loosely correspond to Canada's so-called "3D approach" to involvement in fragile states, which blends diplomatic, defence, and development efforts designed to form coordinated engagement.[3]

THE CANADA-HAITI RELATIONSHIP

Canada's sustained engagement with Haiti, and our perceived comparative advantage can be explained in terms of five factors. First, with 8.3 million citizens, the Caribbean's most populous nation is viewed as presenting challenges in several social and political spheres. The movements of its sizeable population have caused concern for Haiti's neighbours and Canada's regional partners, particularly the United States and the Dominican Republic. Political instability and economic decline have contributed to mass migration, illegal immigration, drug and weapons trafficking, and the spread of HIV/AIDS.

Second, our reputation in Haiti is grounded in the "perceived neutrality, established trust, and non-colonial history of Canadian cooperation throughout the Caribbean" (Canada, 2004b: 11). Whereas Washington's crusading democratizing spirit has been marked by interventions and occupations, Canada has refrained from such heavy-handed missionary adventures. Although, as Tom Keating (2001: 208) rightfully notes, "That is not to say that Canadians have completely avoided the missionary spirit. They tended, however, to leave this to those missionaries inspired by matters of the spirit." Also important is Ottawa's long-term diplomatic relations with Haiti and its uninterrupted flow of development assistance.

Third, the influence of the large Haitian diaspora in Canada, that has brought approximately 100,000 families to live here, mostly in Quebec, should not be understated. According to the 2001 Census, there are approximately 54,000 Haitian-born immigrants in Canada, about 46,000 in the city of Montreal (Simmons et al., 2005: 4–6). The Canadian International Development Agency (CIDA) notes that the diaspora "has been a significant driver behind Canadian support to Haiti" (Canada, 2004b: 11). For instance, Canada's military intervention in 1994 was influenced by "concerns emanating from the Haitian community in Montreal and the perceived need to address these 'francophone' interests in the government's foreign policy" (Keating, 2001: 220).

Fourth, Haiti's relevance to Canada is linked to our sustained interest in a Free Trade Area of the Americas agreement (Canada, 2004b). Given its "influential demographics," Haiti is viewed as a potentially important trading partner.[4]

And fifth, our engagement with Haiti can be explained by Canada's longstanding commitment to, and participation in the intergovernmental organization la Francophonie.

It is important to note that Quebec pursues its own relations with Haiti through its provincial ministries and from its position as an independent member of la Francophonie. Past bilateral meetings have been held between Quebec's National Assembly and the Haitian Chamber of Deputies and Senate (Council on Hemispheric Affairs, 2006). In addition, a number of collaborative efforts in education, health, economic cooperation, police, and energy were undertaken in the 1990s. As such, Haiti is the top beneficiary of Quebec's Direction de l'aide internationale (Ibid.), and the majority of Canadian non-governmental organizations (NGOs) working in Haiti are based in the province.[5] Since 1997 Quebec has funded almost 60 projects at a cost of c$3.86 million. Trade between Haiti and Quebec totalled approximately c$23 million in 2002 (c$21 million in Quebec exports), representing close to 60 percent of all Canadian exports to Haiti that year (Quebec, 2006).

PROMOTING DEMOCRACY

In the 1990s, we witnessed a readiness on the part of Canadian policy-makers and citizens to promote democratic governance beyond our borders (Axworthy and Campbell, 2004). At the same time, some of our activities on this front – specifically our behaviour during Haiti's 2004 crisis – have been controversial. It is therefore appropriate, indeed warranted, that we review these actions and how they may affect our long-term relationship with Haiti and our hemispheric standing on democracy. While Washington's position fits with its longstanding and vocal anti-Aristide lobby, and France's position with its intense disapproval of Aristide's reparations campaign, it is less clear why Canada tacitly supported the unconstitutional removal of an elected president. It is not implausible that we "bent to US will"[6] on this issue, given Canada's respectable past practice on Haiti. Our behaviour is all the more puzzling given that Canada has made the promotion of representative democracy a centrepiece of its hemispheric agenda.

Our record in this area is impressive. In 1990, Canada was instrumental in gaining approval for the establishment of a Unit for the Promotion of Democracy within the Organization of American States (OAS).[7] We were influential in securing support for the Santiago Commitment to Democracy and the Renewal of the Inter-American System and its accompanying Resolution 1080, in which member-states agreed to "adopt efficacious, timely and expeditious procedures to ensure the promotion and defense of democracy" (OAS, 1991). Canada also supported the 1992 Washington Protocol – an amendment to the OAS Charter that made representative democracy a necessary condition for participation in OAS activities. Furthermore, Canadian diplomacy advanced and supported multilateral initiatives aimed at restoring democracy in Haiti in 1991, Peru in 1992, Guatemala in 1993, and Paraguay in 1996 (Thérien et al., 2004). Canada was also involved in the development of the region's Inter-American Democratic Charter (adopted in 2001) and supported its application following Venezuela's *coup d'état* in April of 2002.

It is worth highlighting that this record on democracy has previously extended to Haiti. Ottawa adopted a strong and purposeful position when Haiti's elected government was first threatened in 1991. Prime Minister Brian Mulroney denounced the coup and supported efforts to overturn it by force if necessary. When different positions emerged among the Friends of Haiti during long, drawn-out negotiations with coup leaders, Canada remained steadfastly opposed to the Haitian army's stalling tactics and was supportive of the exiled president. While some members of the American administration were suspicious of Aristide and willing to accommodate the military regime, Canada pushed for "an unconditional guarantee of his return to power" (Keating, 2001: 216). But despite its support for constitutional rule in the region and particularly in Haiti, Canada consciously chose to let Haiti's elected government fall on 29 February 2004. I will not present a detailed account of the circumstances surrounding Aristide's ouster in this paper,[8] but will instead focus on last-ditch diplomatic efforts to resolve the crisis and Canada's role in those negotiations.

International efforts to broker a solution to the crisis centred on the Friends of Haiti, the Caribbean Community (CARICOM), and the OAS. Canada served as a prominent actor in support of multilateral solutions, including the three-year OAS attempt to mediate talks between Aristide and opposition groups. CARICOM, which took on a leading role one month before the government's collapse, engineered a plan to establish a series of short-term, confidence-building measures which would lead to new elections. The proposal was supported by Canada and accepted by Aristide on 31 January 2004 (Canada, 2004a), but its terms were rejected by the "Democratic Platform" – a coalition of political parties and citizen groups that had been demanding Aristide's departure since December 2003 (ICG, 2004: 9).

An armed rebellion erupted on 5 February. In the face of escalating violence, Canada joined the international community in promoting the unambiguous message presented by US Secretary of State Colin Powell at a 13 February press conference: "We all have a commitment to the democratic process in Haiti and we will accept no outcome that is not consistent with the constitution. We will accept no outcome that, in any way, illegally attempts to remove the elected President of Haiti" (United States, 2004). The security situation worsened despite a flurry of diplomatic activity, with members of the Haitian National Police (HNP) abandoning their posts in several cities and former army and paramilitary troops joining the insurgency. On 20 February, a high-level delegation that included Canadian representatives attempted to break the political deadlock with a new version of CARICOM's earlier proposal. Once again, the opposition rejected it. On 22 February, Powell reiterated the international community's support for a negotiated solution, proclaiming "We cannot buy into a proposition that says that the elected president must be forced out of office by thugs and those who do not respect law and are bringing terrible violence to the Haitian people" (cited in Bogdanich and Nordberg, 2006). While a clear condemnation of violent tactics was evident in Powell's statement, Aristide's request for peacekeeping troops was denied, with international actors making any such assistance contingent on the brokering of a political settlement. Given the refusal of the opposition to negotiate and the inability of the HNP to defend the government, such a posture meant a collapse of the regime. Haiti scholar Robert Fatton (2006: 20–1) explains what happened next: "Rather than compelling the opposition to accept it, which would have weakened Aristide's powers and generated a government of national unity, the White House ominously 'called into question [Aristide's] fitness to continue to govern' and urged 'him to examine his position carefully, to accept responsibility, and to act in the best interest of the people of Haiti.'"

Washington's refusal to back a negotiated power-sharing agreement represented an official abandonment of Aristide, and Canada's silence indicated tacit approval. The Haitian president had no choice but to accept exile (Fatton, 2004). It is worth noting that Ottawa's position contrasted sharply with CARICOM's, which immediately demanded an investigation into the circumstances leading to the government's fall upon hearing of Aristide's departure.

Some were not surprised by Canada's stance. Domestic critics accused the Canadian government of helping to lay the groundwork for Aristide's removal. In a 15 March 2003 article published in *L'Actualité*, reporter Michel Vastel described a January 2003 brainstorming session hosted by Denis Paradis, at that time Secretary of State for Latin America, Africa and la Francophonie. Key officials from the United States and France attended, but no Haitian government official was present. Paradis denies Vastel's claim that meeting participants agreed that "Aristide must go."[9] In Parliament, Liberals, insisting that 'regime change' was not discussed at the 2003 meeting, rejected NDP calls for an investigation into the circumstances of Aristide's forced departure. The official narrative is that Aristide resigned – *point final*.[10]

Canada's failure to support Haiti's constitutional government, regardless of Aristide's well-known flaws, is of no small significance, especially given our stated commitment to representative democracy in the region. After years of building a reputation as a credible and respected actor in the Americas, falling into line with France and the United States was not a prudent decision. But a bigger issue than our reputation is the realization that allowing Aristide to fall could encourage the emergence of "a new US doctrine on 'failed elected leaders,' whereby leaders which Washington finds objectionable are allowed to fall with the hope that a more amenable replacement will take their place" (Cameron, 2004). US scholar Michael Shifter concurs, noting that the Haiti case "sets a very disturbing precedent for the entire region" (cited in Lobe, 2004). Moreover, such a doctrine directly counters the intent of the Inter-American Democratic Charter championed by Canada and signed by OAS member-states in 2001. This is not a complex issue: if Canada wants to be viewed as an international arbiter and influential diplomatic actor in the region, it needs to stand behind the norms it helps to craft.

How should Canada have acted in this situation? One might have expected our position to mirror that of CARICOM's, as articulated by Jamaica's Minister of Foreign Affairs and Foreign Trade K.D. Knight: "We will not accept a coup d'état in any form. Any change in Haiti must be through constitutional means ... This should not be construed as uncritical support for the President of Haiti. It is for democracy in Haiti" (United States, 2004). Moreover, Canada should have expressed its frustration with the UN Security Council for its lack of willingness to take immediate action in response to the Haitian government's calls for assistance, especially since the UN-body ultimately authorized the deployment of a multinational interim force as part of its Resolution 1529 on the very day of Aristide's forced departure (CARICOM, 2004).

A transitional government headed by then-Supreme Court Chief Justice Boniface Alexandre as president and Gérard Latortue as prime minister was installed immediately following the collapse of the Aristide government.[11] At this point, Ottawa's commitment to Haitian democracy and constitutional authority re-emerged with spirited vigour. Although some observers argued that conditions were not conducive to free and fair elections (Fatton, 2006: 22), Canada immediately pledged its robust support to these processes so the transitional government could be replaced as soon as possible with one elected by Haitians.[12] Ottawa spent approximately c$30 million for electoral observers and the deployment of Canadian security forces around the country, and Elections Canada led an International Mission for Monitoring Haitian Elections to observe and evaluate the process.

While the elections did not solve Haiti's numerous problems, they constituted a first step toward addressing the countries many difficulties. Lionel Hurst, former Ambassador to Antigua and Barbuda, was correct when he asserted that "only through the system of democratic elections of a government can Haiti progress"[13] – an objective that Canada has made valuable contributions to.

POVERTY REDUCTION AND ECONOMIC DEVELOPMENT

Over half of all Haitians (56 percent) live on less than US$1 per day, making its poverty "deeper and more pervasive than in the rest of Latin America" (Sletten and Egset, 2004: 20). Haiti's peasant farmers constitute the most destitute segment of the population, with rural residents accounting for 75 percent of the country's poor; only one-quarter of this segment has access to safe water and only one-sixth to basic sanitation (Erikson, 2004: 4). Haiti also suffers the starkest division between rich and poor of any Caribbean country.

In this section, I will use a poverty reduction lens to judge Canada's and others' economic development strategies in Haiti. This emphasis is in part normative and in part due to the importance that peacebuilding and development experts assign to this goal. For instance, the International Crisis Group (2005) notes that much of the violence which plagues Haiti is due to the "chronic failure to tackle the poverty, social deprivation, and exclusion that endanger most of the population." In sum, donors have accepted that poverty and inequality are among those factors leading to violence, insecurity, and political instability. Indeed, in a recent strategy paper on Haiti, CIDA argues that the primary challenge is to find and implement strategies that will foster poverty reduction (Canada, 2004b).

To its credit, CIDA has engaged in serious discussion and analysis of Haiti's predicament. Perhaps driven by the disappointing results of post-1994 development strategies, it has re-evaluated its program and developed a new approach to the country's needs.[14] CIDA now appears willing to accept a higher level of risk, uncertainty, and the possibility of setbacks and lack of progress in cases like Haiti – a more realistic starting point and therefore a positive development. Moreover, CIDA now concedes that the strict conditionality imposed on Haiti after the disputed elections of 2000 in order to promote better governance and specific macroeconomic policies did not produce the desired reforms and instead contributed to the 2004 crisis (Ibid.).

The three-fold strategy for economic renewal now being advanced by Canada and the international community consists of building stronger links with members of the Haitian diaspora, strengthening the private sector, which is viewed as the primary engine of economic growth, and re-establishing Haiti's assembly manufacturing export sector. A broad aid instrument known as the Interim Cooperation Framework (ICF) supports the approach. In 2004, Canada was instrumental in creating this us$1.085 billion aid plan, which coordinates all assistance to Haiti.[15] Ottawa provided approximately c$180 million in aid between April 2004 and March 2006. More than c$150 million has been devoted to projects and programs that reflect ICF priorities, which continue to receive support from the Conservative government under the leadership of Stephen Harper.[16] In the following sections, I suggest that the three foci of the development plan make it unlikely that the lot of Haiti's poor will be improved. This expectation arises from the plan's failure to address the needs of the country's rural majority.

The Diaspora: A New Darling of Development Agencies

As noted earlier, this sizeable and vocal group has pressed the Canadian government for continued support to Haiti. Sociologist Jean-Claude Icart has characterized the Haitian diaspora as more organized and active than ever before (Council on Hemispheric Affairs, 2006). While very little is known about the number of active Haitian-Canadian voters and their preferences, the population's geographic concentration does appear to give it considerable political weight. At least two key Liberal politicians involved in the 2004 Haiti drama lost their seats in recent federal elections: former Minister of Foreign Affairs Pierre Pettigrew lost his Papineau riding and former Canadian Secretary of State for Latin America, Africa and la Francophonie, Denis Paradis, lost his Brome-Missisquoi riding.[17]

In December 2004, the Ministers of Foreign Affairs and International Cooperation hosted a conference in Montréal to recognize the diaspora's role in promoting development and democracy in Haiti.[18] The meeting was intended to mobilize its members in support of the Interim Cooperation Framework rather than to solicit input into development priorities, which indicates a muted influence on policy. In short, for the moment Ottawa appears to view the diaspora as a useful implementer rather than a policy generator.

Haiti receives approximately us$1.5 billion per year in remittances from diaspora members – a large and consistent source of income that often exceeds the contributions of all international actors combined

(Council on Hemispheric Affairs, 2006). Clearly, the grouping has the potential to be a powerful economic force. Remittances sent to Haitian families in 2002 were at least six times greater than the sum of development financing from the United States, France, Canada, the Inter-American Development Bank (IADB), the World Bank, the EU, and the UN. Moreover, as Carlo Dade (2006a: 90) points out, these remittances are not in the form of loans, therefore "they impose no future financial obligations on the government of Haiti."

The diaspora is also proving to be a source of trained professionals that Haiti lacks due to the massive outflow of migrants since 1993, as well as a source of expertise for international development agencies seeking advice and individuals with local language skills. CIDA has been incorporating the diaspora into the reconstruction process by working with a Montreal-based federation of Haitian Hometown Associations known as the Regroupement des organismes canado-haïtien pour le développement (ROCAHD) in support of Haitian community development.

Despite these promising developments, there is much debate in the literature on the economic development potential of diasporic remittances (see Goldring, 2003; Fagen and Bump, 2005; Orozco et al., 2005). Despite their ability to keep Haiti afloat (particularly during crisis periods) and to improve the living conditions of individual families and certain communities in which large concentrations of recipients reside, national poverty and inequality statistics remain unchanged. Even Dade (2006a: 90), a strong believer in the diaspora's development potential, notes that making these contributions take on a transformative role will not be automatic. Action on a number of fronts is still required and efforts on the part of traditional development actors (e.g., multilateral development banks) are needed to help create the necessary conditions and incentives for progress in this area.

Boosting Haiti's Private Sector

President Préval views his country's development as heavily dependent on private sector investment, which explains his courting of key Haitian private sector actors and his inclusion of private sector delegations in three post-election foreign trips (ICG, 2006: 9; Préval, 2006). Though the country's private sector remains fragile and weak, it is a major development objective of the Canadian government. For instance, Ottawa supports the Institut de la Francophonie pour l'administration et la gestion dans la Caraïbe – an initiative of *Agence Universitaire de la Francophonie* designed to train Haitian business leaders inside Haiti. Canada also acted as host for the first ever meeting between IADB President Enrique V. Iglesias and members of the Haitian private sector to discuss the latter's role in rebuilding Haiti (see IADB and CIDA 2005).

This focus is not without its challenges, however, the foremost being the suspicion with which international development agencies view the Haitian private sector. Haitian business elites have long been suspected of being more interested in turning a quick profit than in long-term economic development (Dade, 2006b), and past links among private sector players, Haitian dictators, the military, and para-military groups continue to cause concern among development agencies. Progressive elements are beginning to alter this perception, but this is a slow process.

Furthermore, there is little data to support the assumption that the poorest Haitians, many of whom make their living in the informal sector or in rural areas, will automatically benefit from a more robust private sector. Even the World Bank, a staunch supporter of private sector development, notes "that the evidence on small and medium enterprise [SME], growth and poverty, 'does not support the contention that SMEs are particularly effective job creators'" (cited in Tomlinson, 2004: 3). The Bank's analysis also reveals that "the size of the SME sector is not significantly associated with the income of the poorest quintile of society, the percentage of the population living below the poverty line, or the poverty gap" (Beck et al., 2003: 4). While prosperous and thriving economies usually have strong SME sectors, "cross-country comparisons do not indicate that SMEs exert a particularly beneficial impact on the incomes of the poor, [nor do they show] a significant relation between SMEs and measures of the depth and breadth of poverty" (Ibid.: 26).

Export Assembly Operations

In line with conventional economic thinking, Canada and other donors are pursuing a strategy that was also emphasized in the 1970s and 1980s – building up Haiti's export-oriented assembly operations. The previous attempt failed to spark economic development; instead, it increased inequality and poverty levels. Jean-Claude Duvalier championed export development manufacturing between 1971 and 1986. Various incentives – a tax holiday of ten years, complete profit repatriation, and a guaranteed non-unionized work force – led to the massive expansion of assembly operations. Exports from light industry grew at an average annual rate of 40 percent during the 1970s, and the number of companies engaged in assembly operations increased from 13 in 1966 to 154 in 1981 (Deere and Antrobus, 1990: 175). By the early 1980s, Haiti was second only to Mexico among US-centered subcontracting territories in the Western Hemisphere, with 240 multinational corporations employing

60,000 Haitian workers (Thomas, 1988: 95). In 1985, one year before Duvalier was forced into exile, Haiti was ranked ninth in the world in the assembly of goods for US consumption. The sector generated more than half of the country's industrial exports and earned one-quarter of its foreign exchange (McGowan, 1997: 5).

Despite this tremendous expansion, the effects on Haiti's overall economy were disappointing, especially in terms of the number of Haitians living at or below the poverty level. The country's debt increased from US$53 million in 1973 to US$366 million in 1980 – double the growth rate for external indebtedness in the entire Caribbean over the same period (McGowan, 1997: 4). Foreign-exchange reserves were exhausted by 1981. Commenting on Haiti's balance of payments, World Bank officials conceded that the assembly industry had, over the long term, made "almost no fiscal contribution" to the economy (Hooper, 1987: 37; Trouillot, 1990: 213).

Repercussions for Haiti's poorest citizens were significant. Faced with a shortfall in revenues from imports (since goods for assembly operations escaped customs duties), the government turned to consumption taxes that adversely affected rural peasants and members of the urban lower classes. Food costs increased sharply as production diminished – one result of the mass exodus from rural areas to Port-au-Prince, the primary site of the manufacturing sector. Between 1975 and 1985, the average price of all foodstuffs more than doubled (Trouillot, 1990: 216). In short, the light industry formula did not spark development or reduce poverty levels. In fact, the rapid spread of urban-based assembly firms reinforced economic polarization between Haiti's rural and urban sectors.

Ignoring the needs of the agrarian sector has been customary in Haiti and reflects a long-term pattern among donors as well. Development plans in the 1990s allocated only 7 percent of assistance to agriculture – the source of income for 80 percent of all Haitians living below the poverty line (ICG, 2006: 11; Morrell et al., 1999). Current donors argue that agriculture in Haiti is neither sustainable nor ecologically sound. To be sure, rural development is a daunting challenge. Haiti's landholdings are small, mainly on steep slopes, making mechanical farming virtually impossible, and close to one-third of all plots are in agriculturally marginal areas. Still, Haiti experts argue that these abysmal conditions make rural development essential, if for no other reason than to prevent the rural poor from slipping further into poverty (Barthélemy, 1989; Fatton, 2002; McGowan, 1997; Morrell et al., 1999). Without support, peasants will continue to stream into the overcrowded slums of Port-au-Prince, where jobs are scarce and poverty is already unbearable.[19] Restoring agricultural production and improving food security for rural households must be established as a strategic priority for international donors who make poverty reduction their primary objective.

Some members of the development community want the US Congress to pass the HOPE Act, which would give articles of clothing assembled in Haiti preferential access to the US market. They believe that such treatment would boost the apparel industry and create jobs. However, studies have shown that even if the export assembly industry were restored to 1980 levels, it would likely provide employment for only 1 percent of the population – about 3 percent of the Haitian work force (Creelman, 1995: 3). Thus, any resurrection of this strategy to reduce poverty in a meaningful way will require significant modifications. For instance, the industry would need to directly affect the rural sector. A decentralized rural industrialization plan that encourages the establishment of labour-intensive industries in different parts of the country, instead of concentrating them in or around Port-au-Prince, could do much to help achieve a rural-urban balance.[20]

Canada showed real leadership when it released its 2003 policy paper "Promoting Sustainable Rural Development through Agriculture," especially since it did so on the heels of substantial cuts in aid to agriculture and rural development by bilateral and multilateral agencies throughout the 1990s. Regrettably, Ottawa decided in 2005 to drop agriculture as a focus of its foreign aid program, which has repercussions for countries such as Haiti where the promotion of sustainable rural development through agriculture is crucial. Aid to peasant agriculture would encourage small-scale producers to remain on the land and improve their livelihoods through production of food for consumption and sale to local markets (CCIC, 2004: 5). To be sure, the new priorities of health, education, good governance, environment, and the private sector are important. However, it is difficult to imagine putting an end to extreme poverty in Haiti without a strong and sustained plan that specifically targets rural areas.

PROVIDING SECURITY

Haiti's ongoing security crisis has gone through a continuous series of dips and spikes over the past 15 years. Canada has sought to effect change in this critical area by contributing to the four UN missions deployed to Haiti throughout the 1990s. Immediately following President Aristide's forced departure, Ottawa committed 550 troops to the MIF for purposes of establishing a secure environment and facilitating a transition to MINUSTAH. The MINUSTAH force, which took control on

1 June 2004, consists of 7,151 soldiers from 15 countries, 1,752 civilian police (CIVPOL) from 35 countries, and more than 2,000 local and international civilian staff (ICG, 2006: 2; Morneau, 2006: 76–7). It is a peace enforcement mission created under Chapter VII of the UN Charter, which means it is expected to "execute offensive actions," something that its early contingents were uncomfortable putting into effect (Morneau, 2006: 76).[21]

Since its deployment, MINUSTAH has had to deal with violence from many quarters: "armed gangs with or without political ties to former President Jean-Bertrand Aristide, rogue police officers, former rebels and demobilized members of the former Haitian Armed Forces (Forces Armées d'Haïti, FAd'H), and organized crime" (Amnesty International, 2005). MINUSTAH was finally able to drive out armed rebels and ex-FAd'H forces from smaller provincial towns after it was fully deployed in 2005. Thus, violence in the country prior to the presidential elections was concentrated in Port-au-Prince's most overcrowded and indigent areas. The security situation has improved somewhat since the elections, with a reduction in kidnappings and other violent crimes. Progress has been attributed to the support Préval has been able to garner from key gang and community leaders in Cité Soleil (ICG, 2006: 7).

Canada's primary contribution to MINUSTAH has been directed to UN-CIVPOL, the entity that is responsible for training the HNP. We contributed about 100 civilian police officers early on, which was later supplemented with 25 retired officers just prior to the presidential election. In addition, the current head of UN-CIVPOL is a Canadian RCMP officer. Police training has been one our most important contributions and a focus since the mid-1990s. It is particularly significant given that Haiti has lacked a professional civilian police force for almost 200 years. Prior to the establishment of the HNP, police were viewed as part of a subservient force under the control of the military; they have long been accused of taking part in systematic human rights abuses (Thompson, A., 2006). The HNP's current importance is amplified by the fact that it is the only law enforcement agency in the country, as the army was disbanded in 1995, and Haiti has no municipal or provincial police forces.

While Canada's policing assistance has been important, its impact has been diminished by serious deficiencies within the HNP and MINUSTAH. The HNP has been plagued by questionable training and unqualified officers, while MINUSTAH has suffered from huge resource and capability gaps, a lack of reliable intelligence, divided loyalties, and conflicting mandates (Amnesty International, 2005; ICG, 2005; Morneau, 2006).

MINUSTAH's standing has also been damaged by a large number of casualties resulting from firefights with armed gangs and a failure to report and/or investigate human rights abuses (Amnesty International, 2005). Some critics have charged the mission with being too heavy-handed, resulting in the deaths of innocent Haitians (Diceanu, 2006). Others have accused it of not doing enough to quell Haiti's ongoing violence (Williams, 2006). According to press accounts, Brazilians in MINUSTAH leadership positions have admitted that the mission has failed to provide widespread security or prevent crime and political murders that continue to plague the country (Klarreich, 2006).

The issue that has received the most attention from peacebuilding scholars and human rights advocates is MINUSTAH's mandate, which consists of three broad objectives: ensuring that conditions are stable enough to advance the political process; assisting the government in reforming the Haitian National Police; and, assisting in disarmament, demobilization, and reintegration programs (OAS, 2005). The conflict stems from having the task of 'assisting' the Haitian National Police while simultaneously having to protect Haiti's citizens from human rights offences by HNP officers. Because of this dual mandate, MINUSTAH has been accused of providing "unquestioning support to police operations that have resulted in warrantless arrests and detentions, unintended civilian casualties and deliberate extrajudicial killings" (Harvard Law Student Advocates, 2005: 48). In addition to accusations of serious human rights violations, the Haitian National Police has also been accused of corruption and involvement in criminal activities (Amnesty International, 2005; ICG, 2005: 14). Assisting a police force with such deficiencies has discredited MINUSTAH in the eyes of many Haitians.

The solution, according to some, is for MINUSTAH to take over the defective force and act as a primary law enforcer. Others have suggested that the UN-CIVPOL officers (including Canadians) should be stationed alongside their Haitian counterparts across the country and take responsibility for discipline of the HNP, in order to effectively deal with misconduct issues (ICG, 2006: 9). Of course the government of Haiti would have to be in agreement with these measures. The transitional government was not. One year prior to the elections, then-Minister of Justice Bernard Gousse proclaimed that limits placed on Haitian police by the UN were illegal and usurped the rights of the Haitian state (cited in ICG, 2005: 19). Furthermore, in March 2005, MINUSTAH soldiers reportedly intervened when violence erupted between pro-Aristide demonstrators and the HNP. While demonstrators expressed gratitude, Haitian government authorities described the intervention as "a breach of MINUSTAH's mandate" (Amnesty International, 2005). This lack of collaboration is less likely to be an issue with the new Préval government but it does underscore the intense sensitivity that

Haitians feel about their sovereignty; indeed, a small but vocal group of nationalists continue to call for MINUSTAH's removal.

Another security problem is the proliferation of small arms and light weapons. The International Crisis Group (2006) suggests that disarmament may be the most pressing issue for the new Préval government. According to the Geneva-based Small Arms Survey, there were nearly 170,000 guns in Haiti in 2004 and 2005, most of them in the hands of criminal gangs, armed civilian groups, and security and law enforcement officers (Muggah, 2005). MINUSTAH head Juan Gabriel Valdes admits that MINUSTAH has made little progress in this area. He suggests that this failure is because, unlike most UN missions, disarmament in Haiti is not a collective problem. MINUSTAH is not faced with an army, militia, or guerrilla group, but armed individuals who perceive their weapons as necessary for self-defence and for providing food for themselves and their families, as well as for attacking others (Thompson, G., 2006). Moreover, there is agreement among peacebuilding agencies that conventional disarmament, demobilisation, and reintegration (DDR) programs are difficult to implement in countries such as Haiti that lack formal peace accords, reconciliation processes, or political agreements (ICG, 2006: 8).

The most worrisome potential outcome of a failed security effort and continued arms proliferation is the re-establishment of the FAd'H. There have been calls for the army's re-establishment ever since Aristide was forced out of office in 2004. This pressure began with the shocking re-branding of the army by former Prime Minister Latortue who referred to the former military and paramilitary rebels who ousted Aristide as 'freedom fighters.' In addition, an alarming number of political and economic elites have indicated their support for the reestablishment of the FAd'H, despite its historical involvement in human rights abuses and lack of strategic purpose. The country is not being threatened by a neighbouring state, therefore its security needs are better focused on specific internal problems. Obvious needs are to strengthen border operations and the Haitian coast guard for the purpose of blocking drug trafficking, and strengthening internal operations for the purpose of reducing crime. Neither task requires a standing army. Given the country's security requirements, finances, and the urgent need to focus on democratization and civilian needs, re-instituting the FAd'H is ill-advised. Moreover, there has not been any open debate about this issue (ICG, 2005: 18). The views of ordinary Haitians must be gathered and considered, and the international community should support the Préval government's consultation efforts.

CONCLUSION

This chapter has considered Canada's foreign policy toward Haiti in three areas: democracy building, development and poverty alleviation, and security. Concerning democracy, I have argued that Ottawa's support of Haiti's electoral process (both the February 2006 presidential and 21 April second round parliamentary elections) was valuable and commendable, but its conduct during President Aristide's removal in 2004 eroded its position as one of the region's most active and committed supporters of democratic governance. My point is not that Canada should have supported Aristide the man, but it should have done much more within its power to support his office and position as a constitutionally elected leader.

Concerning development – that is, reducing poverty and inequality and building a viable economy – Canada's principal aid agency (CIDA) appears positioned to implement some innovative thinking as part of its bilateral program. However, Canadian leaders have decided to follow the lead of other major donors in applying a predominantly urban-based development strategy. This approach proved unsuccessful in the 1970s and 1980s, when the Haitian government overlooked its rural sector in favour of promoting export processing zones. The argument here is not that foreign donors should orient the bulk of their aid and loans to the agricultural sector. Given the level of environment degradation, over population, and increased division of landholdings, agriculture will never become Haiti's primary engine of economic growth (Maingot, 1996: 195–8). However, if poverty reduction is indeed a primary objective for Canada and other international donors, restoring agricultural production and improving food security for rural households must be made a strategic priority.

Concerning security, the overall level of violence in Haiti has decreased, but tensions remain high and the political peace fragile. Peacebuilding scholars and practitioners agree on two things, that security is the first step in a long process of social and economic reconstruction, and that the HNP cannot provide security without outside help in the form of training and monitoring. Canada is making a strong effort in this area, especially in terms of training, but more assistance will be required. It is expected that Haiti will have approximately 6,000 police officers by the end of President Préval's term in office, but the country needs at least 15,000 officers to be truly effective (ICG, 2006: 9). However, Morneau (2006: 72) notes that even 15,000 would leave Haiti's 8.5 million residents under-policed; in comparison, New York City has 40,000 officers for its 8 million residents.

There are significant opportunities for Canadian leadership in Haiti, especially in the areas of security and policing. Canada's policy in the

Americas can best be described as autonomy without ruffling US feathers. Helping the Préval government establish security fits well with this agenda. As Christopher Sands notes in this volume, when it comes to our relationship with the United States, Canada has greater flexibility on third-country issues. Such issues may therefore constitute the best way to strengthen our relationship with the wary mammoth. If Sands is correct, he provides a powerful argument for increasing our aid and presence in Haiti, since it would be in accordance with Washington's interests.

Following from this, it also makes more sense to devote peacebuilding resources to Haiti (given that stability is far from assured and MINUSTAH requires strengthening) than it does to Afghanistan. Prime Minister Stephen Harper's visit to Afghanistan may have played well in the United States, but Canadians remain unconvinced, as public commitment to that effort remains tepid.[22] In fact, Canadians appear to be more comfortable with sending troops to Darfur than to Afghanistan: the former reflecting our values (a humanitarian ethos) and the latter our interests (strengthening relations across the 49th parallel) (Travers, 2006). The allure of Haiti is that our involvement there speaks to both – assisting an extremely poor country in our own (and Washington's) backyard. Most importantly, our peacebuilding efforts in Haiti, a country with which we have a long-standing relationship, would not be intertwined with Washington's dubious 'war on terror.'

NOTES

1 It is worth noting from the outset that the C$180 million pales in comparison to the C$2 billion Canada has spent in Afghanistan. These statistics are cited in Trudeau (2006).

2 The friends of Haiti include Argentina, Bahamas, Belize, Canada, Chile, the Dominican Republic, Guatemala, Mexico, and the United States, as well as a small number of European states: Germany, Spain, France, and Norway.

3 This 'whole-of-government' approach is outlined in Canada's five-part, *International Policy Statement: A Role of Pride and Influence in the World*, of April 2005.

4 Canadian exports to Haiti include meat, fish and other seafood, vegetables, paper and cardboard, and electric materials. We import textile articles, fish and shellfish, cocoa, fruits, and string.

5 For an engaging discussion of the split between Canada's left-leaning NGOs who work on Haiti, see Hodgson (2006).

6 This phrasing comes from Robert McRae, who suggests that the reason that we tend to be in accord with US foreign policy is not because we "bend to

US will" but because "similar impulses animate a good deal of our international policies" (McRae, 2005: 68–9).

7 The UPD was renamed the Office for the Promotion of Democracy (OPD) and placed under a newly created Department for Democratic and Political Affairs (DDPA) in September 2004. The head of the OPD has always been a Canadian.

8 A comprehensive account of the events leading up to Aristide's ouster in 2004 are provided in ICG (2004). For an excellent account of the US role, see Bogdanich and Nordberg (2006). For a critical account of Canada's role, see Engler and Fenton (2005).

9 For a transcription of the Vastel's interview on CBC Radio, *The Current*, 6 August 2004, see: <http://dominionpaper.ca/weblog/2004/08/cbcs_the_current_discusses_canadas_coupplotting_in_haiti.html>

10 For a good account of House of Commons debates on Haiti, see Fenton (2004).

11 This action was authorized by UN Security Council Resolution 1529, of 29 February 2004.

12 Both presidential and legislative elections took place on 7 February 2006, but a second round of parliamentary elections was held on 21 April 2006.

13 Cited from an interview for CBC Radio, *The Current*, 14 August 2004.

14 CIDA's new approach to Haiti is also heavily influenced by OECD DAC research on aid allocation to fragile states as well as the World Bank's Low Income Countries Under Stress (LICUS) initiative.

15 The ICF was set to expire in September 2006 but has been extended to December 2007.

16 Harper met with President-elect Préval in May 2006 pledging C$48 million to promote good governance and democracy over the next five years. C$30 million is new money over and above the C$190 million already pledged. C$20 million will be devoted to local development initiatives, C$5 million to strengthening parliament; C$5 million to a local fund that supports good governance and human rights, and C$18 million will help pay down Haiti's debt to the IADB. For detailed breakdown of funds, see: <http://www.acdi-cida.gc.ca/CIDAWEB/acdicida.nsf/En/JOS-5913146-MYN>; On 3 June 2006, the government announced an additional C$15 million, from the Global Peace and Security Fund to be administered by Foreign Affairs Canada, to help strengthen democratic institutions in Haiti.

17 Interestingly, Denis Coderre, former Prime Minister Paul Martin's special advisor for Haiti, retained his seat by a wide margin of over 5,000 votes.

18 Then Prime Minister Martin opened the two-day meeting. For the final report, see: <http://www.focal.ca/pdf/Rapport%20Final%20Haïti.pdf>

19 The rural exodus since 1986–87 has increased Port-au-Prince's population by 20.7 percent leading to tremendous sanitation problems (due to insufficient urban infrastructure) and a further swelling of the informal sector. Both have been linked to increases in urban-based violence since late 2003 (McGuigan, 2006: 38).

20 For a similar argument on Ecuador, see North and Cameron (2000).

21 Originally authorized for six months, the mandate has been extended and is expected to be renewed in the future.

22 A poll conducted in May 2006 by the Strategic Counsel for CTV and the *Globe and Mail* found that 54 percent of Canadians were against the deployment of troops, with 23 percent being strongly opposed.

REFERENCES

Amnesty International. 2005. "Haiti: Disarmament Delayed, Justice Denied," 28 July. 9 May 2006. Available at: <http://web.amnesty.org/library/Index/ENGAMR360052005>

Axworthy, Thomas, and Leslie Campbell. 2004. "Advancing Democracy Abroad: A Proposal to Create the Democracy Canada Institute," Conference paper for *Canada's Role in International Assistance to Democratic Development*, The Institute for Research on Public Policy, Ottawa, 10 September.

Barthélemy, Gérard. 1989. *Le Pays en dehors: Essai sur l'univers rural Haitien.* Montreal: Le Centre International de Documentation et d'Information Haïtienne, Caraibeene et Afro-Canadienne (CIDIHCA).

Beck, Thorsten, Asli Demirguc-Kunt, and Ross Levine. 2003. *Small and Medium Enterprises, Growth, and Poverty: Cross-Country Evidence.* Washington, DC: The World Bank.

Bogdanich, Walt, and Jenny Nordberg. 2006. "Mixed U.S. Signals Helped Tilt Haiti toward Chaos," *The New York Times*, 29 January.

Cameron, Maxwell. 2004. "We're Failing Elected Leaders," Editorial, *The Globe and Mail*, 9 March, A15.

CARICOM. 2004. Statement issued by CARICOM Heads of Government at the Conclusion of an Emergency Session on the Situation in Haiti, Kingston, Jamaica, 3 March. Available at: <http://www.haiti.org/Whatsnew/press_release_03_02_04.htm>

Canada. 2003. "Promoting Sustainable Rural Development through Agriculture," *Canada Making a Difference in the World*. Ottawa: Canadian International Development Agency (CIDA). Available at: <http://www.acdi-cida.gc.ca/INET/IMAGES.NSF/vLUImages/agriculture/$file/Agriculture-e.pdf>

– 2004a. "Canada Participates in CARICOM Meeting to Address Situation in Haiti," News Release 7. Ottawa: Department of Foreign Affairs and International Trade (DFAIT), 21 January.

– 2004b. "Canadian Cooperation with Haiti: Reflecting on a Decade of 'Difficult Partnership,'" Strategy Paper for the OECD. Ottawa: Canadian International Development Agency (CIDA), December. Available at: <www.oecd.org/dataoecd/41/45/34095943.pdf>

CCIC. 2004. "A Food Security Perspective on Canada's International Trade and Development Assistance Policies," Discussion Paper for the Government of Canada's International Policy Review. Ottawa: Canadian Council for International Cooperation (CCIC).

Council on Hemispheric Affairs. 2006. "Canada's Aid to Haiti: Commendable or Making Amends for a Discredited Anti Aristide Strategy?" *COHA Report*, 30 March. Available at: <http://www.coha.org/NEW_PRESS_RELEASES/New_Press_Releases_2006/COHA%20Report/COHA_REPORT_06.04_Canada_Haiti.htm>

Creelman, Matthew. 1995. "Haiti: US Plan for Economic Recovery Depends Heavily on Private Sector Reactivation," *Chronicle of Latin American Economic Affairs* 10, no. 18 (4 May): 1–4.

Dade, Carlo. 2006a. "The Role of the Private Sector and the Diaspora in Rebuilding Haiti," in Yasmine Shamsie and Andrew S. Thompson, eds. *Haiti: Hope for a Fragile State*. Waterloo, ON: Wilfrid Laurier University Press and The Centre for International Governance Innovation, 85–98.

– 2006b. Telephone Interview with Author, Waterloo, 7 May.

Deere, Carmen Diana, and Peggy Antrobus, eds. 1990. *In the Shadow of the Sun: Caribbean Development Alternatives and U.S. Policy*. Boulder, CO: Westview Press.

Diceanu, Alex. 2006. "Haiti Deserves Better from the United Nations," *Peace Magazine* 22, no. 2 (April-June): 16–8.

Engler, Yves, and Anthony Fenton. 2005. *Canada in Haiti: Waging War on the Poor Majority*. Halifax: Fernwood Press.

Erikson, Daniel P. 2004. "Haiti: Challenges in Poverty Reduction," Conference Report. Washington, DC: Inter-American Dialogue.

Fagen, Patricia, and Micah Bump. 2005. "Remittances from Neighbors: Trends in Intra-Regional Remittance Flows," in Inter-American Development Bank, ed. *Beyond Small Change: Making Migrants' Remittances Count*. Washington: IADB.

Fatton, Robert, Jr. 2002. *Haiti's Predatory Republic. The Unending Transition to Democracy*. Boulder, CO: Lynne Rienner.

– 2004. "Upheaval in Haiti," PBS TV Interview, *Newshour*, 1 March. Available at: <http://www.pbs.org/newshour/bb/latin_america/jan-june04/haiti_3-1.html>

– 2006. "The Fall of Aristide and Haiti's Current Predicament," in Yasmine Shamsie and Andrew S. Thompson, eds. *Haiti. Hope for a Fragile State*. Waterloo, ON: Wilfrid Laurier University Press and The Centre for International Governance Innovation, 15–35.

Fenton, Anthony. 2004. "The Canadian Connection," *ZNet*, 11 March. Available at: <http://www.zmag.org/content/showarticle.cfm?ItemID=5140>

Goldring, Luin. 2003. "Re-thinking Remittances: Social and Political Dimensions of Individual and Collective Remittances," *CERLAC*

Working Paper Series. Toronto: Centre for Research on Latin America and the Caribbean.

Harvard Law Student Advocates for Human Rights and Centro de Justiça Global. 2005 *Keeping the Peace in Haiti? An Assessment of the United Nations Stabilization Mission in Haiti Using Compliance with Its Prescribed Mandate as a Barometer for Success*. Independent Report, March. Available at: <http://www.law.harvard.edu/programs/hrp/clinic/documents/Haiti_English_Final.pdf>

Hodgson, Jim. 2006. "Dissonant Voices: Northern NGO and Haitian Partner Perspectives on the Future of Haiti," in Yasmine Shamsie and Andrew S. Thompson, eds. *Haiti. Hope for a Fragile State*. Waterloo, ON: Wilfrid Laurier University Press and The Centre for International Governance Innovation, 99–110.

Hooper, Michael S. 1987. "Model Underdevelopment," *NACLA Report on the Americas* 21, no. 3 (May): 32–9.

IADB and CIDA. 2005. "The Role of the Private Sector in Rebuilding Haiti," Conference Report. Inter-American Development Bank (IADB) and Canadian International Development Agency (CIDA), Meech Lake, QC, 9–10 September.

International Crisis Group (ICG). 2004. "A New Chance for Haiti?" *Latin America/Caribbean Report*, no. 10 (18 November).

– 2005. "Spoiling Security in Haiti," *Latin America/Caribbean Report*, no. 13 (31 May).

– 2006. "Haiti after the Elections: Challenges for Préval's First 100 Days," *Latin America/Caribbean Briefing*, no. 10 (11 May).

Keating, Tom. 2001. "Promoting Democracy in Haiti: Assessing the Practical and Ethical Implications," in Rosalind Irwin, ed. *Ethics and Security in Canadian Foreign Policy*. Vancouver: UBC Press, 208–26.

Klarreich, Kathie. 2006. "Policing Haiti," Web Posting, *Time.com*, 5 January. Available at: <http://www.time.com/time/world/article/0,8599,1146293,00.html>

Lobe, Jim. 2004. "Role in Haiti Events Backfiring on Washington," *Inter Press Service*, 12 March. Available at: <http://www.commondreams.org/headlines04/0312-03.htm>

Maingot, Anthony P. 1996. "Sovereign Consent versus State-Centric Sovereignty," in Tom Farer, ed. *Beyond Sovereignty: Collectively Defending Democracy in the Americas*. Baltimore and London: The Johns Hopkins University Press, 189–212.

McGowan, Lisa. 1997. *Democracy Undermined Economic Justice Denied: Structural Adjustment and the Aid Juggernaut in Haiti*. Washington: The Development Gap.

McGuigan, Claire. 2006. Agricultural Liberalisation in Haïti. London: Christian Aid, March.

McRae, Robert. 2005. "International Policy Reviews in Perspective," in David Carment, Fen Olser Hampson, and Norman Hillmer, eds. *Canada Among Nations 2004: Setting Priorities Straight*. Montreal & Kingston: McGill-Queen's University Press, 55–72.

Morneau, Jacques. 2006. "Reflections on the Situation in Haiti" in Yasmine Shamsie and Andrew S. Thompson, eds. *Haiti: Hope for a Fragile State*. Waterloo, ON: Wilfrid Laurier University Press and The Centre for International Governance Innovation, 71–84.

Morrell, James R., Rachel Neild, and Hugh Byrne. 1999. "Haiti and the Limits to Nation Building," *Current History* 98, no. 626 (March): 127–32.

Muggah, Robert. 2005. "Securing Haiti's Transition: Reviewing Human Insecurity and the Prospects for Disarmament, Demobilization and Reintegration," *Small Arms Survey*, Occasional Paper, no. 14 (November).

North, Liisa L., and John D. Cameron. 2000. "Grassroots-based Rural Development Strategies: Ecuador in Comparative Perspective," *World Development* 28, no. 10 (October): 1751–66.

Organization of American States (OAS). 1991. The Santiago Commitment to Democracy and the Renewal of the Inter-American System, OAS General Assembly, AG/DOC. 2374/91.

– 2005. "Human Rights Developments in the Region: Haiti," in *Annual Report of the Inter-American Commission on Human Rights 2004*. Washington, DC: Inter-American Commission on Human Rights (OEA/Ser.L/V/II.122, Doc. 5 , rev. 1), 23 February.

Orozco, Manuel, Lindsay Lowell, Michah Bump, and Rachel Fedewa. 2005. "Transnational Engagement, Remittances and their Relationship in Latin America and the Caribbean," *Report to the Rockefeller Foundation*. Washington, DC: Institute for the Study of International Migration, Georgetown University.

Préval, Rene Garcia. 2006. "Less Poverty, More Hope," *Miami Herald*, 29 March.

Québec. 2006. "Haiti: Relations with Québec," *Rélations internationales Québec*. 27 April. 9 May 2006. Available at: <http://www.mri.gouv.qc.ca/en>

Simmons, Allan, Dwaine Plaza, and Voctor Piche. 2005. "The Remittance Sending Practices of Haitians and Jamaicans in Canada," Report to CIDA. Toronto: Centre for Research on Latin America and the Caribbean.

Sletten, Pal, and Willy Egset. 2004. "Poverty in Haiti," *Fafo-paper* 31. Oslo: Institute for Applied Social Science (Fafo).

Thérien, Jean-Philippe, Gordon Mace, and Myriam Roberge. 2004. "Le Canada et les Amériques: la difficile construction d'une identité régionale," *Canadian Foreign Policy* 11, no. 3 (Spring): 17–37.

Thomas, Clive Y. 1988. *The Poor and the Powerless: Economic Policy and Change in the Caribbean*. New York: Monthly Review Press.

Thompson, Andrew S. 2006. "Haiti's Tenuous Human Rights Climate," in Yasmine Shamsie and Andrew S. Thompson, eds. *Haiti. Hope for a Fragile*

State. Waterloo, ON: Wilfrid Laurier University Press and The Centre for International Governance Innovation, 51–70.

Thompson, Ginger. 2006. "Fear and Death Ensnare UN's Soldiers in Haiti," *The New York Times*, 24 January, A1.

Tomlinson, Brian. 2004. "The UNDP Commission on the Private Sector and Development. Unleashing Entrepreneurship: Making Business Work for the Poor," *CCIC Commentary* (March). Ottawa: Canadian Council for International Cooperation, 1–10.

Travers, James. 2006. "For Harper, It's Either Darfur or Afghanistan," *Toronto Star*, 13 May, F2.

Trudeau, Alexandre. 2006. "Our Third Chance," CBC Radio Documentary, *The Current*, 2 May.

Trouillot, Michel-Rolph. 1990. *Haiti. State Against Nation: The Origins and Legacy of Duvalierism*. New York: Monthly Review Press.

United States. 2004. Press briefing by Secretary of State Colin Powell and Honoured Guests, 13 February. Washington, DC: Department of State. Available at: <http://lists.state.gov/SCRIPTS/WA-USIAINFO.EXE?A2=ind0402b&L=dospress&H=1&O=D&P=2150>

Williams, Carol J. 2006. "Mission Missing Its Mark," *Los Angeles Times*, 9 January. Available at: <http://www.latimes.com>

12 Canada and Quebec on the World Scene: Defining New Rules?

NELSON MICHAUD

On 19 December 2005, Stephen Harper made an important election stop in Quebec City in an effort to strengthen local support for two of his candidates. At mid-course in the campaign, both Josée Verner (in the riding of Louis-St Laurent) and Maxime Bernier (of Beauce) enjoyed strong support in their communities. The timing and location of the visit was thus strategic, as it offered the Conservative leader an opportunity to launch the party's Quebec agenda before a receptive audience and at a time when Liberal support was slipping even further in the province. The time was right for Harper to be bold in Quebec, and he set out to consolidate this support and turn it into much needed Tory seats.

Built on the theme of "open federalism" (Harper, 2005), the speech was essentially a call to Quebec's autonomist voters who believe in the respect of the separation of powers as constitutionally defined; to those who are not inclined to support separation, but are nevertheless uncomfortable with a centralist federal government; to those who do not want to vote for the Liberals (especially after the sponsorship scandal); and to those who used to turn to the Bloc Québécois due to the lack of alternatives. The speech was an attempt to introduce the Conservative Party as a viable option for moderate Quebec voters, having largely ignored the province in their election preparations until then,[1] and in light of the traditional absence of the New Democratic Party (NDP) as an alternative on the Quebec political radar screen.

Sensing a momentum elsewhere in the country, especially after the insinuations that Ralph Goodale, the Liberal finance minister, had leaked information about his latest budget to the benefit of a few, Harper had no choice but to make a move in order to ensure some gains in Quebec – his credibility as a national leader and eventually as prime minister was at stake. He needed Quebec seats to win the election including, if successful in this regard, a few competent members to invite to the Cabinet table. The Quebec City Chamber of Commerce speech was his best chance to hit these two targets. Additionally, the geographic location was optimal for Harper to reach his goals, as the Quebec City area had shown some interest in Mario Dumont's right wing Action Démocratique party in the latest provincial elections and by-elections, and ridings on the south shore had been identified for some time as a fertile ground for conservative hopefuls (Drouilly, 1998).

What is surprising to some extent is that in a speech that was obviously loaded with phrases crafted to address domestic concerns and aimed at echoing Brian Mulroney's 1984 Baie Comeau declaration, which invited Quebec back to the Canadian family table, Harper included a major commitment towards Quebec's role on the international scene, redefining what was up to then a cornerstone of Canadian foreign policy dogma.

Leaving aside any prudence dictated by Privy Council Office (PCO) and Foreign Affairs officials, Harper declared that under his government, Quebec would get a seat at the United Nations Educational, Scientific and Cultural Organization (UNESCO) following the model agreement that is operational in la Francophonie. Analysts were quick to point out that such a promise was beyond the purview of the Canadian government; the organization's own rules do not allow such an arrangement to take place, since it does not recognize 'participating government' status. Notwithstanding the actual format the agreement would be translated into, the intent was clear: Harper wanted to leave his imprint on a forty year old debate regarding Quebec's international role and settle the issue to the satisfaction of Quebec's autonomist voters.

Undoubtedly, and regardless of the longevity of the Harper government, any action taken regarding this question would shape not only the federal relations with Quebec, but also the development of Canadian foreign policy. To fully explain the significance of this new direction, this chapter examines the basis on which these requests from the Quebec government rest. Next, it will identify the grounds on which any federal response can be based, and the potential answers that are available. Finally, as Harper was swift to act on this and several other questions, the last part of this chapter will look at the solution he has offered, the reaction of the Quebec government, and the prospects for the future of this policy.

QUEBEC'S INTERNATIONAL ROLE

The debate that Harper hoped to put to rest can be summed up in a simple question: what shape (if any) should Quebec's international presence and actions take? This question has lingered in the political landscape for several years, but recent influences of globalization have contributed greatly to its renewed significance.

One effect of globalization has been the increase in the number of international norms and standards states must consider when they legislate. These norms and standards have steadily impinged on the constitutionally defined jurisdictions of federated entities, compelling these entities to react. Specifically, this external pressure has incited several federated entities, including Quebec, to be active on the international scene and to exercise an upstream influence on the setting of these international standards, in view of having these norms take into account their respective values and identity.

Although the quest for an international presence has been rejuvenated by globalization, it is nevertheless part of a long-standing interest the Quebec government has expressed over the years. Therefore, to answer the initial question of this section, one must first consider historical precedents. Specifically we must recognize that Quebec's pursuit of an international identity is not simply the opportunistic reaction by a determined minority with a set agenda to the arrival of propitious circumstances.[2]

Quebec's international presence dates back to the nineteenth century, when commercial agents were sent to London, Dublin, Paris, and later Brussels. In those days, Canada had to operate from the British legations around the world (or through Quebec's agents!) since the country was not allowed to conduct its own foreign relations. These relations remained under the Empire's responsibility and under London's management until the adoption of the Statute of Westminster in 1931. Quebec's agents were the precursors of today's *délégués* and *délégués généraux* who are contemporary Quebec representatives around the world.

These first attempts were followed, in 1940, by the opening of a trade office in New York City by Adélard Godbout's Liberal government. The rationale for this initiative largely rested on the need to help the province recover from the Great Depression. Despite his reluctance towards any international action, Union Nationale[3] Premier Maurice Duplessis kept the office open. These meagre operations were to be sustained, a few years later, by the wind of change brought by the Quiet Revolution.

When Quebecers elected Jean Lesage and his Liberal "Thunder Team" in June 1960, the province was ready for a major transformation. The modernization of its governance through the establishment of a professional public service was at the heart of the movement and these sweeping changes were not possible without relying on some other governments' expertise. In order to facilitate these needed exchanges, the Quebec government signed agreements with, first, the French government. The initiative met strong opposition from Ottawa, and it is this opposition that is at the heart of the debate Harper hoped to seal in history books with his 19 December commitment. It is then not surprising if observers and analysts with a sense of history commented that the contemporary pros from Quebec and cons from the Pearson building and the PCO were bearing a tone of familiarity when compared to those advocated in Paul Gérin-Lajoie's and Paul Martin Sr.'s time.

In those days, the opposition from Ottawa to Quebec's initiatives was harsh, and grew stronger in 1968 when Quebec received an invitation directly from an African country (Gabon) to participate in an international summit on education, a matter under its sole jurisdiction.[4] The incident turned into diplomatic discord, with Canada nearly severing its links with the offender, although the original invitation was made at the behest of France. It also helped spur the Canadian government into consolidating its international aid programs by establishing the Canadian International Development Agency – whose headquarters were conveniently located on the Quebec side of the Ottawa River – and to direct it to spend greater attention to French speaking West African countries.

The rationale for Quebec's international involvement has been worded by Paul Gérin-Lajoie, then Quebec minister of Education and deputy premier, in an April 1965 speech, delivered before the Consular corps based in Montréal.[5] He reiterated his doctrine a few weeks later in Quebec City at a dinner hosting European scholars, and it was at the Legislative Assembly in 1967, during the second reading of the bill instituting the Ministère des relations intergouvernementales, that he phrased his thoughts in the way that he is still cited today: Quebec's international relations are defined as "the external prolongation of its domestic fields of jurisdiction" (Quebec, 1967).

This doctrine has been the constant basis on which Quebec's international presence has been developed since then, notwithstanding the political stripes of the governing party. The present government is no different in this matter. In a speech delivered at the École nationale d'administration publique in February 2004, Premier Jean Charest (2004) paraphrased the Gérin-Lajoie doctrine in stating that "ce qui est de competence du Quebec chez nous, est de competence du Quebec partout."[6] Since then, this new motto has been used time and again by Charest himself, by Monique Gagnon-Tremblay, his minister of international relations, and by Benoît Pelletier, his minister of Canadian intergovernmental affairs.

The source of this long standing policy was André Patry, a constitutional lawyer and artisan of the Quiet Revolution (Aird, 2005). Patry anchored the policy postulate on decisions rendered by the Judicial Committee of the Privy Council in the 1930s. These rulings clearly established that provinces have full responsibility in the application and implementation of international treaties and standards in their own fields of jurisdiction. This interpretation is based on the silence of the Canadian Constitution on questions of international relations and foreign policy and on unambiguous jurisprudence related to section 92 that defines which questions fall under the provincial legislative responsibilities.[7] It is on these constitutional grounds that Quebec built its international action.

As a result, for almost forty-five years, Quebec has established a network of delegations that covers key regions where its interests are at stake. This network has experienced continuous support from consecutive Quebec governments, except when difficult fiscal circumstances forced Lucien Bouchard's Parti Québécois (PQ) administration to close several posts in the pursuit of his 'zero deficit' objective. The most recent policy, tabled by Monique Gagnon-Tremblay at the end of May 2006, calls for an increased Quebec presence and representation abroad in countries such as the United States and Germany. In addition, new office are to be opened in India and Brazil, and more resources allocated to representation in China (Quebec, 2006).

The Quebec government has also entered into over 550 international agreements, with more than 300 of them still in effect. In 1985, Prime Minister Mulroney and Premier Pierre-Marc Johnson resolved a long standing problem by defining the status that allowed Quebec an autonomous participation at the meetings and in the institutions of la Francophonie. Finally, in May 2002, Quebec's National Assembly became the first Westminster-type parliament in the world to grant itself the legislative powers to study and vote on the implementation of international treaties.[8]

As we may appreciate, Quebec's international role rests on an interpretation of the Canadian constitution, which leaves room for provincial international involvement; with time, its practice has evolved and been refined. It is at this point that globalization comes into play, setting new standards on matters that are dealt with at the level of federated entities, challenging the role of Canadian provinces, Mexican states, or even Austrian Länder. These sub-national actors must avoid being left aside, and they must seize the opportunities for development that globalization offers. These opportunities define a new modernity and Quebec (as well as all other federated entities) cannot take the risk of ignoring it. The question then arises; is this a sufficient reason to justify further international activity on the part of Quebec? The Charest government seems to think so. This is why it petitioned Ottawa to obtain recognition for an international role better suited to its interests.

In so doing, Quebec ministers Monique Gagnon-Tremblay and Benoît Pelletier expressed opinions that were dissenting from Ottawa's traditional credo of 'one country, one voice.' By the end of the summer and during early fall 2005, they had claimed for some time and with insistence that Quebec should be more involved in the crafting of Canada's international stance on questions of provincial jurisdiction. Moreover, they defended Quebec's right to express itself in some fora where matters that come under its constitutional responsibility are discussed; areas such as culture, language, education, health care, and labour.

The Quebec government had some foundations upon which to build its position: During the 2004 electoral campaign, Paul Martin Jr. (2004) had promised to provide an answer to Quebec's wish to play a more active role in the international defence of its domestic and jurisdictional interests. However, the *International Policy Statement* that his government issued about a year later turned 180 degrees (see Canada, 2005). A clash between Ottawa and Quebec was unavoidable and it happened as Pelletier and Martin's Quebec lieutenant, Minister of Transportation Jean Lapierre, exchanged harsh words on this issue, via the media.[9]

As an ultimate attempt to better define the Quebec government's demands and structure requests it addressed to Ottawa, Monique Gagnon-Tremblay issued, in mid-September 2005, a document that outlined what the government's five priorities were concerning Quebec's participation in international fora:

1 Getting access to all information and ensuring an upstream participation in the development of the Canadian position;
2 Having a representative being recognized as a full member of the Canadian delegation, Quebec having the exclusive responsibility regarding her or his designation;
3 Being recognized as having the right to express itself and speak from its own voice within international fora when matters related to its constitutional responsibilities are discussed;
4 Being recognized as having the right to grant its approval before Canada signs or declares itself part of a treaty or of an international agreement that relates to matters of Quebec's jurisdiction;
5 Being recognized to have the right to express its own stance when Canada appears before international organizations' control authorities, if it is a party to the case or if its interests are at stake. (Quebec, 2005b)

The document also mentions that, in the specific case of the UNESCO, Quebec is asking for a review of the Canadian mission's mandate so that it is the Quebec government that is responsible for conducting the consultation with its civil society (Ibid.). According to Gagnon-Tremblay's own statement, all this would be done with the objective of reinforcing Canada's international stance and role (Quebec, 2005a).

Following the publication of the document, Quebec ministers Gagnon-Tremblay and Pelletier met with their federal counterparts, Pierre Pettigrew and Lucienne Robillard, in October, but no solution was in sight. This dead end dialogue of the deaf characterized the debate in December 2005, when Harper presented his policy platform in Quebec City.

POTENTIAL ANSWERS

As mentioned earlier, Harper's offer to have Quebec represented at UNESCO was enthusiastic but not feasible. Unlike la Francophonie, UNESCO recognizes only UN members as full fledged participants, a demand that, obviously, Quebec does not fulfill. Several solutions came first to mind. Amendments to the UNESCO charter were among them. However, this represented a long, complex, and high risk solution that offered meagre hopes of reaching favourable results. There was also the possibility of getting Quebec an 'associate membership,' but this would have meant that, to meet UNESCO's criteria for such membership, Quebec would have to recognize that it had no control over its own foreign relations, a counterproductive outcome that would have erased forty years of work towards the establishment of an international role of its own.[10]

A look at procedures other federated entities have established in dealing with this problem offers some possible options beyond the two mentioned above, which were among the first identified by those involved in the Canadian debate. This approach presents the advantage of anchoring potential solutions in established and recognized practices, a valuable asset in the crafting of foreign affairs. As well, by comparing the practices of other international non-sovereign state actors, it is possible to theorize about these practices and define an applicable solution that is characterized by objective, rather than political, dimensions.

There are many examples that we can draw from in order to illustrate how federated entities can exercise influence in the international context. These examples can be classified on a matrix defined by two question-oriented parameters. First, does the federated entity exercise its influence directly or indirectly, that is, mediated through the federal state? And second, are the tools used to exercise this influence defined within the country's constitution or are they regulated through administrative arrangements? Figure 1 provides a reading of this matrix with specific examples that apply.

Belgium, for instance, presents a prime example of a federal constitution that explicitly allows its regions and communities to exercise a direct influence on the international scene, when matters discussed in a

Figure 1
Type of International Roles by Federated Entities

Frame

		Constitutional	Administrative
Influence	Direct	*Type*: **Emancipated** *Example*: Belgium	*Type*: **Autonomous** *Example*: Canada (la Francophonie)
	Mediated	*Type*: **Integrated** *Examples*: Austria, Germany, South Africa, Switzerland	*Type*: **Consensual** *Example*: Australia

given international forum primarily pertain to the federated entity's jurisdiction. As Comeau (2006) reports, in some instances, the federal government merely enjoys an observer's role.

For its part, Canada offers a fine example of direct influence that is administratively framed. Although limited since it refers to a specific forum (la Francophonie), this administrative bilateral agreement was reached between Ottawa and three provinces (Quebec, Ontario, and New Brunswick) who wished to take part in this forum's activities. The agreement allows the provinces to obtain a 'participating government' status, in accordance with the organization's rules.

Some federated entities influence the shaping of international norms and standards through an application, to international policies, of the participation they enjoy in federal policymaking. For instance, in Germany, in Austria, in South Africa, or in Switzerland, federated states have their voice heard in policymaking at the federal level, a right that is constitutionally enshrined. For example, this is done through the Bundesrat in Austria and in Germany as well as in the National Council of Provinces in South Africa. This process allows German Länder to be instrumental in bringing the subsidiarity principle to the Maastricht Treaty. It is in Switzerland where we find perhaps the best example of highly organized participation in foreign policymaking from federated entities. There, its cantons influence foreign policymaking within the framework of a specific law that allows them to get involved and through the Conference of Canton Governments, where trans-border and trade issues are discussed. Also, these sub-national entities play a role in the European Union and in la Francophonie.

Finally, other federated states rely on administrative agreements that allow them to exercise an indirect influence on international issues. In the case of Australia, the nation's constitution explicitly makes foreign policy a responsibility of the federal government. Notwithstanding this restriction, Australian states acquired a role for themselves on the international scene in order to defend those interests that came under their own jurisdiction. However, following a judgment of the Australian High Court, the Canberra government was recognized as the sole international voice for the country, to the extent that, on these questions, it would have been required to legislate in areas under the Australian states' jurisdiction. Given this constitutional deadlock, the governments accepted to enter into agreements for the purpose of establishing rules governing the international influence each of them is interested in carrying.

As we can appreciate from this very brief overview, Quebec's international involvement is not a unique case. More and more federated entities need to have their say and exercise their influence on the international context and there are precedents that help understand how this can be done. What then was available to the Harper government in terms of having the 19 December commitment being fulfilled?

If we agree that the 'Autonomous' role cannot be implemented for the reasons given above, there remains three types of role worthy of consideration. However, solutions that are constitutionally framed (that is, the 'Emancipated' and the 'Integrated' types), are not easy to implement in the Canadian context. The difficulty is of a political nature, for it would require amending the Canadian Constitution to include sections defining federal and provincial international responsibilities, and thus the opening of a constitutional Pandora's box.

At first glance then, the best available option seems to be the consensual role based on an administrative arrangement that is matched with a mediated influence. However, this solution is not totally optimal, for the mediation might be perceived as a source of uncertainty as long as it rests on the good will of the actors of the day. Where then is the solution to be found?

The constitutional routes being too unpredictable to be travelled, I suggest that a hybrid solution of an administrative nature is probably the best option available. This solution partly refers to a direct influence exercised by a federated entity speaking from its own voice, but where the direct content is partly mediated in format because of the necessity of expressing it within a larger (sovereign federal) framework due to UNESCO's operating rules. Entering into a long term agreement of this nature, which would give Quebec the opportunity for autonomous interventions and a direct say from within the Canadian delegation, could therefore best answers its demands as framed by the

Charest government and in accordance with both Quebec's established international role and the organization's internal constraints. The key element here, for both Quebec and Canada – and as a matter of fact, for all provinces who would deem it appropriate to exercise this option – is that the action therein instituted would lower the level of political uncertainty and tensions by providing a predictable and stable framework from which to work. In short, this would neither mean breaking ranks with a bang, nor blindly falling into step.

SOLUTION OFFERED AND PROSPECTS

This solution is indeed the one that Stephen Harper and Jean Charest considered as an acceptable common ground.[11] The December commitment made by the Tory leader in Quebec City and reiterated in the Speech from the Throne (Canada, 2006b) was enshrined into a policy agreement signed by Harper and Charest on 5 May 2006 in the Legislative Council Chamber of Quebec's National Assembly (Canada, 2006a). The solution is indeed of an administrative nature, but it gives Quebec the possibility to have its own voice heard and exercise a direct influence, although from within the Canadian delegation, which is the main difference from what is implemented in la Francophonie.

The agreement answers every one of the five demands expressed by Minister Gagnon-Tremblay in her September 2005 document. Moreover, the agreement breaks new ground in terms of the international recognition a federated entity might enjoy. First, the Quebec permanent representative is granted diplomatic status. Second, Quebec "will have the right to address the sessions, to complete the Canadian position, and give expression to the voice of Quebec" (Ibid.). And, should there be a disagreement between positions defended by both governments, the federal government might have the last say, but in terms of implementation "Quebec alone will decide if it proceeds with implementation in areas of its responsibility" (Ibid.). With respect to this third clause, one understands well that Canada has no advantage of entering into an international agreement that will not be implemented.

From a domestic point of view, the agreement also ushers in new definitions within Canada's federal framework. First, it specifically recognizes that Quebec's uniqueness "leads it to play a special role internationally" (Ibid.). This is the first time that the federal government not only recognizes this fact in an official document, but also that it uses it as the basis for its policy. This in itself could very well be the final settlement of the forty year old dispute concerning Quebec's international presence, which from this point on can hardly be contested by federal actors. As well, the agreement cannot be modified unless both parties agree to it; this, in itself, implements a stable and predictable context in which both actors will operate, and it puts to rest the practice based on the good will of the actors of the day.

There is no doubt that this agreement has, to some extent, clipped the wings of the sovereigntist movement on the issue of international representation. Of course, there were claims that only a sovereign Quebec could enjoy all attributes associated with a full-fledged membership. However, even former PQ Minister of International Relations Louise Beaudoin, although critical, has admitted that this was an "avancée" – a step forward – for Quebec (cited in Radio-Canada, 2006). Others have complained that the Quebec representative should not be part of the Canadian delegation, but rather be housed in the Délégation générale du Quebec in Paris and report to the Délégué général. In fact, this complaint is ill-founded. The Quebec representative will receive his or her mandate directly from the minister and not from a paradiplomatic hierarchy, which indeed gives more weight to the Quebec spokesperson in his or her dealings within the Canadian delegation.

What does lie in the future and what can result from this agreement? From the Quebec perspective, it is noteworthy that the agreement was echoed at the first opportunity. Less than three weeks after the signature, Monique Gagnon-Tremblay issued her international policy statement, a major revamping exercise that was long overdue. In this government-wide policy program, it is made clear that the progress made with UNESCO is a first step towards a wider international involvement of the Quebec government in international organizations where constitutional responsibilities of federated entities are discussed and standardized (Quebec, 2006: 28–9).

From the federal perspective, the agreement figures prominently in all analyses as an important feature Harper can count on in his pursuit for increased support in Quebec. At the electoral level, it might indeed bring in some dividends, mainly in Quebec. However, it is from a structural point of view that I see a longer term influence. Both the recognition of Quebec's specificity that needs to be expressed in international fora and the fact that the agreement "may not be modified or terminated without the consent of the signatories" (Canada, 2006a), no doubt define new rules in terms of Canadian foreign policy and Quebec's international role. Moreover, it articulates a new component of an asymmetrical, open federalism that both Harper and Quebec federalists were looking for.

CONCLUSION

This chapter evolved from a question that Stephen Harper more than likely asked himself as he prepared for his stop in Quebec City, at the mid-point of a long electoral campaign: What shape (if any) should Quebec's international presence and actions take? This analysis found part of the answer in the survey of historical precedents and rationale used to establish Quebec's role in the world.

The new challenges brought about by globalization, namely the need of federated entities to influence international standards before they force their governments to amend laws, by-laws, and policies falling under their constitutional jurisdiction, make this role more pertinent than it has ever been. The experiences of other federations help define the different types of international roles a federated entity can have. On the basis of the consequent typology of roles it is possible to devise a hybrid that could solve Harper's dilemma of providing Quebec a UNESCO voice (if not a seat), while surmounting the stumbling blocks coming from the international organization's internal rules. The administrative crossbreed we arrived at allows a direct influence for Quebec to voice its own concerns while simultaneously embedding that voice within a mediated framework that is in tune with the international institutions' requirements. This solution, that I have first theoretically defined, is the one that ultimately lies behind the agreement Stephen Harper and Jean Charest signed on 5 May 2006.

The result obtained did not satisfy all parties. Quite expectedly, sovereigntists have not expressed their approval, as previously mentioned. In some other parts of the country, the usual claim of frustration that 'Quebec gets it all' was heard. Some have expressed their fear that this policy would encourage actions that will challenge Canadian unity. Others have suggested that this arrangement would undermine Ottawa's hard work aimed at preserving Canada's identity on the international stage at a time when its role is being increasingly challenged by emerging middle powers seeking to share the declining influence of that group in an increasingly unipolar world.

While only time will tell if these concerns are indeed well-founded, there are already ample indications that the pessimistic view is incorrect. History shows that Canada's place in the world has never been jeopardized by the requests of the Quebec government. In fact, a decade of neglect on the part of Ottawa has been much more damaging to Canada's prestige[12] than forty-five years of Quebec's international presence. As well, the obstinate federal refusal to reduce the constraints imposed on the international role of provinces is more likely to tarnish Canada's global image. A continued stubbornness in this regard could see treaties signed by Canada in areas of provincial responsibility go unimplemented, as it would be the sole responsibility of the provinces to put such agreements into action. If Canada does not live up to its treaty obligations, what type of international image would it then project?

How did the Harper government negotiate this agreement within its own bureaucracy? Did it put in place its own administrative mechanisms to ensure that the accord will be successfully implemented? And, from an analytical point of view, will the typology used here offer a framework for predicting how other federated entities might acquire the tools necessary for some form of international presence? Further research on this issue will be needed to help resolve these questions.

In any case, one element of this debate remains. Several studies conclude that there is a well-defined necessity for federated entities, such as Quebec, to be involved in the international arena. This involvement will be beneficial to both Quebec and Canada if it is carried on within a stable and predictable environment. This is what the agreement on UNESCO offers. It would then be a mistake to consider it only as the fulfilment of an electoral promise.

This being said, other questions come to mind. Among them, one might ask if the agreement can be considered as a blueprint for what the Harper government sees as 'open federalism,' a more flexible approach that goes back to the spirit of Georges-Étienne Cartier's federation. If such is the case, it will be interesting to see where the next application of this renewed federalism will be implemented – will it be the answer to the alienation of provinces, such as Harper's Alberta, that feel 'governed from the centre?' As well, of great interest will be the next fields to which this new approach will be applied; the environment perhaps, or the economy? In such important cases, it will be important to determine the international impact of this new way of conducting foreign policy. Finally, it might be surprising to see that the Harper government regarded solving the question related to Quebec's international presence as a priority. If this was more than the mere fulfilment of an electoral promise, does this mean that wherever Harper finds a way to implement his version of open federalism, he will act swiftly to demonstrate the feasibility of his plan? And what would this mean in terms of Canadian foreign policy?

Finally, from an international perspective, there is no doubt that, more importantly, this agreement is also an instrument that defines new rules from which federated entities may operate to defend their interests in a globalized world. The document even suggests that Canada and Quebec will "explore, in relation to the work of UNESCO, innovative ways and possible mechanisms by which the Organization might better take advantage of the contribution of federated states in meeting its objectives" (Canada, 2006a). This might very well be the first, but by no means the least, of Stephen Harper's input in the restructuring of international influences in a world order that needs to be better adapted to the new challenges states and societies face.

NOTES

1 Examples of this include undersampling or even no sampling of Quebec in the polls conducted by the party prior to the elections, the allotment of (scarce) resources with a clear priority to other regions of the country, and even potential candidates of calibre having been offered no support whatsoever and told to put their name on the ballot and hope for the best.

2 For a more complete historical overview and an extensive topical bibliography, see Michaud (2004: 128).

3 Québec's conservative party from the 1930s up until the 1980s.

4 See Martin, Sr. (1985: ch. 18); and Morin (1987). From these readings, one can appreciate both sides of the coin from actors who were involved in the process.

5 For a thorough review of the Gérin-Lajoie doctrine, see Paquin and Beaudoin (2006).

6 "What is of Quebec's jurisdiction at home is of Quebec's jurisdiction at large" (author's translation).

7 The only section that deals with international questions is s.132 and it adresses the obligation the Dominion has towards treaties signed by the Empire; however this section became obsolete with the Statute of Westminster in 1931.

8 This applies to 'treaties of importance' signed by Canada, but that deal with questions of provincial jurisdiction.

9 For an example of these exchanges, see Castonguay (2005).

10 Surprisingly, this solution was and still is warmly supported by Parti Québécois members and MNAs, including constitutionalist Daniel Turp who considered this avenue to be "very much advantageous" (Castonguay and Robitaille, 2006).

11 This could look like an ex post facto analysis. However, I defended the same approach in November 2005, in my presentation, "Quebec's Role on the International Stage: Out of Place and Out of Time?" to the Canadian Defense and Foreign Affairs Institute conference in Ottawa.

REFERENCES

Aird, Robert. 2005. *André Patry et la présence du Québec dans le monde*. Montréal: Vlb éditeur.

Canada. 2005. "Diplomacy," in *Canada's International Policy Statement: A Role of Pride and Influence in the World*. Ottawa: Department of Foreign Affairs and International Trade (DFAIT), 19 April.

– 2006a. *Agreement between the Government of Canada and the Government of Québec concerning the United Nations Educational, Scientific and Cultural Organization (UNESCO)*. Ottawa: Office of the Prime Minister, 5 May. Available at: <http://www.pm.gc.ca/eng/media.asp?category=5&id=1153>

– 2006b. *Canada's New Government: Turning a New Leaf*. Speech from the Throne. Ottawa: Office of the Governor General, 4 April. Availabe at: <http://www.sft-ddt.gc.ca/default_e.htm>

Castonguay, Alec. 2005. "Lapierre dénonce Pelletier," *Le Devoir*, 20 October. Available at: <http://www.ledevoir.com/2005/10/20/93038.html>

Castonguay, Alex, and Antoine Robitaille. 2006. "Harper ne pourra tenir sa promesse: Le Québec n'aura pas de délégué à l'UNESCO," *Le Devoir*, 10 February. Available at: <http://www.ledevoir.com/2006/02/10/101741. html>

Charest, Jean. 2004. Allocution du premier ministre du Québec à l'ÉNAP, Québec, 25 February. Available at: <http://www.premier.gouv.qc.ca/general/ discours/archives_discours/2004/fevrier/dis20040225.htm>

Cohen, Andrew. 2003. *While Canada Slept: How We Lost Our Place in the World*. Toronto: McClelland and Stewart.

Comeau, Paul-André. 2006. *Régionalisation et relations internationales en Europe*, forthcoming.

Drouilly, Pierre. 1998. *Le Québec mou*. Montreal: Centre René-Lévesque, 21 November.

Harper, Stephen. 2005. Allocution prononcée devant la Chambre de commerce de Québec, Québec City, 19 December.

Martin, Paul Sr. 1985. *A Very Public Life: So Many Worlds*, vol. 2. Toronto: Deneau.

Martin, Paul Jr. 2004. Address by the Prime Minister on the occasion of a luncheon hosted by the Laval Chamber of Commerce, Montreal, 17 May. Available at: <http://www.pco-bcp.gc.ca/default.asp?Language=E&page= archivemartin&sub=speechesdiscours&doc=speech_20040517_207_e.htm>

Michaud, Nelson. 2004. "Le Québec dans le monde: faut-il redessiner les fondements de son action?" in Robert Bernier, ed. *L'État québécois au XXIème siècle*. Québec: Presses de l'Université du Québec.

Morin, Claude. 1987. *L'Art de l'impossible: La diplomatie québécoise depuis 1960*. Montréal: Boréal.

Paquin, Stéphane, and Louise Beaudoin, eds. 2006. *Histoire des relations internationales du Québec depuis la Révolution tranquille*. Montréal: Vlb éditeur, forthcoming.

Quebec. 1967. *Débats de l'Assemblée législative du Québec*, vol. 5, no 49. Québec: Legislative Assembly, 13 April.

– 2005a. "Monique Gagnon-Tremblay et la participation du Québec dans les forums internationaux," Press Release. Québec: Ministère des relations internationales, 14 September. Available at: <http://www.mri.gouv.qc.ca/fr/ ministere/communiques/textes/2005/2005_09_14.asp>

– 2005b. "Québec in International Forums: Exercising Québec's Constitutional Rights at International Organizations and Conferences," *Québec's International Initiatives*, no. 1 (October). Québec: Ministère des

relations internationales. Available at: <http://www.mri.gouv.qc.ca/en/pdf/
action_internationale1.pdf>
– 2006. *Politique internationale du Québec: La force de l'action concertée.*
Québec: Ministère des relations internationales. Available at: <http://www.
mri.gouv.qc.ca/fr/pdf/Politique.pdf>
Radio-Canada. 2006. "La voix du Québec à l'UNESCO," *Maisonneuve en
direct*, 5 May. Available at: <http://www.radio-canada.ca/radio/maisonneuve
/05052006/72626.shtml#commentaires>
Welsh, Jennifer. 2004. *At Home in the World: Canada's Global Vision for
the 21st Century.* Toronto: Harper Collins.

PART FOUR

Competing Policy Priorities

13 Meeting the China Challenge:
Developing a China Strategy

WENRAN JIANG

Canada's relationship with China has been moving forward with some momentum over the past year, and at the time when the Conservatives took over from the Liberals after the federal election of early 2006, a new China strategy had been developed and discussed at the cabinet level. A change in governing party traditionally brings a new domestic agenda and an overhaul of Canadian foreign policy. The Conservatives, however, put very little emphasis on foreign policy in their election platform, and Prime Minister Stephen Harper's minority government, has shown no hurry in revealing an overall Conservative foreign policy framework. So questions on how the Harper cabinet will handle some of its most pressing foreign policy issues and Canada's important bilateral relations remain to be answered.

In this chapter, I first look at the state of Canada's relations with China around the time of the Conservative-Liberal transition in 2006. This is also a good occasion to make an assessment of the Liberal government's China policy in the past thirteen years. Next, I examine a range of issues and options that may affect the direction of the new Tory government's China policy in both the domestic and international contexts. Finally, I propose a roadmap for a pro-active China strategy that can maximize Canadian interests not only in the world's fastest growing economy specifically, but also in the Asia Pacific region generally.

THE STATE OF CANADA-CHINA RELATIONS

The change of government in early 2006 marked the end of an era in Canadian foreign policy. In contrast to the time when the Liberals took over from the Progressive Conservatives in 1993, Canada's relations with China have deepened in many aspects and can be summarized by the following four major characteristics.[1]

First, the Liberals gradually developed a set of foreign policy priorities that put considerable weight on engaging China over the past thirteen years. Prime Minister Jean Chrétien and his successor Paul Martin both pursued closer economic relations with Beijing. The "Team Canada" approach, developed by the Chrétien cabinet with much hope and hype, was first applied to furthering economic and trade relations with China. The idea was to have provincial premiers and hundreds of Canadian business executives follow the prime minister on a mission to Canada's major trade partners to demonstrate a new commitment by the federal government to making Canada more competitive in a globalizing world. In addition, Ottawa perceived that China and other East Asian nations, where the government had driven much of the country's economic growth agenda, would be more receptive to Canadian businesses when they were part of an official effort. But trade figures show that Canada's exports to China did not register a significant increase from the early 1990s to the early 2000s. Team Canada, an innovative idea and well executed set of visits, may have forged some good contacts with China for long-term benefits, but it did not translate into any immediate boosts in bilateral trade (Roy, 2004). Structurally pulled by the strong growth of the US market, Canada's economic ties deepened with its neighbour south of the border rather than others across the Pacific.[2]

Prime Minister Martin, although implementing much of Chrétien's China policy, began to re-package it as a part of his own ambitious foreign policy agenda (Martin, 2005). China, together with India and Brazil, were identified as the most dynamic emerging markets. Developing closer ties with these countries was on the priority list of Canada's foreign relations. Policy consultations and foreign policy documents such as the Martin government's international policy review were designed to have a new vision of engagement with China and other major developing economies.

Ottawa's efforts to seek closer ties with China coincided with Beijing's relentless pursuit of high economic growth and its successful entry into the World Trade Organization (WTO) in 2001, which has generated clear economic and trade gains for Canada-China relations. In the past fifteen years, bilateral trade has increased with unprecedented speed. From 1993 to 2000, Canadian exports to China only increased 100 percent, while imports jumped 350 percent. But since 1998, both exports to and imports from China have at least tripled. From 2001 to 2004, Canada's total exports grew 40 percent while imports increased 60 percent; and in

2005, Canadian exports went up only 2.2 percent, while imports grew 42 percent. So what is the overall balance sheet for the Liberal government's trade policy performance with China? While bilateral trade volume increased dramatically, which is good news, Canada's exports to China are not keeping pace with its imports. Indeed, the gap increased even more in 2005 (Roy, 2004; 2005).

Second, the Liberal government managed to upgrade Canada's political relations with China through a number of important phases. As documented by Jeremy Paltiel, the Chrétien cabinet, after coming to power in 1993, quickly moved to restore relations with Beijing, which were damaged by the Chinese government's crackdown on student demonstrations in 1989. Measures such as Chrétien's summit with Chinese President Jiang Zemin in late 1993 and the appointment of Raymond Chan as the very first Minister of State for Asia-Pacific facilitated the warming of the bilateral relationship (Paltiel, 1995). These measures were then followed by the Team Canada initiative in 1994.

The Chinese leadership responded with a number of its own initiatives. By 1997, Beijing optimistically labeled its relationship with Ottawa as a "trans-century comprehensive partnership" (Evans, 2005: 151). During his visit to Canada in late 2003, when Chrétien was handing over the prime minister's position to Martin, Chinese Premier Wen Jiabao proposed that both sides establish a Strategic Working Group (SWG) to further cooperation between the two countries. Martin endorsed the idea, and by early 2004, a Canadian Strategic Working Group, centered on the Department of Foreign Affairs and International Trade (DFAIT) and with the participation of other federal and provincial government agencies and China experts across Canada, was up and running. Initially, multilateralism and energy cooperation were identified as key priorities of the group and later on trade and investment promotion was added to the list. When Chinese President Hu Jintao visited Ottawa in the fall of 2005, the two sides officially elevated the bilateral relationship from 'cooperative partnership' to 'strategic partnership' – a status reserved for Beijing's most important and trustworthy international partners. But other than an announcement of this new stage of bilateral cooperation, there was little substance given by either side. The Chinese press gave more coverage to the new strategic partnership than the Canadian media, and Ottawa gave little indication that it had more to say beyond its goodwill for better ties between the two countries. Yet, in this push for closer political and economic relations, important questions have been left unanswered: What is the Canadian definition of a 'strategic partnership' with China? How are its contents to be defined? And what does it mean for Canada's other truly strategic partnerships such as the North Atlantic Treaty Organization (NATO) and its relations with the United States?

Third, both the Chrétien and Martin cabinets made closer energy ties with Beijing one of their top China policy objectives. During his first Team Canada mission to China in November 1994, Chrétien signed a Nuclear Cooperation Agreement on the peaceful uses of nuclear energy. This agreement, along with Memoranda of Understanding (MOUs) between Atomic Energy of Canada Ltd. and the China National Nuclear Corporation, laid the groundwork for the sale of two CANDU 6 reactors to be built at Qinshan, outside Shanghai. This deal was followed by the signing of a number of agreements and memoranda that included the energy and related sectors during Chrétien's second Team Canada mission to China in early 2001. Chrétien went to China again in 2003 to commemorate the completion of the Qinshan project's two CANDU 6 reactors. The project, which was completed under budget and ahead of schedule, was marked by a high degree of cooperation between the two countries and among the participants. It was celebrated as an example of advanced Canadian nuclear technology that meets China's growing electricity needs.

These exceptions notwithstanding, it is difficult to conclude that there was much progress in bilateral energy cooperation during the Chrétien years. Overall bilateral trade figures do not particularly demonstrate tangible expansion in the energy sector, except in two particular categories – bituminous coal and peat.[3] There was much thunder and little rain as far as Chrétien's larger federal initiatives in the energy sector were concerned.

The Martin years in office (late 2003 to early 2006) happened to coincide with a surge in China's demand for energy and other resources. Following the rapid increase in world oil prices, Alberta's potentially huge oil sands production became more attractive, and there were signs that at last the two countries would engage in some substantial cooperation. As proposed by Premier Wen Jiabao during his visit to Ottawa in late 2003, Canada and China developed The Common Paper of the Canada-China Strategic Working Group, with the following bilateral priorities in the energy area: Canada and China to strengthen their bilateral dialogue on energy in the context of the 2001 MoU between the Department of Natural Resources of Canada (NRCan) and the National Development Reform Commission of China (NDRC); both sides to maintain regular dialogue and an exchange of views on oil and gas developments, including oil sands activities; NRCan, NDRC and other relevant departments or agencies to explore collaboration in the research and development of oil sands technology and advanced nuclear technologies, and to pursue joint projects in energy efficiency and cleaner energy, engaging other players as appropriate (Canada, 2003).

This initiative was followed by high-level visits by Canadian leaders with an agenda to push for energy cooperation with China. In a further push to the federal initiative, Alberta's Premier Ralph Klein went to China in 2004, with a focus on selling Alberta's energy potential and attracting Chinese investment. Martin's official visit to China in January 2005 identified three cooperation priorities in energy and related areas. According to *Canada-China Statement on Energy: Cooperation in the 21st Century*: "In particular, the two countries have identified oil and gas, nuclear energy, energy efficiency, and cleaner energy (including renewables) as priority areas where they will work together to advance their longer term mutual interests, in accordance with their respective laws and regulations" (Canada, 2005).[4]

With Chinese energy companies beginning to invest in Alberta's oil sands and to purchase Canadian energy firms' overseas assets (as discussed below), Martin seemed to have more enthusiasm for Canada's alternative energy market in China and India. It was to the surprise of many when Martin, clearly frustrated with the slow progress in Canada's negotiation with the United States over the soft lumber dispute, threatened that Canada might seek other potential energy markets rather than only depending on sending Canadian crude south of the border. These developments raised a new set of questions on whether Chinese participation in the exploitation of Canada's vast and strategically important oil sands reserve is being welcomed, whether there are security considerations for Chinese government-backed companies investing in Canada, and if Ottawa may potentially use its status as the largest supplier of US crude imports as a card in Canada-US trade disputes.

Fourth, China's human rights issues, which dominated Canadian public perceptions of China and then Progressive Conservative Prime Minister Brian Mulroney's China policy around 1989, gradually faded away in Canada-China relations under the Liberal watch. Even under the leadership of Minister of Foreign Affairs Lloyd Axworthy, who emphasized the promotion of human rights, Canada took a low-key approach to China on its human rights record (Frolic, 1997). The Liberal idea of an engagement strategy with China on human rights was not to pursue open confrontation but to use more subtle and indirect means to influence Chinese behaviour. Chrétien himself was on record saying that he would not go to a big country like China to lecture it on how to run things. Thus, Ottawa committed funding and established various programs aimed at improving 'good governance,' and set up a government-level annual human rights dialogue. Although the issue of human rights has for the most part fallen to the sidelines and given way to more emphasis on economic relations, it still resurfaces from time to time, often during high-level bilateral visits.

These developments in Canada-China relations will in one way or another affect the formation of the Harper government's China policy, that is, if it lasts long enough as a minority government to formulate a China policy at all. With the Liberals still recovering from their election losses and going through a major leadership renewal process, the Conservatives may not face serious policy challenges in the House of Commons in the near future. By the summer 2006 parliamentary recess, the new government had managed to push a number of Conservative campaign promises through Parliament, thus consolidating rather than eroding its base of public support. The question is where will the Conservatives start when they construct either an overall foreign policy framework or a specific strategy for China?

CONSERVATIVES MEETING THE CHINA CHALLENGE

Over the course of the past two election campaigns the Conservatives built up a winning domestic agenda. As others have pointed out (see Kirton; Chapnick, this volume), however, the same cannot be said about foreign policy. It is one thing to neglect Canada's foreign relations during the election campaign due to the lack of attention from the public and the media, but a governing party cannot continue for long without seriously considering the basic direction of where it intends to take Canada in the world. While in some foreign policy areas it is easier to tell where the current minority government stands, such as its inclination to forge close relations with the United States, its commitment to a strong military, and its hostility toward the Kyoto Protocol, it is not clear at all where it stands on a range of other issues – China being one of them.

This opacity is not surprising because the Conservatives do not have many alternatives from which to select a China policy of their own any time soon. Of course the new government may also simply need more time to think through a range of issues in Canada's relations with China. The challenge facing the Harper government in terms of a new China policy is to identify and weigh carefully the available options.

One way for a new Conservative China policy is to seek continuity by re-packaging what the Liberals have done so far. That includes, as discussed in part one of this chapter, a closer economic and political relationship, a positive attitude toward Chinese investment in Canada's energy sector, and a less confrontational approach on human rights issues. It is certainly easier to re-package what's in place than to re-invent a whole new China policy. The advantage of doing so is to keep the momentum of fast-growing bilateral economic relations, which has propelled China to second place in the ranks of Canada's largest trading partners in the past few years. The bilateral talks on promoting mutual investments will continue without complications, and there will likely be no interruption in the ongoing negotiations for designating Canada as an open destination for the rapidly expanding numbers of Chinese tourists.[5] Recycling the status quo is also the option by default – if the new government does nothing to change the course, which is so far the case, bilateral relations will move forward along the existing track.

But there are also risks and tensions for the Conservatives to go along with a 'business-as-usual,' 'continuity-as-first-choice' approach in its China policy. It may make the new government look as if it lacks new ideas and initiatives to deal with important international players like China. More importantly, some Conservative Members of Parliament may have reservations about following the Liberal route on China. After all, the Conservatives were at odds with the Liberals over their China policy on a number of issues when it was the main opposition party in parliament. Occasionally, these disagreements surfaced to become major domestic and international events. One example is when China's former premier, Zhao Ziyang, who was sympathetic to student demonstrators in the Tiananmen Square in 1989 and lost his position after the crackdown, died during Prime Minister Martin's official visit to China in January 2005. Conservative MP Jason Kenny (currently Parliamentary Secretary to the Prime Minister) openly clashed with Martin in Beijing, accusing him of being soft on human rights issues and criticizing him for not going to Zhao's home to pay his respects. Another Conservative MP, Jim Abbott, introduced a private members bill in the spring of 2005, calling for Canada to have an elevated relationship with Taiwan. Bill C-357, known also as the "Taiwan Affairs Act," went through the first reading of the government before it was shelved under pressure from overwhelming concerns of its negative implications. But so far neither of those two areas, human rights or Taiwan, has re-emerged to mark a Conservative departure from the Liberal's China policy.

What did cause great media attention and a major diplomatic row between the new Conservative government and Beijing was national security. Foreign minister Peter MacKay first raised the question, claiming that the Canadian government was "very concerned about economic espionage" from China. "It is something we want to signal that we want to address, and to continue to raise with the Chinese at the appropriate time," MacKay said (cited in CTV, 2006). It appears that his concerns were not based on new evidence. Rather, the origin of the Chinese spy charges came out of a 2003–2004 report from the

Canadian Security and Intelligence Services. It did not name China directly but suggested that there could be up to 1,000 Chinese agents and informants operating in Canada for the purpose of collecting economic, scientific, and military information, among other secrets.

The Chinese response was strong. Chinese foreign ministry spokesman Qin Gang said China had not been engaging "in any so-called economic espionage activities in Canada." The Chinese Ambassador to Canada Lu Shumin declared on CTV, "There is no Chinese espionage in Canada," and warned, "These kinds of accusations do not help the relationship and are not conducive to the development of this strategic partnership between the two countries" (Ibid.). Harper, firmly backing his foreign minister, insisted that MacKay's comments were well-founded: "We have some concerns with certain activities of the Chinese government in this country and we do intend to raise them at the appropriate time" (Ibid.). Almost as quickly as it appeared, the incident and the diplomatic confrontation went away with little follow-up. It is difficult to conclude from this event that a departure from the previous China policy was about to occur. After all, the 'appropriate time' to which both MacKay and Harper referred for raising the espionage issue with Beijing has not arrived, even though by the time this book went to print, there had been already two letter exchanges at the prime minister level and two letter exchanges at the foreign minister level between Ottawa and Beijing.[6]

Another option for the Conservatives to develop their own China policy, if the re-packaging of the Liberal ideas is deemed undesirable, is to seek continuity from the Conservative legacy of the past. In terms of a historical basis for a new Conservative China policy, the Tories may find a number of precedents during the time of Prime Minister Brian Mulroney. It was during the Mulroney years that Canada began to deliver large amounts of aid to China through the Canadian International Development Agency (CIDA). When the Chinese authorities repressed the 1989 Tiananmen student movement, the Mulroney government, supported by all the other parties, responded with a number of measures, ranging from sanctions to the suspension of CIDA aid to giving special landed immigrant status to Chinese students who were studying in Canada at the time. But times have changed, and China's situation is different from the years when the last Conservative government was in power. The Liberal government under Paul Martin had decided that when its current programs expired, CIDA would not run any new programs in China. The responses to the dramatic event of 1989 occurred under special circumstances, reducing their value as policy precedent. While the Harper cabinet may learn some operational principles from the Mulroney Conservatives on China policy, there are few policy implementation models that can be useful to the new government.

Going beyond the domestic context, the Harper government can also seek models of conservative China policy frameworks from other international like-minded-governments. Australia's current conservative government may serve as an example on how to engage China. It has aggressively entered the Chinese market, offering Beijing its vast energy reserves and other resources. At the same time, it has also managed to foster a close relationship with the United States over issues such as the Iraq War, while maintaining independence and distance from Washington when it comes to dealing with China. However, another conservative government, currently serving in Washington, presents a China policy model with a more negative view of Beijing. Some dominant figures in the Bush administration view the rise of China primarily as a threat to US interests around the world. Given the espionage comments by Peter MacKay, who has confessed admiration for Condoleezza Rice, it will not be surprising if the Harper government move its China policy more along the line of the US China policy.

The bottom line is that there is no easy formula to follow for a new China policy. It will be a learning process for the Harper government to manage Canada's relations with China. It is also obvious that a new China policy, if there is one to be developed, has to be considered in the context of a number of new factors, both domestic and international.

First, how is the government to cope with a rapidly rising China and understand the challenges it will present to Canada in the twenty-first century? Much has been discussed about the importance of China to the world economy, to the international order, and to the future of Canada's well-being, and the need for a paradigm shift in Canada's China policy (Evans, 2005). Both Canada and China see each other as vast markets with great opportunities. But the existence of markets alone does not automatically translate into benefits. China's market is huge, but all the countries around the world want to take advantage of it. In contrast to the Australian and many European governments, Ottawa has not been as aggressive and as competitive in promoting Canada in the Chinese market to really capitalize on its potential. The Canadian government needs to broaden its range of activities in China and to better organize Canadian expertise on China. After more than three decades since the establishment of Canada's diplomatic relations with China, there is a growing body of experts at different levels of government; with the fast expanding bilateral trade, there are a growing number of China-related businesses and business associations across the country; and there is also an increasing number of academics who have close links with China. Yet these groups are not sufficiently organized or coordinated to provide a government-business-academic network that can identify challenges that Canada must face in responding to a rising China.

Second, and a more specific challenge, is how to respond to the moderate but potentially growing Chinese investment in Canada's energy sector. With its sharp increase in energy demand, China is now paying much attention to Alberta's oil sands, and its state-owned energy companies are also buying Canadian energy firms' overseas holdings. The following is a list of Chinese investment and acquisition activities from the spring of 2005 to the end of the year:

April: China National Offshore Oil Corp. (CNOOC) paid c$150 million for a one-sixth stake in MEG Energy Corp., an Alberta startup company in the oil sands. This was China's first major investment in Canada's vast oil sands industry.

April: Two days later, PetroChina International Co. Ltd. signed an MOU with Canada's giant pipeline company Enbridge Inc., promising cooperation in the c$2.5 billion Gateway pipeline from Alberta to the Pacific Coast that may supply China with at least 200,000 barrels of crude a day once completed.

May: China's Sinopec Group agreed to buy a 40 percent stake in the proposed 100,000 barrel a day Northern Lights oil sands project for c$105 million, with a potential investment scale up to c$2 billion.

August: China National Petroleum Corp. (CNPC), the largest Chinese oil company, agreed to pay US$4.2 billion to purchase PetroKazakhstan Inc., a Calgary-based firm with large operations in Kazakhstan. This is so far the largest overseas acquisition by any Chinese company.

September: Andes Petroleum, controlled by CNPC and Sinopec, purchased Canadian energy exploration firm EnCana's assets in Ecuador for US$1.42 billion.

December: CNPC and India's Oil and National Gas Company (ONGC) jointly acquired 37 percent of Petro-Canada's Syrian assets for c$676 million.

The small leap forward in 2005 for Canada-China energy relations has continued. Sinopec has reportedly looked into buying Calgary-based Nations Energy for US$2 billion since January 2006. These expanding energy ties all speak to the Chinese leadership's apparent anxiety regarding energy security. Visiting Ottawa last fall, Chinese President Hu stated that the Chinese government intended to support the investment by China's large energy companies in Canada while Martin told his guest that Chinese investments in Canadian energy sectors are welcome as long as they meet necessary Canadian requirements. This view is also shared by the Alberta business sector, a major supporter for the core members of the Harper government. Premier Klein is a strong advocate for China's increasing investment in Alberta's energy sector. He made a trip to China in the fall of 2004, and one of his priorities was to meet with top executives of large Chinese energy companies and to mobilize their investment in Alberta's booming oil sands sector. "We continue to impress upon Chinese oil companies that there are opportunities [in Alberta], that the only oil isn't in Venezuela, or Australia or Indonesia or Brazil, that there is a very safe and reliable source of oil here," Klein assured the Chinese during his trip (cited in Kyne, 2004). Being one of top trading partners of Alberta, China, and close ties with it, enjoys wide support among Alberta's business community. Almost all of the major Chinese investments and acquisitions in the Canadian energy sector in the past few years have been with Alberta-based companies. Canada's most dynamic province in economic development is also home of major figures of the Harper government, which might be under some pressure not to dramatically change course on Canada's China policy. But Harper is trying to build himself up as a man of principle and man who keeps his word. If he intends to carry out his party's criticism, while in opposition, of the Martin government on trading human rights for economic benefits with Beijing, he may act to change the current engagement priorities with China. An indication of that development may be from the release of an assessment report on the current state of Canada-China human rights dialogue (Burton, 2006). If Harper chooses to raise the issue of espionage with the Chinese government as he promised he would, the bilateral relationship will certainly take another turn for confrontation. A potential dilemma for the Conservatives is that if they limit future Chinese investment based on political or national security concerns, they may be at odds with their own support base in Alberta's business community.

Third, and a very new dimension in Canadian politics, is the rise of the Chinese diaspora's participation in Canadian domestic politics. For a minority government that is so focused on expanding its base in order to win a majority in the next federal election, the Chinese immigrant community is one of the most important voting blocks that must be considered. In contrast with the older generation of Chinese immigrants, second and third generation Chinese-Canadians and many new Chinese immigrants are well-educated, linguistically skilled, high-income earning professionals who have integrated well into Canada's social mainstream. They are politically sensitive and their level of political participation is high. These new generations of Canadians and a fast-growing new Chinese immigrant group demonstrated their effectiveness in the last federal election both as individual candidates affiliated with different political parties and as an interest group. As individual participants, there were nineteen candidates of Chinese origin who stood for election from all major political parties; with five of them winning their seats in parliament. Both of these numbers are unprecedented in Canadian history. As an ethnic group, their voice helped convince Stephen Harper to promise an apology for the notorious 'head tax' and forced the Liberal Party to reverse its original stand and make the same promise. Subsequently Prime Minister Harper followed through on his pledge, and offered some financial recompense as well. While emerging as a strong domestic political force, the network of Chinese immigrants coming from the mainland is also growing in strength. Most of them continue to keep very close ties with their families, former colleagues, and friends in China even when they are well settled in Canada. Many of them are also eager promoters of Canada-China relations. This group, while loyal new citizens of Canada, also has a deep sense of attachment to China, thus some of them are often irritated by what they perceive as unjust and biased criticisms of China. The Conservatives may not even be aware that when Peter MacKay made his serious but general charges of Chinese espionage, not only the government in Beijing took offence. Many professionals of Chinese origin in Canada felt they might be the target of Chinese spy charges simply because they are Chinese and have extensive contacts with their home country. After the MacKay remarks, one famous scientist, who is of Chinese origin but grew up in Canada, speaks no Chinese, and currently works in the United States, told this author that he would now think twice before applying for a job in Canada. Many who share such sentiments feel the Canadian government should either prosecute the spy cases it claims with evidence it has or it should not make such vague and general statements that have little evidence to back them up. The question is whether such complaints will influence voting decisions at the time of election. Will the Tories tread carefully on such issues in the future, not so much because of the response from Beijing but out of strategic consideration for voters of Chinese origin at home? How Chinese immigrants help to restructure Canada's perspective of China and how they may affect Canadian foreign policy toward China are indeed newly emerged issues that call for further study.

ROADMAP FOR A PRO-ACTIVE CHINA POLICY

These new challenges, as analyzed in the last section, require some hard thinking and will present some complexities for a potential Conservative China policy. But it is important to realize that Ottawa must go beyond partisan politics for the sake of pursuing broader Canadian national interests. Thus, the faster the new Harper government works out a China policy blueprint, the better Canadian interests will be served at home and abroad. Canada's pro-active China policy today should have the following components.

First, the Harper cabinet should rise above party politics and endorse some of the solid progress in Canada's China policy under the Liberal government. Re-package as they wish, but a new Conservative agenda of engaging China cannot and should not begin from scratch. At the time of the Liberal-Conservative transition in early 2006, a China strategy was already being discussed at the cabinet level. From various sources, we have learned that DFAIT, in consultation with other government institutions, had developed a comprehensive China strategy. As a major review of Canadian engagement with China, it is said to have included many measures that would strengthen the Canadian presence within China. Harper and his caucus should re-visit this document as early as possible, and adapt it to their foreign policy interests. To improve their chances of success, the government should seek greater input from businesses, individuals, and the Chinese diaspora in Canada, possibly through the use of public hearings or pubic forums, and actively pursue the implementation of this strategy abroad.

Second, the new government should free itself from the human rights versus trade argument. If past experiences are any indication, Canadians tend to repeat this familiar debate whenever there is a high-level bilateral meeting with China. Opposition politicians, editorial pundits, and some non-governmental organizations will criticize the government for emphasizing economic interests over human rights violations in China, the party in power will counter such criticism by raising human rights concerns in the summit agenda, and the Chinese will play along to accommodate what they see as a formality. Once the meetings end, most of the human rights issues disappear from news coverage and little follows in terms of government policies.

Such a 'spotlight' approach to human rights in China is both superficial and ineffective. The rejection of this false dichotomy between trade and rights is long overdue. As Charles Burton (2006) notes in his assessment of the annual Canada-China human rights dialogue, the mechanism that Ottawa claimed to be a major achievements in engaging China on human rights issues is basically useless. Neither the Canadian side nor the Chinese side really benefited. The failing grade should serve as a wakeup call that a new and more effective approach is needed on Canada's human rights engagement with China. There are signs that the Harper government may be more ideologically committed to emphasizing human rights issues when dealing with Beijing, and yet there is also the traditional pro-business side of the Conservatives that pull it toward market-driven interests. The real issue for Canada is not to choose either rights or trade but how it can effectively engage China on both fronts. With the complexities of the Chinese reality in mind, new Canadian human rights policies on China must embody the following three principles: that economic prosperity and the promotion of human rights in an open society are not and should not be mutually-exclusive goals; that Canada's future economic cooperation with China must firmly rest on the foundation that China is moving toward a democratic society ruled by law; and that Canada is ready to extend a helping hand to achieve these goals.

Third, energy cooperation with China should be promoted, for strategic reasons as well as for profits. With all the Chinese investments and acquisitions in Canada in 2005, Canada has yet to strike a major deal with China, in contrast to what Beijing has done with other countries. China and Iran are currently working to finalize a deal worth up to US$100 billion, which will ensure Iranian energy supplies to China for the next 25–30 years. In 2003, Chinese President Hu Jintao signed energy deals worth up to US$40 billion during his trip to Australia. Large scale, long-term cooperation between Canada and China in the energy and environmental sectors has profound strategic implications. Among them, it will benefit both countries economically; it will guide a rising China's energy policy toward a more environmentally-friendly direction, producing less acid rain and air pollutants; and it will align Beijing's foreign policy towards more peaceful and less confrontational international partnerships, thus serving the comprehensive security interests of Canada and the rest of the world. A preliminary study by Alberta Economic Development also finds that potential Canadian crude export to Asia will reduce oil tanker traffic at the Strait of Malacca substantially in the next decade, thus contributing to the balancing of energy supply distribution. Ottawa should make it clear that Chinese investments in the Canadian energy sectors are welcome as long as they meet necessary Canadian requirements as specified in the Investment Canada Act. Concerns have been raised about whether Chinese investments in Canada, carried out mainly by state-backed energy companies, may constitute an intrusion to Canadian sovereignty and threat to Canadian strategic interests (Hester, 2006). Further measures or restrictions targeted particularly at Chinese investments whether Canada's energy and resource sectors will certainly be a sign of the new government's departure from the Martin government's efforts in promoting energy cooperation with China.

At the same time, Canada must ease US concerns in this area. One persistent American worry is simply selfish – its own energy interests. Every barrel of Canadian oil going to China will be seen as one less headed for the United States which, in turn, has to import oil from other parts of the world that are likely more hostile to Washington. It is a zero-sum game. What is good for Canada or China may not be good for the United States. To that concern Canada has a market-oriented answer: Canada has plenty of oil and its production capacity is more than enough to satisfy the US market, thus China is simply a new export market. Promoting Chinese investment in Alberta during his visit to China in 2004, Alberta Premier Klein projected that new investment in oil sands would quadruple the current daily oil output by 2010. "That would be equivalent to the total demand for all of China," Klein claimed, "What we're suggesting ... as China searches the world to find secure and reliable supply of oil [is] they should be looking here [in Alberta]" (cited in Kyne, 2004). John McCallum, minister of national revenue in the last Martin Cabinet, echoed Klein by claiming that Canada could export as much as 450,000 barrels of oil per day to China in six years. "Beyond the 450,000 barrels of [crude] oil per day is the much more important point that this is the future of the global economy and it's fundamentally in our interests that we become a part of it," McCallum said while visiting Beijing in 2005 (cited in Reuters, 2005).

But to American strategic planners, there are political implications beyond economics. Canada and Venezuela, together supplying one third of the crude imports to the United States, may have more leverage over Washington with their oil potentially also going to China. In addition, Chinese control or partial control of resources in these countries may weaken Canada-US relations, and may fuel anti-Americanism in Latin America. Canada certainly should not play the China card in its relations with the United States. Not only would such a ploy be unseemly and severely compromise Canada's reputation and relations in Washington it also would fail to advance Canada's negotiating position with the Americans. Instead, if Ottawa can build a strong, transparent working relationship with China, Canada may have the potential to reduce confrontations between the United States and China.

Fourth, Canada's strategic goal of engaging China should include persuading Beijing to play a more constructive role in Afghanistan where Canada is now deeply involved. As the leader of the Shanghai Cooperation Organization (SCO), China's influence in Central Asia has grown substantially in recent years. As SCO is expanding to include observers from Afghanistan, Iran, India, and Pakistan, Ottawa must assume a bold role of mediation between multiple players in the region. If Canada can successfully obtain support from China and eventually from the SCO for international efforts to rebuild Afghanistan, the process itself may facilitate the reorientation of the SCO, reduce suspicions of Washington toward the SCO's strategic postures, and contribute to stability in Central Asia and the Middle East. The sooner the mission in Afghanistan is accomplished, the sooner Canadian troops will return home. To achieve that goal, Ottawa must tread carefully on the issue of Taiwan. It should maintain a policy of status quo and support stability across the Taiwan Straits.

It was thirty-six years ago that Prime Minister Pierre Trudeau took to bold step of officially recognizing the People's Republic of China and re-establishing diplomatic relations. Today, Canada needs a similar strategic mindset in crafting a China policy that moves the bilateral relationship forward, in an effort to benefit both countries in the new century.

NOTES

1 For an excellent overview of Canada's relations with China over the past few decades and the necessity for a new China engagement strategy, see Evans (2005).

2 For more on Team Canada missions and evaluations, see Hampson, Molot and Rudner (1997).

3 Data includes the following industries: oil and gas extraction, peat extraction, coal mining, electric power and petroleum. Canada did not export electric power or petroleum industry products to China in the years 1995 to 2004. Available at: <http://strategis.ic.gc.ca/sc_mrkti/tdst/engdoc/tr_homep.html>

4 The author has been involved with the energy theme of Canada's Strategic Working Group on China. With funding from DFAIT, the government of Alberta, and the private sector, the author led the University of Alberta efforts to organize three major Canada-China energy cooperation conferences between November 2004 and May 2006.

5 There are signs of such a trend in the appointment of David Mulroney, who has been running Canada's Asia Pacific profile in the Foreign Affairs for a long time, as Harper's advisor on foreign policy, and David Emerson's appointment as the Minister of Industry in charge of the Pacific Gateway project.

6 This is from the author's conversation (June 2006) with a senior Canadian diplomat who prefers to remain anonymous.

REFERENCES

Burton, Charles. 2006. "Assessment of the Canada-China Bilateral Human Rights Dialogue," Report prepared for the Department of Foreign Affairs and International Trade. Available at: <http://spartan.ac.brocku.ca/~cburton>

Canada. 2003. *Common Paper of the Canada-China Strategic Working Group.* Beijing: Canadian Embassy in Beijing, December. Available at: <http://www.beijing.gc.ca/beijing/en/1612.htm>

– 2005. *Canada-China Statement on Energy: Cooperation in the 21ˢᵗ Century*. Ottawa: Privy Council Office, January. Available at: <http://www.pco-bcp. gc.ca/default.asp?Language=E&Page=archivemartin&Sub= newscommuniques&Doc=news_release_20050120_396_e.htm>

– 2006. *Trade Data Online*. Ottawa: Industry Canada, 18 March. Available at: <http://strategis.ic.gc.ca/sc_mrkti/tdst/engdoc/tr_homep.html>

China. 2005. *Chart of Import and Export Commodities By Countries/Regions (2005 January to December)*. Beijing: Ministry of Commerce, Department of Planning and Finance. Available at: <http://gcs.mofcom.gov.cn/aarticle/ Nocategory/200602/20060201484766.html>

CTV. 2006. "Chinese Ambassador Rejects Espionage Claims," *CTV.ca News*, 20 April. Available at: <http://www.ctv.ca/servlet/ArticleNews/story/ CTVNews/20060420/china_espionage_060420/20060420?hub=World>

Evans, Paul. 2005. "Canada and Global China: Engagement Recalibrated," in Andrew F. Cooper and Dane Rowlands, eds. *Canada Among Nations 2005: Split Images*. Montreal & Kingston: McGill-Queen's University Press, 150–68.

Frolic, Michael. 1997. "Re-engaging China: Striking a Balance between Trade and Human Rights," in Fen Osler Hampson, Maureen Appel Molot and Martin Rudner, eds. *Canada Among Nations 1997: Asia-Pacific Face-Off*. Ottawa: Carleton University Press, 323–47.

Hampson, Fen Osler, Maureen Appel Molot and Martin Rudner, eds. *Canada Among Nations 1997: Asia-Pacific Face-Off*. Ottawa: Carleton University Press.

Hester, Annette. 2006. "State Corporations Must Play by Our Rules," *National Post*, 28 March.

House of Commons, Standing Committee on Foreign Affairs and International Trade (SCFAIT). 2005. *Evidence*. 38ᵗʰ Parliament, 1ˢᵗ Session, 27 October. Available at: <http://www.parl.gc.ca/InfocomDoc/38/1/FAAE/Meetings/ Evidence/FAAEEV60-E.HTM>

Kyne, Phelim. 2004. "INTERVIEW: Canada's Alberta <http://www.gov.ab.ca/ premier/missions_asia.cfm>

Martin, Paul. 2005. "Making a Difference: Foreword from the Prime Minister," in "Overview," *Canada's International Policy Statement: A Role of Pride and Influence in the World*. Ottawa: Department of Foreign Affairs and International Trade.

Paltiel, Jeremy. 1995. "Negotiating Human Rights with China," in Maxwell Cameron and Maureen Appel Molot, eds. *Canada Among Nations 1995: Democracy and Foreign Policy*. Ottawa: Carleton University Press, 165–86.

Reuters. 2005. "Canada to export 450,000 bpd of oil in 6 yrs," 16 October. Available at <http://www.chinadaily.com.cn/english/doc/2005–10/16/ content_485265.htm>

Romero, Simon. 2004. "Not Elk, But Oil: China's Canadian Hunt," *New York Times*, 24 December.

Roy, Francine. 2004. "Canada's Trade with China," *Canadian Economic Observer*, June. Available at: <http://www.statcan.ca/english/ads/11-010-XPB/jun04.pdf>

– 2005. "Canada's Trade and Investment with China," *Canadian Economic Observer*, June. Available at: <http://www.statcan.ca/english/ads/11-010-XPB/pdf/jun05.pdf>

York, Geoffrey. 2006. "Rights Dialogue in China Blasted as Futile; Canadian Deplores Empty Annual Ritual," *Globe and Mail*, 16 June.

14 The New Strategic Positioning
of Canada within North America:
The Energy Factor

ISIDRO MORALES

In some ways Prime Minister Stephen Harper and his minority Conservative government inherited a mixed legacy from its predecessor. On the one hand, a strong dollar, low inflation and unemployment rates, and comfortable budgetary surpluses provide a solid economic foundation for the country. On the other, Canada's main trading and political partner, the United States, has become increasing inclined to impede the flow of goods, services, and people in the face of increased sensitivity to security concerns. In the area of energy, however, economics and security have colluded to bolster the strategic position of Canada within North America.

High international oil prices have spurred the development of huge non-conventional petroleum reserves in Western Canada at the same time that the United States has come to view security and energy as intrinsically linked. Although both Canada and the United States are rich in coal and uranium resources, as well as in renewable energy resources (water, wind, solar), oil and gas remain at the core of the energy security agenda of the United States and constitute the major energy resource imported from its northern neighbour. Western Canada's potential to compensate for the eventual decline of Mexican and Venezuelan energy exports to the United States, and to become the largest, safest, and most reliable energy producer in North America, would alleviate some of the concerns about energy security that have become conspicuous in the United States after the terrorist attacks of 11 September 2001.

To fulfill this potential, both Canada and the United States must sort out their national and continental programs to blend effectively market-oriented mechanisms (i.e. incentives for developing conventional and non-conventional resources in an era of 'expensive oil') with the somewhat contradictory additive of strong regulatory intervention and jurisdictional division. If the regulatory and environmental concerns can be sorted out between, primarily, Alberta, Ottawa and Washington, Western Canada will be strongly positioned to deepen its integration with the oil and gas markets of the United States. Deeper integration, in turn, will draw attention to questions about the security of the infrastructure, the pipelines and electricity transmission grids, that link continental energy markets. This chapter examines the main features and challenges of this new strategic positioning of Canada's energy reservoirs in North America.

The first part of this chapter will explain how security concerns have recently returned to the US energy policy agenda, and how Canadian energy resources have become a pillar of the bilateral strategic partnership following the events of 9/11. The second part will explore how the development of both non-conventional and conventional energy resources in Western Canada has matched US strategic and security expectations. Finally, the third part will review how corporate and industry organizations in the two countries have internalized security measures to protect the energy grid at the regional and cross-border level. Although the 'privatization' of security cooperation remains in the domain of electricity transmission and interconnection, this could eventually become a model to be adapted in the oil and gas continental grid.

US MARKET-BASED ENERGY SECURITY GOVERNANCE AND THE STRATEGIC POSITIONING OF CANADIAN NON-CONVENTIONAL RESOURCES

In recent years, Canada has become a major oil power since the official recognition of its massive reserves of tar sands, from which bitumen (a heavy, low gravity oil) and synthetic oil are obtained. With the equivalent of 178 billion barrels (bb) of proven reserves, oil sands have made Canada (primarily Alberta) the second largest hydrocarbons reserve in the world, second only to Saudi Arabia (NEB, 2004a: 4). Table 1 compares Canada with the rest of North America in terms of its energy stock and potential. Taking current levels of production and expected consumption into account, the United States and Mexico are expected to deplete their respective proven reserves in less than ten years, while Canada will be able to fuel another 195 years of its consumption. It is worth noting the depletion of Mexico's proven reserves follows two major reclassifications made by Petróleos Mexicanos (PEMEX), the state-owned monopoly, in order to comply with international standards. The projected collapse is

Table 1
Estimated World Oil and Natural Gas Reserves

Estimated Oil Reserves in billion barrels (end of 2004)

	Proven Reserves	World Percentage	R/P Ratio	Reserve Growth	Unconfirmed Reserves	Total Reserves
United States	21.9	1.7%	7.1	76.0	83.0	180.9
Canada	178.8	14.0%	195.0	12.5	32.6	223.9
Mexico	14.6	1.1%	10.6	25.6	45.8	86.0
North America	215.3	16.9%	39.3	114.1	161.4	490.8
Venezuela	77.2	6.0%	70.8	NA	NA	NA
Former Soviet Union	77.8	6.1%	NA	137.7	170.8	386.3
Middle East	729.6	57.1%	81.6	252.5	269.2	1251.3
WORLD TOTAL	1277.7	100.0%	40.5	730.2	938.0	2946.8

Estimated Natural Gas Reserves in trillion cubic feet (end of 2005)

	Proven Reserves	World Percentage	R/P Ratio
United States	192.5	3.0%	10.4
Canada	56.0	0.9%	8.6
Mexico	14.5	0.2%	10.4
North America	263.3	4.1%	9.9
Venezuela	152.3	2.4%	*
Former Soviet Union	2058.8	32.4%	76.7
Middle East	2546.0	40.1%	*
WORLD TOTAL	6348.1	100.0%	65.1

Source: *World Energy Outlook 2005*, International Energy Agency, OECD, and BP *Statistical Review of World Energy 2006*, British Petroleum.

* More than 100 years

NA Not available

R/P Reserve to production ratio: Estimate of years remaining in reserves at current production and expected consumption levels also explained by the inability of the company to compensate for the depletion of its stock with additional reserves. In the Western Hemisphere, only Venezuela has comparable proven reserves and whose crude output is similar to that of heavy oils coming from Canada. Apart from that, conventional, cheap, light crude reserves still lay primarily in Persian Gulf producing countries (see Table 1).

That said, Canada has become geopolitically well positioned to develop and exploit its huge reserves of non-conventional crude. Its production could potentially compensate for an eventual decline in Mexican exports to the US,[1] and the country has the opportunity (and will) to move from a gross crude oil importer to a storehouse and powerhouse (Shook, 2005). Current geopolitical conditions and prevailing security concerns of the United States are favourable to these developments. Indeed, following the disruption of relations with oil producing nations in the Middle East, spurred by the US-led wars in Afghanistan and in Iraq, it has become clear that energy security and the pursuit of 'safe oil' have risen up the list of priorities of both foreign and domestic policy in the United States.

Controlling risk and uncertainty is very much at the heart of the emerging US energy strategy. Risk is perceived in terms of unexpected shocks affecting the stability of energy supplies (mainly oil and gas). Such shocks could be unleashed by natural depletion (such as the decline of energy stocks in reservoirs), natural disasters (such as hurricanes and flooding), geopolitical changes (such as political instability in oil producing countries), or structural disruptions (such as malfunctions, accidents, or explosions in refineries, tankers, pipelines and storage facilities). These supply shocks create uncertainties in energy markets, with risk being a key factor in the determination of world oil prices as well as a constraint on the effectiveness of policy options such as the introduction of alternative fuels, the funding of new investments, and the exploration of high-prospect (and more stable) drilling areas. So far, the best strategy for the Bush administration to address these risks and uncertainties has been the development of conventional and non-conventional energy resources domestically, or within low risk areas.

The market-driven approach of the Bush administration to govern energy flows into the US is anchored in an optimistic perception of the fundamentals of energy markets. At present, high oil prices are not perceived to be fuelling inflation and hampering economic growth, as was experienced during the oils shocks of the 1970s and 1980s. It seems rather that the current American administration expects a new era of 'expensive oil' (where prices could float in the US$40–50 per barrel range for the next 25 years), during which several energy options could become possible. Continued higher than normal oil prices could support the development of 'non-conventional' hydrocarbon resources (tar sands, synthetic oil, shale oil, coal-bed methane, etc), provide a new boost to nuclear energy alternatives or coal consumption, and foster the growth of renewable sources of energy and the feasibility of synthetic fuels. Technological advances have made many of these sources viable inputs into electricity generation. The Energy Policy Act (EPA) of 2005 launched a number of incentives for such initiatives (see United States, 2005). In other words, the Bush administration is betting on a transformation to a new era in which oil is a major, but merely one, component of a diversified energy resource mix, where synthetic oil and other alternatives can enter the market (EIA, 2006).

The rationale by which expensive oil is not perceived as a vulnerability (as has been the case in the past) lays in the fact that the US economy is becoming less and less dependent on oil intensive industries such as steel, paper, cement, and chemicals, and that economic growth in the following years will come from service industries (currently 80 percent of US GDP) and non-energy intensive manufacturing. These trends combined with a decline in energy intensity ratios (i.e. less and less energy is needed per unit of GDP), technological innovation, and growing population and labour productivity, have forecast that the US economy will continue growing at an average rate of 3 percent in real terms over the following twenty-five years, in spite of the prevalence of high oil prices (EIA, 2006: 63)

Another optimistic supposition of the Bush administration is that international oil prices will remain high because of economic influences – major consumers and importers such as the United States, China, and India will maintain their growing energy demands during periods of high economic growth. Since OPEC countries remain the residual suppliers, the development of additional spare capacity in these countries remains crucial for the evolution of prices. If OPEC production returns to pre-crisis levels, and the spare capacity of Persian Gulf countries increases, there will be a downward influence on oil prices, pushing OPEC onto the defensive, as was the case during the mid-1980s.

However, the increase in spare capacity is expected to lag behind growth in demand. In addition, the estimates of the US Department of Energy do not take into account the geopolitical fundamentals that also explain the decline of oil-producers' capacity (or potential decline of shipments to the US), including formal embargoes of oil imports from Iran, deteriorating relations with producers such as Venezuela, civil conflict in Iraq, and the uncertainties generated by the prosecution of the war against terror in oil-producing regions such as the Middle East. In other words, market influences are heavily intertwined with American post-9/11 geopolitical calculations and actions pursued in the Persian

Gulf region. In that sense, a period of 'expensive oil' may be an opportunity for the US and its partners (mainly in Europe and Asia) to share the costs of restructuring the economics and geopolitics in the Middle East. Since the partners of the US are not as well positioned to deal with high energy prices, market influences may eventually increase American leverage to deal with security concerns in conventional oil producing states.[2] Within this perspective, market mechanisms remain the most effective way for the US to deflect the costs of a major transformation away from conventional oil-producing countries in the Persian Gulf, towards non-conventional oil, gas and fuel markets (in which American companies have a stake), and to articulate a new 'oil security' diplomacy to increase American leverage vis-à-vis other major importing countries. It should also be noted that current proposals calling for a NATO energy strategy or even the creation of an 'Energy NATO' (see Gallis, 2006) would allow not only for the US to broaden its energy concerns internationally, but would also give Canada a strategic role beyond North America with other industrialized economies.

The strategic role that Canada is called to play in this new security agenda becomes clear when it is recognized that during the transition to new energy sources, and in spite of all policy efforts, the United States will remain addicted to oil and gas. According to most recent available data, it is predicted that oil and gas will still amount to 61 percent of overall US energy consumption in the year 2030. In this scenario, gross oil imports will amount to 64 percent of petroleum consumption, while gas imports will account for 21 percent of overall gas consumption (EIA, 2006: 64). Canada is currently the major supplier of oil and gas to the United States. As shown in Table 2, 16.3 percent of gross US oil imports in 2005 came from Canada, while imports from Mexico and Venezuela (the other two major Western Hemisphere suppliers) respectively provide around 15 and 12 percent. However, due to a lack of consensus on the best strategy not only to maintain, but also to increase Mexico's oil and gas production,[3] Mexican exports could decline in the short term. Although the United States remains the major outlet for exports coming from Venezuela, domestic conflicts in the energy sector and mounting tensions with the United States have made the future of Venezuelan exports uncertain.

These developments help explain why a Security and Prosperity Partnership (SPP) was launched in 2005 by the three governments of North America, a partnership in which energy cooperation became a major pillar. This trilateral initiative was certainly led and envisioned by the US, and upholds the spirit of previous trade agreements linking Canadian and American interests.

In fact, the Canada-US Free Trade Agreement (CUSFTA) set the original framework for energy relations between the two countries. CUSFTA

Table 2
United States Annual Crude Oil Imports by Source (2005)

Country	Thousand Barrels	Percent
Canada	599,681	16.34%
Mexico	565,919	15.42%
Saudi Arabia	524,714	14.30%
Venezuela	449,196	12.24%
Nigeria	386,872	10.54%
Iraq	189,657	5.17%
Angola	164,183	4.47%
Other	790,181	21.52%
All Countries	3,670,403	100.00%
Important Groups		
Persian Gulf Countries	796,094	21.69%
OPEC	1,738,271	47.36%

Source: United States Department of Energy <www.eia.doe.gov>

eliminated barriers to cross-border energy trade, prohibited dual pricing (by discriminating between domestic and foreign producers), and committed Canada to maintain its share of energy exports to the United States (based on the previous three years) in the event of a major reduction in overall supply. When the North American Free Trade Agreement (NAFTA) came into force in 1994, the Canada-United States energy commitments were renewed while Mexico maintained its state monopoly in its domestic energy sector, and liberalization was only introduced in its cross-border trade of gas and electricity. The CUSFTA and NAFTA agreements thus framed the progressive liberalization of energy markets between Canada and the United States, contributing to an emerging but incomplete continentalization of the industries.

In 2001, Presidents Bush and Fox, and Prime Minister Jean Chrétien, created the North American Energy Working Group (NAEWG), an interministerial task force charged with the responsibility of sharing information and data to enhance energy trade and interconnections within North America. In June 2005, SPP working groups called for the creation of a "policy environment" in which a sustainable supply and efficient use of energy could be promoted. It also recognized that energy had become "critical to the prosperity and security" of the three nations (SPP, 2005). In other words, the major goal of the strategic energy partnership of North American is to keep both Canada and Mexico as reliable and safe partners of the United States, as long as market signals and incentives guide the development of their respective production and trade interconnections. It could also be argued that the United States is highly interested in increasing, not only in maintaining, its import share from these two countries in the foreseeable future.[4]

The fact that the energy grids of Canada and Mexico are highly interconnected with US markets has resulted in somewhat of a continentalization of American homeland security interests. The United States is interested not only in the steady development of both conventional and non-conventional sources of oil and gas of its North American partners; it is also interested in the safety and integrity of any critical infrastructure that delivers energy to its major markets. However, in contrast with other regional post-9/11 security concerns such as border surveillance, migratory flows, or air defence which require different degrees of state involvement and inter-agency collaboration, the security of energy flows and interconnections is still perceived as assured if market signals drive the major decisions of stakeholders (consumers, producing companies, energy developers, etc.). In other words, the securing of energy markets in North America relies on market-oriented incentives operating within a regulatory system defined at the sub-national, national, and (increasingly) continental levels. This dynamic will be explored later in the chapter.

FEEDING THE US ADDICTION: CANADA'S ROLE AS THE LARGEST CONTINENTAL SUPPLIER

The Prospects for Developing Non-conventional Oil Resources

In 2004, overall Canadian crude production reached 2.5 million barrels (mb) per day, of which 90 percent came from Western Canada. Most of Canada's conventional and non-conventional crude oil reserves and natural gas stocks are located in the Western Canadian Sedimentary Basin (WCSB), a vast region encompassing most of Alberta, and parts of British Columbia and Saskatchewan. This does not mean that reserves and production located offshore in Eastern Canada are to be underestimated. In fact, conventional oil production from the Maritime Provinces is anticipated to increase and compensate in part for the decline of conventional crude production in the WCSB. However, conventional production from the Eastern provinces is also anticipated to peak in the mid-term; thus, production from oil sands will be the main source to compensate for the depletion of conventional oil (NEB, 2005b: 20–8). Currently, oil sands provide 1 mb per day, and according to Alberta's Minister of Energy

Greg Melchin, this amount could reach 3 mb per day over the next decade and possibly grow to 5 mb per day by 2030 (McFall, 2006).

The distinction between conventional and non-conventional crude oil is not simply academic. Extraction methods are more complex and costly for non-conventional crude.[5] The raw material is bitumen, a high viscosity hydrocarbon with elevated concentrations of sulphur and metals, which makes it more useful for asphalts and residual fuels. Lighter blends are preferred because they have higher yields of "white products" such as gasoline, the demand for which dominated the demand for crude oil. Unfortunately, synthetic light blends are the most expensive to produce from unconventional sources.

Supply costs for bitumen range between c$10–19 per barrel; upgrading for synthetic fuels boosts the cost to c$28. While supply costs could either increase or decrease over time, due to investment and technological innovation the trend is toward a cost reduction.[6] Currently, experts estimate that a return on investment from oil sands becomes possible if crude oil remain above a us$25 baseline (McFall, 2006).[7] If prices remain above us$40 per barrel in real terms over the long term, as predicted in the most recent forecasts of US energy agencies, a boom in oil sands production is anticipated.[8] However, we cannot underestimate the geopolitical rationale underlying the new expensive oil scenarios, as highlighted earlier in this chapter. If for any reason oil producing Persian Gulf countries are successful in increasing their current production capacity of cheap conventional oil, prices will be more volatile, as they were during the early 1980s. If such volatility were to return, Alberta and the federal government would both be keen to have a stabilizing role in international oil markets, as a non-OPEC player, to limit price fluctuations to a us$25–30 per barrel range.

If prices remain attractive enough, there will be no major 'structural barrier' impeding the development of this major source of non-conventional oil. With the established bilateral relationship enshrined by CUSFTA, Canada and the US have worked cooperatively to liberalize their oil and gas markets for increased interoperability, and to increase available supply. Currently, major American (and Asian) firms are investing heavily in the development of the Alberta oil sands.[9] Public officials from Western provinces are fully devoted to the development of their natural resource wealth. As the Premier of Alberta Ralph Klein has expressed, Canadian resources have become geopolitically "more competitive" because Alberta offers a safe, predictable, and stable fiscal regime compared to the Middle East or other regions.[10]

Table 3 summarizes US projections of Canadian non-conventional oil production over the next twenty-five years. While conventional production declines, this is more than compensated for by the increase in non-conventional oil production. According to this 'reference case scenario,' overall Canadian production could reach 5 mb per day in the next twenty-five years if average oil prices range between US$40–50 in real terms. If prices are higher, non-conventional oil could amount to almost 5 mb per day on its own, as optimistically predicted by Premier Klein, or half that amount if international prices are lower. In other words, non-conventional production in Canada will remain sensitive to world oil prices. However, with a production level of 4–5 mb per day, a level similar to that of Iran in past years,[11] Canadians will have the opportunity to play a major role in international oil markets. In February 2006, a record 95 percent of WCSB's 773 drilling rigs were engaged in exploration and development activities and it is anticipated that the fleet will increase to 850 by the end of that year (D'Arcy, 2006). If this pace is maintained, the supply of synthetic oil will increase as forecasted.

The possible evolution of Mexican production is also shown in Table 3, as it is assumed Mexico will freeze, or even reduce, its export share in the short term, due to financial and infrastructure limitations. In this case, net Canadian exports will be able to compensate for the Mexican decline, as previously discussed, and will be able to gain a larger share of the US energy import market. However, it is estimated that in the long run Mexico will increase its conventional production to a similar level as Canada, and together, the two countries will have the capacity to influence world oil prices. Thus, there is room to build solid, long-term cooperation between Canada and Mexico to realize their shared goal of oil price stability.

The Infrastructure and Regulatory Challenges

Infrastructure shortages and sectoral and horizontal regulatory measures must be addressed before future large-scale development and export of non-conventional oil can occur. Currently, nearly all Canadian crude exports are destined for the US, as the development of the WCSB has traditionally relied on the growing fuel consumption in the American Midwest. Exports to these areas are assured through a network of seven pipelines travelling north to south, the largest of which is Enbridge, which carries around 72 percent of Western Canada's crude oil shipments. This pipeline crosses the Western provinces and goes directly south to Chicago. This pipeline interconnection has effectively created a cross-border economic region between Western Canada and the American Midwest. With no major pipeline above the Great Lakes, Central and Eastern Canadian provinces are supplied by either oil from the Maritime provinces or imported oil from a number of foreign suppliers.[12] Thus, according to official estimates, the anticipated growth of

Table 3
North American Petroleum Supply: US Department of Energy Reference Case

	2004	2010	2015	2020	2025	2030	*Annual Growth Rate 2004–30*
CRUDE OIL PRICES[1]							
Imported Low Sulphur Light	40.49	47.29	47.79	50.70	54.08	56.97	1.3%
Imported Crude Oil Price	35.99	43.99	43.00	44.99	47.99	49.99	1.3%
PRODUCTION (CONVENTIONAL)	*million barrels per day*						
United States	8.41	9.39	9.62	9.51	9.13	8.92	0.2%
Canada	2.40	1.66	1.43	1.45	1.45	1.43	−2.0%
Mexico	4.10	3.97	4.19	4.48	4.78	5.01	0.8%
TOTAL (CONVENTIONAL)	80.50	86.09	89.98	95.68	100.87	106.29	1.1%
PRODUCTION (NON-CONVENTIONAL)[2]	*million barrels per day*						
United States	0.22	0.48	0.72	0.94	1.31	1.50	7.6%
Canada	0.92	1.79	2.32	2.67	3.16	3.58	5.4%
TOTAL (NON-CONVENTIONAL)	1.96	4.91	6.92	8.02	9.73	11.52	7.1%
TOTAL PRODUCTION	82.46	91.00	96.90	103.70	110.60	117.80	1.4%

Source: World Energy Outlook 2006, Energy Information Administration, OECD. With projections to 2030, US Department of Energy.

(1) 2004 US$ per barrel

(2) Includes lease condensates, natural gas plant liquids, and other hydrogen and hydrocarbons for refinery feedstocks.

oil production from bitumen in Western Canada will foster an increase in exports to the US, while little can be used in the Central provinces as there is no effective method of delivering it. The current transport infrastructure is heavily integrated with American pipelines that serve their major markets. Thus there is little economic incentive to shoulder either the huge costs of building a pipeline over the Great Lakes or the opportunity costs of supplying domestic consumption instead of selling Albertan oil on more lucrative international markets.

The continental trade in oil is also affected by the distinction between conventional and non-conventional sources. Currently, 27 percent of total Canadian supply is synthetic oil, while heavy blends comprise a further 41 percent. Heavy blends have been absorbed by US refineries located in the Midwest, and will continue to be as some refineries located in this key area are increasing their output capacities for processing 'sour' crude (NEB, 2005b: 33). If oil sands production continues to grow, however, new processing outlets must be reached. According to some market analysts, it makes sense for oil sands producers to access the major refinery cluster located in Texas and on the Gulf of Mexico, as there they already have the economies of scale to process heavy blends (Hawkins, 2004). Another possible outlet is the Pacific Coast, through which Canadian oil could be transported to fuel-hungry California or to ports for shipping to Asia.

Current investments and strategic plans seem to indicate that a combination of these three options is the solution for the mid term. Enbridge is scheduled to open the first phase of a new line in 2008 which would link its terminal in Chicago with St. Louis, a point from which it will be possible to further connect with the Gulf of Mexico refinery cluster. The company also has plans for piping up to 400,000 bd to the Pacific Coast in British Columbia by 2010. The pipeline could be co-financed with Chinese capital in order to open an export outlet to Asia (see Jiang, this volume). Other pipeline companies, including the famous TransCanada (operating a major west-east gas line), are also planning to incrementally increase their transmission capacities in order to profit from the anticipated boom in non-conventional oil (NEB, 2005b: 41). The expected boom has also prompted the planning and construction of new refineries.[13] A new one is about to be constructed in southern California, which in principle could be supplied by oil coming from Mexico. Since Mexican authorities could not guarantee a ten-year supply of crude, Canadian suppliers have shown interest. This interest clearly shows that the expansion of Canadian exports to the southern US and the Gulf of Mexico will directly compete with Mexican and Venezuelan oil, as these countries also export great volumes of heavy blends within the region.

Apart from infrastructure logistics, the further deepening of energy markets between Canada and the United States must manage regulatory and environmental constraints. Transmission lines and import connections are regulated at the federal level in the two countries. State and provincial authorities regulate most energy matters. The mix of jurisdictions risks both regulatory confusion and political interference.[14] However, the most controversial issues have been raised by environmental groups. Since the exploitation of oil sands is itself an energy-intensive activity, requiring a high consumption of natural gas and water in order to upgrade bitumen, environmental and advocacy groups are pressing for stricter supervision of the tar sands development by Canadian agencies. Recently, the Sierra Legal Defence Fund, followed by other organizations, asked for an appeal to the Supreme

Court of Canada in order to broaden the federal government's environmental review of the oil sands project (*Oil Daily*, 2006).

In fact, the real environmental battle that Albertans and WCSB's producers will confront will be when Ottawa and the provinces set the policies for dealing with the reduction of greenhouse gas (GHG) emissions. In September 2002, the Chrétien Liberal government announced that it would ratify the Kyoto Protocol, thereby committing Canada to reduce GHG emissions to a target of 6 percentage points below the 1990 emissions level. For Albertans, this commitment signalled the return of federal regulation in the oil and gas industry and they have consequently opposed the international agreement. Their concerns stem from the cost that environmental policies, such as a carbon tax, could impose on oil sands producers although their by-products may be less pollutant. Some estimates suggest that environmental commitments could add an additional US$6 per barrel to supply costs of non-conventional oil (Brownsey, 2005: 216).[15]

As of May 2006, Stephen Harper's government has been explicit in that it will be impossible to comply with Kyoto's reduction targets, as Canada has increased its emissions more than 20 percent above the 1990 benchmark levels. Budget cuts have also been announced which will affect existing climate change programs advanced by the previous administration in support of the Kyoto commitments (Struck, 2006). Minister of the Environment Rona Ambrose (2006: A19) has spoken on the need to draft a realistic, "made-in-Canada" solution to GHG emissions instead of worrying about international targets. This policy shift is comparable to the stance taken by the Bush Administration in the US, and has great support from the Conservatives' base in Western Canada. This does not mean that the Canadian government is planning to withdraw from the agreement, rather it will develop, with other countries, other options "within the treaty" to control emissions (Fisher, 2006). This 'new approach' on GHG emissions has gained the support of oil producers in Alberta and has not completely alienated environmentalist groups. Working out a made-in-Canada environmental policy within Kyoto may be the compromise the Conservatives need to mollify both oil producers (in the West) and environmentalists (generally seen as concentrated in Central Canada), thereby improving their chances of electoral success (see Schwanen, this volume).

Maintaining the Supply of Conventional Natural Gas in the Short to Mid Term

Currently, 97 percent of Canada's natural gas production comes from the WCSB and just 3 percent from the Atlantic Provinces. However, it is estimated that 23 percent of recoverable reserves lie in the Arctic, mainly in the Mackenzie River Delta (NEB, 2004b: 3). Canadian domestic consumption is estimated to continue growing, partly on the basis of oil sands development, which currently consumes 10 percent of Canada's natural gas production (NEB, 2005a: 20). Since gas production from the WCSB appears to be flattening, Canadian agencies plan to develop Arctic reserves and construct a major pipeline to connect the Mackenzie River Delta with Alberta's gas lines in order to maintain the current supply of natural gas. Hearings are already underway to reconcile energy interests with environmental concerns, land claims, and native rights. If the Mackenzie pipeline comes into operation (scheduled for 2011), it will be the major infrastructure route to maintain growing levels of gas exports to the US.

In contrast, Canadian estimates indicate that conventional gas production from the WCSB will begin a fairly dramatic decline after 2008. From then on, this decline is estimated to be compensated by frontier gas from offshore production on the East Coast, non-conventional gas (obtained mainly from coal), the Mackenzie River Delta, and growing imports into Canada of liquefied natural gas (LNG) (see NAEWG, 2005: 82). There are at present eight proposals for LNG import facilities, mostly located in the Atlantic provinces and Quebec, scheduled to start operations at the end of the decade. The siting and development of these terminals will also exacerbate regulatory and environmental concerns at the provincial and federal levels, since re-exports to the US are also scheduled from some of those terminals.

Overall, the EIA's most recent forecast estimates that net Canadian gas exports to the US will decline (from a peak reached in 2001 to the levels of the early 1990s) just before gas from the Arctic region comes on stream. Even with Arctic production, net gas exports will continue to decline and will only stabilize when non-conventional (mostly coal bed) gas becomes economically feasible, which US estimates suggest will occur after the year 2020. Therefore, Canadian gas exports will not be enough to supply the growing demand for gas imports commanded by the US power generation industry (EIA, 2006: 86). With declining net Canadian exports of conventional gas and the future of Mexico's gas production uncertain, the development of LNG terminal clusters throughout North America has become a strategic issue for the growing demand for natural gas in the three industrial economies (see NEB, 2005a: 15; and IEA, 2004: 86). The presence of LNG terminals either in Canada or Mexico has become part of the spotlight within the US-led SPP initiative. Currently, there are five terminals located along the East Coast and the Gulf of Mexico which provide for growing LNG imports to the United States and whose capacity will increase in the years to come. It is projected that US imports of LNG will grow from less than 1 trillion cubic feet (tcf) in 2005 to more than 4 tcf in year 2030.

FOSTERING REGULATORY CONVERGENCE TO SECURE CRITICAL TRANSMISSION INFRASTRUCTURE

The safety of infrastructure and any other transmission mechanisms linking the US to foreign energy flows has become, after 9/11, a major American goal in the protection of the homeland. Since oil and gas markets between Canada and the United States are fully integrated through pipeline interconnections, the security of this infrastructure has become critical. Key oil producing reservoirs (encompassing large volumes of downloading and storage operations), such as those located offshore in the Gulf of Mexico, could eventually become the target of terrorist attack by surface, air, or cyber-network (Norman, 2004). Local, state/provincial, and federal authorities must be prepared for such a scenario, and must be able to coordinate efforts with their foreign counterparts when infrastructure and transmission lines cross national borders.

With the US Department of Homeland Security in charge of the protection of critical infrastructure, it seems that a combination of market incentives in the energy field, combined with stronger regulatory oversight, has become the model for ensuring security, at least at the preventive level. The model is being built upon the experience of regional electricity organizations for ensuring the reliability of the grid and its interconnections. This is the case of the North American Electricity Reliability Council (NERC), currently encompassing eight regional electricity organizations (REOs) who ensure most of the power generation and transmission in both Canada and the US. Founded in 1968 as a response to previous major power outages, the goal of NERC is to coordinate the activities of the different REOs to establish standards and oversight mechanisms to prevent transmission failures. The organization of NERC already reflects the way power generation and transmission operates between Canada and the US.

Twenty years ago, electricity markets were heavily regulated at the local, state, and federal levels in the United States. As electricity is not a commodity like other energy products (i.e. it cannot be stored, and it must be produced at the time of its consumption), markets became very localized and heavily dependent on the vertical integration of power companies. The situation changed once the federal government initiated the liberalization of electricity generation and transmission across the United States. Markets became more regionally oriented, with strategic interconnections among them. The regionalization of electricity markets did not stop at the 49th parallel, as numerous REOs included Canadian provinces. The Western Electricity Coordinating Council encompasses not only the Western states of the US, but British Columbia and Alberta as well. The US based Midwest Reliability Organization includes Saskatchewan and Manitoba, while Ontario and Quebec are members of the Northeast Power Coordinating Council, which also represents the interests of the US East Coast states. NERC has remained a private organization with voluntary membership and no enforcement mechanism to ensure the security and reliability of the electricity grid. When markets were locally based and regulated, private companies were able to internalize the costs of protecting the security and reliability of their operations. It was in their interest to do so, and localized price controls covered the additional costs. Once competition began to grow at the generation and transmission levels, it became less clear how to fund and operate the security of the grid. In fact, deregulation created a sort of regulatory patchwork of jurisdictions that overlapped or competed with the different levels of government (Nervius and Vancko, 2005). While markets moved towards a regional and even trans-national configuration, infrastructure and transmission development remained stuck at the state level. This dissonance provoked, among other things, a lag between the construction of transmission lines and the growth of energy demands.

The governance of the electricity grid hit a major crisis in August 2003, when the largest electricity blackout in the history of North America occurred without warning. It started with three daytime shutdowns at power plants in Michigan, mid-Ohio, and Cleveland, and quickly cascaded into a major outage affecting around 50 million customers in the United States and Canada (United States, 2003: 1–4). The joint Canada-US taskforce that was created to identify the causes of the blackout concluded that human errors were the major origins of the crisis, including the inability of system operators to visualize events on the system, ineffective operation communications and coordination, inadequate training of operators, and inadequate reactive power resources (NERC, 2004). In other words, reliability standards already agreed to by NERC members were not respected and there was no way to ensure their adherence and enforcement.

As a consequence of this crisis, NERC advocated for major regulatory reform to ensure the security of the continental electricity network. They called for the creation of a full oversight organization which would issue reliability standards, the enforcement of which would be assured through a mechanism of incentives (for those who comply) and fines (for those who do not). This proposal was incorporated in the 2005 EPA and in the trilateral SPP initiative. Indeed, the EPA called for the creation of an Electricity Reliability Organization committed to the harmonization of the industry's security standards, its oversight, and enforcement. At the same time, the EPA enlarged the jurisdictional duties of the federal regulatory body, the Federal Energy Regulatory Commission (FERC), to impose sanctions on organizations or firms who fail to comply with security standards and provisions. FERC also became the primary authority to design and establish National Interest Economic Transmission Corridors through which inter-state transmission lines will be constructed to meet the growth and geographic changes in energy consumption. In the June 2005 SPP report, the three governments of North America called for the conversion of NERC into a continental organization, in which Mexico would initially join as an observer. NERC has already submitted its proposal to become the new North American Electricity Reliability Organization (NERO). If FERC agrees to this (and it most likely will), current NERC reliability standards will become obligatory nation-wide in January 2007 and enforceable through a joint NERO-FERC collaboration. Two major consequences derive from this major regulatory breakthrough.

The first implication is that NERO will play a major role in policy harmonization to ensure the reliability of the electricity grid and its interconnections, this time at the continental level. NERO will continue to be a cluster of private firms and associations, but will now also encompass some publicly-owned electricity utilities, as it is the case in both Canada and Mexico. In the years to come, its role will not only be to ensure the reliability of transmission grids in order to prevent blackouts, but also to progressively internalize the security of the entire grid to anticipate and avoid any physical or cyber terrorist attack.

The second implication of this regulatory breakthrough is the empowerment of FERC as a backup authority in transmission matters and other energy decisions. Since FERC will be the ultimate authority to determine sanctions in cases of non-compliance with reliability or any other security standards, it will most probably request a similar role to federal energy regulatory bodies in Canada and Mexico. In other words, FERC will soon become the leading regulatory body to set standards and levels of jurisdiction for similar regulatory bodies in Canada and Mexico. These two countries still have highly regulated and vertically integrated electricity markets. However, when FERC opens the US transmission grid to any power company, it asks for reciprocity. Thus, Canadian companies exporting to the US are required to open access to their transmission grids to American companies. This has prompted the provinces of British Columbia and Quebec – in an effort to enlarge their export markets – to introduce transmission rates modelled on the

FERC tariff. Currently, the federal government and the rest of the provinces are discussing the best way to accommodate their respective access regulations with those currently prevailing in the US (see Doern and Gattinger, 2003: 84–88). Now that FERC has become more powerful for the supervision of the power grid, regulatory practices existing in electricity markets in both Canada and Mexico will have to adapt to the new continental trend.

NERO's role in assuring the reliability and eventually the security of electricity provision in North America could become a standard for how the combination of a market-based approach (involving multiple stakeholders, incentives and fines) with a strong regulatory approach (where electricity is seen as a necessity) including regulatory coordination at the regional level (to take place within SPP), could be implemented in the oil and gas fields. This sort of 'privatization' of security operations have proved to be more functional and cost effective for regulators, since market organization and stakeholder involvement is very similar in the United States and Canada within the oil and gas sectors.

CONCLUSIONS

Harper's Conservative government came to office at a time when the economic and political significance of oil wealth is increasing. The primary resource economy in Western Canada is once again fuelling growth across the country and is about to solidify the region as the biggest and safest powerhouse in North America, and a key player in international energy markets. At a juncture where international oil prices are expected to remain high, and the security of oil and gas supplies and infrastructure interconnections have become a 'homeland' priority for the United States, Canada's strategic energy position has become quite unique. Only Mexico could stand in a similar position, although its potential is significantly smaller.

The political and economic consequences of expanding oil wealth remain to be seen. It is clear that the oil and gas markets will be further continentalized in the years to come. Regional markets and infrastructure interconnections are the main driving forces in this process. Canadian non-conventional oil could eventually compensate for a short-term decline or disruption of heavy blends imported from Mexico or Venezuela. New export markets are being developed overseas, mainly in China and Japan. However, the evolution of oil sands production will remain highly sensitive to technological innovations and oil price fluctuations. Under current conditions, private firms have the incentives to invest in new technologies to reduce the costs of synthetic oil production, but have no say in the evolution of world oil prices. The latter responds to macroeconomic behaviour in major oil consuming and importing countries, and to the evolution of US-led 'transformational' diplomacy in the Persian Gulf. That is why it will become crucial for Ottawa to develop a policy approach vis-à-vis world oil markets, aimed at ensuring the stability of prices to encourage the long term development of its huge oil reserves. Mexico could become a major partner in this process.

The development of Canada's energy reserves brings with it both domestic and foreign policy challenges and opportunities. Domestically the shift in economic activity will eventually be reflected in a shift in political power as well, strengthening the traditional political base of the Conservative Party. This shift in domestic political power will undoubtedly have implications of the conduct of foreign policy, especially in the areas of trade, energy, and the environment.

The foreign policy implications and questions are also intriguing. While integration with the American market seems to fit in well with the Harper government's foreign policy so far, the accompanying need for regulatory harmonization and incorporation into a continental security framework that embraces more than just energy reliability may create some political discomfort at home. It will also be interesting to see how the growing demand for energy in Asia will intrude on more harmonious relations with the United States. Asian investment in energy allows Canada to develop new markets, a potentially sensible strategy of market diversification, but one that may be viewed with less enthusiasm in the United States. In addition, while closer energy links with Asia may assist in opening the door for wider commercial relations, they may also embroil Canada in a host of thornier issues such as human rights in China. In a wider sense, will Alberta's energy wealth trickle up and facilitate a more expansive role for Canada in international affairs, providing the financial resources for a more muscular security and development program? Will this enhanced capacity allow us to be more active and play a leadership role in global and regional affairs? Or will our integration with the United States dilute perceptions of our independence (especially in the Americas)? Our provision of secure energy resources to the United States may frustrate those who want to use energy as a weapon against them, at the same time possibly allowing the Americans to react more aggressively without fear of energy-based reprisals. It remains to be seen whether the Harper government will be willing or able to articulate a sort of 'oil diplomacy' to capitalize on the opportunities of Canada's energy potential. If he wins a majority mandate in the near future, however, learning how to play Canada's energy card will have to become one of his government's priorities.

NOTES

1 This may happen in the short to mid term if PEMEX does not make the necessary investment to maintain current production trends.

2 This seems to explain, for instance, the closer links Washington is building with oil producing former Soviet nations, such as Azerbaijan, from which a gas pipeline is proposed in order to reduce European dependency on Russian gas.

3 The uncertainties about the future of Mexico's oil and gas production have become a security concern for the United States. Although Mexico remains a reliable oil partner – a non-OPEC country, with most of its exports concentrated in the US market, and refusing to use oil as a 'bargaining weapon' – the decline of its oil reserves, a surge in imports on natural gas, and the lack of consensus in the political class for modernizing and boosting PEMEX's activities, have seriously compromised the future of Mexican oil exports. See Morales (2006).

4 According to some authors, it is irrelevant for the US to reduce its oil imports from the Gulf producers (21.7 per cent of its imports in 2005), since oil markets are global and fully integrated (see Cordesman and Al-Rodhan, 2005). This is true in terms of the evolution of crude oil prices. Any disruption in any part of the world is immediately transmitted to all importing countries. However, in terms of strategic options, US growing reliance on 'high risk' countries or areas could become a liability. Since the fall of the Shah, the US does not import oil from Iran. Washington has imposed sanctions – through oil embargos – to Iraq and Libya. If the 'War on Terror' is going to last, as it has been repetitively announced by the Bush administration, Washington will be keen to keep and/or increase its oil imports from 'out of risk' regions.

5 For all the technical procedures involved in oil sands productions, see NEB (2004a).

6 For supply costs of Canadian oil sands, see NEB (2004a: 7). In the past decade, costs for bitumen were in the range of US$30–35 dollars per barrel (McFall, 2006).

7 A US$30 range is established by American experts, see EIA (2006: 52).

8 According to United States EIA estimates, the higher the price, the higher the volume that will be produced from non-conventional oil. In Mexico, the opposite trend is anticipated, since Mexico's PEMEX is still a rent-seeking company which will attempt to optimize the value of its oil according to the fluctuation of prices. See EIA (2006: 182).

9 Currently, US firms Imperial Oil, Exxon, Mobil, Chevron, and Conoco Philips are operating in the country. Japanese and Chinese firms have also shown their interests in the WCSB resources. The participation of these firms is facilitating the expansion of transmission and refinery capacities in the United States. See IEA (2004: 80); and Kumagai (2006).

10 The Government of Alberta has clearly identified the fiscal incentives for investors participating in oil sands development. Since the 1990s, the government

takes a 1 percent royalty of the gross revenue of a company until it had a pay out of all of its capital. Once this is done, royalties amount to 25 percent. See McFall (2006).

11 From 1972 to 1978, that is, before the downfall of the Shah, Iran's production of crude oil was above 5 mb per day. Although Iranian production was below 3 mb per day during the 1980s, in 2005 it reached 4.05 mb per day. See British Petroleum (2006).

12 In 2004 Canada imported 950 000 barrels per day mainly to supply the consumption of Central and Eastern Canada. The country remains, however, a net oil exporter.

13 Canada is currently exporting 500,000 barrels per day of petroleum products. This amount could dramatically increase if oil companies find it cost effective to build new refineries in Canada for upgrading bitumen and exporting fuels to the US.

14 For a more detailed analysis on how different levels of jurisdiction and regulatory authorities interact on specific energy issues between the two countries see Ziff (2004).

15 For the Alberta-made GHG plan, see Lucas (2005: 293–310).

REFERENCES

Ambrose, Rona. 2006. "Mandate to Clean Up Air, Water, Soil," *Toronto Star*, 1 March, A19.

British Petroleum. 2006. "Historical Data Series from 1965," *Statistical Review of World Energy 2006*. Available at: <http://www.bp.com/productlanding.do?categoryId=91&contentId=7017990>

Brownsey, Keith. 2005. "Alberta's Oil and Gas Industry in the Era of the Kyoto Protocol," in Bruce Doern, ed. *Canadian Energy Policy and the Struggle for Sustainable Development*. Toronto: University of Toronto Press, 200–22.

Cordesman, Anthony, and Khalid R. Al-Rodhan. 2005. "The Changing Risks in Global Oil Supply and Demand: Crisis or Evolving Solution?" First working draft. Washington, DC: Center for Strategic and International Studies, 3 October.

D'Arcy, Jenish. 2006. "Captives of Industry: The West's Resource Boom Is Making It Too Easy for Ottawa to Ignore a Growing Eastern Economic Crisis," *Western Standard*, 24 April.

Doern, Bruce G., and Monica Gattinger. 2003. *Power Switch: Energy Regulatory Governance in the Twenty-First Century*. Toronto: University of Toronto Press.

Energy Information Administration (EIA). 2006. *Annual Energy Outlook 2006: With Projection to 2030*. Washington, DC: Department of Energy (US).

Fisher, Doug. 2006. "Silent Spring: If Scientific Circles Agree on the Fundamentals of Global Warming, Why Isn't the Environment One of the Conservatives' Top Priorities?" *Ottawa Citizen*, 9 April.

Gallis, Paul. 2006. "NATO and Energy Security," *CRS Report for Congress*, 21 March. Available at: <http://www.opencrs.com/document/RS22409/>

Hawkins, David J. 2004. "Canadian Bitumen Stands Poised to Expand to US Markets," *Oil and Gas Journal* 102, no. 219 (2 August): 52–7.

International Energy Agency (IEA). 2004. *Energy Policies of IEA Countries: Canada, 2004 Review*. Paris: Organisation for Economic Cooperation and Development (OECD).

Kumagai, Takeo. 2006. "Japan Weighs Running Canadian Synthetic," *Platts Oilgram News*, 13 March.

Lucas, Alastair. 2005. "The Alberta Energy Sector's Voluntary Approach to Climate Change: Context, Prospects, and Limits," in Bruce Doern, ed. *Canadian Energy Policy and the Struggle for Sustainable Development*. Toronto: University of Toronto Press, 293–310.

McFall, Kathy. 2006. "Feeding the American Addiction," *Platts Energy Economist*, 1 March.

Morales, Isidro. 2006. "The Politics of Energy Markets in North America: The Challenges and Prospects for Enhanced Cooperation in a Continental Partnership," in Isabel Studer and Carol Wise, eds. *Reflections on North American Integration: NAFTA, FTAA and the Doha Round*, forthcoming.

National Energy Board (NEB). 2004a. *Canada's Oil Sands: Opportunities and Challenges to 2015*. Calgary, AB: Government of Canada, May.

– 2004b. *Canada's Conventional Natural Gas Resources. A Status Report*. Calgary, AB: Government of Canada, April.

– 2005a. *Short Term Outlook for Natural Gas and Natural Gas Liquids to 2006*. Calgary, AB: Government of Canada, October.

– 2005b. *Short-term Outlook for Canadian Crude Oil to 2006*. Calgary, AB: Government of Canada, September.

Nervius, David R., and Ellen P. Vancko. 2005. "Ensuring a Reliable North American Electric System in a Competitive Marketplace," Paper prepared for the US-Canada Power System Outage Task Force, 15 August.

Norman, Brian S. 2004. "Gulf of Mexico: Offshore Energy Infrastructure at Risk?" in Michael W. Ritz, et al. *The Homeland Security Papers: Stemming the Tide of Terror*. Alabama: USAF Counterproliferation Center, February, 55–109.

North American Electric Reliability Council (NERC). 2004. "Conclusions and Recommendations," *Final NERC Report, August 14, 2003 Blackout*, 13 July. Available at: <http://www.nerc.com/~filez/blackout.html>

North American Energy Working Group (NAEWG). 2005. *North American Natural Gas Vision*. Washington, DC, January. Available at: <http://www.pi.energy.gov/pdf/library/NAEWGGasVision2005.pdf>

Oil Daily. 2006. "Groups Seeks Oil Sands Review," 29 March.

Security and Prosperity Partnership of North America (SPP). 2005. *Report to Leaders*, Trilingual Version, June. Available at: <http://www.spp.gov/report_to_leaders>

Shook, Barbara. 2005. "Northwest Territories Want to Get into the Energy Act," *Natural Gas Week*, 21 March.

Struck, Doug. 2006. "Canada Alters Course on Kyoto; Budget Slashes Funding Devoted to Goals of Emissions Pact," *The Washington Post*, 3 May.

United States. 2003. *Electricity Restructuring: 2003 Blackout Identifies Crisis and Opportunity for the Electricity Sector.* Washington, DC: General Accounting Office, November.

– 2005. *Energy Policy Act of 2005.* News Release. Washington, DC: Senate Committee on Energy and Natural Resources. Available at: <http://energy.senate.gov/public/_files/PostConferenceBillSummary.doc>

Ziff. Paul. 2004. "Cross-Border Regulatory Collaboration in Its Context: Energy Balances and Energy Policy," in David N. Biette, ed. *Moving Toward Dialogue: Challenges in Canada-U.S. Energy Trade.* Washington, DC. Woodrow Wilson International Center for Scholars, September.

15 Canada and the Kyoto Protocol: When Reality Sets In

DANIEL SCHWANEN

Unless Canada is willing to purchase billions of dollars worth of greenhouse gas emissions 'credits' internationally between now and 2012, it will run afoul of its obligations under the Kyoto Protocol (KP) to the United Nations 1992 Framework Convention on Climate Change (FCCC). Under the KP, which was signed in 1997 and entered into force in February 2005, Canada took responsibility for reducing emissions of greenhouse gases (GHG)[1] by six per cent relative to what emissions in Canada were reckoned to be in 1990. It is now clear that, during the 'commitment period' of 2008–12 – during which the promised reductions must be achieved on average – Canadian emissions will remain wildly above the promised target.

The KP requires countries whose domestic emissions will be above their Kyoto targets to purchase emission reduction 'credits' (called Assigned Amount Units) from other countries whose domestic emissions will have come in below their Kyoto target. Countries may also receive credit, counting toward their Kyoto targets, for projects undertaken by private or public entities within their borders that certifiably reduce emissions in another country. But the number of such projects undertaken so far by Canadian entities is very small.

Thus, in practice, in order to comply with its Kyoto obligations, Canada will have to purchase credits worth between $1.6 and $3 billion[2] – money that will likely be paid to Russia and the Ukraine, countries whose emissions reductions will, on current trends, easily meet or exceed their Kyoto commitments. How will the government of the day explain to Canadians that such a large sum, certainly equivalent to a major new social program or tax cut, will be sent abroad to reward other countries for good environmental behaviour that Canada promised but was not able to emulate?

Canada's inability – or unwillingness – to implement effective domestic GHG emission reduction policies in order to follow through on its KP promises has been painfully evident for some time now. Along with many others, I have been deeply sceptical of Canada's ability to meet the targets to which it had committed under the Protocol (Schwanen, 1997; *Globe and Mail*, 1997: A24). It was clear to me then, and it is now a matter of record, that the government of the day had not properly evaluated what these targets would mean for Canada. Indeed, at the time Canada solemnly reaffirmed its commitments by ratifying the KP in December 2002, it can be said that objective conditions known at the time made it very unlikely that Canada could fulfill its promises, at least not through domestic reductions. Using comparative country data, this chapter will illustrate why it was unrealistic to expect that Canada could meet its Kyoto targets with domestic greenhouse gas reductions. Readers may interject that it is easy to indulge in hindsight. However, most of the points I will make on this score simply illustrate, with recent data, that Canada's targets relative to those of other countries, were hard to reconcile with objective conditions that were known at the time of their adoption. This in turn helps explain – but does not condone – why Canadian governments since then have been reluctant to take any significant measures that would move Canada toward the targets.

I will then turn to the key factors that will come into play as Canada re-examines its approach to the problem of reducing greenhouse gas emissions globally. Clearly, the minority Conservative government that came to power following the January 2006 federal election has begun this re-examination. But it is equally clear that our situation in view of the looming Kyoto commitment period would have required any government to do the same.

The issue of what to do, practically speaking, about greenhouse gas emissions can be effectively tackled only within a very long-term framework, but a framework that requires early action as well as a clear sense of direction in order to reap long-term benefits. While the environment was barely on the radar screen during the 2006 federal election, it is highly unlikely that the policy debate will be similarly avoidable in any future election contest this decade, as the issue of Canada's non-compliance with the KP is now out in the open. Any party hoping to form a majority government in the years ahead will be asked to explain what it intends to do with respect to climate change and how its plan to abate GHG emissions meshes with other elements of its platform and with Canadians' priorities in general. In that light, a final

Table 1
Greenhouse Gas Targets and Emissions (1990–2003)

	Kyoto Targets (on 1990 levels)	Change in Emissions (by 2003)	Difference
North America	percentage points		
Canada	−6.0	24	+30.0
United States	−7.0	13	+20.0
Asia and Oceanic			
Australia	8.0	23	+15.0
Japan	−6.0	13	+19.0
New Zealand	0.0	23	+23.0
European Union[1]	−8.0	−1.1	+6.9
Austria	−13.0	17.0	+30.0
Belgium	−7.5	1.0	+8.5
Denmark	−21.0	7.0	+28.0
Finland	0.0	22.0	+22.0
France	0.0	−2.0	−2.0
Germany	−21.0	−18.0	+3.0
Greece	25.0	26.0	+1.0
Ireland	13.0	26.0	+13.0
Italy	−6.5	12.0	+18.5
Luxembourg	−28.0	NA	NA
Netherlands	−6.0	2.0	+8.0
Portugal	27.0	37.0	+10.0
Spain	15.0	42.0	+27.0
Sweden	4.0	−2.0	−6.0
United Kingdom	−12.5	−13.0	−0.5
Other Europe			
Iceland	10	−8.0	−18.0
Liechtenstein	−8	NA	NA
Monaco	−8	NA	NA
Norway	1	9.0	+8.0
Switzerland	−8	0.0	+8.0
Turkey			
Countries in Transition[2]			
Bulgaria	−8	−50.0	−42.0

Table 1
Greenhouse Gas Targets and Emissions (1990–2003) *(continued)*

Croatia	–5	–6.0	–1.0
Czech Republic	–8	–24.0	–16.0
Estonia	–8	–51.0	–43.0
Hungary	–6	–32.0	–26.0
Latvia	–8	–59.0	–51.0
Lithuania	–8	–66.0	–58.0
Poland	–6	–34.0	–28.0
Romania	–8	–46.0	–38.0
Russian Federation	0	–39.0	–39.0
Slovakia	–8	–28.0	–20.0
Slovenia	–8	–2.0	+6.0
Ukraine	0	–46.0	–46.0

Source: Japan (2006: Tables 1–3); and United Nations (2005: Table 5).
(1) Based on EU15, prior to May 2004 expansion.
(2) Former Soviet and Eastern European states in transition to a market economy

substantive section of the paper will assess possible policy stances from the viewpoint of their domestic economic and political feasibility, and of their implications for meeting, modifying or exiting from our international commitments.

WHAT WERE WE THINKING?

Relative to other countries that committed to constraining their GHG emissions under the KP, the so-called Annex B parties,[3] Canada had strayed from its target the most by 2003, with the exception of Austria, as plainly seen in Table 1.

International Reality Check

While the numbers speak for themselves in terms of absolute discrepancy between promise and reality, three points are worth making with respect to the target that the Canadian government committed to, in relation to the obligations that other Annex B parties entered into under the KP.

First, the best 'performers' relative to their promises have been former planned state economies that were, at the time of the signature of the KP, 'in transition' toward a market economy. It is not minimizing the issue of environmental degradation in market economies to say that centrally planned economies were notoriously much worse for the environment. The reason, in purely material terms, is plain: these economies used up enormous amounts of resources to produce what in the more innovative developed market economies would take far less.

Second, while the European Union made a commitment as a bloc to reduce its emissions by eight per cent (or by two per cent more than Canada), widely divergent GHG emission targets were allowed for each EU member country, under what is called the European "bubble." This allowed for specific economic circumstances, for example fast anticipated economic growth in one country or planned changes in sources of energy supplies, to be taken into account in the forward-looking European approach, in effect allowing great flexibility geared to each member country's situation.

Third, the United States and Australia subsequently refused to ratify the KP, yet they did "better" than we did in the sense that they did not stray as widely as Canada from the emission limits they had agreed to at the time of Kyoto. Their situation illustrates that the mere fact of a country not partaking in the KP is not in and of itself a sign that its legislators are unconcerned with human-induced impacts on the climate, or that they are doing nothing about it. Both Australia and the United States have engaged in a range of research and public discussions on this issue that Canadians could have certainly benefited from ourselves.

The practical importance of these basic observations for policy choices can be illustrated by using a simple identity, called the Kaya identity, which breaks down GHG emissions into four distinct multiplicative components, as follows:

1 The GHG intensity of energy consumption (GHG/E)[4]
2 The energy-intensity of output (E/GDP)
3 Output per capita (GDP/Pop)
4 Population (Pop)

Total emissions in the economy are the product of the four components, thus:

Pop x (GDP/Pop) x (E/GDP) x (GHG/E) = GHG

Using this identity, it is possible to explain the difference in GHG emissions growth between two countries over time, as is demonstrated in Figure 1. Here, the contribution of each component of the Kaya identity is illustrated to show the difference in emissions growth between Canada and, respectively, Germany, the United Kingdom and the United States, between 1990 (the Kyoto base year for most greenhouse gases) and 2003 (the most recent year for which data were available at the time of writing).

A number of observations about Canada's position relative to these three countries can be made from Figure 1. First, both Germany and the United Kingdom benefited from a large switch toward less carbon-intensive sources of energy, specifically from coal to natural gas, due to the development of North Sea gas fields in particular. The magnitude of this switch in energy source in both countries during that time period was unique among major industrial countries. Not to diminish other tough measures that also resulted in reduced emissions in these countries (such as reduced subsidies for coal), but Canada certainly did not have the physical opportunity to implement such a switch in energy sources over such a short period of time.

Germany was 'assisted' in its ability to reduce emissions by another factor, namely that it was able to include the emissions of the former East Germany in its base year 1990. The collapse in dirtier East German industries after 1990 is manifest in Figure 1 by the much more substantial reductions in energy per unit of GDP that Germany (including East Germany) was able to achieve during the period, relative to Canada and the other two countries discussed here. Still looking at Canada's emissions growth relative to that in Germany and in the United Kingdom, we see from Figure 1 that a large part of the difference is simply due to the fact that Canada's population continued to grow throughout the period, while the population growth of Germany and of the UK were nearly stagnant. To be clear, while the reductions in emissions committed to by the United Kingdom (12.5 percent) and Germany (21 percent) were greater on the surface than Canada's (6 percent), on a per capita basis, in actuality Kyoto required Canada's reduction to be in the order of 20 percent. This is higher than the UK's reductions and comparable to Germany's, and Canada did not have the benefit of the two structural factors discussed that allowed sharply reduced carbon-intensity of output in these two economies.

Meanwhile, other European countries whose profile were more comparable to Canada's in terms of population growth or that otherwise experienced fast-growing economies, for example Spain or Ireland, were allowed substantial emissions increases under Kyoto (respectively 15 percent and 13 percent), implicitly benefiting under the EU 'bubble' from the significant reductions promised by the UK and Germany. The above observations certainly do not amount to an economic analysis of the relative cost of reducing emissions in Canada, the United Kingdom, or Germany, and hence it is not meant as a discussion of the reductions that Canada should have been able to promise if it had made the same national effort as Germany or the UK. The point is that the UK and Germany had already practically 'locked in' their promised reductions by the time the Kyoto Protocol was signed, thanks to factors mostly exogenous to any new policy designed to reduce greenhouse gas emissions. Thus, from its early commitments, Canada was forced to play catch up.

Figure 1
Greenhouse Gas Emissions Growth 1990–2003:
Factors Explaining Difference between Canada and Other Countries

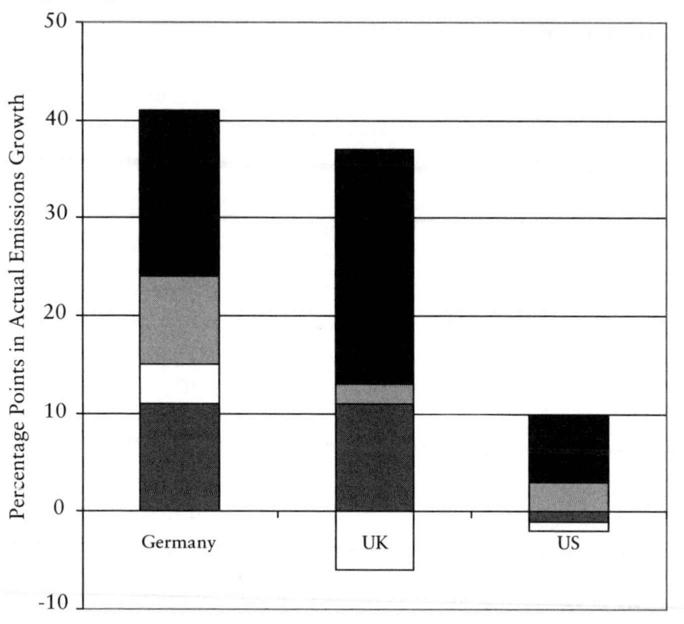

Source: OECD, World Resources Institute, and author's calculations.

As for the United States, it has displayed unspectacular but real progress on fuel efficiency and fuel switching. A striking feature of the US climate change policy framework in recent years, particularly since 2001 under the administration of President George W. Bush, has been the leadership role played by American states in setting goals for greenhouse gas emissions reductions and in enforcing them. At the federal level, US policies have focused heavily on reducing emissions per unit of output, or what is called greenhouse gas intensity, and on tax incentives to encourage the use of renewable energy and the development of energy-efficient technologies. These initiatives have also placed a greater focus on research into the causes and effects of climate change. In this regard, the focus is clearly on the potential of technology for deep, long-term emissions reductions.

The Bush administration's specific goal is to reduce the greenhouse gas intensity of the economy (GHG emissions per dollars of real GDP, i.e. the product of the first and second variables in the Kaya equation) by 18 percent between 2002 and 2012. However, this is probably not an objective requiring a great effort to attain, as it simply reflects recent trends: the greenhouse gas intensity of the United States economy fell by 22 percent between 1990 and 2003, even as total emissions grew due to overall growth in economic output. Meanwhile, a number of American states have taken concrete measures to reduce greenhouse gas emissions on their own, and some have even set quantitative targets for overall emissions that, by definition, constitute much more ambitious goals than those set by the federal government. A key example is California. With an economy larger than Canada's, the state has worked aggressively to set a series of short-term (2010), medium-term (2020) and long-term (2050) goals for the reduction of its own GHG emissions to 2000 levels, 1990 levels and to 80 percent below 1990 levels, respectively. The main tools proposed for achieving these targets are regulatory: greenhouse gas vehicle standards (treated as distinct from federally-set fuel economy standards, a position contested by the automobile industry), a required portion of renewable energy sources in the overall power generation portfolio of the state, and various other energy efficiency standards (California, 2006).

Beyond these measures, however, a proper comparison between the performance of the US and Canada in GHG abatement needs to take another consideration into account. Specifically, during the same period, the traditionally robust American industrial sector – a much more emissions-intensive sector than that of services – shrank rather than expanded. This fact can be explained in part as American imports of manufacturing products from China and Mexico (two countries whose emissions are unconstrained by the Kyoto Protocol) boomed during that period. In contrast to the United States, as well as to Germany and the United Kingdom, Canada's industrial sector – the sector producing all goods other than agricultural – remained strong during that period (see Figure 2). This is an outcome that Canadian federal government actively pursued and welcomed in the late 1980s and 1990s, through policies such as the negotiation of free trade with the United States, the introduction of the Goods and Services Tax (which replaced the manufacturers' sales tax), and even (implicitly) with the historically low value of the Canadian dollar that prevailed through most of that period. Canada also actively pursued population growth through immigration. The desired outcome of these various policies was clearly not taken into account when setting our Kyoto targets, even though it was well-known that they would affect greenhouse gas emissions. In short, there was inconsistency between our environmental and our economic goals.

Figure 2
Changes in Industry Employment of Selected Countries (from 1990 levels)

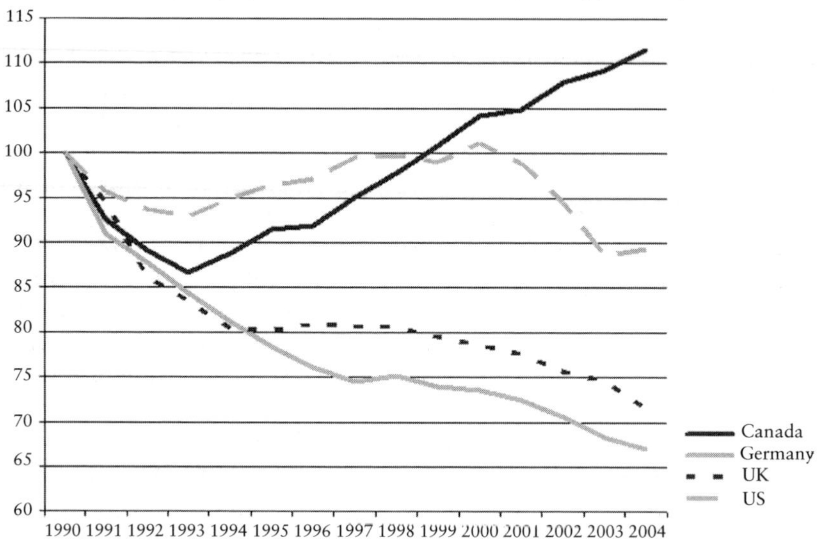

Source: OECD Labour Force Statistics 1984–2004, and author's estimate of East German employment decline 1990–1991.

Domestic Reality Check

Given the environment for energy prices at the beginning of the twenty-first century, it is not surprising that Canada's energy resources are being developed rapidly, and this trend looks to be set for the foreseeable future (see Gold, 2006: B12; Waldie, 2006: B8). These developments are playing a large part in Canada's current and projected overall economic prosperity (see Jiang; Morales, this volume). For example, even though the combined share of the Canadian population remained steady at 13 percent for the two hydrocarbon-rich provinces of Saskatchewan and Alberta between 1990 and 2003, and that federal revenues as a share of GDP are low in these two provinces as compared to others, they nevertheless accounted for 20 percent of the growth in federal revenues between 1990 and 2003 (Statistics Canada, 2006; author's calculations). However, this prosperity is also intrinsically linked with the country's difficulty in coming even close to the KP target for the 2008–12 period, with Alberta and Saskatchewan combined accounting for 57 percent of Canada's overall GHG emissions growth between 1990 to 2003 (see Figure 3). The growing need for electrical power in these provinces (with coal and other fossil fuels being a key source of generation), the growth of the

Figure 3
Canadian Greenhouse Gas Emissions Increase by Region (1990–2003)

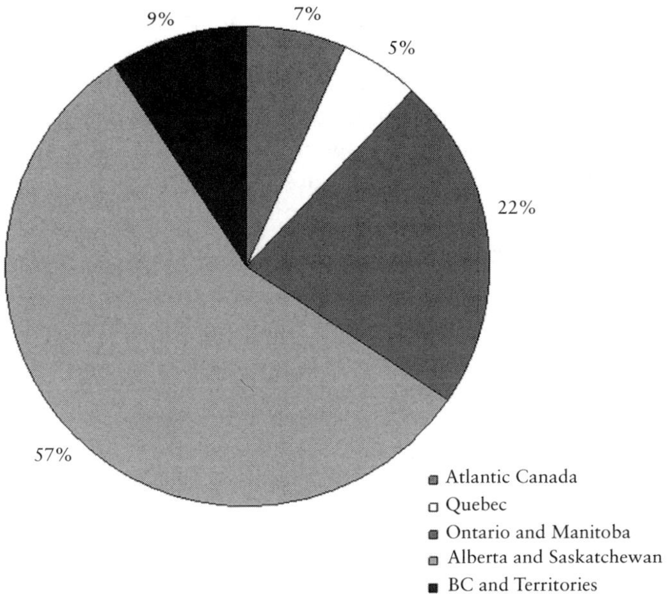

Source: Environment Canada, "Canada's Greenhouse Gas Emissions Inventory," Annex 11.
Available at: <http://www.ec.gc.ca/pdb/ghg/inventory_report/2003/report/toc_e.cfm>

hydrocarbon industry in general and of the oil sands in particular, as well as the growth of agriculture, have all been important sources of emissions growth in these two provinces combined.

Canada's position on what action needs to be taken domestically to address Kyoto is seriously hampered by the regional concentration of carbon energy resources and use in Canada. The reality is that the provinces are sharply divided over what needs to be done – and no one wants to pay an excessive price. Alberta can afford gold-plated government services relative to other provinces as a result of its oil-price induced prosperity, at relatively low tax rates. Hence, its representatives are extremely sensitive about statements to the effect that the production of hydrocarbons might be curtailed directly, such as would be the case under a comprehensive carbon tax, for example. Additionally, the country's federal constitutional framework assigns provincial legislatures exclusive power to make laws in relation to the "development, conservation and management of natural resources and forestry resources in the province." It also sets out a shared responsibility for the environment with the federal government, among other constitutional considerations. This means that under

Canadian constitutional law, ratifying a treaty such as the Kyoto Protocol is an entirely different venture than actually implementing it.[5]

Statements by the joint federal-provincial meetings of energy and environmental ministers that were issued both before and after Kyoto continuously shied away from referring to mandatory reductions. Once the federal government hinted at mandatory targets (Canada, 2002), Canadian provinces and territories felt the need to jointly stress the importance of new technologies, incentives for renewable and other clean energy sources, and of maintaining Canadian competitiveness. They demanded that a national policy ensure that "no region or jurisdiction shall be asked to bear an unreasonable share of the burden," and that "the costs and impacts on individuals, businesses and industries ... be clear, reasonable, achievable, and economically sustainable" and furthermore that federal funding be available to ease any negative impact (Canadian Intergovernmental Conference Secretariat, 2002). The provinces were actually taken aback by the targets announced at Kyoto by the federal government (Smith, 1998), and clearly as a group, they stuck not only to a low common denominator in the approaches they recommended, but increasingly wished to put constraints on any national policy in terms of the distribution of the burden of reducing emissions.

These constraints, reflecting the political and economic reality on the ground, loomed large in Canada's plan to address its obligations under the KP, "Project Green," which was finally made public in 2005, just over seven years after Canada signed the Protocol. The centerpiece of that plan was a compulsory plan aimed at reducing the intensity of emissions per unit of output (not absolute emissions) from large final emitters (LFEs), accounting for over half of Canada's GHG emissions. The required intensity reductions differed by industry. Note how the emphasis was put on intensity of emissions per output (rather than on actual emission reductions), which reflects a concern that mandated actual emissions reductions across the board would hurt economic output and that it is more realistic to seek reductions through continuous reductions in the carbon-intensity of output over time. This is a similar philosophy as that espoused by the US federal government, except that in the Canadian case rewards were given for those who exceeded the target, and conversely, those who did not were penalized. Credits would accrue to emitters reducing their intensity below target, which they could sell to others, those whose emissions were over target (and who were obliged to show that they had acquired such credits or equivalents from non-LFE sources, or that they had invested equivalent sums in a fund investing in cleaner technologies). Given the focus of the LFE scheme on intensity rather than on actual emissions, and the fact that other major sources of emissions, such as transportation fuels, were only peripherally covered by the plan, the federal government also promised to set aside significant sums, $4–5 billion over five years, to finance further reductions at home and purchase credits abroad.

These and other aspects of the plan are analyzed by Wigle (2005) and Jaccard (2006). They conclude that the plan as conceived is cost-ineffective, and that actually achieving the Kyoto targets was going to cost far more than the government anticipated. In any event, reaching the targets would require a large reliance on the purchase of cheaper emission reductions abroad, through the Kyoto clean development mechanism (CDM) for example.

The provinces, meanwhile, have been elaborating their own plans in light of what they deemed feasible within their respective jurisdictions. The two very different plans of Alberta and Quebec reflect the very diverse circumstances of these two provinces. Alberta, mindful of the importance of fossil fuels to the booming provincial economy, issued what it calls the first climate-change specific legislation in Canada. It has set for itself a longer-term target of reduced GHG-intensity of output, through measures such as government power coming in large part from green and renewable sources, and a requirement that all new coal-fired power plants in the provinces use available "clean as gas" standards that would cut their emissions in half relative to prevalent technologies. The province figures that this plan will only reduce emissions by 20 million tonnes by 2010 and 60 million tonnes by 2020 relative to a "business-as-usual" scenario (still leaving Alberta's emissions 39 percent and 27 percent above their 1990 level by 2010 and 2020 respectively) (Alberta, 2002). Quebec, mindful of its position as an abundant provider of cheap, 'clean' renewable hydro-electric power and as a net consumer rather than supplier of hydrocarbons, actually embraced the Kyoto targets in its plan, and is focusing on renewable energy, tougher California-style emissions standards, new technologies and adoption of best practices for industry (as in the case of Alberta), as well as on reducing methane emissions from garbage dumps. Nevertheless, because the province is already a very low GHG emitter per GDP relative to Alberta and has experienced weaker economic growth, the total reductions in the Quebec plan relative to a 'business-as-usual' scenario in the province in 2012 is 14 million tonnes, less than Alberta's during the same time frame.

Due to this recent action at the provincial level, the statement that "governments in the US have, in fact, taken far more significant action to reduce GHG emissions than have governments in Canada" (Bramley, 2002: 1), is probably less accurate than it was five years ago. But that is thanks to another similarity with the US situation: Canada's climate change policy is being increasingly 'provincialized.'

CLIMATE CHANGE POLICY
CONSIDERATIONS FOR
A MAJORITY GOVERNMENT

As Canada's embarrassment over the Kyoto fiasco becomes clear against the backdrop of the looming Kyoto 'commitment period,' it seems likely that the next one or two federal elections will feature some robust public exchanges on the climate change question, quite unlike the January 2006 election. Environmental issues barely made it on the radar screen during the latter, perhaps because the ruling Liberals (in a minority government situation) did not wish to draw attention to their weak record on climate change, while the challenging Conservative Party possibly did not wish it advertised that it lacked a well-developed policy on the issue. But the Conservatives, who appeared to shock environmentalists and some sections of the public by admitting publicly, soon after their taking over the reins of government (also in a minority situation) that the Kyoto targets were "impossible, impossible" to achieve (Sallot, 2006) are now under pressure to spell out, if not their entire philosophy on the question, at least what they intend to do with respect to the obligations that Canada has undertaken internationally. The Liberals, who may be eager to distance themselves from an appearance of being adrift toward the end of their long spell in power from late 1993 to early 2006, will be under pressure to say how their commitment to Kyoto – firm on the surface – was allowed to slip into near-insignificance in practice. After two consecutive minority governments of differing political stripes, each with sharply divergent public stances on Canada's ability to reach its Kyoto targets, what should Canadians ask of political parties vying for a majority in the next election?

1) A Clear Stance on the Global Environmental Problem

All political parties would probably do well by reaffirming where they stand on the science of global warming. By remaining a party to the FCCC with the United States and over 180 other countries, Canada acknowledges that human activities have substantially increased the atmospheric concentration of greenhouse gases, contributing on average to a warming of the Earth that is potentially harmful to ecosystems and human societies. Article 2 of the FCCC also spells out the goal of eventually stabilizing greenhouse gas concentration in the atmosphere, while in

Article 3 Canada agrees that "lack of full scientific certainty should not be used as a reason for postponing" measures "to anticipate, prevent or minimize the causes of climate change" when it is threatening to cause "serious or irreversible damage," although such measures should be "cost-effective" (United Nations, 1992).

In other words, by adhering to the FCCC, Canada is saying that it believes there is a problem, and it subscribes to a set of reasons why Canadians would want to take action, in concert with other nations and in a cost-effective way, to address human impact on the climate – even if we believe that human activities' role in global warming has not been proven beyond a reasonable doubt. If we do not believe that global warming is occurring, or we believe that global warming poses a risk but we are willing to tolerate it on our and other nations' behalf – in which case we might confine ourselves to investments that mitigate the effects of global warming, rather than attempt to abate the warming per se – then we should not remain within the FCCC.

It is unlikely, especially in the current political climate, that a major political party would want to openly question the scientific consensus that global warming is human-induced. There is little political capital in engaging in mud-slinging over science,[6] and in any event experience tells us that one can believe that there is a problem and still end up taking as little action as someone who is sceptical about the problem, but wishes to be seen as doing something about it.

2) A Clear Statement on the Main Policy Principles

Indeed, as we have seen, it is one thing to acknowledge – even only implicitly through continued adherence to the FCCC – that there is a problem that we could and should do something about. In practical policy terms, deciding what "cost-effective" actions can be taken, and who needs to take them, are two other things altogether. This analysis will look at both issues in turn.

Roughly speaking, the first of these issues, cost-effectiveness, refers to whether it is possible to reduce greenhouse gas emissions at a low enough cost that this cost will be palatable domestically. The key issues here are what I call the '3Ts' of cost-effective greenhouse gas reductions: timing, taxes (or trading), and technology.

The second issue, responsibility for reducing emissions, refers to the question of how these costs should be distributed. While distinct, the two issues are closely linked from a policy-maker's perspective, in that the lower the expected overall costs, the easier the political distribution of the responsibility of these costs will be.

Thus, the political battle will be centred on how the parties view the respective role of the '3Ts' in their policy arsenal, and how they see the costs being distributed. Here again, it will be possible, and very likely profitable, for the parties to state their policy positions based on a clear link between principles and policy.[7] In the United States, Congress has long ago given its answer to that question. For example, in 1997 (prior to the negotiation of the Kyoto Protocol), the US Senate passed a resolution by a rather overwhelming 95-0 vote, which declared that:

the United States should not be a signatory to any protocol to, or other agreement regarding, the United Nations Framework Convention on Climate Change of 1992, at negotiations in Kyoto in December 1997 or thereafter which would: (1) mandate new commitments to limit or reduce greenhouse gas emissions for the Annex 1 Parties, unless the protocol or other agreement also mandates new specific scheduled commitments to limit or reduce greenhouse gas emissions for Developing Country Parties within the same compliance period; or (2) result in serious harm to the US economy. (United States, 1997)

The resolution, with its massive Senate endorsement, prevented then – President Bill Clinton, a strong supporter of the Protocol, from even submitting it to Congress for ratification. This marked the beginning of a process that led to US President George W. Bush's rejection of the Protocol in March 2001. This decision left Canada hanging high and dry as the lone country in the Americas to agree to commit to reduction targets.

It is now time for Canadians to step back and define our own position in respect to these same questions. Perhaps a concrete way of approaching this would be to approach our policy stance on Kyoto specifically, and on greenhouse gas emission reduction in general. This should be done within a framework that ensures coherence with our other positions and policies on national and international issues that are deeply inter-related with the question of controlling greenhouse gas emissions, including: immigration, trade, economic growth, and economic well-being in general.

3) A Clear Stance on Who Bears Responsibility for Costs

While the question of how to reduce emissions, once a target has been agreed upon, is certainly an issue of momentous economic significance, it is much more amenable to being addressed with well-understood policy tools, and thus much more circumscribed, than the question of who actually should bear responsibility for reducing greenhouse gas emissions. The United States Congressional Budget Office states the policy problem in a depressingly comprehensive and clear fashion:

Policymakers may be faced with the extraordinarily complicated task of managing a resource that no one owns, that everyone depends on, and that provides a wide range of very different – and often public – benefits to different people in different regions over very long periods, benefits for which property rights would be very difficult to define, agree on and enforce. (United States, 2003: 25)

By signing the Kyoto Protocol in 1997, Canada seemingly agreed on the division of GHG emission reductions among countries. Nevertheless, as we have seen, little thought was put into whether we could bear that particular share of responsibility – and for little environmental benefits to boot. Taking a fresh look at the international situation, it can be perfectly logical for a Canadian government to believe in global warming caused by human activity (or at least to officially subscribe to that position), and to want to do something to address this question, but not in a way that puts an unacceptably high or inequitable burden on Canada.

Certainly, if Canada did something, and others did not, then one question would be why we are allowing other countries to 'free ride' at our expense – particularly since Canada's contribution would only have a minuscule impact on abating any increase in global temperature. Why should we bear a particular burden, for essentially no environmental result (or worse, if industry simply moves to countries where greenhouse gas reduction targets are non-existent)?

That may not be a high-minded question, but it needs to be confronted as part of a comprehensive policy statement by the Canadian government. It must be addressed if only because of looming negotiations over future targets applying to the post-Kyoto commitment period, or alternatively because of unacceptable costs of burden-sharing could be invoked as a primary reason for why we would want to withdraw from the KP altogether. In this context, the largest elephant in the room remains the developing world, whose carbon dioxide emissions will by 2015 collectively overtake those of the developed world (EIA, 2006: Fg. 65). In spite of vast efforts from China to improve its energy efficiency and introduce tough vehicle emissions standards as well as introduce cleaner coal technology, emissions from that country alone over the next twenty-five years will dwarf the reductions that were agreed to under the Kyoto Protocol (Bradsher and Barboza, 2006).

As a party to the FCCC, Canada agrees that rich countries bear more responsibility, at least in the sort-term, for initiating cutbacks in GHG emissions. Indeed, from the point of view of the well-known equity principle of 'ability to pay' or 'polluter pay' (the latter often taken in a historical sense), the view that developing countries would not initially have to meet hard limits on their emissions makes some sense. Nevertheless, the complete exemption of developing economies from the existing KP is certainly now becoming a 'wedge' issue that could completely stall attempts at defining a post-Kyoto compromise. Nationally, there is anything but consensus because it is abundantly evident that, if reductions were to be made domestically, given current technology, the impact would be highly differentiated regionally – an outcome that Canadian premiers and the federal government have consistently said would be unacceptable. This is where reducing costs as much as possible becomes important and where the '3Ts' come into play.

4) Clarify Position on Timing, Taxes, and Technology

Given the ultimate goal of stabilizing the concentration of GHG in the atmosphere at a level judged non-threatening, the KP targets are obviously a step in the right direction, but it is one that in and of itself will only have a minute impact. In order to accomplish the stabilization goal, it will be necessary to achieve deep reductions in actual emissions globally and over a period of time extending decades beyond the KP first commitment period. Thus, certain models show that, up to a point, it does not matter whether we reduce emissions now, as long as we are able to reduce them very deeply later, and take action to that effect.

We also know that significant GHG emission reductions, if they are to be achieved without a catastrophic halt to economic activity, will require extensive changes in our lifestyles and sources of energy, or will require the use of new technologies altogether, or possibly a combination of all three. The organizational structure of our economies will in particular require significant changes to our public and private capital stock, including our stock of research and development. It is a well-known result in economics that the cost of a capital investment will dramatically increase if it must be compressed over a very short period of time. Hence, the preference of economists for long-term solutions to climate change, that would for example involve giving incentives to adopt the cleanest available technologies and practices in the course of the normal replacement cycle for capital equipment (which can of course vary from a few years to many decades depending on the type of plant or equipment). In turn, while regulation has its place in many circumstances, the best incentive is a price signal, provided either by the tax system or by a system that 'caps' overall emissions at a certain level, but otherwise does not dictate where emissions should occur – only that emitters beyond, say, a certain quota, pay the tax or acquire credits from those who were able to reduce below the quota. While one system controls the price in the hope of controlling quantity, and the other controls quantity and lets the price of credits settle where it will, both systems can ensure that emissions are reduced first where it is cheapest to do so.[8]

The main point is that change, if it is not to be costly, must be allowed to happen over time, but that it will not happen without the proper signal, ideally a price signal. Recent articles by Mark Jaccard (2006a; 2006b) and a study by the very credible National Roundtable on the Economy and the Environment suggest that recent technological advances can go very far in achieving the deep emissions reduction over time, justifying a long-term approach rather than a narrow focus on Kyoto, but not justifying the absence of more robust price signals that would induce investors to embrace these new technologies.

POLICY IMPLICATIONS

At the May 2006 workshop launching a dialogue between all UNFCCC parties on long-term cooperative action, Canada reiterated its belief in the need to reduce GHG emissions globally (United Nations, 2006). From that particular point of departure, however, Canada's submission at the workshop, and a comprehensive speech by Canada's environment minister given shortly thereafter (Ambrose, 2006), indicate that the federal government is leaving all its options open as to what approach, exactly, it intends to adopt in addressing the climate change issue. In general, both documents strongly suggest that Canada is seeking more future room for manoeuvre than it is currently afforded under the KP.

In practice, the option is open for Canada to simply withdraw from the KP, which it can do after providing notification under Article 27 of the Protocol. This indeed Canada would have to do, under current arrangements, if it cannot meet its target, and is unwilling to purchase credits abroad under the scenario outlined at the beginning of this article (or, unrealistically, quickly become the dominant player in projects that reduce emissions in developing countries) and, additionally, is unwilling to face the KP penalties for non-compliance. The latter, it should be said, can easily be construed as providing an inducement for countries that have not met their targets (individually or collectively in the case of countries under the European "bubble"), to abandon the KP altogether.

There is what could be called a 'first strike you're out' policy. This consists of suspending the offending country's ability to acquire emissions reduction credits either through international emissions trading or by receiving credits for helping or cooperating with another country to reduce emissions there (admittedly, this would happen after the country itself would refuse to use such mechanisms to acquire enough such credits to meet its target). There is, to be sure, an 'expedited' reinstatement procedure for countries that 'rectify the problem.' At the end of the day, however, if a country does not meet its target, it must make up the difference between its actual emissions and its KP target, plus a 30 percent penalty, in the second commitment period (beyond 2008–2012). However, since negotiations on what exactly the second commitment period will consist of are just beginning in 2006, this prospective penalty seems like an incentive for countries that are not meeting their KP to not commit to doing much in any subsequent commitment period.[9]

It is a fair bet that, whether because of high prices or because of policy-induced constraints on emissions, we will be living in a more carbon-constrained world. Assuming that Canada remains part of an international effort to reduce GHG emissions in quantifiable ways, it would certainly be unfortunate if it could not somehow continue to acquire credits in return for assisting emission reductions abroad through the various mechanisms allowed and verified under the KP, even as it misses its own KP target. The reality is that any significant amount of GHG emissions reduction can be achieved much more cheaply this way than by reducing emissions domestically, and for an equivalent environmental benefit. If we assume that markets, such as the markets sustained by the Kyoto mechanisms, will continue to put a positive value on verified emission reductions, Canadian companies that develop, sell, share or use clean technologies could reap large benefits from Canada's continued access to these mechanisms (Castonguay, 2003). But getting out of Kyoto, or being kicked out, reduces that possibility.

How does one square being neither willing nor able to meet one's Kyoto targets, but perhaps wishing to benefit from the Kyoto international credits system and trading mechanisms, or similar mechanisms? One factor that must be taken into consideration is that, again assuming a carbon-constrained world in the future, the current cost of acquiring credits now could be attractively low, at least as long as Russia and others in a similar position are willing to sell rather than "bank" their permits. In that light, Canada should be clear on what is feasible and acceptable on its part and on the part of its trading partners for the second commitment period.

In my view, negotiations for the second commitment period will be much more arduous than those that led to the initial KP targets, because they will be based on experience and much more realistic assumptions. The cost of 'real' policy-induced incremental reductions will now begin to bite more in Europe, as the effect of easy greenery has dissipated, and countries like Spain are taken to task by others for exceeding even their relatively generous allowance. Sharp increases in electricity prices shocking consumers and chasing businesses are well within the realm of possibilities. Of course, new countries have joined the European Union since the KP was signed, countries for which further emission reductions will still be easier than for most EU-15 countries, and Europe is already thinking of a new "bubble" for the second commitment period, that would allow, under one scenario, continued large increases for Spain and Portugal (Wagner and Michaelowa, 2005). But its partners, including Canada, are likely to be querying why these arrangements within Europe, that leave more room for the more dynamic economies to increase their emissions, would not mean that a similar regard for objective economic conditions should apply to other fast-growing economies such as Canada's. And it seems that positions have solidified on the issue of hard commitments by developing countries to reduce their GHG emissions, with more Annex B countries, including Canada, saying emphatically that they should be held to firmer commitments, in line with both their increasing contribution to the problem and their greater ability to pay. If the targets are set more realistically in the second commitment period, it may be advantageous for Canada to remain in the Protocol.

However, given the current Canadian GHG emissions level relative to the KP requirements, and given the KP enforcement mechanisms, seeing how Canada could remain within the KP while suffering only acceptably small costs requires a fair bit of imagination. One possibility would be to see whether a mechanism could be established whereby Canada could 'borrow' from the same 'bank' where other countries whose emissions coming under their targets could leave their various Kyoto credits should they decide not to sell them. This could be done if Canada believes that it can beat its targets the next time, and that it will be able to repay the bank in actual emissions reductions. In other words, Canada may not want to purchase 'hot air' from Russia or the Ukraine, but it could see whether it could borrow some, and protect itself against adverse price fluctuations in the price of these credits by entering into forward arrangements on the various carbon credit markets. A more aggressive version of this idea would be for Canada to enter into talks with Russia (or the Ukraine) on jointly implementing Kyoto, which is allowed under the agreement between two parties when both are under emissions caps. This would involve Canada and Canadian entities committing to helping Russia reduce its emissions in the future through, for example, technology agreements, assuming that this is allowed under the still-evolving rules for Joint Implementation.

These scenarios will certainly appear fanciful, but while the KP may prove to be a dead-end for Canada, at this point Canada should still explore all options it has to remain in that game, in anticipation of a more realistic second commitment period in which it could take continued full advantage of the Kyoto mechanisms. If Canada is ultimately forced to reject Kyoto as impractical, then it need not adopt the minimalist course set by the US government, although, as a continuing party to the FCCC, it should certainly attempt to complement the US efforts to find technological solutions to the GHG emissions problem. It could also join the United States in the Asia-Pacific Partnership on Clean Development and Climate (that also includes Australia, China, India, Japan and South Korea), whose main aim is to voluntarily support the development and introduction of cleaner and more efficient technologies among its partners, on a voluntary basis but so as to achieve "practical results" (Justus and Fletcher, 2006:14).

Unless the provinces saw Canada leaving the KP as a signal that they can themselves become disengaged from their existing GHG reduction plans, it is likely that federal disengagement from Kyoto will mean that by default the provinces would begin occupying the centre stage of Canadian policy on the climate change issue, as the states do in the United States. However, a more economically and administratively difficult (but politically and environmentally rewarding) position might be for the federal government to support a 'provincial +' approach that is at least pro-active in supporting provincial efforts, and mindful of the fact that efficiency requires that emissions reductions are implemented where they are the cheapest.

It is my assumption here that options that significantly increase the federal tax take are not politically attractive, and that there will be no federally-set mandatory reduction targets (that will have lost part of their *raison d'être* by Canada being outside of Kyoto). Instead I assume that the federal government will still want to encourage real emissions reductions that are not only compatible with provincial implementation plans, but go beyond what each province can achieve individually (and that will, in effect, aid the provinces in achieving their set goals). I am also assuming that the federal government will want to encourage technological, clean and renewable developments, without attempting to pick 'winners' in that regard (from experience, always a dangerous policy route). In that case, the federal government could promote a twofold national goal of ensuring that there is a single market for GHG emission reduction credits in Canada, and that these credits are as much as possible tradable with instruments on existing national or international voluntary-based markets such as that of the Chicago climate exchange or the fledgling Montreal exchange. This would make sense, given that a number of US states and Canadian provinces, as well as individual LFE's in both countries, are committed to abating greenhouse gas emissions in some measurable fashion, which will create both a supply and a demand for such credits. The wider the market geographically, the greater the opportunities for cheap emissions reductions, and if successful within Canada and North America, the experiment could be extended to the Asia-Pacific Partnership.

Achieving this would require action to ensure greater comparability of provincial policies and to make a national registry mandatory. Comparability of diverse provincial actions would definitely be a tough nut to crack, but is certainly feasible. While Alberta has a 50 percent reduction goal and Quebec has an absolute reduction target compatible with Kyoto, efforts by Quebec may not be as meaningful as those in Alberta, because of the existing higher GHG intensity economic growth there. If there is a common understanding of efforts to reduce GHG, for example, if Quebec's hard targets are converted into intensity targets, encouraging the comparability and registration of a variety of provincial, state and private commitments within a single carbon market scheme could provide the ties that bind all schemes together, even though these would have been defined at the local level and implemented in light of local conditions. The government could even be a buyer of last resort on this market, whose existence would more than incidentally assist in financing research and development (at least in the sense that a value would be put on emissions reductions, encouraging research and adoption of cleaner practices), in effect arbitraging the difference between "effort-based" R&D that can result in reductions in the future and current "results-based" emissions reductions. Thus, while not meeting the KP targets, the approach could be that of a compendium of provincial plans, which would make sense on the ground given vastly different circumstances, plus an overlay of federal encouragements, combining classic market and federalism approaches. It is even possible to envisage over time extending such a mechanism to the rest of the Asia-Pacific Partnership, or even a link between this mechanism and the Kyoto-based mechanism.

In a more daring vein, it might be smart to engage in a comprehensive and public examination of the range of Canadian taxes and subsidies that may affect greenhouse gas emissions. Perhaps a commission with a broad mandate could examine areas where tax, subsidy or even regulatory reform may have a positive impact both on reducing emissions and other pollution, and could also help with economic efficiency. For example the commission would examine the impact of the tax regime for mining or of Canada's agricultural subsidies on GHG emissions, in light of course of Canada's overall competitive position in these sectors. The result of such an exercise might be a reorientation of Canada's tax system towards more broad-based environmental taxes (a direction already envisaged in chapter 9 of the Technical Committee on Business Taxation in the mid-1990's), and away from environmentally-damaging subsidies that, especially if the revenue they raised was directed toward productivity-enhancing tax cuts, could make great strides in reducing GHG while protecting the economy.

CONCLUSION

Assuming continued adherence to the UNFCCC, I conclude in this paper that Canada should attempt to remain within the Kyoto Protocol, provided it can do so on reasonable terms with respect to the consequences of not meeting its GHG reduction targets. At the same time, Canada should aggressively be looking for more balanced and achievable goals by all parties if and when future commitments are undertaken. This assumes of course that there continues to be a true commitment, emulating that in provinces as diverse as Alberta and Quebec, for some quantifiable GHG abatement. Such a true commitment to reduce GHG emissions requires quantifiable targets and a monetary signal (or enforceable regulations), rather than purely voluntary measures. Here again, whether or not Canada remains party to Kyoto, an important federal role would be to support, and, as necessary, augment, quantifiable provincial plans to reduce GHG emissions. This role would also include being a catalyst for the emergence of a national carbon market by taking the lead on the comparability and proper verification of emissions-reduction measures across provinces, and ensuring that they are somehow linked to an international emissions-reduction market, if not the Kyoto mechanisms themselves. Such an approach could certainly be combined with a more or less comprehensive examination of the role that existing taxes and subsidies play in generating GHG emissions that are both environmentally and economically undesirable. This would of course require convincing the public that the KP targets were not well thought-out, and in any event are not particularly meaningful environmentally, but that the government is nevertheless committed to bringing about quantifiable emissions control, and eventually, abatement, in a way that does not make short shrift of oil and gas as a strategic Canadian asset. In short, the public needs to be convinced that Canada is contributing to a long-term solution – the only type that will count in the end.

NOTES

The author would like to thank Kelly Jackson, Jennifer Jones, and Andrew Schrumm for their editing and excellent research assistance, as well as the participants at the *Canada Among Nations* authors' workshop (April 2006) and the Food for Thought session (May 2006) both held at CIGI in Waterloo. Ontario for their valuable comments on earlier versions of this paper

1 Most greenhouse gases occur naturally in the atmosphere, and indeed by "capturing" heat that would otherwise be radiated back into space, they have been essential to maintaining the hospitable climate necessary to life on Earth as we know it. However, human activity is leading to increased concentration in the atmosphere of such naturally occurring greenhouse gases as carbon dioxide, or CO_2 (through the burning of oil, natural gas, coal and wood), methane (production and transportation of coal, natural gas and oil), nitrous oxide (agricultural and industrial activities and combustion of solid waste and fossil fuels) as well as inducing, through various industrial processes, the presence in the atmosphere of other greenhouse gases that are not naturally occurring, to levels that are inducing potentially harmful climate change (United States, 2006).

2 Canada's domestic GHG emissions will almost certainly be at least 200 million tonnes over its Kyoto target by the commitment period. Capoor and Ambrosi (2006: i) report average international prices for Certified Emissions Reductions recognized under the KP at US$7.23 per tonne of CO_2 equivalent in 2005, climbing to US$11.45 per tonne in the first three months of 2006, or some $13.00 Canadian. Bramley (2005: 9) states there is a common belief that prices will tend to rise with the approach of the Kyoto deadline. But one issue with that scenario is precisely that countries may not stick to their targets as a rise in price bites on their industries and individual customers. Jaccard (2006a: 20) assumes that the international price for international credits facing Canadian buyers will be C$8.00 in 2008–2012. The numbers I mention reflect a lower bound of 200 million tonnes x C$8.00 ($1.6 billion) and an upper bound of 230 million tonnes time C$13.00 ($3.0 billion).

3 Technically speaking, these are countries that are listed under Annex B to the Protocol; this list is virtually the same as that of Annex I parties to the FCCC, which entered into force in 1994. The latter countries made nonbinding commitments to reduce their emissions to 1990 levels by the year 2000. Turkey is a significant case of an Annex I country that did not undertake obligations under Annex B of the KP.

4 Not all GHG emissions stem from energy consumption, thus this first factor in the equation only approximates the GHG intensity of energy consumption per se. For purpose of the comparison among the four countries shown in Figure 1, using CO_2 emissions – that are more closely linked to energy

consumption – instead of overall GHG emissions would have made no difference, except that the UK would have looked slightly worse on the carbon-intensity front (United Nations, 2005: Tables 5 and 7).

5 For a quick overview of the constitutional issues involved, see Macdonald and Lakoseljac (2002).

6 This is not to imply that the scientific debate isn't important, but that it is of little weight relative to powerful movies, such as Al Gore's 2006 documentary, *An Inconvenient Truth*. A national poll of Canadians conducted in 2006 showed 72% agreed with the statement that "Global warming will have become the greatest crisis facing mankind" by 2020. (Van Rijn, 2006).

7 Gain in the sense that political parties can avoid being put in a damaging situation if they appear to not have a stance on, or a plan to address, these issues.

8 For a review of the basic features of regulation, taxes and emissions trading as a way of reducing emissions, see for example Schwanen (2000).

9 For a brief description of the Kyoto compliance mechanisms, see United Nations (2006).

REFERENCES

Alberta. 2002. *Albertans and Climate Change: Taking Action*. Calgary, AB: Ministry of the Environment, October.

Ambrose, Rona. 2006. Speaking Notes for the Minister of Environment Canada on Clean Air Day, Canadian Club, Ottawa, 7 June.

Bradsher, David, and David Barboza. 2006. "Pollution from Chinese Coal Casts a Global Shadow," *New York Times*, 11 June.

Bramley, Matthew. 2002. *A Comparison of Current Government Action on Climate Change in the U.S. and Canada*. Drayton Valley, AB, and Toronto: Pembina Institute for Appropriate Development and World Wildlife Fund-Canada.

– 2005. *Future Financial Liability for Greenhouse Gas Emissions from New Large Industrial Facilities in Canada*. Dayton Valley, AB: The Pembina Institute, October.

Brethour, Patrick. 2006a. "Alberta Eyes Greater Share of Oil Wealth," *Globe and Mail*, 3 June, B1.

Brethour, Patrick. 2006b. "Guess Who (Quietly) Likes Québec's Carbon Tax Plan?" *Globe and Mail*, 19 June, B1.

California. 2006. "Executive Summary," in *Climate Action Team Report to Governor Schwarzenegger and the California Legislature*. Sacramento: California Environmental Protection Agency, Climate Action Team.

Canada. 1997. *Report of the Technical Committee on Business Taxation*. Ottawa: Department of Finance, Technical Committee on Business Taxation.

– 2002. *Climate Change Plan for Canada*. Ottawa: Minister of Supplies and Services.

– 2005. *Canada's Greenhouse Gas Inventory, 1990–2003*. Ottawa: Environment Canada. Available at: <http://www.ec.gc.ca/pdb/ghg/inventory_report/2003_report/toc_e.cfm>

– 2006a. *Advice on a Long-term Strategy on Energy and Climate Change*. Ottawa: National Round Table on the Environment and the Economy, June.

– 2006b. "Dialogue on Long-Term Cooperative Action to Address Climate Change by Enhancing Implementation of the Convention," Workshop, Working Paper no. 16, Bonn, Germany, 15–16 May.

Canadian Intergovernmental Conference Secretariat. 2002. "Provincial and Territorial Statement on Climate Change Policy," Issues at the Joint Meeting of Energy and Environment Ministers, Halifax, 28 October.

Capoor, Karan, and Philippe Ambrosi. 2006. *State and Trends of the Carbon Market 2006*. Washington, DC: World Bank and International Emissions Trading Association, May.

Cazorla, Marina, and Michael Toman. 2000. "International Equity and Climate Change Policy," *Climate Issue Brief* 27. Washington, DC: Resources for the Future, December.

Castonguay, Alec. 2003. "La facture Kyoto, Qui paie? Qui empoche?" *Revue Commerce*, May, 31–6.

Energy Information Administration (EIA). 2006. *International Energy Outlook 2006*. Washington, DC: Department of Energy (US), June.

Globe and Mail. 1997. "Common Sense About Global Warming," Editorial, 31 October, A24.

Gold, Russell. 2006. "As Prices Surge, Oil Giants Turn Sludge into Gold," *Globe and Mail*, 27 March, B12.

Jaccard, Mark. 2006a. "'Dirty Fuel' May Be Ontario's Clean Answer," *Globe and Mail*, 4 April.

– et al. 2006b. "Burning Our Money to Warm the Planet," *C.D. Howe Institute Commentary* 234. Toronto: C.D. Howe Institute, May.

Japan. 2006. *CDM and JI in Charts*. Tokyo: Ministry of the Environment and Institute for Global Environmental Strategies. Available at: <http://www.iges.or.jp/en/cdm/pdf/charts.pdf>

Justus, John R., and Susan R. Fletcher. 2006. "Global Climate Change," *CRS Issue Brief for Congress*. Washington, DC: Library of Congress, Congressional Research Service, 12 May.

Macdonald, Donald, and Natasha Lakoseljac. 2002. "There's More at Stake Than Kyoto," *Globe and Mail*, 17 December, A23.

Quebec. 2006. *Le Québec et les changements climatiques: Un défi pour l'avenir*. Québec, QC: Ministère du Developpement durable, de l'Environnement et des Parcs, June.

Sallot, Jeff. 2006. "Scrap the Kyoto Plan, Ambrose says," *Globe and Mail*, 8 April.

Schwanen, Daniel. 1997. "Confronting the Greenhouse Challenge: Matching Protection with Risk," *C.D. Howe Institute Commentary*, no. 99. Toronto: C.D. Howe Institute, October.

– 2000. "A Cooler Approach: Tackling Canada's Commitments on Greenhouse Gas Emissions," *C.D. Howe Institute Commentary*, no. 141. Toronto: C.D. Howe Institute, April.

Smith, Heather. 1998. "Canadian Federalism and International Environmental Policy Making: The Case of Climate Change," *Working Papers Series*, vol. 1998, no. 5. Kingston, ON: Institute of Intergovernmental Relations, Queen's University.

Statistics Canada. 2006. *Provincial Economic Accounts 2005 (Preliminary Estimates)*. Catalogue 13–213. Ottawa: Statistics Canada.

United Nations. 1992. *United Nations Framework Convention on Climate Change*. FCCC/INFORMAL/84. Available at: <http://unfccc.int/resource/docs/convkp/conveng.pdf>

– 1998. *Kyoto Protocol to the United Nations Framework Convention on Climate Change*. Kyoto: Framework Convention on Climate Change. Available at: <http://unfccc.int/resource/docs/convkp/kpeng.pdf>

– 2005. *National Greenhouse Gas Inventory Data for the period 1990–2003 and Status of Reporting*. Montreal: Framework Convention on Climate Change (FCCC), October. FCCC/SBI/2005/17. Available at: <http://unfccc.int/resource/docs/2005/sbi/eng/17.pdf>

– 2006. "Compliance under the Kyoto Protocol." Bonn: Framework Convention on Climate Change (FCCC). Available at: <http://unfccc.int/kyoto_mechanisms/compliance/items/3024.php>

United States. 1997. "Byrd Hagel Resolution," Senate Res. 98, 105th Congress. Washington, DC: Library of Congress. Text available at: <http://www.nationalcenter.org/KyotoSenate.html>

– 2003. *The Economics of Climate Change: A Primer*. Washington, DC: Congress of the United States, Congressional Budget Office, April.

– 2006. "Global Warming," EPA *Global Warming Site*. Washington, DC: Environmental Protection Agency. Available at: <http://yosemite.epa.gov/oar/globalwarming.nsf/content/index.html>

Van Rijn, Nicolaas. 2006. "Global Warming Top Worry: Poll," *Toronto Star*, 30 June, A1.

Wagner, Fabian, and Axel Michaelowa. 2005. "Burden Sharing Targets for the EU Bubble in the Second Commitment Period: CO_2 from the energy Sector," in Klaus-Dieter John and Dirk Rübbelke, eds. *Klimapolitik in einer erwiterten Europäischen Union*. Aachen: Shaker-Verlag, pp. 79–102.

Waldie, Paul. 2006. "Canada's Crude Output Expected to Double by 2020," *Globe and Mail*, 18 May, B8.

Wigle, Randall. 2005. "Canada, Public Economics and Climate Change." Paper presented to the Canadian Public Economics Study Group, May.

16 Canadian Aid to Africa: Assessing 'Reform'

DAVID R. BLACK

Since the start of the new millennium, the international aid regime has undergone a protracted process of reform and renewal. At the centre of this process has been aid to Africa, now widely portrayed as exceptional because it is the one continent that has become poorer, on average, over the past thirty years, with manifold economic, social, political, and security challenges accompanying this protracted relative decline.[1] A, perhaps *the*, high point of this trend was reached in the summer of 2005, with the confluence of transnational (and celebrity) activism through the Live 8 phenomenon and the extraordinary attention given to Africa by the G8 at the Gleneagles Summit (see Group of Eight, 2005).

The Canadian government, its principal aid agency, the Canadian International Development Agency (CIDA), and various Canadian civil society organizations have actively participated in these trends. Indeed, there have been moments when Canada has been a leader among northern governments in the renewed focus on Africa, though rarely in the context of the aid regime. Yet it is the latter that has historically been the largest and most consistent point of contact between Canada and Africa. This chapter therefore seeks to take stock of Canada's renewed aid policies and programmes towards Africa. More specifically, it addresses three questions. First, what has changed – and what has not – in this period of renewal and reform? Second, what is the normative and substantive essence of the changes that *have* occurred? And third, how sustainable is the trend towards renewed interest in and engagement with Africa through the Canadian aid programme? Will the trend towards sustained growth and engagement persist, or is a new period of backsliding in the offing? In short, the paper draws on the incisive analysis of Denis Stairs, among others, to argue that considerably *less* has changed than the previous Liberal government's own rhetoric would lead one to believe. Nevertheless, there are changes of real importance that have been consolidated through this period, bringing Canadian aid programming more closely in line with shared understandings and modalities embodied in the "new aid agenda" (Killick, 2004), with its 'third way' understandings and approaches. These changes raise important doubts concerning the prospects for meaningful 'ownership'[2] of development policies by recipient governments and societies. Moreover, while the Harper Conservatives have good reason to minimize change and disruption to aid programming in a minority context, the signs are that on balance, a majority Conservative government would be less interested in aid and in Africa than its Liberal predecessors, thus bringing the medium term sustainability of the trend of recent years into question.

Before these themes and prospects can be addressed, however, it is important to remind ourselves of where Canadian aid to Africa has come from – and in particular of the sorry state from which it emerged at the end of the 1990s. It is to this brief account of recent history that I first turn.

RENEWAL FROM WHERE? THE DISMAL 1990S

In the absence of robust trade and investment relations,[3] Canada's links with African countries have historically depended on aid-based relationships for much of their substance. However, in the austerity years of the 1990s, Canadian aid spending suffered draconian cuts, even by comparative international standards. Official development assistance (ODA) is estimated to have decreased by 33 percent in real terms between 1988/89 and 1997/98, compared with a 22 percent decline in defence spending and cuts of 5 percent to all other programs in the same period (see Morrison, 1998: 413). The aid to Gross National Product (GNP) ratio declined from 0.49 percent in 1991/92 to 0.25 percent in 2000, dropping Canada well down the Organisation for Economic Co-operation and Development (OECD) donor 'league table' (16th of 22 states in 2000). Aid to Africa was hit hardest of all, with declines in bilateral aid between 1990 and 2000 of 7.2 percent for Africa, 3.5 percent for the Americas, and 5.3 percent for Asia (de Masellis, 2003: 78).

The disarray caused by these cuts to Canadian aid programming throughout the continent was considerable, and surely signaled to African counterparts as well as other donors a lack of commitment to long-term relationships. For CIDA – an agency that was already relatively weak in political and policy terms, caught as it was between a wide range of domestic, intra-governmental and transnational cross-pressures (see Black and Tiessen, 2006; Wood, 2005) – it may be surmised that the cuts of the 1990s would have strongly reinforced a sense of vulnerability and a parallel tendency towards risk aversion. These tendencies have doubtless strengthened the already-strong urge to embrace and participate in the trend towards coordinated and collaborative donor programming (Program Based Approaches) – a theme to which I will return in section three. From the vantage of the mid-1990s, moreover, there was little reason for optimism concerning a renewal of support for development assistance in general, and to Africa specifically. Under attack from critics on both the left and the right, the political support base for aid was at a historically low ebb (see Thérien and Lloyd, 2000: 26–34) and it seemed entirely plausible to project a continued long-term decline in both development assistance and, concomitantly, Canadian interest in Africa.

Any such projections, however, were confounded by a number of factors over the remainder of the decade. Of most immediate relevance was the orchestration and steady popularization of a 'new aid agenda,' consensus, or paradigm. Jean-Philippe Thérien and Carolyn Lloyd (2000: 24–6) have traced this trajectory of renewal through the OECD's 1996 publication of *Shaping the 21st Century: The Contribution of Development Co-operation*. This momentum was reinforced by the adoption of the Millennium Development Goals (MDGs) at the Millennium Summit of the United Nations in 2000.[4] The 'new aid agenda' also reflected wider trends in public management and policy thinking, bearing on both the conceptualization and implementation of development assistance. In line with the trend towards third way politics in the industrialized north, key development agencies recognized after a decade-and-a-half of Structural Adjustment Policies that marketization, deregulation, and liberalization alone could not secure long-term development, and with it, stability and prosperity. While mainstream development thinking remained neo-liberal at its core, the emergent post-Washington Consensus came to the view that both social development and capable public institutions ('good governance') were essential – and that development assistance was necessary for both. On the management side, the new agenda reflected a broad consensus (at least discursively) on best practices, summarized by Bernard Wood (2005: 12) as:

– applying the basic principles of local ownership
– building capacity to ensure sustainability

- striving for more genuine partnerships in the face of imbalances in bargaining power
- civil society and private sector engagement alongside government
- an integrated approach to take account of political, economic, social and institutional dimensions of development, and
- a results-based approach (focused on partner countries' priorities among the MDGs) with built-in monitoring and evaluation programmes and some mechanisms of mutual accountability.

Accompanying these normative and intellectual trends were the beginnings of renewed investment in the resources required to give these various principles and priorities a fighting chance of success. Somewhat tardily, CIDA fell into line with both the direction of reform and the renewal of aid spending in the first years of the new millennium (see Canada, 2002).

This trend was reinforced, in Canada and elsewhere, by a couple of related policy and political developments. The first was the impetus towards humanitarian interventionism and a much more expansive peacekeeping/making/building agenda. In Canada, this came to be subsumed by the high-profile human security agenda championed by foreign minister Lloyd Axworthy from 1996 to 2000. Here and elsewhere, it was sharply reinforced by the widespread collective shame associated primarily with the developed world's historic failure in the face of the Rwandan genocide. In short, one could not profess to be concerned with human security and sustainable peacebuilding without being led, inevitably, to a renewed focus on development and the aid levers that could be pulled in its pursuit (see Brown, C., 2001) – as well as an understanding that irresponsible aid could be positively destructive, as it had been in Rwanda (see Uvin, 1998).

Finally, while it was not the most important factor, it is worth noting the importance of the personal, or idiosyncratic variable in Canada, responding in turn the residual streak of "humane internationalism" in Canadian society (see Pratt, 2000). Axworthy's personal preoccupation with the sources of the human security deficit, notably in Africa, has already been flagged. More significantly, the renewal of interest in Africa generally, and aid to Africa specifically, was decisively reinforced by then-Prime Minister Jean Chrétien's born again internationalism in the twilight of his long political career, capped by his personal insistence on focusing the G8's attention on African issues at the Kananaskis Summit that he chaired in 2002 (see Fowler, 2003; Black, 2004). In order to make this initiative credible in the shadow of seven prior years of austerity-induced aid cuts, this personal diplomacy was accompanied by an announced commitment to a doubling of foreign aid through annual

8 percent increases at the Monterrey Summit on Financing for Development, only months before the Kananaskis Summit. Even more instrumentally, it was underpinned by a c$500 million Canada Fund for Africa to (in the candid prose of a key CIDA document) "provide a showcase for Canadian leadership in pursuit of effective development through a series of large-scale, flagship initiatives in support of NEPAD [New Partnership for Africa's Development] and the G8 Africa Action Plan" (Canada, 2002: 26). It is worth emphasizing these idiosyncratic influences not only because of their explanatory importance, but also because they are the necessary backdrop for a consideration of how the advent of a Stephen Harper-led Conservative government from January 2006 may affect the prospects for aid to Africa.

Thus the foundations for reform and renewal were laid; but how significantly different have been the programmatic structures built upon them?

HOW MUCH HAS (NOT) CHANGED?

The latest and most authoritative statement of the government's ostensible new direction in Canadian aid policy, towards Africa and elsewhere, is contained in the Development chapter of the five-part April 2005 *International Policy Statement: A Role of Pride and Influence in the World* (IPS). The IPS, in turn, consolidates trends arising out of a multi-year process of rethinking the aid programme, going back to the release of a CIDA discussion document entitled "Strengthening Aid Effectiveness" in 2001 (see Black and Tiessen, 2006). Apropos Africa, the IPS reiterates the former government's 2005 budget commitment to double Canada's aid to the continent between 2003–04 and 2008–09 – i.e., more rapidly than the general doubling of aid (to c$10 billion from $5 billion) between 2001 and 2010. Along with continued progress towards better management of the aid programme, it most famously announces that Canada's aid will in the future be more concentrated in both country and sectoral terms, focusing on twenty-five core "Development Partners" and five sectors "directly related to achieving the MDGs": good governance, health (with a focus on HIV/AIDS), basic education, private sector development, and environmental sustainability. Gender equality is designated as a sixth, cross-cutting theme "to be addressed systematically in all of our programming." The emphasis on concentration is a continuation of a trend first initiated in 2002, and responds to long-standing criticism of Canada's aid programme as "the most widely dispersed in the world." It also reflects a more general trend in the New Aid Regime towards supporting "enhanced partnership countries" (in the words of the G8's Africa Action Plan) that are thought to be particularly well equipped to use aid effectively, owing to perceptions of relatively better governance. In the Canadian case, the IPS states that core 'Development Partners' are to be selected on the basis of three criteria: level of poverty (i.e., only relatively poor countries were selected); ability to use aid effectively (through sound economic management, structural policies, policies for social inclusion and equity, and public sector management and institutions); and "sufficient Canadian presence to add value" (notably Canada's relative donor rank and the scale of our current aid effort). In relation to the focus of this paper, fourteen of twenty-five designated Development Partners are African (see Tables 1 and 2). The IPS announced, to considerable acclaim, that "at least two thirds of bilateral resources" would be concentrated in Development Partner countries.

It is not clear how stable these partnerships are to be – that is, how readily states can and will be promoted or demoted, like teams in European football league tables. There is provision, moreover, for continued support to ongoing bilateral relationships, middle-income countries 'in transition,' and other ODA-eligible countries, in order to retain a degree of flexibility regarding bilateral recipients. Finally, the IPS reserves "a special type of bilateral programming [in a coordinated, 'whole of government' fashion] for a manageable number of failed and fragile state situations – countries in or emerging from crisis and of overriding strategic importance ..." (Canada, 2005: 24). It is within this category that assistance to the Sudan and, to a lesser degree, the Democratic Republic of Congo in Africa is situated, as well as CIDA's largest assistance programmes in Afghanistan and Iraq and its substantial commitment to Haiti (see Shamsie, this volume).

This latter category gives rise to an initial concern. While there is no questioning the importance of engagement to support both urgent humanitarian and developmental demands in, for example, Sudan/Darfur – indeed the previous government has been rightly criticized for a response that is, relative to its expansive rhetoric, "conservative, limited, and symbolic" (Nossal, 2005: 1025) as well as tardy – there is a problem with the highly selective and apparently time-limited approach taken to dealing with these sorts of "failed and fragile states." As Robert Matthews has noted, a serious commitment to the related imperatives of peace and development in the Sudan will involve long-term engagement through a process that is bound to be arduous and challenging – yet the Canadian government has provided no indication, within the new foreign policy framework, of a commitment extending beyond the next two years (Matthews 2005: 1059–64). Moreover, as the focus of Canada and the 'international community' has been drawn to the Sudan, other less strategic but critical peacebuilding processes just beyond the immediate crisis

Table 1
Canadian Aid Commitments in C$ million to Sub-Saharan Africa (SSA)
for core Development Partners.

Country	2004	2003	2002	2001	2000
Benin	9.25	3.36	4.52	2.09	2.62
Burkina Faso	12.81	10.33	19.81	6.07	2.27
Cameroon	48.13	20.74	82.52	4.90	1.89
Ethiopia	133.24	12.86	19.90	11.16	12.52
Ghana	223.81	25.13	8.52	16.44	12.77
Kenya	14.76	10.26	3.43	6.58	9.17
Malawi	7.38	17.39	4.54	16.66	27.86
Mali	39.74	41.81	32.94	2.85	14.63
Mozambique	54.94	35.05	5.86	11.13	2.76
Niger	10.69	0.17	1.92	3.40	5.09
Rwanda	3.36	1.19	2.63	9.89	11.78
Senegal	12.34	9.65	38.94	8.73	15.74
Tanzania	57.63	22.33	4.58	7.36	7.07
Zambia	13.27	8.61	8.99	9.80	17.43
TOTAL	641.35	218.88	239.10	117.06	130.83
TOTAL ODA TO SSA	791.75	415.00	434.40	190.12	232.03
PERCENTAGE	81.00%	52.70%	55.00%	61.57%	56.38%

Source: International Development Statistics (IDS) Online <www.oecd.org/dac/stats/idsonline>

stage – such as that in Sierra Leone – may effectively drop off the Canadian policy map, certainly in terms of development assistance. Yet in the Sierra Leonean and other similar contexts, a responsible policy response consistent with the "responsibility to rebuild" (ICISS, 2001: 39–45) surely demands that immediate relief and crisis responses be followed up with longer-term peacebuilding commitments. The IPS provides no clear provision or guidance concerning this imperative.

A second problem is that in the end, the extent of *real* change is far less than the statements contained in the IPS imply. On this point, I am in the debt of Denis Stairs, who has carefully scrutinized the announced changes in the IPS on country and sector concentration against the numbers and priorities which preceded it (see Stairs, 2005). On country concentration, he finds not only that the concentration of two-thirds of bilateral assistance in twenty-five countries affects a relatively small percentage of overall aid spending (less than 35 percent of the

Table 2
Canadian Aid Disbursements in c$ million to Sub-Saharan Africa (ssA)
for core Development Partners

Country	2004	2003	2002	2001	2000
Benin	6.63	5.59	2.40	1.75	3.32
Burkina Faso	16.18	11.40	8.63	5.88	8.32
Cameroon	43.18	20.43	80.29	5.44	6.34
Ethiopia	59.48	38.02	6.88	12.38	10.94
Ghana	48.54	20.64	12.39	11.23	16.21
Kenya	18.10	7.98	7.25	3.81	5.40
Malawi	16.20	16.66	8.54	10.96	6.69
Mali	44.14	25.20	13.62	8.97	12.67
Mozambique	27.34	26.70	9.02	13.88	7.99
Niger	7.55	6.76	5.27	2.30	2.58
Rwanda	6.05	10.82	5.58	6.68	6.67
Senegal	24.56	17.61	9.78	8.63	11.31
Tanzania	32.71	34.33	8.25	8.38	11.64
Zambia	24.98	17.53	12.21	8.94	8.41
TOTAL	375.64	259.67	190.11	109.23	118.49
TOTAL ODA TO SSA	566.58	463.22	356.53	182.31	179.67
PERCENTAGE	66.30%	56.06%	53.32%	59.91%	65.95%

Source: International Development Statistics (IDS) Online <www.oecd.org/dac/stats/idsonline>

total), but that two-thirds of bilateral aid spending was *already* concentrated in 25 countries – albeit a somewhat different list than the twenty-five Development Partners announced in the context of the IPS (Stairs, 2005: 12–16). In particular, three of the four largest bilateral recipients – Afghanistan, Iraq and Haiti – are re-located to the failed and fragile state category, allowing some room for a substantial growth of resources to those moved into the top twenty-five, including a disproportionately large number of African states. Still, the extent of real change is less than meets the eye.

Similarly, there are questions concerning both the durability and clarity of the five/six sectors of concentration. As David Morrison has noted, foreign aid programming priorities have been particularly prone to "frequent twists and turns," and "like other donors, but with more alacrity than most, CIDA has associated itself with new fashions and policy thrusts" (Morrison, 1998). After reflecting on the breadth and ambition of the "sectors of concentration" set out in the IPS, Stairs concludes that "Simply put, it is next to impossible to conceive of *any* development assistance activity that could not be defended by reference to one or more of the items on the operational matrix the IPS lays down" (Stairs, 2005: 22–3). There is no question that CIDA's latest set of sectoral priorities is (like previously-announced priorities) highly malleable and permissive. Nevertheless, this argument should not be overstated. As I will suggest in the next section of this paper, the priorities set out in the IPS have been pursued with somewhat greater consistency and effect than many of their predecessors, in ways that are having an enduring, though uncertain, impact on both recipient states and societies, and north-south development "partnerships."

A final way in which there is less real change embedded in the IPS than one might have expected or hoped for is with regard to the widely-touted need to decentralize programming presence and authority to the field, or "strengthen Canada's development presence on the ground" (Canada, 2005: 30). This decentralization is seen by many commentators as a necessary step to strengthen the contextual understanding, responsiveness and overall effectiveness of aid programming. Indeed as Bernard Wood recounts in a recent paper, CIDA was initially a pioneer in this area, undertaking a major process of decentralization in the late 1980s and early 1990s before abandoning this promising but expensive initiative in the face of budget cuts and bureaucratic resistance (Wood, 2005: 16–19). More recently, several major donors (most ambitiously the UK's Department for International Development) have moved towards more decentralized programme authority and delivery mechanisms. The IPS is CIDA's most recent expression of its intentions in this regard, but like earlier statements is so vague on this point as to be almost meaningless in policy terms. Moreover as Wood notes, without significantly larger concentrations of resources in key bilateral recipients, the increased costs of decentralized delivery are not likely to be worth the anticipated benefits.[5] So we are left, once again, with a process of reform that reflects a high level of caution and, on the whole, amounts to less than it appears to promise.

Yet in emphasizing what has *not* changed there is a risk of overlooking the significance of what *is* new – the most systematic and sustained expressions of which are unfolding in Canada's relationships in and with African countries. It is therefore to these new and changing aid relationships that I now turn.

So what *has* changed? There are at least three key ways in which the IPS both reflects and reinforces significant change in the nature or essence of Canadian aid towards Africa, particularly pertaining to the privileged class of Development Partners. Each reflects, in turn, the alacrity with which Canadian aid policy has followed key trends in the New Aid Regime.[6] These are its thematic foci; the basis on which it has selected Development Partners; and the increasingly collaborative and coordinated modalities by which it is delivering much of Canada's aid.

Notwithstanding the malleability and flexibility of the IPS sectoral priorities, as emphasized in the previous section, there is a certain coherence and consistency that has emerged over the past decade reflecting a kind of 'global third way' vision within the international aid regime. This post-Washington Consensus remains fundamentally neo-liberal, insofar as it combines a firm commitment to market-led economic growth on a global scale, and the fuller participation of developing countries in these dynamics. Yet it combines this foundational commitment with a renewed emphasis on ensuring that the benefits of this process extend to the poor and that the exclusion of marginalized groups is ameliorated. These latter priorities are most clearly embodied in the MDGs.

While CIDA's programming is less fulsome in its commitments to poverty alleviation and ending marginalization than some other statements of this vision (see Commission for Africa, 2005: 66), it is perfectly consonant with the general approach taken in the New Aid Regime. Thus, not only is there a renewed emphasis on 'basic needs' and social development, through the prioritization of health, basic education, and gender, but these priorities are combined with, and portrayed as dependent upon, the successful pursuit of good governance reforms and private sector development. This emphasis can be seen, for example, in the projects of the Canada Fund for Africa, with its governance commitments to Parliamentary strengthening ($9 million), local governance ($6 million), and especially public sector capacity building ($28 million) and its even larger commitments to trade and investment facilitation (totaling $130 million) and "bridging the digital divide" ($35 million – see Canada, 2004: 16). It can also be seen in key bilateral programming relationships, such as that in Ghana where, according to indicative program spending disbursement and budget figures, support for governance and private sector development have become the two largest categories of aid spending at an estimated $15.46 million and $15.12 million respectively in 2005.

Moreover, these same two examples – one regional, the other bilateral – illustrate a more general tendency within governance programming to privilege the more technocratic side of good governance reforms, emphasizing the administrative reforms necessary for 'sound economic management' and a more efficient public sector, *versus* the more expansive and less predictable process of supporting more comprehensive dynamics of democratization and human rights promotion (see Arthur and Black, 2006). To be sure, these two dimensions of governance reforms are both present in Canadian aid programming (Canada, 2005: 13). In practice however, it seems that greater weight has been given to the former.[7]

The point of these brief observations is not to pass judgement on these sectoral priorities. Rather, it is simply to highlight that in establishing them, Canada (through CIDA) is following a clear, transnational trend that is firmly within the parameters established by the international financial institutions, as well as the collective preferences of G8 governments, and which is more ideological and contested than its proponents in CIDA and elsewhere acknowledge (see Brown, S., 2005).

These tendencies are reinforced by the criteria applied to the selection of core Development Partners – particularly the second, concerning "ability to use aid effectively"(Canada, 2005: 23). The fact that the only concrete measure which is flagged for making this judgement – the World Bank's controversial *Country Policy and Institutional Assessment* (CPIA) for evaluating "a country's policies and institutional framework to support poverty reduction, sustainable growth, and effective use of development assistance" (Canada, 2005: 23) – indicates, at least, that such judgments will be compatible with the World Bank's. The failure to include respect for human rights among the criteria for selection suggests, moreover, that technocratic governance criteria are privileged over more expansive and ambitious considerations of rights and democracy. Finally, the criteria applied raise the spectre that CIDA's selection of 'enhanced partnership countries' will contribute to a transnational donor herd dynamic, creating both aid favourites and aid orphans on the basis of contestable criteria. This is a possibility that needs more research and bears close observation over the next few years.

Finally, and perhaps most significantly, the move to designate core Development Partners – a move that, as noted previously, has its origins in the selection of nine countries[8] for increased aid investment in late 2002 – has opened the door to the greatly increased use of coordinated and collaborative donor mechanisms for the delivery of aid. These so-called Program-Based Approaches (PBAs) include both Sector-Wide Approaches (SWAPs), and large-scale Budgetary Support (BS) initiatives. A review of selected CIDA Country Development Programming Frameworks (CDPF's) for designated Development Partners[9] indicates that they are being extensively used in these countries. Indeed, the longer-term and larger-scale commitments implied in the designation of Development Partners are a clear precondition for participation in collaborative PBAS, given their relatively long time horizons and the responsibilities of 'burden sharing' with other donor agencies. For example, CIDA has made a C$93 million commitment to the Ghana

Poverty Reduction Strategy – Budget Support (GPRS-BS) programme for 2004-9, along with nine other major donors. While this is a very large commitment for CIDA, it translates for 2005 into a US$13.3 million pledge, out of the total commitments of US$285 million (with a World Bank share of US$125 million) (Dodoo, 2005: 4).

Much stock has been placed in these types of budgetary support initiatives and other PBAs.[10] In Ghana for example, various budgetary support activities (both bilateral and multilateral) now account for about 70 percent of CIDA's bilateral programme. They involve large-scale, multi-year agreements to transfer funds to public sector authorities at national, sectoral and district levels in recipient countries, on the basis of agreed-upon frameworks linked to World Bank-approved Poverty Reduction Strategy Papers (PRSPs). They are thus seen by proponents as combining the promotion of governance reforms with the pursuit of basic human needs and poverty alleviation objectives through the combination of accountability (to donors as well as recipient-country 'stakeholders') and the fostering of local ownership, since they are premised on district, sectoral and central government authorities applying the resources committed to their own policy priorities, and then accounting for their performance in implementing these priorities.

Budgetary support is controversial however, both within and beyond CIDA. Some see this approach in general, and multi-donor budget support in particular, as the most promising way yet of fostering recipient ownership in the process of governance reform. In the Ghanaian case, for example, CIDA informants cited encouraging evidence that the government of Ghana was increasingly able and willing to 'push back' in exchanges with donor agencies on policy priorities – a dynamic that is facilitated, in principle at least, by collaborative donor arrangements that allow it to push back against one collective rather than having to engage multiple institutional 'partners' across a wide front. This is one dimension of the broader argument that PBAs reduce the transaction costs of donor-recipient relationships (Killick, 2004: 18-24). Others see the effective implementation of this type of programme as being critically dependent upon thoroughgoing public service and public finance reforms, as well as decentralization, to ensure that the policies designated for support can be effectively implemented and the large infusions of funds effectively tracked. Yet such technocratic governance reforms can be enormously difficult to implement, encountering both inertia and active resistance from those for whom existing governance processes work advantageously.

Finally, civil society and academic critics mount a deeper critique of budgetary support and other similar PBAs. Some argue that there is simply a lack of evidence to support the 'common sense' that such collaborative structures and processes reduce transaction costs (Killick, 2004). Others argue that the widely-endorsed 'good' of donor coordination can in fact significantly *reduce* effective recipient ownership, because multi-donor budget support is usually premised on policy and governance conditionalities emanating principally from the World Bank and IMF, which risk averse medium-sized donors like CIDA tend to rally behind. From this perspective, collectively imposed conditionalities are the most powerful of all (an argument that may be understood by analogy with the challenges of negotiating with collectives like the European Union[11]). Such critics take little comfort from the fact that budgetary support is tied to nationally 'owned' PRSPs, because they regard the breadth and quality of participation in the negotiation of these vital gatekeeping documents as highly limited (see Tomlinson, 2004 for elaboration). These are powerful arguments that place issues of ownership, partnership and accountability – major themes within the 'new paradigm' of best practices for management of aid cited above – into sharp relief.

In the end, it is probably too soon to tell how effective most of these novel modalities will be in fostering ownership, accountability, and more effective and responsive poverty alleviation. Their achievements will certainly vary between different country contexts and donor consortia. However, several factors would seem to be crucial in determining their longer-term implications for both recipients and donors. A first factor is the need for stronger policy research capacity in recipient countries, within and beyond government. For policy ownership to be meaningful, it must reflect understandings of the principal development challenges that are rooted in carefully researched and contextually grounded studies by country-based and other southern researchers. This requirement points towards the importance of re-investing in the research and tertiary education sectors of developing country partners – a focus which CIDA's emphasis on basic education largely excludes.

Second, CIDA and other donors must be supportive of structures, processes, and actors that enhance democratic accountability. In many cases this is a very long-term project, requiring patience and commitment. The point, however, is that for PBAs to be understood as genuinely responsive to the needs and priorities of the poor majority, it must be clear that these citizens have a meaningful degree of influence on the political life and policy processes of the country in question. Consequently a greater relative emphasis must be placed on the broader, and riskier, dimensions of governance reforms related to democracy-building and human rights promotion, with all the debate, discussion, and contestation these terms imply.

Finally, in order for CIDA to play a significant and autonomous role in the shaping of PBAs, it must have both the intellectual/research capacity and field presence, sustained over an extended period of time, to engage with and, where necessary, challenge the priorities and interpretations of both recipient country governments and other, more powerful donor agencies. In turn, this imperative points to the question of whether Canada's enhanced commitments to African 'partners' will be sustained and built upon over the medium to long term, through financial commitments and decentralized personnel for example. It is to this question that I finally turn.

HOW SUSTAINABLE IS CANADA'S RENEWED AID COMMITMENT IN/TO AFRICA?

Writing in the run-up to the Gleneagles G8 Summit and the Live8 mobilization surrounding it, Tim Shaw (2005: 20) cautioned in June 2005 that "Africa's day in the sun may be fleeting," suggesting that there was a limited moment of opportunity to advance the Commission for Africa's package of human development, human rights, and security initiatives towards the continent. In Canada, moreover, we have since seen the election of a new Conservative minority government. What, then, do these passages – beyond the Gleneagles/Live8 transnational mobilization for Africa, and beyond the Martin Liberals – portend for Canada's renewed aid focus on Africa?

The sensible answer, of course, is that it is too soon to tell – not least because the medium-term survival and consolidation of the Harper government is far from assured. What can be done, however, is to survey the range of precedents, influences, and calculations that are likely to come to bear on both a Conservative minority and, prospectively, majority government.

On the record, the Conservatives have had very little to say about their approach to development assistance. Their election platform, for example, opines that a Conservative government will:

- Articulate Canada's core values of freedom, democracy, the rule of law, human rights, free markets, and free trade – and compassion for the less fortunate – on the international stage;
- Advance Canada's interests through foreign aid, while at the same time holding those agencies involved in this area accountable for its distribution and results; and
- Increase spending on Overseas Development Assistance beyond the current projected level and move towards the OECD average level. (Conservative Party of Canada, 2006: 45)

These vague and somewhat contradictory intentions can be contrasted with the precise and ambitious targets for enhancing the capacity and prestige of the Canadian armed forces that follow in the next plank of the platform. Parsing these statements more closely, there is nothing here to suggest an understanding of, or interest in, the deeper causes or implications of global poverty. The combined emphasis on "compassion for the less fortunate," with its resonance in motives of Christian charity, and on an interest-based calculus for the deployment of aid suggests a limited and instrumental approach. Similarly, the emphasis on accountability for its distribution and results speaks to the deep skepticism that opinion surveys suggest predominates among core Conservative voters concerning the value of aid, and the ability of those agencies responsible for its distribution (notably CIDA) to do so effectively.[12] At the same time, the third point above speaks to the Conservatives' concern with international burden sharing and respectability among Canada's western peers.

Among the current Conservative caucus and leadership, there seems to be a generally low level of interest in and support for a strong Canadian role in global development rooted in a "logic of solidarity" (Noel and Thérien, 1995: 552). Such indifference would be consistent with the current leadership's lack of interest in, and intellectual support for, socially redistributive public policy at the domestic level, and is one of the key ways in which the new Conservative Party seems to be markedly different from its Progressive Conservative predecessors, with their influential Red Tory element. One looks in vain among the current crop of Conservative parliamentarians for successors to the articulate and outspoken voices of 'humane internationalism' found in the Mulroney PC caucus and government, such as David MacDonald, William Winegard, Walter McLean, Joe Clark and, periodically at least, Brian Mulroney himself.

This is not to suggest that there are no countervailing influences. One, already noted above, is the strong conservative Christian element within the current party, and its potential responsiveness to appeals based on compassion and charity. A second, arguably more potent, influence is the government's base in the business community, especially extractive industries. Canadian mining and mining supply companies, for example, have become major players in Africa, and are projected to invest close to $15 billion in current and new projects over the 2006–11 period (Bradet, 2006). In addition, Deepak Obhrai, the Parliamentary Secretary to the Minister of Foreign Affairs with special emphasis on Africa and the Asia-Pacific, is a businessman by background who was born in Tanzania. Thus, it is likely that CIDA's current emphasis on private sector development and on governance, as it relates to the regulatory environment for private sector activity, will resonate among significant elements within the party and government.

Third, although support for aid is generally soft, even among its supporters, it does enjoy more support in Quebec than in other parts of the country (Noel et al., 2004). In the Conservatives' quest to win more voters in that province, therefore, it would seem impolitic to tamper too significantly with aid spending levels, at least in a minority context. In this regard, it is noteworthy that the current Minister of International Cooperation responsible for CIDA, Josée Verner, is also Chair of the Quebec Conservative caucus and was a key Harper advisor on Quebec prior to the 2006 election. It remains to be seen how strong a presence she will be at the Cabinet table, but given CIDA's long history of comparatively weak Ministers her appointment may reflect positively on the agency's prospects. Similarly, the Conservatives' ongoing quest to present a more moderate image nationally as a key step towards winning an electoral majority counsels against any moves that could be seen as an attack on aid and, indirectly, the least fortunate of the world, thereby giving ammunition to those arguing that they are simply heartless neoconservatives in disguise. Finally, as noted above, this is a government that does seem preoccupied with international respectability among its western peers in particular, and with building a reputation for keeping its commitments. These dynamics, too, mitigate against any abrupt changes of course on aid to Africa.

It is not surprising, in light of this configuration of influences and calculations, that the Conservatives' first budget was essentially a 'stand pat' one in terms of aid, maintaining previous Liberal projections but "for the first time since the late 1990s (offering) no new aid commitments ... and not even a mention of international cooperation in Finance Minister Flaherty's first budget speech" (Tomlinson, 2006). So long as its minority status persists, it seems unlikely that this situation of what we might term persistence through indifference will change significantly.

Over the longer term however, and if a majority is secured, more substantial changes are likely. Canada will 'do its part' in world affairs largely through a more robust defence and security capacity. Aid will be thought of primarily as an obligation of international citizenship and, more particularly, as an adjunct of foreign economic and security policy priorities conceived largely within the frame of reference of the western alliance. Africa is likely to become less important in the calculus of a more narrowly-interest based foreign policy. The Conservative government cannot quickly or respectably retreat from the steps its predecessors have taken towards a more robust re-engagement with Africa through Canada's development assistance programmes. Depending on its longevity and electoral success however, we should anticipate another 'ebb tide' for official interest in development assistance to Africa (Morrison, 1998).

NOTES

The author would like to thank Malcolm Savage for his able and timely research assistance in the preparation of this chapter.

1 For one of the more comprehensive accounts of these conditions and challenges, see Commission for Africa (2005).
2 'Ownership' has become a ubiquitous but also ambiguous construct in the international aid regime. Everyone agrees that aid projects and programmes need to be locally/nationally owned to be sustainable; yet there is much controversy over how (and whether) this can be achieved.
3 For example, in 2001, total Canadian trade (exports and imports) with Africa amounted to roughly C$3.82 billion – less than 0.5 percent of Canada's total foreign trade, at C$716.61 billion (de Masellis, 2003: 99–101; see also Black, 2004).
4 The eight MDGS, targeted to be achieved between 1990 and 2015, are: to halve extreme poverty (those living on less than a dollar a day) and hunger; to achieve universal primary education; to promote gender equality and empower women by eliminating gender disparities in education; to reduce child mortality by two-thirds; to reduce by three-quarters the maternal mortality ratio; to reverse the spread of HIV/AIDS and the incidence of Malaria and other major diseases; to ensure environmental sustainability; and to develop a global partnership for development. Perhaps needless to say, these targets will be badly missed in Africa on current trends.
5 Wood argues that, given both additional costs associated with field-based personnel and the need for a critical mass of decentralized officers, country programmes would need to be in the range of $50–200 million annually to make the effort worthwhile. As Table 2 makes clear, very few of CIDA's announced Development Partners currently even approach this threshold.
6 For an early analysis of this tendency, see Black et al. (1996).
7 This conclusion is tentative at this stage, requiring a more comprehensive analysis of CIDA's bilateral programming in Africa to be made more definitively.
8 Including six African countries: Ethiopia, Ghana, Mali, Mozambique, Senegal, and Tanzania. All have been carried over to the 2005 list of 14 African Development Partners.
9 Specifically Ghana, Mali, Mozambique, and Tanzania.
10 Much of the next several paragraphs is drawn from Arthur and Black (2006).
11 See also Rogerson (2005) on the hazards of "cartelization" in the aid industry.
12 For elaboration on these tendencies, see Noel et al. (2004: 38–43).

REFERENCES

Arthur, P. and David R. Black. 2006. "The Benefits of an Indirect Approach: The Case of Ghana," in Jennifer Welsh and Ngaire Woods, eds. *Aid for Good Governance: Learning from Experience*, forthcoming.

Black, David R. 2004. "Canada and Africa: Activist aspirations in straitened circumstances," in Ian Taylor and Paul Williams, eds. *Africa in International Relations*. London: Routledge Press.

– and Jean-Philippe Thérien with Andrew Clark. 1996. "Moving with the Crowd: Canadian Aid to Africa," *International Journal* 51, no. 2 (Spring): 259–86.

– and Robert Tiessen. 2006. "Canadian Aid Policy: Parameters, Pressures, and Partners," in Luc Bernier and Nelson Michaud, eds. *The Administration of Foreign Affairs*. Toronto: University of Toronto Press, forthcoming.

Bradet, Lucien. 2006. "Canadian Mining Investments in Africa," *Canadian Council for Africa*, 11 January, 9 May 2006. Available at: <http://www.ccafrica.ca/archives/messages/060111.htm>

Brown, Chris. 2001 "Africa in Canadian Foreign Policy 2000: The Human Security Agenda," in Fen Osler Hampson et al., eds. *Canada Among Nations 2001: The Axworthy Legacy*. Don Mills, ON: Oxford University Press, 192–212.

Brown, Stephen. 2005. "'Creating the World's Best Development Agency'? Reading Between the Lines of Canada's International Policy Statement," Unpublished paper. Ottawa: University of Ottawa.

Canada. 2002. "Canada Making a Difference in the World: A Policy Statement on Strengthening Aid Effectiveness." Ottawa: Canadian International Development Agency (CIDA).

– 2004. "New Vision, New Partnership: Canada Fund for Africa." Ottawa: Canadian International Development Agency (CIDA).

– 2005. "Development," in *Canada's International Policy Statement: A Role of Pride and Influence in the World*. Ottawa: Department of Foreign Affairs and International Trade (DFAIT).

Commission for Africa. 2005. *Our Common Interest: Report of the Commission for Africa*. London: Foreign and Commonwealth Office (UK), 11 March.

Conservative Party of Canada. 2006. *Stand Up for Canada: Federal Election Platform*, 13 January. Available at: <http://www.conservative.ca/media/20060113-Platform.pdf>

de Masellis, Luigi Scarpa. 2003. "Statistics," in *Canadian Development Report 2003: From Doha to Cancun, Development and the WTO*. Ottawa: North-South Institute.

Dodoo, Charles. 2005. "Disbursements: How It Works," Multi-Donor Budgetary Support Secretariat, *Multi-Donor Budget Support Newsletter* 1, no. 1: 4.

Elliott, Larry. 2002. "Africa Betrayed: The Aid Workers' Verdict," *Guardian Weekly*, 10 July, 5.

Fowler, Robert. 2003. "Canadian Leadership and the Kananaskis G8 Summit: Towards a Less Self-Centred Foreign Policy," in David Carment et al., eds. *Canada Among Nations 2003: Coping with the American Colossus*. Don Mills, ON: Oxford University Press, 219–41.

Group of Eight. 2005. "G8 Agreement on Africa," G8 Leaders Summit. Gleneagles, Scotland, 8 July. Available at: <http://www.fco.gov.uk/Files/kfile/PostG8_Gleneagles_Africa,0.pdf>

Guardian Weekly. 2002. "Africa Let Down by the Rich," Comment, 10 July, 12.

International Commission on Intervention and State Sovereignty (ICISS). 2001. *The Responsibility to Protect*. Ottawa: International Development Research Centre.

Killick, Tony. 2004. "Politics, Evidence and the New Aid Agenda," *Development Policy Review* 22, no. 1 (January): 5–29.

Matthews, Robert O. 2005. "Sudan's Humanitarian Disaster: Will Canada live up to its responsibility to protect?" *International Journal* 60, no. 4 (Autumn): 1049–64.

Morrison, David R. 1998. *Aid and Ebb Tide: A History of CIDA and Canadian Development Assistance*. Waterloo, ON: Wilfrid Laurier University Press.

Noel, Alain, and Jean-Phillipe Thérien. 1995. "From Domestic to International Justice: The Welfare State and Foreign Aid," *International Organization* 49, no. 3 (Summer): 523–53.

– and Sébastien Dallaire. 2004. "Divided over Internationalism: The Canadian Public and Development Assistance," *Canadian Public Policy* 30, no. 1 (March): 29–46.

Nossal, Kim Richard. 2005. "Ear Candy: Canadian Policy toward Humanitarian Intervention and Atrocity Crimes in Darfur," *International Journal* 60, no. 4 (Autumn): 1017–32.

Pratt, Cranford. 2000. "Alleviating Global Poverty or Enhancing Security: Competing Rationales for Canadian Development Assistance," in Jim Freedman, ed. *Transforming Development: Foreign Aid in a Changing World*. Toronto: University of Toronto Press, 37–59.

Rogerson, Andrew. 2005. "What If Aid Harmonization and Alignment Occurred Exactly as Intended? A Reality Check on the Paris Forum on Aid Effectiveness," Draft Paper. London: Overseas Development Institute, 28 January.

Shaw, Timothy M. 2005. "Canada and Africa: Does a commitment Exist That Can Outlast the Moveable G8 Agenda?" *Literary Review of Canada* 13, no. 5 (June): 18–20.

Stairs, Denis. 2005. "Confusing the Innocent with Numbers and Categories: The International Policy Statement and the Concentration of Development

Assistanc," Research Paper Series. Calgary, AB: Canadian Defence and Foreign Affairs Institute (CDFAI), December. Available at: <http://www.cdfai.org/currentpublications.htm>

Thérien, Jean-Philippe, and Carolyn Lloyd. 2000. "Development Assistance on the Brink," *Third World Quarterly* 21, no. 1 (February): 21–38.

Tomlinson, Brian. 2006. "A CCIC Review: May 2006 Federal Budget," *Canadian Council for International Co-operation* (CCIC), 9 May 2006. Available at: <www.ccic.ca>

– and Pam Foster. 2004. "At the Table or in the Kitchen? CIDA's New Aid Strategies, Developing Country Ownership and Donor Conditionality," Briefing Paper. CCIC/Halifax Initiative, September. Available at: <http://www.ccic.ca/e/docs/002_aid_2004–09_at_the_table.pdf>

Uvin, Peter. 1998. *Aiding Violence: The Development Enterprise in Rwanda*. Hartford, CT: Kumarian Press.

Wood, Bernard. 2005. "Managing Canada's Growing Development Cooperation: Out of the Labyrinth," Paper prepared for, "Strategic Directions in Canada's Aid Policy," conference of the Global Economic Governance Programme, Oxford University, October. Available at: <www.globaleconomicgovernance.org>

17 Canada, Hippocrates, and
the Developing World: Toward
a Coherent Foreign Policy for Canada

ROY CULPEPER

The central argument of this chapter is that *development* has become
profoundly related to all the major preoccupations of foreign policy,[1]
including areas as diverse as defence, international trade and investment, diplomacy, immigration, the global environment, and international health. Rather than merely constituting one of the '3Ds' (along
with defence and diplomacy) development provides the 'connecting tis-
sue,' so to speak, between these seemingly disparate dimensions of foreign policy (see North-South Institute, 2005a).

Consider the close interrelationship between development and international commerce: Canada's trade and investment relations become
more active and complex as developing countries grow and evolve into
emerging market countries. Development is also clearly linked to international security and defence, even more so in the post-11 September
2001 world. Indeed, Afghanistan, an impoverished 'fragile state' which
gave rise to the Taliban regime and provided a berth for al Qaeda, had
a key role in the terrorist attacks of 9/11. But vanquishing the Taliban
and instability in that country is now inextricably linked to a development strategy that will wean the economy from the production of
opium and generate sustainable livelihoods.

Development has an obvious and manifold role in international
health issues as well. The HIV/AIDS pandemic continues to wreak most
of its devastation among the world's poorest countries and people, particularly in sub-Saharan Africa. The pandemic cannot be arrested
through drug treatments alone. Considerable investment is also required to improve the capacity of the health and education sectors to
deal more effectively with the pandemic in the worst affected countries.

At the same time, however, it is also true that development cannot possibly inform foreign policy in its entirety. For example, development has little to do with the bilateral relations between Canada and the United States – though it should give structure to those aspects of the relationship concerning global issues. Nor can it fully encompass all the complex inter-relationships among states that include developing countries. For example, the tensions between Israel and its neighbours, or between India and Pakistan, are due largely to historical, political and cultural factors, although it could be argued that tensions could subside with greater social and economic development in those regions.

Nonetheless, because it arguably underlies most of the major issues confronting the world today, there are compelling reasons to situate development at the centre of foreign policy, particularly for a middle-power country such as Canada. If it is to occupy this role, it is important to consider the meaning of development in order to relate it to the several different strands of foreign policy.

WHAT IS MEANT BY 'DEVELOPMENT'?

The growing recognition of the role of development in international affairs follows from the evolution in our understanding of how that term is understood. According to Amartya Sen (1999: 3), "Development can be seen … as a process of expanding the real freedoms that people enjoy." Sen's concept of development is much broader than the more traditional focus of development policy – on growth in gross national product, income per capita, or industrialization.

Although such economic indicators clearly are important, Sen argues that these are possible means toward, rather than the ultimate ends of, development. These ends include freedom *from* material wants (such as poverty, hunger and disease) and fear (of oppression, violence, and so on). Equally they include freedoms *to* participate fully in social and political life as a citizen and individual, maximize individuals' potentials through educational opportunities, vote, express views openly and associate with fellow citizens.

Not coincidentally, Sen regards democratic rights and freedoms as integral to a broader conception of development. Most of all, Sen emphasizes that development is thoroughly dependent on the free agency of people (including the empowerment of women in particular) to effectively shape their own destiny and help each other, rather than being "passive recipients of the benefits of cunning development programs" (Sen, 1999: 1–11).

Other critics of traditional notions of development emphasize the notion of the interdependence between human welfare and the ecology of the planet. For environmental critics such as David Suzuki, Vandana Shiva and Wolfgang Sachs, 'sustainable development' is the only kind of development that is morally defensible or even physically possible (see Suzuki and Gordon, 1991).

Since 11 September 2001, the concept of 'security' (especially in the United States) has come to refer particularly to the war against terrorism. However, perspicacious writers such as Regehr and Whelan (2004) argue in favour of a much broader concept in which development and democracy form part of a comprehensive "human security envelope" along with diplomacy, disarmament and defence.

Sen's notion of agency can be applied not just to people and individuals, but also to developing countries as entities. As Nancy Birdsall put it recently, "Development is ... largely determined by poor countries themselves, and outsiders can play only a limited role. Developing countries themselves emphasize this point, but in the rich world it is often forgotten" (Birdsall et al., 2005: 136–7).

Understood in this way – as a holistic process in which the agency of developing countries and their people is pre-eminent – there are important implications for the role of development in foreign policy in the twenty-first century. First, much more is at stake than 'economic development' promoted via effective aid programs and trade policies that work for the poor. Social and political development, associated with individual and collective rights and freedoms, are at least as important. So are peace and security, without which there can be no development, and vice-versa. The issues of environmental sustainability are also intertwined with development. What is entailed is a broad-based foreign policy agenda. Development is too complex and important simply to be left to foreign aid; rather, foreign policy must be infused with development objectives in all its critical dimensions if it is to be effective and coherent.

Second, and somewhat paradoxically, even a coherent foreign policy involving components such as trade, defence, aid, and the environment, can play only a limited role if we take the agency (or ownership) of developing countries seriously.

RICH COUNTRIES' COMMITMENT TO DEVELOPMENT

Turning to the question of the 'limited' role of rich countries in the development process, the following points are worth noting. First, rich countries can and do influence development in a number of important (if ultimately limited) ways through various dimensions of their foreign policy. As Birdsall (et al., 2005) points out, more and better aid and greater trade access to industrial country markets can be significant ways of helping poor countries. But these traditional policy channels are greatly overrated in terms of their contribution to poverty reduction in particular, and their development impact more generally.

Other relatively neglected foreign policy channels linking rich and poor countries deserve far more attention, such as more liberalized migration, and technology transfer that actually serves the interests of the developing country recipient. For example, the development of medicines aimed at preventing or curing tropical diseases is not high on the priority list of Northern pharmaceutical companies, but could have a very high payoff for developing countries and their people.

It is one thing to recognize the multi-dimensional foreign policy links between rich and poor countries. However, an even more difficult challenge is to design a coherent policy given the multiplicity of these links. There are numerous examples of rich countries giving foreign aid with one hand and taking away with the other via trade restrictions and subsidies that damage poor countries. Such inconsistencies include the immigration policies of rich countries, which provide assistance for the health sectors of impoverished countries at the same time as they recruit skilled professionals such as doctors and nurses who are in chronically short supply (Ward, 2006: A23).[2]

'Policy coherence' between various foreign policy channels is much talked about, not least by the purveyors of development assistance (see OECD, 2005). But little has been done even by way of designing a conceptual framework to bring the key ingredients together. A recent step in this direction has been the Center for Global Development's (CGD) development of a Commitment to Development Index (CDI) that ranks the efforts of rich countries by evaluating and conflating their policies in seven distinct areas (see Roodman, 2005):[3]

- quantity and quality of foreign aid
- openness to developing country exports
- policies that influence investment
- migration policies
- environment policies
- security policies, and
- support for creation and dissemination of new technologies

The index has been applied to each of the 21 member countries of the Organisation for Economic Co-operation and Development's (OECD) Development Assistance Committee. Each country is graded in its performance in each of these seven areas; the sub-indices are then averaged to obtain an overall index of the country's commitment to development.

Not surprisingly, the traditionally best-performing aid donors also do well on the CDI. In 2005, the top three are Denmark, Sweden, Netherlands; Norway is fifth; Finland seventh. Canada is tenth, in the middle of the pack, tied with the UK but just ahead of the US. Canada has a relatively low score on its aid component;[4] high scores on trade and investment; and average scores in migration, environment, security and technology (although with Finland it scores the highest on technology among the 21 countries).

The CDI's component indexes are quite subjective – i.e. they are scored according to the judgment of CGD analysts – thus they are also contentious. One can certainly quarrel with the specific numbers and hence the country rankings assigned by the CDI. The main point, however, is that there are many "vectors of development" connecting rich and poor countries besides aid, and that the whole is often much less than the sum of the parts as a consequence of the lack of policy coherence. The CGD's bottom line in the 2005 survey is that all rich countries could do much better. Even Denmark, ranked number one in the index, scores average in four of the seven policy areas (Roodman, 2005: 3).

THE ISSUE OF DEVELOPING-COUNTRY OWNERSHIP

But policy coherence is much easier said than done. Why? Fundamentally it is because policy must be coherent around a set of agreed objectives or priorities. And this is difficult in democratic and pluralist societies, since reasonable people with different interests and perspectives will disagree about priorities.

In the realm of development, what objectives or priorities should policies be coherent around? A compelling case can be made that the Millennium Declaration (MD) and the Millennium Development Goals (MDGs) should constitute the objectives around which to build coherence – that is, Canada's aid, trade, investment, etc., policies should all be consistent with the MD and MDGs.

These objectives are not perfect – indeed many have criticized them as grossly inadequate, for example, with respect to gender issues (see North-South Institute, 2005a; 2005b). However, the MD/MDGs should be regarded as a minimalist platform for development. Moreover such a framework has the additional advantage of international endorsement – thus providing the basis for coherence internationally as well as domestically – among rich countries and with developing countries.[5]

At the risk of contradicting my own argument, it is important to acknowledge another critique of the MD/MDGs, however, emanating from developing countries. Even though the goals and principles of the

MD/MDGs may be commendable (if imperfect), imposing them on developing countries vitiates Sen's fundamental principle of agency, or (to use the World Bank's term) the principle of developing country "ownership." This issue goes to the heart of the current development debate. The most important thing developed country outsiders can do is to allow developing countries the policy space to design and implement a strategy that fits their unique economic, social and political circumstances.

Instead, rich countries (usually fronted by the Bretton Woods Institutions and the World Trade Organization) have gone to great lengths in the past to impose a policy framework on developing countries. In the 1980s, the policy framework was structural adjustment; in the 1990s, it was the Washington Consensus. In the current decade, it is Poverty Reduction Strategies and the MDGs. The imposition of policies by outside agencies has been more evident in the case of smaller, poorer, or debt-distressed countries with weak bargaining power than in countries with greater autonomy such as China and India. Even a relatively wealthy country such as South Korea was subjected to policy conditionality during the Asian Financial Crisis of 1997–8.

Critics such as Joseph Stiglitz (2002) and Dani Rodrik (2003) argue that if developing countries had latitude to design and implement policies that fit their circumstances, these may diverge somewhat from the orthodoxy favoured by the Bretton Woods institutions and their major shareholders. Rodrik goes further in arguing that the most successful developing countries (for example China, Korea, Viet Nam, and more recently India) have generally followed heterodox development strategies that involved state intervention and ownership and a cautious approach to economic liberalization. Such strategies have been at odds with the prevailing doctrines of the Bretton Woods institutions and the WTO.

Of course, in the real world the chances are that some developed countries might take exception to the pursuit of unorthodox economic strategies by developing countries, or with their political regimes. And when it comes to the poorest, aid-dependent countries, donors are typically in a strong bargaining position to dictate policies to recipient countries. In turn, government leaders and officials from such countries tend to recognize who is calling the tune in terms of policy priorities and directions, and fashion their policies accordingly.

THE HIPPOCRATIC RULE

Clearly, there are many pitfalls to the conceptualization and design of a coherent foreign policy centred on development. Some derive from competing interests in rich countries that may be at odds with development objectives. Examples include opening developing country markets to

Canadian exports and promotion of mining investments whose operations may be harmful to local communities. Yet other pitfalls lie in the potential incompatibility of rich country policies (even coherent ones) with developing-country ownership. Ultimately, a perfectly coherent policy is a chimera.

But do these impediments render significantly greater policy coherence impossible? At a minimum, a good case can be made that rich countries (particularly aid donors) should follow a Hippocratic rule: 'first, do no harm.' Such a rule may serve to considerably enhance the coherence of a foreign policy framework centred on development, or at least reduce its incoherence.

In practical terms, what this implies for Canada is greater consistency among the various elements of foreign policy with overarching development objectives. One possibility would be to put all the elements of foreign policy to an 'MDG test': for example, does Canada's policy of recruiting health professionals from developing countries contribute toward the achievement of the MDGs?[6] If there are good reasons to believe that such immigration policies would erode the achievement of the MDGs, they would fail the Hippocratic test and should be replaced by policies that at least do no harm.

But it would not suffice to focus simply on the bilateral policies of Canada and other rich countries. The Hippocratic test also requires rethinking about the policies and conditionality as practiced by the multilateral and global organizations. The policies most in need of rethinking relate to distributional equity. In other words the distributional implications of alternative development policies need much more care than they have had in the past. Remarkably, this is the key message of both the World Bank (2005) in its recent *World Development Report* and the UNDP (2005) in its *Human Development Report*.

Concern about distributional equity stems from a number of sources.[7] First, income is becoming more unequally distributed within most countries in the world. Second, there is much evidence to suggest that widening disparities are due to the nature and speed of economic liberalization (which is the handmaiden of globalization). Policies aimed at spreading the benefits of globalization more equitably by being more inclusive of women and girls, achieving universal primary and secondary education, etc., are simply not working to reduce inequalities.

Third, there is a growing body of literature that suggests that high income (and other) inequality impairs economic growth.[8] Moreover, with any given aggregate rate of growth, the poorest benefit more if inequalities are low than if they are high; put differently, it takes a much higher (and possibly unachievable) rate of growth to reduce poverty where disparities are wide than where they are narrow.

The revisionist thinking about the relationship between growth and income distribution overturns the older, trickle-down orthodoxy that there is a 'trade-off' between equity and efficiency. If too much emphasis is put on distribution, it was felt, this would only slow down economic growth, and the poor (who should simply be patient) will only suffer more in the long run. Today, the World Bank (2005) argues that equity is complementary to long-term prosperity, and that some forms of redistribution can increase economic efficiency.

Cornia (2005) places much of the blame for increasing inequality on policy changes inspired by liberalization and globalization. As a consequence, strongly market-oriented policies such as liberalization and privatization should be treated with considerably more caution than in the last two decades, and more attention should be given to ameliorating the distributional impact of any policy or set of policies. Free markets have a habit of rewarding the rich and discriminating against the poor. The objective of global institutions and international policy should not be to achieve distributional equality, which is both impossible and undesirable, but at a minimum to prevent widening disparities and preferably to narrow them.[9]

ENHANCING DEVELOPING-COUNTRY OWNERSHIP AND AUTONOMY

Let me come back to the question of how developing countries may best determine their own development. If we accept the centrality of ownership and recognize the need for diversity in developing countries' strategies according to their needs and circumstances, the principal issue is how domestic ownership and diversity can be upheld when resources are externally provided.

It is no accident that the large Asian economies, drawing primarily on their own resources, have forged their own development strategies. The same goes for most other East Asian economies, which have featured astonishingly high and sustained savings rates. High domestic savings and investment rates have led to high growth rates and rapid poverty reduction. But they have also enabled East Asian countries to purse their own, domestically designed, development strategies.

The opposite can be said about the aid dependent countries of sub-Saharan Africa, in which domestic resource mobilization has been low and falling over time. Not only has growth been low and poverty incidence rising; aid dependence has also militated against domestic ownership and has strictly limited the policy space for heterodox or made-at-home strategies. South Africa, in any case one of the most advanced countries in the continent, has managed to retain a greater measure of independence by eschewing a borrowing relationship with the World Bank and IMF.

Ironically, "mobilizing domestic financial resources for development" was among the six leading actions called for, and the first to be listed, in the March 2002 Monterrey Consensus. The declaration said that "a critical challenge is to ensure the necessary internal conditions for mobilizing domestic savings, both public and private, sustaining adequate levels of public investment and increasing human capacity." It went on to say that "An effective, efficient, transparent and accountable system for mobilizing public resources and managing their use by Government is essential. We recognize the need to secure fiscal sustainability, along with equitable and efficient tax systems and administration, as well as improvements in public spending that do not crowd out productive private investment" (United Nations, 2002: 3–4).

Notwithstanding the prominent place given to domestic resource mobilization at the Monterrey Conference, it has not particularly been an issue for priority action either by donors or developing countries. Other issues that have been given greater priority, such as enhancing governance, building capacity, strengthening democracy, reducing indebtedness and ensuring that future debt remains within sustainable limits, are all intrinsically related to, and can be facilitated by, greater domestic resource mobilization.

Moreover, certain economic reforms urged upon developing countries, such as trade liberalization via tariff reduction or elimination, can have the unintended consequence of undermining domestic resource mobilization, since tariffs constitute a major revenue source in poor countries. Similarly, tax reforms and the creation of a more enabling environment for business resulting in tax concessions can seriously erode the fiscal base (see Martin and Rose-Innes, 2004).

Ultimately better governance, lower indebtedness and strengthened capacity require, among other things, dependable revenues for the state and its agencies. The Hippocratic rule in this case suggests that 'harm' consists in weakening the long-term revenue-raising capacity of the state, and undermining domestic resource mobilization more generally.

CHALLENGES FOR THE GOVERNMENT OF CANADA

It cannot be said that a coherent foreign policy has been a hallmark of Canadian governments of any political stripe. Nor has the place of development in Canada's foreign policy been an exalted one; its traditional place can more accurately be described as 'low man on the foreign policy totem pole.' In a way, development cooperation has primarily represented a species of charitable activity for the world's poorest countries and people, undertaken by the government on behalf of all Canadians.

The Liberal governments of Jean Chrétien and Paul Martin undertook several reviews of Canada's foreign policy between 1993 and 2005. But none of these really set out to articulate a policy that was coherently organized around an explicit set of objectives.

The International Policy Review launched by Prime Minister Martin in December 2003 came closest in its attempt to bring the '3Ds' of diplomacy, defence and development into greater harmony with each other and with trade, the environment, and other international policy issues. However, when the review emerged in April 2005 as the government's *International Policy Statement*, it took the form of four department specific chapters (on Diplomacy, Defence, Development, and Commerce) along with an Overview. What emerged was less a coherent foreign policy than four silos, with little provided in the Overview in the way of a unifying framework.

Each of the substantive chapters calls for a 'whole-of-government' approach. This at least suggests that Canada's international policies be made consistent with one other. However, in the absence of a unifying policy framework, the danger here is that in practice the focus of a whole-of-government approach will depend principally on the discretion of the Canadian missions in particular countries. At worst, such an ad hoc approach can easily fall prey to exigencies of the war against terrorism or the geopolitical priorities of the United States. It is not surprising that evidence from the field suggests that 'policy coordination' among departments results principally in the exchange of information.

The approach set out in this chapter would represent a fundamental divergence from foreign policy as practiced by both Liberal and Conservative governments. It proposes a coherent foreign policy framework for Canada, one centred on a holistic concept of development. The basic premise of this approach is not a normative one – namely, that development should be at the centre of foreign policy for moral reasons. Rather, it is a positive one: development, understood as a broad concept about human welfare, is in fact integrally related to all the principal dimensions of foreign policy.

To summarize, the principal points of this chapter are:

– First, that Canada's engagement with the world, through its diplomacy, trade and investment policies, through environment, immigration, international security and technology policies, and of course through its aid program, will be driven to a hitherto unprecedented extent by what happens, for good or ill, in the developing world. That being the case, there are compelling reasons to structure a coherent foreign policy around a set of development objectives such as those articulated in the Millennium Declaration and the Millennium

Development Goals.[10] At a minimum, Canada should seek to ensure that none of its foreign policies do harm by constraining the achievement of the MDGs or contributing to an erosion of economic or social development standards.

– Second, Canada should be working with other donors, the Bretton Woods institutions and the World Trade Organization to secure policy space for developing countries to pursue domestically owned and differentiated strategies. This will require far more latitude for heterodox development policies by the industrial countries. It also requires far more attention to widening economic disparities within countries.

– Finally, to bolster the policy autonomy of developing countries, Canada should also be working with international agencies and developing country governments to try to enhance domestic resource mobilization, thereby underpinning domestic ownership and reducing aid dependence.

In short, this chapter has argued that Canadian foreign policy needs to be anchored in a commitment to an enhanced development agenda. At a minimum, this anchor should embody the Hippocratic principle of 'first, do no harm.' More ambitiously, it might include proactive efforts to make all Canada's foreign policy endeavours coherent around the objectives of peaceful, sustainable and equitable development, and to work with developing countries toward building a more stable and representative international system. The penetration of development issues into international policies makes such a commitment unavoidable if we are to achieve a more coherent and effective foreign policy. By constructing the principles of this agenda jointly with others, we would be making development a shared, and more enduring, priority.

NOTES

The author is grateful for comments on earlier versions of this chapter presented to the annual foreign policy conference of the Canadian Institute of International Affairs in Vancouver, and to the workshop of this volume's contributing authors in Waterloo. He would also like to thank his colleagues Lois Ross and Bill Morton for their comments.

1 It may be better to use the term 'international policy' rather than 'foreign policy' which is actually hampered by its traditional meanings. The Liberal government under Paul Martin deliberately chose the former in launching its "International Policy Review." Notwithstanding this precedent the term 'foreign policy' is used here since 'international policy' does not have the currency that it should have.

2 Ward's article refers to the *World Health Report 2006* which indicates that 18,556 African-trained doctors are working in OECD countries, compared to 82,417 working in their own countries.

3 Most of the components require some explanation – for example, highly tied aid reduces the quality of aid and is commensurately penalized in the index. The trade index collapses each country's tariffs and subsidies into a flat tariff representing the total effect on developing countries; the lower the flat tariff, the higher the index. The investment index gauges the efforts of rich countries to stimulate foreign direct investment and portfolio investment in developing countries while screening out projects likely to do environmental damage or harm workers. The migration component rewards rich countries accepting developing country migrants, but gives more points for unskilled than skilled workers. The environment component looks at what rich countries are doing to reduce their disproportionate exploitation of the global commons, including their efforts to reduce greenhouse gases and their complicity in environmental destruction in developing countries. The security component tallies the financial and personnel contributions of rich countries to UN- and NATO-approved peacekeeping interventions, while penalizing arms exports to authoritarian regimes. Finally, the technology index rewards policies that support the creation and dissemination of innovations of value to developing countries.

4 Canada's low aid score is due to the fact that its aid is highly tied, not very selective, and fragmented.

5 The North-South Institute (2005a) made an argument to this effect in its brief to the federal government on its *International Policy Statement* (IPS). Unfortunately, the IPS stopped short of providing coherence on the basis of the MD/MDGS (or on any other basis for that matter) although to its credit the 'Development' chapter spoke of a "whole-of-government" approach. The whole review process for the IPS was ultimately flawed in that it did not provide a unifying policy framework for coherence – illustrated by the very fact there were separate chapters for development, diplomacy, defence and commerce, and none for finance.

6 There are three MDGS on health: reduce child mortality, improve maternal health, and combat HIV/AIDS, malaria and other diseases.

7 For an exhaustive survey of these issues, see Cornia (2005).

8 Examples of this emerging literature are: Persson and Tabellini (1994); Aghion and Williamson (1998); Aghion, Caroli and García-Peñalosa (1999); and Cornia (2005); and World Bank (2005).

9 The Hippocratic test in this case should go beyond using the MDGS, which focus on the benchmark of $1-a-day poverty. Instead, the test should be whether policies would worsen income or other measures of distribution.

10 While I advocate our aid program reaching the aid target of 0.7 percent of GNI by 2015, my main point is that we cannot put all our policy eggs in the

aid basket. There is also a danger in regarding the achievement of the 0.7 percent target, or of the first Millennium Development Goal (reduction by 50 percent of the incidence of absolute poverty) as a development victory. Rather, these are more properly seen as milestones toward much more important achievements.

REFERENCES

Aghion, Philippe, and Jeffrey G. Williamson. 1998. *Growth, Inequality and Globalization.* Cambridge: Cambridge University Press.

Aghion, Philippe, Eve Caroli, and Cecilia García-Peñalosa. 1999. "Inequality and Economic Growth: The Perspective of the New Growth Theories," *Journal of Economic Literature* 37, no. 4 (December): 1615–60.

Birdsall, Nancy, Dani Rodrik and Arvind Subramaniam. 2005. "How to Help Poor Countries," *Foreign Affairs* 84, no. 4 (July-August): 135–52.

Cornia, Giovanni Andrea, ed. 2005. *Inequality, Growth and Prosperity in an Era of Liberalization and Globalization.* Oxford: Oxford University Press.

Martin, Matthew, with Cleo Rose-Innes. 2004. "Private Capital Flows to Low-Income Countries: Perception and Reality," in *Canadian Development Report 2004: Investing in Poor Countries.* Ottawa: North-South Institute, 28–50.

North-South Institute. 2005a. "Human Security, Equitable and Sustainable Development: Foundations for Canada's International Policy." Ottawa: The North-South Institute (January).

– 2005b. *Canadian Development Report 2005. Towards 2015: Meeting our Millennium Commitments.* Ottawa: The North-South Institute.

Organisation of Economic Co-operation and Development (OECD). 2005. "Paris Declaration on Aid Effectiveness," High Level Summit, Development and Co-operation Directorate (DAC). Paris: OECD, 2 March.

Persson, Torsten, and Guido Tabellini, 1994. "Is inequality Harmful for Growth?" *American Economic Review* 84, no. 3, 600–21.

Regehr, Ernie, and Peter Whelan. 2004. "Reshaping the Security Envelope: Defence Policy in a Human Security Context," Working Paper, *Project Ploughshares* (November).

Rodrik, Dani. 2003. *In Search of Prosperity: Analytic Narratives on Economic Growth.* Princeton, NJ: Princeton University Press.

Roodman, David. 2005. "The 2005 Commitment to Development Index: Components and Results," *CGD Brief.* Washington, DC: Center for Global Development (August). Available at: <http://www.cgdev.org/content/publications/detail/3647>

Sen, Amartya. 1999. *Development as Freedom.* New York: Alfred A. Knopf.

Stiglitz, Joseph. 2002. *Globalization and Its Discontents.* New York: W.W. Norton and Company.

Suzuki, David T. and Anita Gordon. 1991. *It's a Matter of Survival*. Cambridge, MA: Harvard University Press.

United Nations. 2002. "Monterrey Consensus," International Conference on Financing for Development. New York: Department of Economic and Social Affairs. Available at: <http://www.un.org/esa/ffd/Monterrey-Consensus-excepts-aconf198_11.pdf>

United Nations Development Programme (UNDP). 2005. *International Cooperation at a Crossroads: Aid, Trade and Security in an Unequal World*. Human Development Report 2005. New York: UNDP.

Ward, Olivia. 2006. "Stop Poaching Doctors, WHO Tells Rich Countries," *Toronto Star*, 8 April, A23.

World Bank. 2005. *Equity and Development: World Development Report 2006*. New York: Oxford University Press and The World Bank.

Contributors

MARIE BERNARD-MEUNIER is the Canadian co-Chair of Atlantik Brücke and the former Canadian ambassador to Germany, The Netherlands, and UNESCO. She is a Special Fellow at The Centre for International Governance Innovation.

DAVID R. BLACK is an associate professor in the Departments of Political Science and International Development Studies, Dalhousie University.

ADAM CHAPNICK is an assistant professor and deputy chair in the Department of Command, Leadership, and Management at the Canadian Forces College.

ANDREW F. COOPER is a professor in the Department of Political Science, University of Waterloo, and the associate director and distinguished fellow at The Centre for International Governance Innovation.

ANN DENHOLM CROSBY is an associate professor in the Department of Political Science, York University.

ROY CULPEPER is the president of The North-South Institute.

CHRISTINA GABRIEL is an associate professor in the Department of Political Science and the Institute of Women's Studies, Carleton University.

FEN OSLER HAMPSON is a professor and director of The Norman Paterson School of International Affairs, Carleton University.

WENRAN JIANG is an associate professor in the Department of Political Science and the acting director of the China Institute, University of Alberta.

JOHN KIRTON is an associate professor in the Department of Political Science and the director of the G8 Research Group at the Munk Centre for International Studies, University of Toronto. His most recent book is *Canadian Foreign Policy in a Changing World* (Thomson Nelson).

DAVID M. MALONE is Canada's High Commissioner to India. He recently published *The International Struggle for Iraq: Politics in the UN Security Council, 1980–2005* (Oxford University Press).

NELSON MICHAUD is an associate professor, the director of the LEPPM (Laboratoire d'études sur les politiques publiques et la mondialisation) and the director of the GERFI (Groupe d'études, de recherche et de formation internationals) at the École nationale d'administration publique.

ISIDRO MORALES is a full time professor at Universidad de las Américas, Puebla, Mexico. During the 2005–2006 academic year, he was Fulbright Professor and Senior Fellow at the Center for North American Studies at American University, Washington DC.

DANE ROWLANDS is an associate professor and associate director of The Norman Paterson School of International Affairs, Carleton University.

CHRISTOPHER SANDS is the senior associate of the Canada Project at the Centre for Strategic and International Studies in Washington, DC.

DANIEL SCHWANEN is director of research and chief operating officer at The Centre for International Governance Innovation.

HUGH SEGAL is the senator for Kingston-Frontenac-Leeds in Ontario and a senior fellow at the School of Policy Studies, Queen's University.

YASMINE SHAMSIE is an assistant professor in the Department of Political Science, Wilfrid Laurier University.

ELINOR SLOAN is an associate professor in the Department of Political Science, Carleton University.

Index